Math Pedia

For Elementary Students

(Grades 3 – 8)

From the Publisher of the bestselling Smart Series

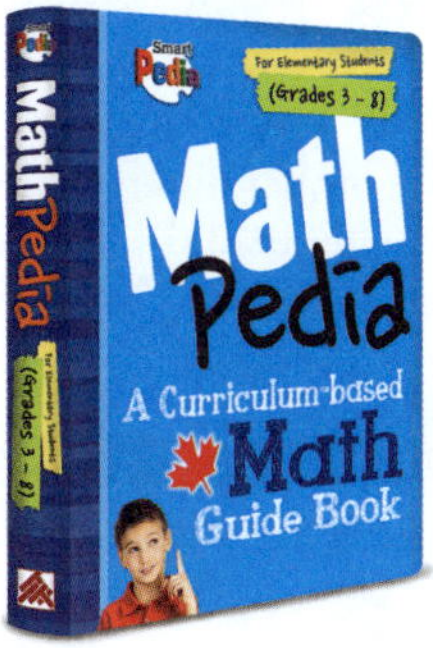

Do you have a hard time with math? Do you feel lost and confused in class? Have no fear, ***MathPedia*** is here! ***MathPedia*** Grades 3 – 8 is your colour-filled guide to making sense of math in school. It covers all the big ideas and major concepts you will encounter in class, providing you with clear definitions and detailed examples every step of the way.

Are you having trouble doing math? No problem! ***MathPedia*** also contains detailed explanations that teach you how to tackle different kinds of math problems using a variety of strategies and techniques. Hints and tips are also scattered throughout the book to provide you with helpful reminders.

MathPedia comes with two sheets of flag tabs for you to mark important pages you want to check back later or write your own reminders.

With ***MathPedia***, you will make sense of math in no time!

Your Partner in Education,
Popular Book Co. (Canada) Ltd.

How to Use This Book

This book is filled with information to help you master math. Look for the highlighted components below. They provide useful information and guidelines.

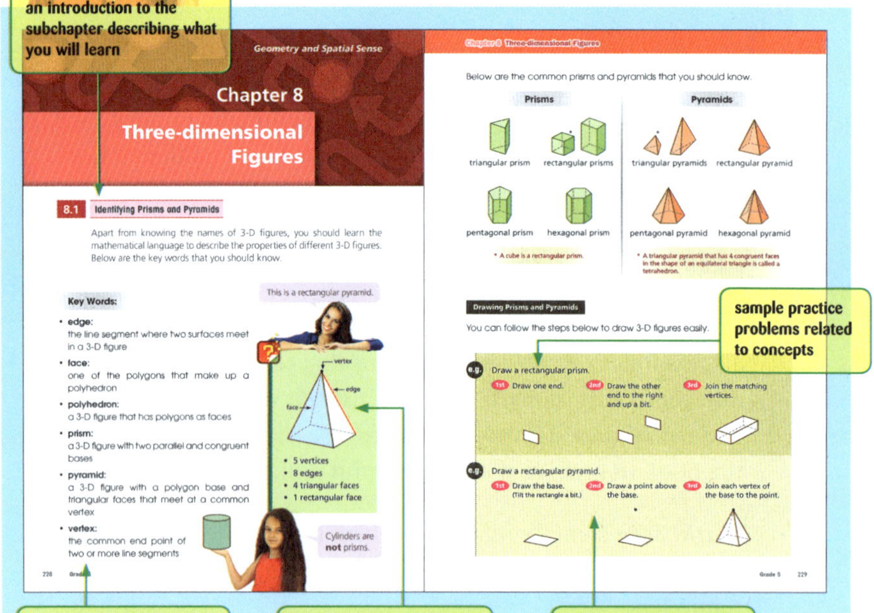

an introduction to the subchapter describing what you will learn

sample practice problems related to concepts

keywords and terms with definitions provided

helpful hints and tip boxes for quick reference

step-by-step solutions to sample problems

contains diagrams and step-by-step instructions on how to solve real-life problems

lists keywords and concepts with definitions and explanations

includes two sheets of flag tabs to mark important pages for quick reference

Table of Contents

Grade 3	**Chapters 1 to 14**	19 – 90
Grade 4	**Chapters 1 to 14**	91 – 166
Grade 5	**Chapters 1 to 12**	167 – 250
Grade 6	**Chapters 1 to 11**	251 – 328
Grade 7	**Chapters 1 to 13**	329 – 402
Grade 8	**Chapters 1 to 11**	403 – 472
Glossary		473 – 478
Photo Credits		479 – 480

See the breakdown of each chapter for each grade on the pages that follow.

Contents

Grade 3

Chapter 1: Whole Numbers to 1000

1.1 Writing Whole Numbers to 1000 20
1.2 Counting Forward by 1's, 2's, 5's, 10's, 25's, and 100's 22
1.3 Counting Backward by 2's, 5's, 10's, and 100's 24
1.4 Comparing Numbers 26
1.5 Rounding Numbers 28
1.6 Composing and Decomposing Three-digit Numbers 29

Chapter 2: Addition and Subtraction

2.1 Adding and Subtracting Using Mental Strategies 31
2.2 Adding and Subtracting Three-digit Numbers 33

Chapter 3: Multiplication and Division

3.1 Multiplying to 7 x 7 36
3.2 Dividing to 49 ÷ 7 37

Chapter 4: Fractions

4.1 Dividing Whole Objects into Equal Parts 39
4.2 Dividing Sets of Objects into Equal Groups 40

Chapter 5: Money

5.1 Counting and Trading Money 42
5.2 Finding Money Amounts 44
5.3 Using Bills and Coins 46
5.4 Adding Money Amounts to $10 47
5.5 Subtracting Money Amounts 49

Chapter 6: Measurement

6.1 Measuring Length in "cm", "m", and "km" 52
6.2 Measuring Capacity in "L" 53
6.3 Measuring Mass in "kg" 55

Chapter 7: Time and Temperature

7.1 Reading and Writing Time 57
7.2 Relating Different Units of Time 58
7.3 Recording and Describing Temperatures 60

Chapter 8: Perimeter and Area

8.1 Finding Perimeter 62
8.2 Finding Area 64

Chapter 9: Two-dimensional Shapes

9.1 Identifying and Describing Angles 65
9.2 Identifying and Composing Shapes 67

Chapter 10: Three-dimensional Figures

10.1 Naming 3-D Figures 69
10.2 Comparing and Sorting 3-D Figures 71
10.3 Constructing 3-D Figures 73

Chapter 11: Locations and Movements

11.1 Describing Movements on a Grid Map 75
11.2 Identifying and Drawing Symmetrical Shapes 76
11.3 Identifying Transformations 78

Chapter 12: Patterning and Algebra

12.1 Identifying and Extending Patterns 79
12.2 Solving Equations and Identifying Properties 81

Chapter 13: Data Management

13.1 Analyzing Graphs 83
13.2 Drawing Graphs 85

Chapter 14: Probability

14.1 Finding the Frequency of an Outcome 86
14.2 Determining Fairness 88

Math Pedia

Contents

Grade 4

Chapter 1: Whole Numbers to 10 000

1.1 Writing Numbers to 10 000 92
1.2 Comparing and Ordering Numbers 93
1.3 Rounding Numbers 95

Chapter 2: Addition and Subtraction

2.1 Adding and Subtracting Using Mental Strategies 97
2.2 Adding and Subtracting Four-digit Numbers 99

Chapter 3: Multiplication and Division

3.1 Multiplying One-digit Numbers 101
3.2 More Multiplying 103
3.3 Dividing by One-digit Numbers 104
3.4 More Dividing 106

Chapter 4: Fractions

4.1 Describing Parts with Fractions 108
4.2 Comparing and Ordering Fractions 110
4.3 More about Fractions 112

Chapter 5: Decimal Numbers to Tenths

5.1 Writing Decimal Numbers 114
5.2 Comparing and Ordering Decimal Numbers 115
5.3 Adding and Subtracting Decimal Numbers 117
5.4 Fractions and Decimals 119

Chapter 6: Money

6.1 Representing Money Amounts to $100 122
6.2 Adding and Subtracting Money Amounts 123

Chapter 7: Measurement

7.1 Measuring Length 126
7.2 Measuring Mass 128
7.3 Measuring Capacity 129
7.4 Measuring Volume 131

Chapter 8: Time

8.1 Measuring Time 133
8.2 Reading and Showing Time on Clocks 135
8.3 Finding Elapsed Time 137

Chapter 9: Perimeter and Area

9.1 Finding Perimeter 139
9.2 Finding Area 141
9.3 Relating Perimeter and Area 143

Chapter 10: Two-dimensional Shapes

10.1 Identifying Angles 145
10.2 Classifying Quadrilaterals 147

Chapter 11: Three-dimensional Figures

11.1 Naming and Describing 3-D Figures 149
11.2 Constructing 3-D Figures 151

Chapter 12: Locations and Movements

12.1 Locations and Movements on a Grid Map 154
12.2 Making and Describing Reflections 155

Chapter 13: Patterning

13.1 Describing Numeric and Geometric Patterns 157
13.2 Solving Equations 158
13.3 Using Properties of Multiplication 160

Chapter 14: Data Management and Probability

14.1 Analyzing and Displaying Data 163
14.2 Finding the Frequency of an Outcome 165

Math Pedia

Contents

Grade 5

Chapter 1: Whole Numbers to 100 000

1.1 Writing Numbers to 100 000 168
1.2 Comparing, Ordering, and Rounding Numbers 171
1.3 Multiplying Two-digit Numbers 173
1.4 Dividing Three-digit Numbers 175

Chapter 2: Decimal Numbers to Hundredths

2.1 Writing Decimal Numbers 178
2.2 Comparing Decimal Numbers 179
2.3 Rounding Decimal Numbers 180
2.4 Adding and Subtracting Decimal Numbers 182
2.5 Multiplying and Dividing Decimal Numbers by 10, 100, and 1000 184

Chapter 3: Fractions and Decimals

3.1 Identifying Fractions and Mixed Numbers 187
3.2 Finding Equivalent Fractions 190
3.3 Relating Fractions and Decimals 193

Chapter 4: Money

4.1 Writing Money Amounts 195
4.2 Solving Problems with Money 198

Chapter 5: Time and Temperature

5.1 Telling Time to the Nearest Second 201
5.2 Finding Elapsed Time 202
5.3 Measuring and Recording Temperatures 204

Chapter 6: Measurement

6.1 Measuring Length Using Standard Units 205
6.2 Finding Perimeter of Polygons 207
6.3 Finding Area of Polygons 209
6.4 Solving Problems Involving Perimeter and Area 211
6.5 Finding Volume of Rectangular Prisms 213
6.6 Measuring Mass 216

Chapter 7: Two-dimensional Shapes

7.1 Identifying Polygons 218
7.2 Measuring and Naming Angles 221
7.3 Classifying Triangles 223
7.4 Constructing Triangles 225

Chapter 8: Three-dimensional Figures

8.1 Identifying Prisms and Pyramids 228
8.2 Identifying and Constructing Nets 231

Chapter 9: Locations and Movements

9.1 Coordinate Systems 233
9.2 Performing Transformations 234

Chapter 10: Patterning

10.1 Identifying and Extending Patterns 236
10.2 Representing Number Patterns 238
10.3 Finding Missing Numbers in Equations 239

Chapter 11: Data Management

11.1 Finding the Mean of a Set of Data 242
11.2 Identifying Discrete and Continuous Data 244
11.3 Interpreting and Making Graphs 246

Chapter 12: Probability

12.1 Determining the Possible Outcomes of an Event 248
12.2 Determining the Probability of an Event with Fractions 250

Math Pedia

Contents

Grade 6

Chapter 1: Whole Numbers to 1 000 000

1.1 Writing Numbers to 1 000 000 252
1.2 Comparing and Ordering Whole Numbers 254
1.3 Prime and Composite Numbers 255
1.4 Order of Operations 257
1.5 Multiplying by Two-digit Numbers 259
1.6 Dividing by Two-digit Numbers 262

Chapter 2: Decimal Numbers to Thousandths

2.1 Writing Decimal Numbers 264
2.2 Comparing and Ordering Decimal Numbers 266
2.3 Adding and Subtracting Decimal Numbers 268
2.4 Multiplying Decimal Numbers 270
2.5 Dividing Decimal Numbers 272

Chapter 3: Fractions and Percents

3.1 Comparing and Ordering Fractions 275
3.2 Percents 277
3.3 Fractions, Decimals, and Percents 279

Chapter 4: Ratios and Rates

4.1 Ratios 282
4.2 Rates 284

Chapter 5: Measurement

5.1 Area of Rectangles 286
5.2 Area of Parallelograms 288
5.3 Area of Triangles 290
5.4 Mass and Capacity 292
5.5 Volume and Surface Area 294

Chapter 6: Geometry

6.1 Geometric Properties of Quadrilaterals 298
6.2 Line of Symmetry and Rotational Symmetry 301
6.3 Measuring and Constructing Angles 303
6.4 Constructing Polygons 305
6.5 Different Views of Solids 307

Chapter 7: Locations and Movements

7.1 Coordinates on a Cartesian Coordinate Plane 308
7.2 Describing Rotations 310
7.3 Creating Tiling Patterns Using Transformations 311

Chapter 8: Patterning

8.1 Identifying, Extending, and Creating Patterns 313
8.2 Graphing Patterns 314

Chapter 9: Equations

9.1 Solving Equations 315
9.2 Formulating Equations 318

Chapter 10: Data Management

10.1 Mean, Median, and Mode 320
10.2 Interpreting Graphs 322
10.3 Making Graphs 324

Chapter 11: Probability

11.1 Finding Probability 325
11.2 Predicting the Frequency of an Outcome 328

Contents

Grade 7

Chapter 1: Multiples and Factors

1.1 Multiples 330
1.2 Factors 333

Chapter 2: Perfect Squares and Square Roots

2.1 Perfect Squares 335
2.2 Square Roots 337

Chapter 3: Integers

3.1 Identifying and Comparing Integers 339
3.2 Adding and Subtracting Integers 342

Chapter 4: Fractions

4.1 Representing and Comparing Fractions 344
4.2 Adding Fractions 347
4.3 Subtracting Fractions 350
4.4 Multiplying Fractions 353
4.5 Dividing Fractions 355

Chapter 5: Decimals

5.1 Adding and Subtracting Decimals 358
5.2 Multiplying Decimals 360
5.3 Dividing Decimals 362
5.4 Relating Decimals, Fractions, and Percents 364

Chapter 6: Proportional Relationships

6.1 Ratios 366
6.2 Rates 368

Chapter 7: Measurement

7.1 Area 370
7.2 Volume 373
7.3 Surface Area 375

Chapter 8: 2-D and 3-D Geometry

8.1 Properties of Quadrilaterals 377
8.2 Properties of Triangles 379
8.3 Congruent and Similar Shapes 381
8.4 Constructing Angles and Bisectors 383

Chapter 9: Locations and Movements

9.1 Transformations 387
9.2 Cartesian Coordinate Plane 388

Chapter 10: Patterning

10.1 Number Patterns 390
10.2 Patterns in Graphs 392

Chapter 11: Algebra

11.1 Algebraic Expressions 393
11.2 Algebraic Equations 396

Chapter 12: Data Management

12.1 Interpreting Graphs 398
12.2 Making Graphs 400

Chapter 13: Probability

13.1 Finding Probability 401
13.2 Predicting Outcomes 402

Math Pedia **Contents** Grade 8

Chapter 1: Numbers

1.1 Exponential Notation 404
1.2 Whole Numbers 406
1.3 Integers 408
1.4 Order of Operations 410
1.5 Common Factors and Common Multiples 412
1.6 Squares and Square Roots 415
1.7 Rational Numbers 417

Chapter 2: Fractions, Decimals, and Percents

2.1 Addition and Subtraction of Fractions 419
2.2 Multiplication of Fractions 421
2.3 Division of Fractions 423
2.4 Multiplication and Division of Decimals 425
2.5 Percents 427
2.6 Equivalent Forms of Fractions, Decimals, and Percents 429

Chapter 3: Proportions and Rates

3.1 Proportions 431
3.2 Rates 433

Chapter 4: Circles and Cylinders

4.1 Constructing Circles 435
4.2 Circumference of Circles 438
4.3 Area of Circles 440
4.4 Volume of Cylinders 442
4.5 Surface Area of Cylinders 444
4.6 Volume and Surface Area of Cylinders 446

Chapter 5: 2-D and 3-D Geometry

5.1 Sorting and Classifying Quadrilaterals 448
5.2 Properties of Similar Figures 450
5.3 Properties of 3-D Figures 453

Chapter 6: Properties of Triangles

6.1 Related Angles 455
6.2 Pythagorean Relationship 457

Chapter 7: Locations and Movements

7.1 Graphing on Cartesian Coordinate Planes 459
7.2 Transformations 460

Chapter 8: Patterning

8.1 Representing Linear Patterns 462
8.2 Graphing Linear Patterns 463

Chapter 9: Expressions and Equations

9.1 Evaluating Algebraic Expressions 464
9.2 Solving Equations 465

Chapter 10: Data Management

10.1 Analyzing Graphs 467
10.2 Representing Data in Graphs 469

Chapter 11: Probability

11.1 Finding Probability 471
11.2 Theoretical Probability and Experimental Probability 472

Grade 3

Chapter 1

Whole Numbers to 1000

1.1 Writing Whole Numbers to 1000

You can use base-ten materials (such as $100 bills, $10 bills, and loonies) or drawings to understand how to write three-digit numbers. You will also learn to write two-digit numbers in words.

Grasping the Place Value Concept

Place value: the value of a digit in a number is based on its position; for example, in the number 365, the digit 3 in the hundreds place means 300.

Place Value Chart

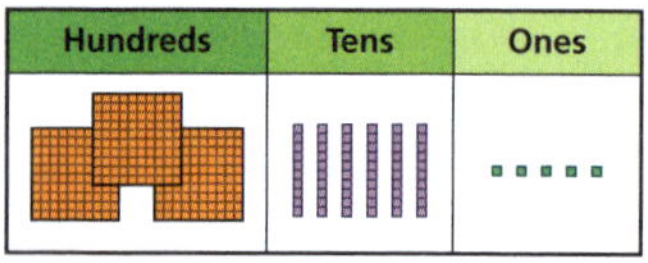

3 hundreds 6 tens 5 ones ← base-ten name

=

H	T	O
3	6	5
300	60	5

= 365

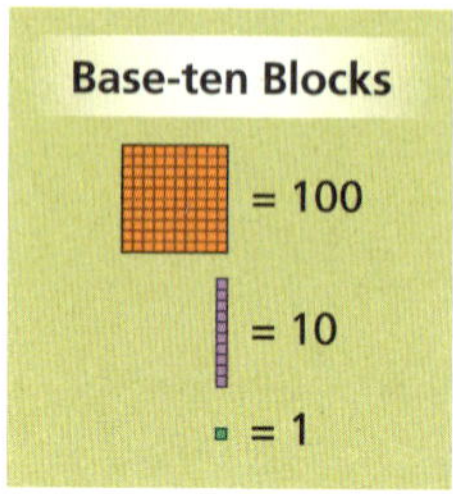

Writing Numbers in Words

Try to identify the spelling pattern in each group of numbers.

From 11 to 19:

eleven, twelve, thirteen, fourteen, fifteen, sixteen, seventeen, eighteen, nineteen

Multiples of 10:

twenty, thirty, forty, fifty, sixty, seventy, eighty, ninety

Don't forget the hyphen.

forty-five cookies

Application

① *A cashier is counting the money in the cash register. There are 2 hundred-dollar bills and 17 rolls of loonies, with 10 loonies in each roll. The cashier records a total of $217. Is the cashier's record correct? Explain.*

Solution:

2 hundred-dollar bills = 2 hundreds

1 roll of loonies = 1 ten

17 rolls of loonies = 17 tens = 1 hundred 7 tens

Add them.
3 hundreds 7 tens
= 300 and 70
= 370

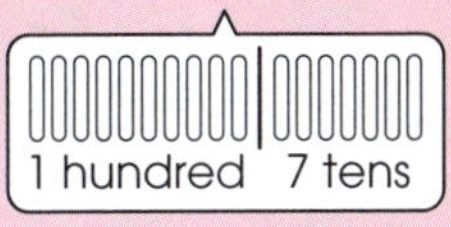

The cashier's record is not correct. The total amount should be $370, not $217.

② *Melissa helped clean the blackboard, but she erased some useful information by accident. Use the clues left on the blackboard to help Melissa rewrite the information.*

Solution:

__nty-six students

It must be either twe**nty** or seve**nty**.

"Seventy-six" cannot be correct because that would mean there are too many students in the class.

So, the answer must be twenty-six.

1.2 Counting Forward by 1's, 2's, 5's, 10's, 25's, and 100's

When you skip count, start at 0. Once you understand the concept of skip counting, start at various numbers to develop your skills.

Here are 3 tools to help you skip count:

1 A hundreds chart

Count by 2's from 64.

61	62	63	64	65	66	67	68	69	70
71	72	73	74	75	76	77	78	79	80
81	82	83	84	85	86	87	88	89	90
91	92	93	94	95	96	97	98	99	100

64, 66, 68, 70, 72...

The coloured numbers run in columns on the hundreds chart.

2 A number line

Count by 5's from 15.

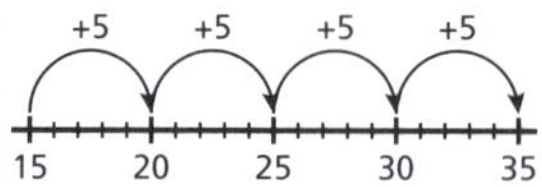

15, 20, 25, 30, 35

Add 5 each time to get the next number.

3 Coins

Count by 10's.

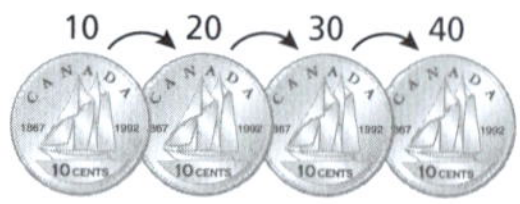

4 dimes make 40¢.

Count by 2's

Start at

- an even number: the digit in the ones place must be 0, 2, 4, 6, or 8.
  e.g. 14, 16, 18, 20, 22...
- an odd number: the digit in the ones place must be 1, 3, 5, 7, or 9.
  e.g. 247, 249, 251, 253, 255...

Count by 5's

Start at

- a multiple of 5: the digit in the ones place must be 0 or 5.
  e.g. 65, 70, 75, 80...
- any number: the digit in the ones place repeats alternately.
  e.g. 132, 137, 142, 147...

Count by 10's, 100's, 25's

- e.g. 214, 224, 234, 244... ← The digit in the tens place goes up by 1 each time.
- e.g. 214, 314, 414, 514... ← The digit in the hundreds place goes up by 1 each time.
- e.g. 150, 175, 200, 225... ← The core pattern is 00, 25, 50, and 75.

Application

① *Julia has 298 stickers in a box. If she buys 3 packs with 100 stickers each and 2 sheets with 2 stickers each, how many stickers will she have in total? Show Julia how to use skip counting to find the answer.*

Solution:

Way 1

Count by 100's (3 times).

298 → 398 → 498 → 598

Count by 2's (2 times).

598 → 600 → 602

Julia has 602 stickers.

Way 2

Add 2 stickers to 298 first.

298 + 2 = 300 ← It makes it easier to count from 300.

Count by 100's (3 times).

300 → 400 → 500 → 600

Add the 2 remaining stickers to 600 to get the answer 602.

② *Look at the coins that Kevin has. Help Kevin use skip counting to find the total value of his coins.*

Solution:

1st Group the coins: 5 quarters, 3 dimes, 2 nickels.

2nd Count by 25's for the quarters (5 times).

0 → 25 → 50 → 75 → 100 → 125

3rd Count by 10's for the dimes (3 times).

125 → 135 → 145 → 155

4th Count by 5's for the nickels (2 times).

155 → 160 → 165

Kevin has 165¢.

1.3 Counting Backward by 2's, 5's, 10's, and 100's

Counting backward can be more difficult than counting forward, so before learning this concept, you should master counting forward. To understand how to count backward, you may count down from 10 with your fingers or walk backward while counting.

Use the methods below to learn the concept of counting backward.

1. Using a hundreds chart

e.g. Count backward by 2's from 80.

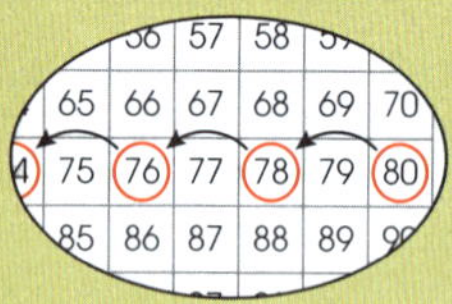

2. Using a number line

e.g. Count backward by 10's from 100.

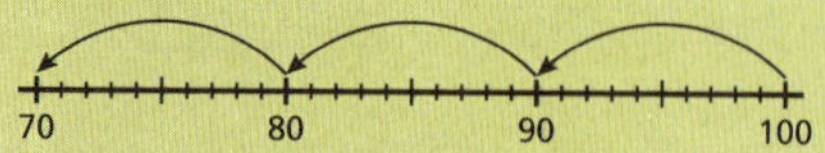

3. Using coins

e.g. Count backward by 5's from 20.

Total: 20¢

Hundreds Chart

1	2	3	4	5	6	7	8	9	10
11	12	13	14	15	16	17	18	19	20
21	22	23	24	25	26	27	28	29	30
31	32	33	34	35	36	37	38	39	40
41	42	43	44	45	46	47	48	49	50
51	52	53	54	55	56	57	58	59	60
61	62	63	64	65	66	67	68	69	70
71	72	73	74	75	76	77	78	79	80
81	82	83	84	85	86	87	88	89	90
91	92	93	94	95	96	97	98	99	100

You can use this hundreds chart to count backward.

Application

① *A stopwatch is counting down from 1 hour. It is set to beep once every 5 minutes. How many times will it beep if it is now at 49 minutes?*

Solution:

1st Draw a number line from 0 to 60.

2nd Start at 60. Count backward by 5's.

3rd Count the number of times the stopwatch beeps after 49.

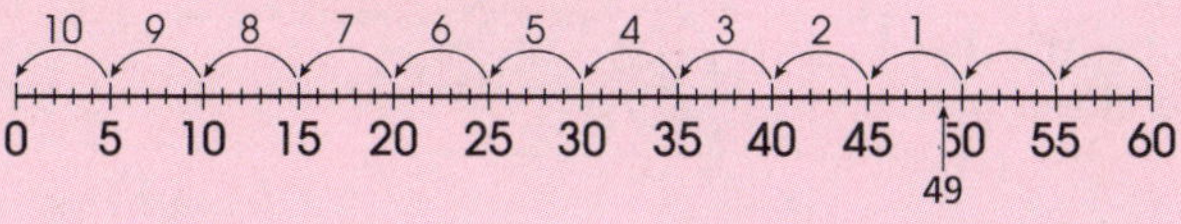

You should count backward by 5's 10 times. So, the stopwatch will beep 10 times.

② I'm going down in an elevator from the 36th floor. The elevator stops every 2 floors. If I get off on the 12th floor, how many stops will there be? On which floors will the elevator stop?

Solution:

1st Draw a number line from 12 to 36.

2nd Start at 36. Count backward by 2's.

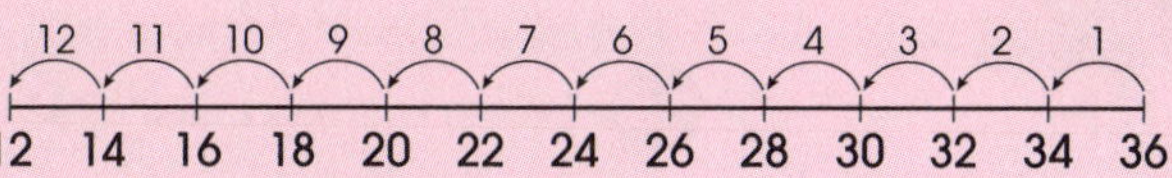

You should count backward by 2's 12 times.

So, the elevator will stop 12 times on floors 34, 32, 30, 28, 26, 24, 22, 20, 18, 16, 14, and 12.

1.4 Comparing Numbers

Use base-ten blocks to learn the concept of comparing numbers and to visualize the exact values of the numbers. Comparing the values of a digit and using a number line are also effective ways to compare three-digit numbers.

Way 1 Using base-ten blocks

1st Draw the numbers using base-ten blocks.

2nd The number that has more big blocks is greater.

e.g. Which is greater, 326 or 263?

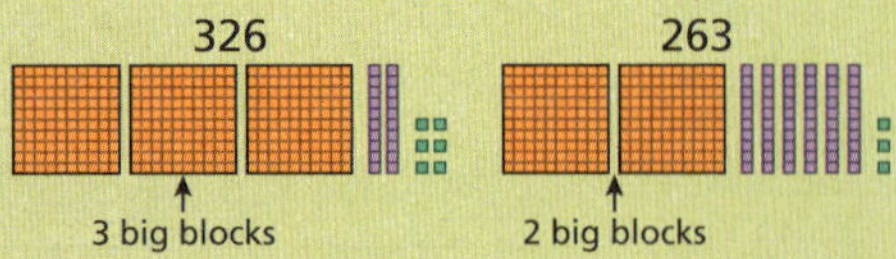

326 is greater.

Way 2 Comparing digits

1st Compare the digits in the hundreds column. If the digits are the same, go to **2nd**.

2nd Compare the tens. If they are the same, go to **3rd**.

3rd Compare the ones.

e.g. Which is greater, 376 or 372?

1st

H	T	O
3	7	6
3	7	2

↑ the same

2nd

H	T	O
3	**7**	6
3	**7**	2

↑ the same

3rd

H	T	O
3	7	**6**
3	7	**2**

↑ $6 > 2$

376 is greater.

Way 3 Using a number line

1st Mark the 2 numbers on a number line.

2nd The number to the right is greater.

e.g. Which is greater, 368 or 421?

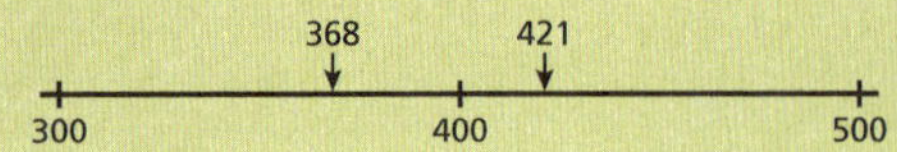

421 is greater.

Application

① *Jack and Andrew played at a game booth. Parts of their scores were covered by ketchup. What are the possible scores of Jack and Andrew if Jack had a higher score?*

Solution:

Jack	*Andrew*
1 __ 0	1 8 __
↑	↑
greater than 180; must be 190	smaller than 190; must be from 180 to 189

So, Jack's score is 190 and Andrew's score is any number from 180 to 189.

② *Lisa, Jason, Terry, and Sandy each got a number for a running race. Sandy had the smallest number. Lisa had the greatest number and it was closest to Terry's. Which number did they each get?*

Solution:

205	316	154	297
Jason	*Lisa*	*Sandy*	*Terry*
	↑	↑	↑
	highest number	lowest number	closest to Lisa's number

1.5 Rounding Numbers

A rounded number is usually easier to work with. For example, it is easier to add 300 than to add 328. Learn to round numbers in everyday situations, such as estimating the total cost of groceries at the checkout. This will help you estimate more easily.

Way 1 Using a number line

Round to the nearest ten.

e.g. 253

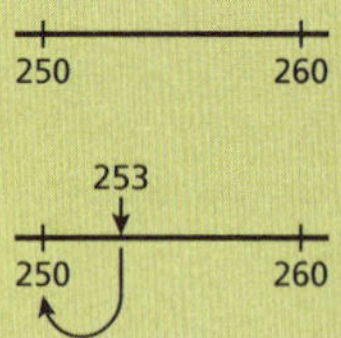

Name the two multiples of **10** that 253 falls between.

Mark 253. 253 is closer to 250.

So, 253 is rounded to **250**.

Round to the nearest hundred.

e.g. 253

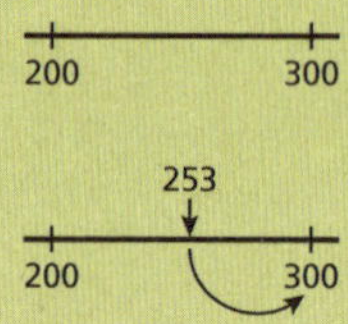

Name the two multiples of **100** that 253 falls between.

Mark 253. 253 is closer to 300.

So, 253 is rounded to **300**.

* If the number is in the middle of the two multiples, round it to the greater multiple.
e.g. 350 rounded to the nearest hundred is 400.

Way 2 Looking at the digit on the right

Round to the nearest ten.

e.g. 253

H	T	O
2	5	3

Look at the digit in the ones column.
It is less than 5, so round 253 down.

So, 253 is rounded to **250**.

Round to the nearest hundred.

e.g. 253

H	T	O
2	5	3

Look at the digit in the tens column.
It is 5 or more, so round 253 up.

So, 253 is rounded to **300**.

1.6 Composing and Decomposing Three-digit Numbers

Remember that numbers can be composed to make larger numbers, and decomposed into smaller numbers. This concept is essential for building a solid foundation for basic addition and subtraction.

Composing Numbers

Use two numbers to compose 405.

Way 1

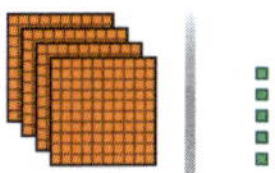

4 hundreds | 5 ones

405

Way 2

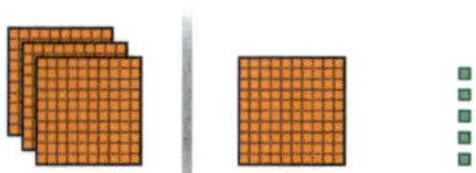

3 hundreds | 1 hundred | 5 ones

405

Compose a number with three numbers.

Use three numbers to compose 405.

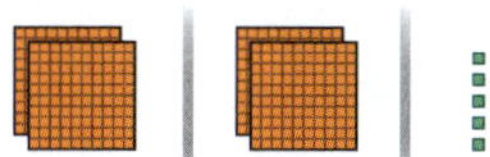

2 hundreds | 2 hundreds | 5 ones

405

These are three of the many ways to compose 405. Try to come up with another way to compose 405.

Decomposing Numbers

Decompose 234 into two numbers.

Way 1

234

2 hundreds | 3 tens 4 ones

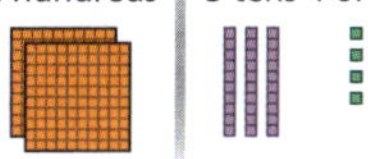

Way 2

234

1 hundred 4 ones | 1 hundred 3 tens

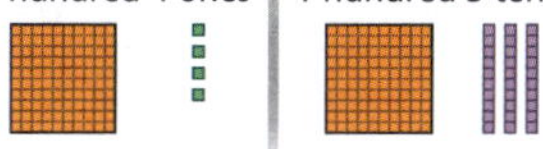

Remember that a number can be decomposed in many ways.

Decompose 234 into three numbers.

234

2 hundreds | 3 tens | 4 ones

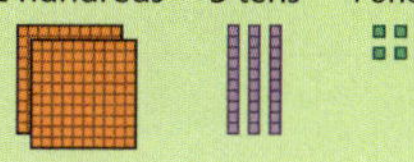

Try to decompose 234 into 1 hundred and 1 hundred 3 tens 4 ones.

1 hundred | 1 hundred 3 tens 4 ones

Application

① *Joshua puts 2 sets of blocks together:*
- 2 hundreds blocks, 7 tens blocks, 5 ones blocks
- 3 hundreds blocks, 5 tens blocks, 6 ones blocks
What number is he composing?

Solution:

2 hundreds	3 hundreds	6 hundreds
7 tens	5 tens	3 tens
5 ones	6 ones	1 one

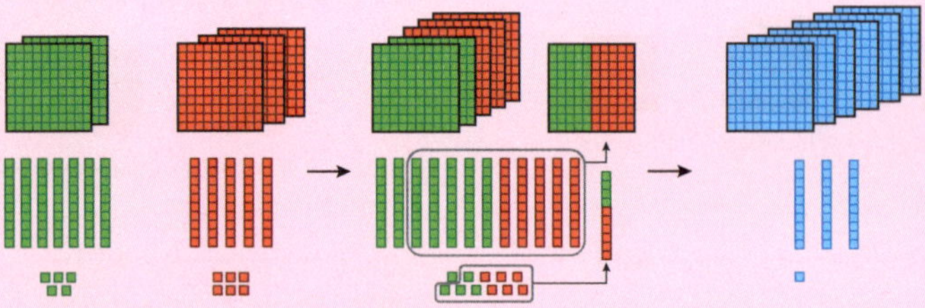

So, Joshua is composing the number 631.

② *A number is decomposed into 216 and 114. What is the number? Use base-ten blocks to solve the problem.*

Solution:

Since the number is decomposed into 216 and 114, the number is composed of 216 and 114.

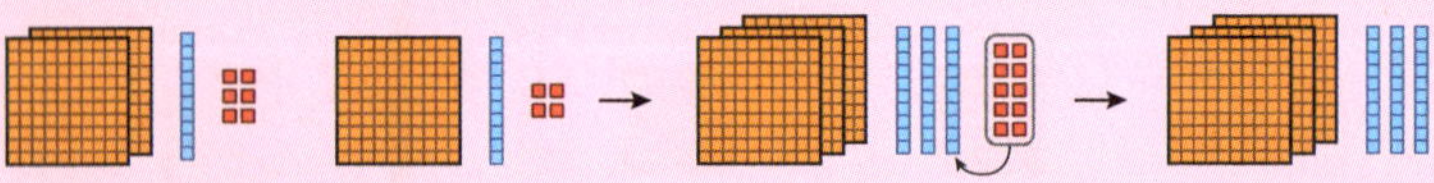

So, the number is 330.

Chapter 2

Addition and Subtraction

2.1 Adding and Subtracting Using Mental Strategies

This unit introduces some mental math strategies. Mental math is essential because it helps build the foundation for more complex math.

Mental Addition

Strategy 1 Splitting

e.g. 29 + 34 = ______

1st Split.

2nd Add.

3rd Combine.

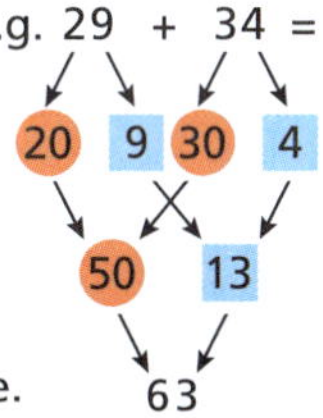

29 + 34 = **63**

Strategy 2 Making a friendly number

e.g. 29 + 34 = ______

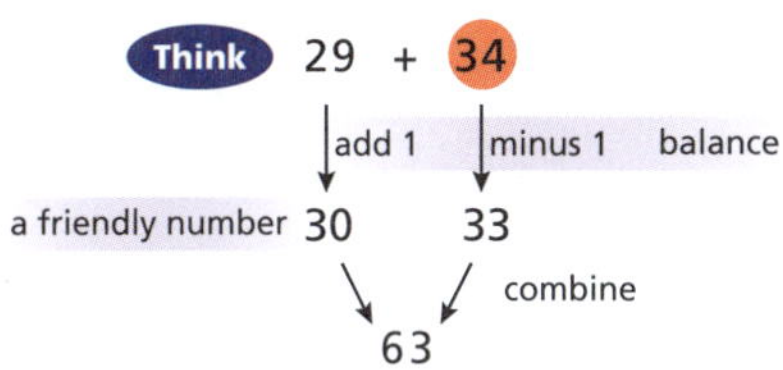

29 + 34 = **63**

Mental Subtraction

Strategy 1 Making the second number friendly

e.g. 51 – 18 = ______

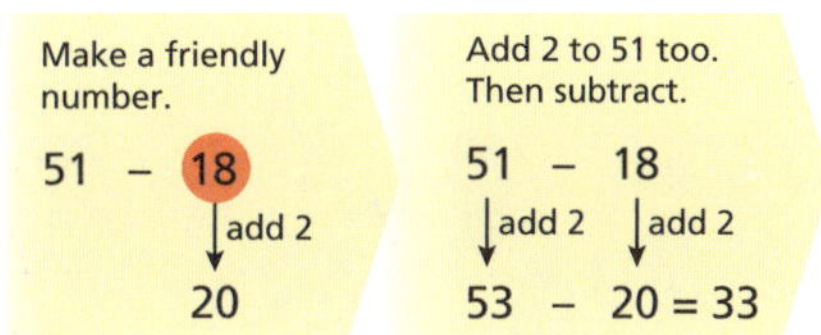

51 – 18 = **33**

Strategy 2 Using a number line

e.g. 51 – 18 = ______

Count on by 10's and then by 1's from 18 until you reach 51.

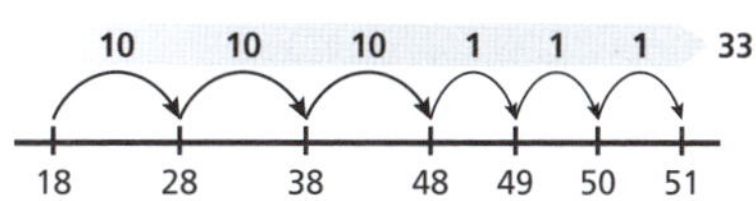

51 – 18 = **33**

Application

Andrea had 57 books and Judy had 26 books. Kelvin borrowed some of their books, so the girls have 69 books left altogether. How many books did Kelvin borrow?

Solution:

Before Kelvin borrowed books : 57 + 26 = 83

After Kelvin borrowed books : 69 | 83 – 69 = ? books that Kelvin borrowed

83 – 69
= 14 (Think: 84 – 70 = 14)

So, Kelvin borrowed 14 books.

2.2 Adding and Subtracting Three-digit Numbers

To understand addition and subtraction of three-digit numbers, you can use base-ten blocks to illustrate the concept of grouping and regrouping. Once you grasp the concept, use a number line or column form to find answers.

Addition

e.g. 364 + 259 = ______

Using Base-ten Blocks

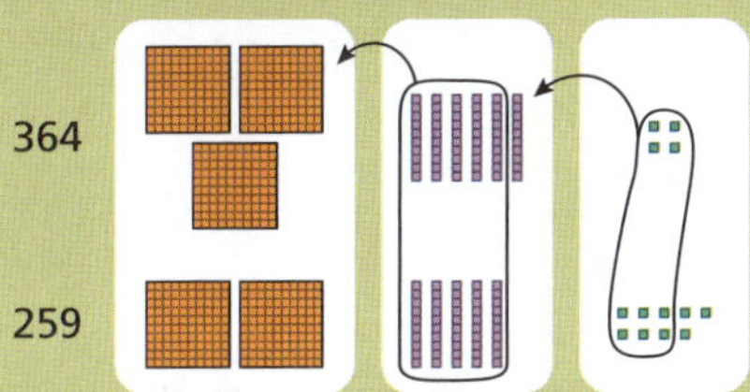

Group the hundreds, tens, and ones separately.

Circle every 10 in each group. Then carry over.

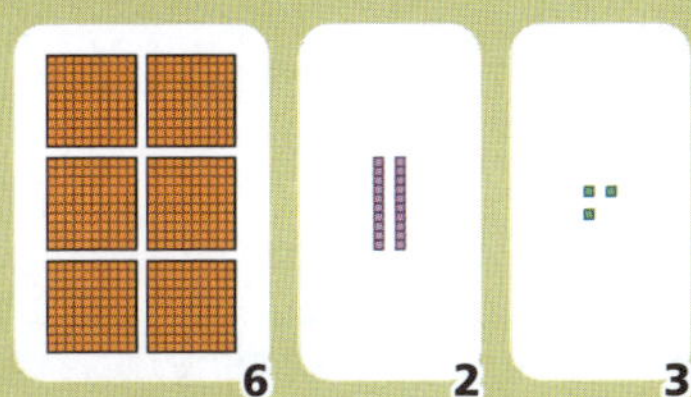

Using Vertical Addition

1st Add the ones.

$$\begin{array}{r} ^{1} \\ 3\ 6\ 4 \\ +\ 2\ 5\ 9 \\ \hline \mathbf{3} \end{array}$$

4 + 9 = 13, so carry 1 to the tens.

2nd Add the tens.

$$\begin{array}{r} ^{1}\ ^{1} \\ 3\ 6\ 4 \\ +\ 2\ 5\ 9 \\ \hline \mathbf{2}\ \mathbf{3} \end{array}$$

1 + 6 + 5 = 12, so carry 1 to the hundreds.

3rd Add the hundreds.

$$\begin{array}{r} ^{1}\ ^{1} \\ 3\ 6\ 4 \\ +\ 2\ 5\ 9 \\ \hline \mathbf{6}\ \mathbf{2}\ \mathbf{3} \end{array}$$

1 + 3 + 2 = 6

Using a Number Line

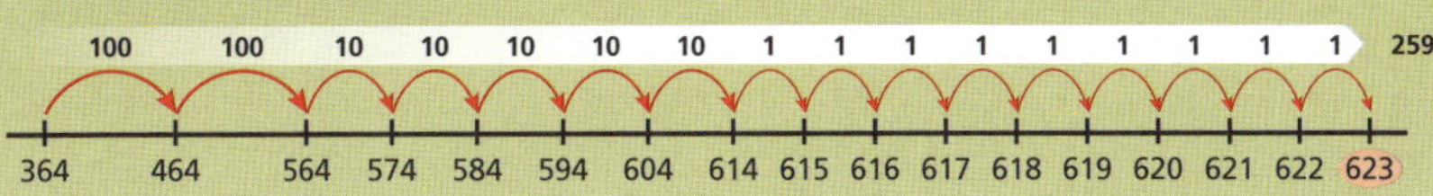

So, 364 + 259 = **623**.

Subtraction

e.g. 415 – 126 = ______

Using Base-ten Blocks

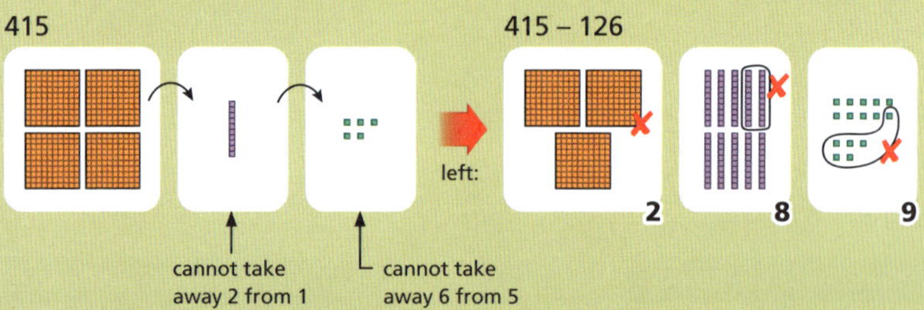

Using Vertical Subtraction

1st Subtract the ones.

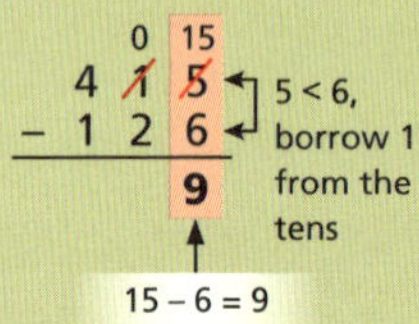

2nd Subtract the tens.

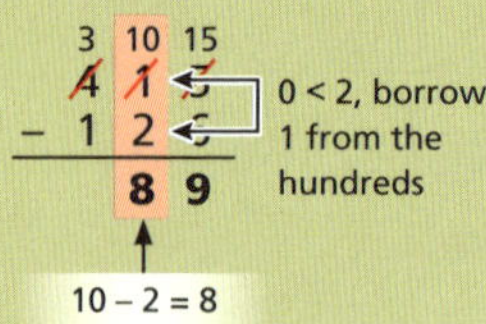

3rd Subtract the hundreds.

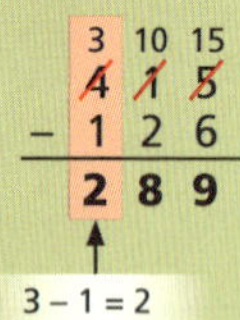

Using a Number Line

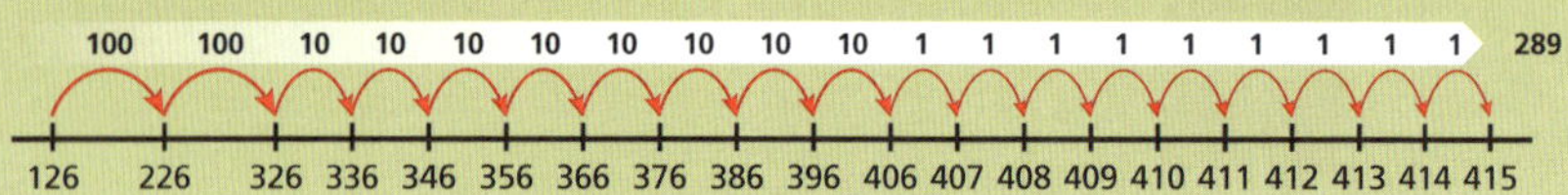

So, 415 – 126 = **289**.

Application

242
812 326

① *Show how to add and/or subtract the three numbers to get 728.*

Solution:

Round all the numbers to the nearest hundred. Then find a combination that will give an answer of about 700.

242 → 200
812 → 800
326 → 300

Think: 800 + 200 – 300 = 700
Try: 812 + 242 – 326 = 728

So, it is 812 + 242 – 326.

②

I collect hockey cards. My goal is to collect 300 cards. I have 2 piles of 100 cards and 8 bundles of 10 cards. How many more cards do I need to reach my goal?

Solution:

2 piles of 100 cards = 200

8 bundles of 10 cards = 80

300 – 280
= 20

To reach his goal, he needs 20 cards.

Chapter 3

Multiplication and Division

3.1 Multiplying to 7 x 7

Multiplication is simply adding a number repeatedly. Therefore, it is a good idea to understand the concept through addition. Once the concept is grasped, memorize the times table, as it is a great tool for doing multiplication and division.

Adding

e.g. 3 x 4 = ____

"3 x 4" means "adding three 4's" (or "adding four 3's").

4 + 4 + 4 = 12

So, 3 x 4 = **12** .

Counting Forward

e.g. 3 x 4 = ____

Start at 0. Count forward by 4 three times.

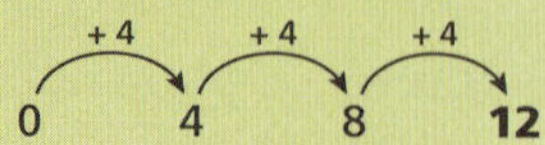

So, 3 x 4 = **12** .

Times Table

	1	2	3	4	5	6	7
1	1 x 1 = 1	1 x 2 = 2	1 x 3 = 3	1 x 4 = 4	1 x 5 = 5	1 x 6 = 6	1 x 7 = 7
2	2 x 1 = 2	2 x 2 = 4	2 x 3 = 6	2 x 4 = 8	2 x 5 = 10	2 x 6 = 12	2 x 7 = 14
3	3 x 1 = 3	3 x 2 = 6	3 x 3 = 9	3 x 4 = 12	3 x 5 = 15	3 x 6 = 18	3 x 7 = 21
4	4 x 1 = 4	4 x 2 = 8	4 x 3 = 12	4 x 4 = 16	4 x 5 = 20	4 x 6 = 24	4 x 7 = 28
5	5 x 1 = 5	5 x 2 = 10	5 x 3 = 15	5 x 4 = 20	5 x 5 = 25	5 x 6 = 30	5 x 7 = 35
6	6 x 1 = 6	6 x 2 = 12	6 x 3 = 18	6 x 4 = 24	6 x 5 = 30	6 x 6 = 36	6 x 7 = 42
7	7 x 1 = 7	7 x 2 = 14	7 x 3 = 21	7 x 4 = 28	7 x 5 = 35	7 x 6 = 42	7 x 7 = 49

3.2 Dividing to 49 ÷ 7

Division is closely related to multiplication. Before trying division, ensure that you have a thorough understanding of multiplication.

Using Counters

e.g. 12 ÷ 4 = ____

Put 12 counters into 4 equal groups.

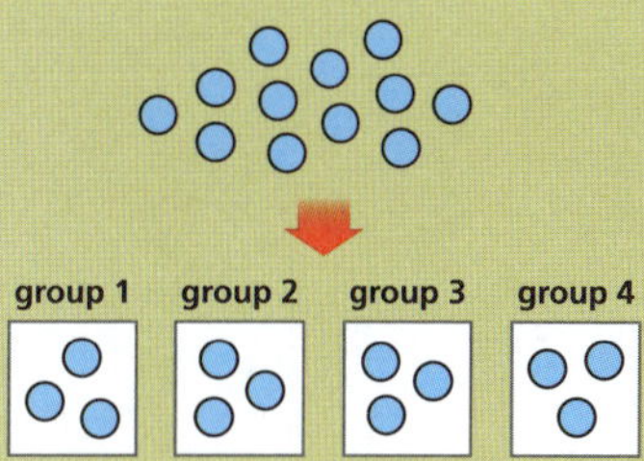

Each group has **3** counters.

So, 12 ÷ 4 = **3**.

Using Subtraction

e.g. 12 ÷ 4 = ____

Subtract 4 from 12 repeatedly until you reach 0.

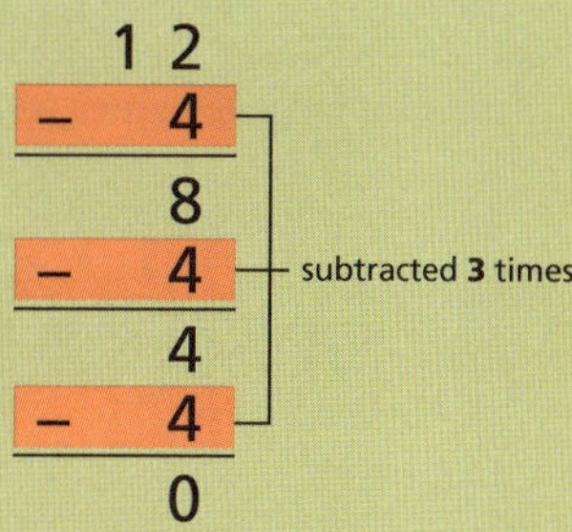

So, 12 ÷ 4 = **3**.

Counting Backward

e.g. 12 ÷ 4 = ____

Start at 12. Count backward by 4 until you reach 0.

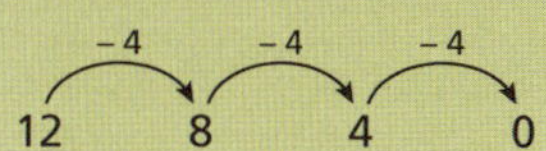

counted backward 3 times

So, 12 ÷ 4 = **3**.

Using Multiplication

e.g. 12 ÷ 4 = ____

Think 4 times what number is 12?

4 x **3** = 12

So, 12 ÷ 4 = **3**.

Application

① *Don wants to build 4 towers of equal height using all of his 15 blocks. Is this possible? If not, how many towers can he build?*

Solution:

Build 4 towers.

So, Don cannot build 4 towers.

Towers he can build:

5 towers of 3 blocks

or

3 towers of 5 blocks

Don can build 5 towers or 3 towers.

② I picked 12 apples and I want to share them equally with my friends. What is the greatest number of friends I can share these with so that each of us gets at least 2 apples?

Solution:

In order to share with the greatest number of friends, each person must get the fewest apples, which is 2.

$12 \div 2 = 6$

6 people can share the apples.

Since the girl gets a share too, she can share the apples with 5 friends.

Chapter 4

Fractions

4.1 Dividing Whole Objects into Equal Parts

This unit focuses on dividing shapes into equal parts. Once you grasp this concept, you will learn to identify and describe parts of a whole using fractional names.

Dividing a Shape

- Dividing rectangles is usually easier than dividing circles.
- There is more than one way to divide a shape.

e.g. Divide each shape into 3 equal parts.

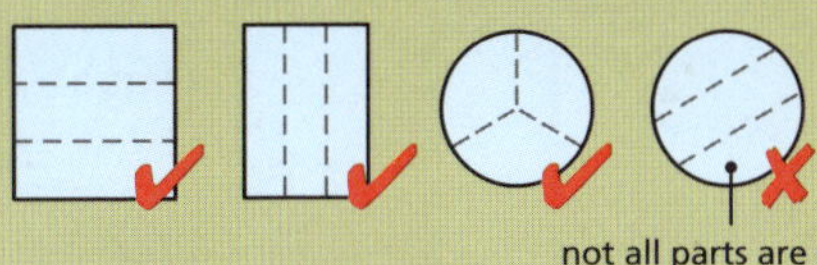

Understanding Fractional Names

e.g. Colour two fourths of the shape.

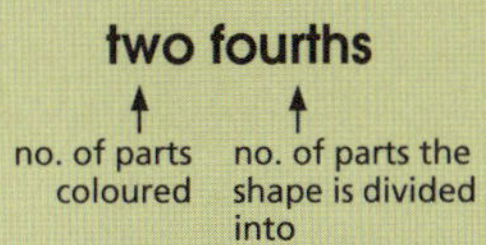

Answer:

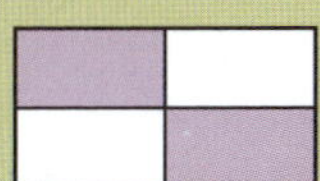

Naming Equal Parts

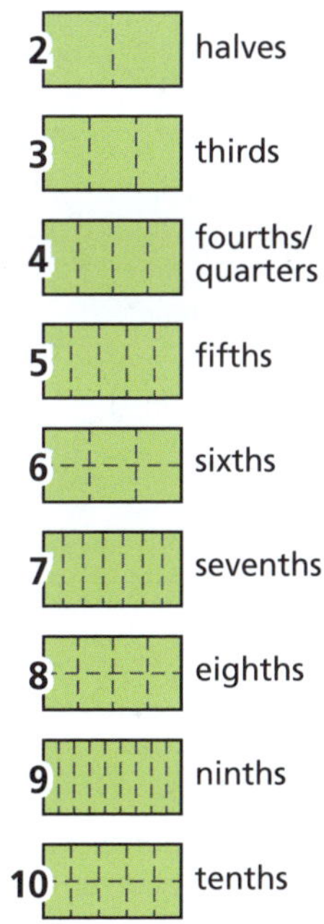

4.2 Dividing Sets of Objects into Equal Groups

At this point, you should be familiar with dividing whole objects into equal parts. You should be able to identify and use fractional names to describe parts of a whole. This unit shares the same concept, but instead of dividing one whole, this unit focuses on dividing a set.

Dividing a Set

When dividing a set of objects, consider the entire set as a whole.

e.g. Put the counters into quarters.

Solution Imagine the counters form a rectangle. Then divide the rectangle into 4 equal parts.

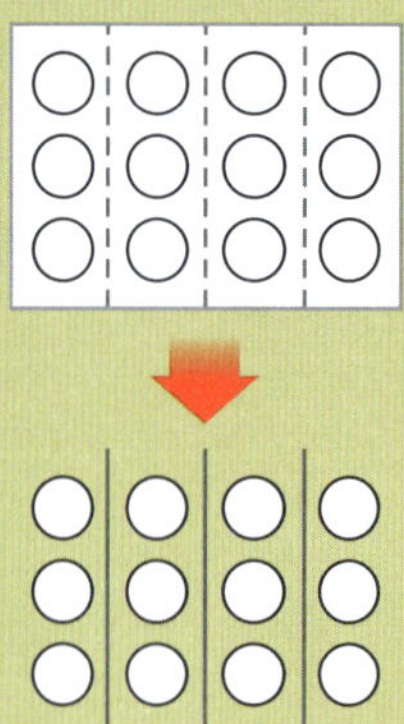

The counters are put into quarters. Each quarter has 3 counters.

Describing Parts of a Set

Fractional names can be used to describe parts of a set of objects.

e.g. What is three quarters of 12?

1st Draw 12 counters and put them into quarters.

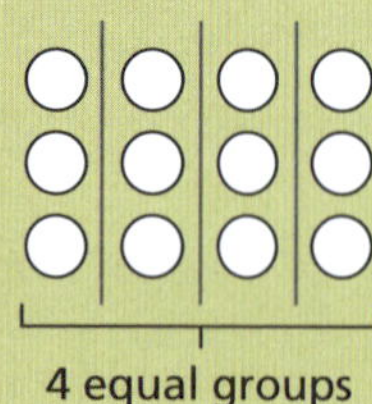

2nd Colour 3 groups.

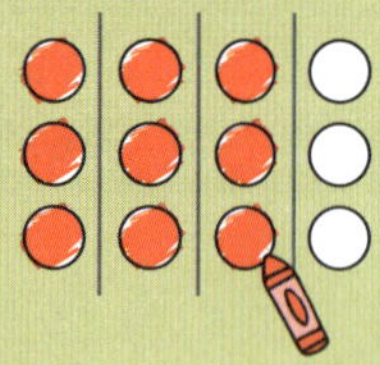

So, three quarters of 12 is 9.

Application

① *Joe dropped a carton of 18 eggs and broke some of them. If 1 more egg had been broken, then Joe would have broken two sixths of the eggs. How many eggs did Joe break?*

Solution:

two sixths of 18 = 6

Joe would have broken 6 eggs if he broke 1 more. So, he broke 5 eggs.

② *A toy costs $12. Anita spent four eighths of her savings to buy the toy. How much did Anita have in her savings before buying the toy?*

Solution:

Anita's Savings

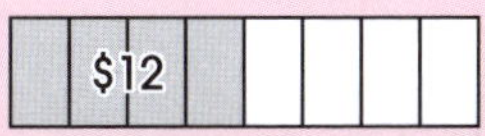

four eighths of her savings = $12
eight eighths of her savings = $12 + $12
= $24

Anita had $24 in her savings before buying the toy.

Chapter 5

Money

5.1 Counting and Trading Money

You should be familiar with the values of bills and coins. In this unit, you will learn to trade bills and coins by skip counting.

Skip Counting to Trade Money

- How many quarters can a loonie be traded for?

Skip count by 25¢ until you reach $1:

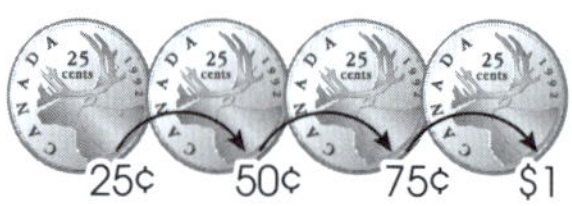

Answer: 4 quarters

- How many nickels can a quarter be traded for?

Skip count by 5¢ until you reach 25¢:

Answer: 5 nickels

To reinforce the concept, prepare some bills and coins to do some trading. Below are some sample questions you may think about.

- How many dimes can I trade for a loonie?
- How many quarters can I trade for 2 toonies?
- I have 10 dimes. How many quarters can I trade for?

Application

① *See how much money Doug has. How many coins can he trade for at most? Name the coins.*

Solution:

Total amount: $5 + $2 + $2 + $1 = $10

To trade for the most coins, Doug should trade for nickels.

$1 = 20 nickels

$10 = 200 nickels

Doug can trade for 200 nickels at most.

② *Jennifer has 20 of the same coin that add up to $2 in total. Which coins does she have?*

Solution:

$2 = 20 coins
$1 = 10 coins ⟵ 10 dimes make $1.

So, her coins are dimes.

5.2 Finding Money Amounts

In this unit, you will learn to find the value of a collection of different bills and coins by skip counting. Use this concept in real-life scenarios and with real coins so that you understand why it is important to learn this concept and how it applies to everyday situations.

e.g. Find the total.

Steps

1st Group the bills and coins of the same kind.

2nd Count the money in dollars first. Start with the bill or coin of the highest value.

3rd Count the money in cents. Start with the coin of the highest value.

4th Add the dollars and cents.

Solution

← 5 dollars

105 cents = 1 dollar 5 cents

Total: 5 dollars + 1 dollar 5 cents = 6 dollars 5 cents

Application

① *Ellen has 1 toonie and 1 quarter. If her mom gives her another coin, what are the greatest and smallest values she can have?*

Solution:

Greatest value

- Mom gave her a toonie.

$2 $2 25¢ 4 dollars 25 cents

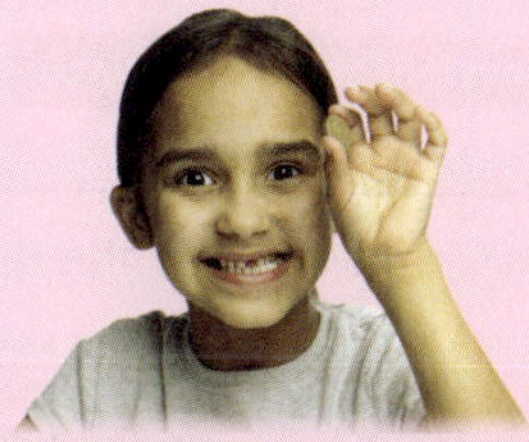

Smallest value

- Mom gave her a nickel.

$2 25¢ 5¢ 2 dollars 30 cents

The greatest and smallest values are 4 dollars 25 cents and 2 dollars 30 cents respectively.

② *Megan wants to make $1 with quarters and dimes. How many ways can she do it? Describe the ways.*

Solution:

Way 1 : quarters only

25¢ 25¢ 25¢ 25¢

Way 2 : quarters and dimes

25¢ 25¢ 10¢ 10¢ 10¢ 10¢ 10¢

Way 3 : dimes only

10¢ 10¢ 10¢ 10¢ 10¢ 10¢ 10¢ 10¢ 10¢ 10¢

Megan can do it in 3 ways: with 4 quarters, with 2 quarters and 5 dimes, or with 10 dimes.

5.3 Using Bills and Coins

This unit focuses on using bills and coins to pay for items. You will learn different ways to make a money amount and how to use the fewest bills and coins to pay for an item.

Showing Money Amounts

There are different ways to show a money amount. Use real bills and coins to help yourself relate the concept to real-life situations.

e.g. Show 9 dollars 45 cents.

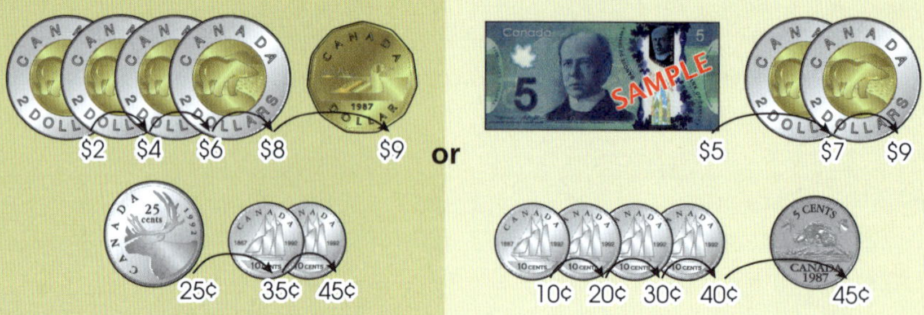

After you grasp the concept, show the same money amount using the fewest bills and coins.

1st Make $9. Start with the bill or coin of the **highest value**.

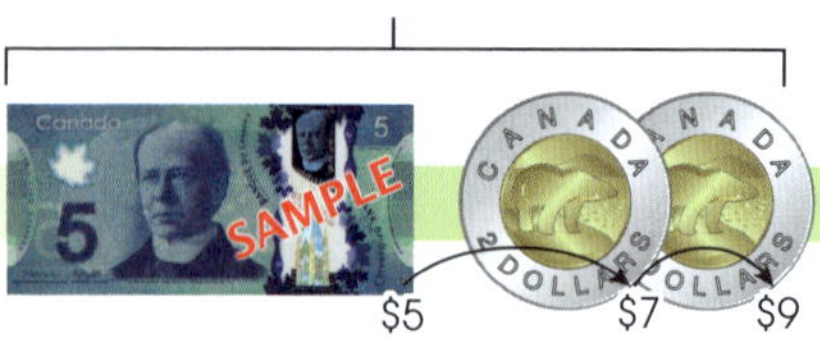

2nd Make 45¢. Start with the coin of the **highest value**.

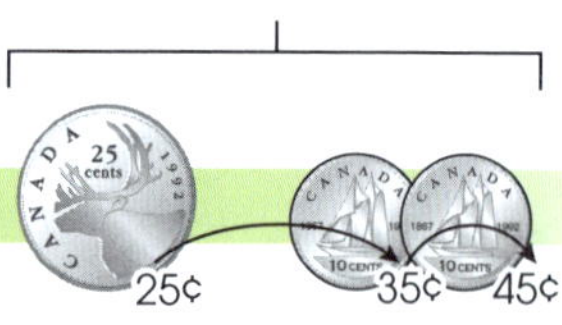

5.4 Adding Money Amounts to $10

Start with the concept of adding using real money in dollars. Then move on to include cents. Do some simple addition while shopping with your parents to improve your understanding of the concept.

Drawing and Counting Money

e.g. Add 6 dollars 20 cents and 1 dollar 85 cents.

1st Draw the fewest bills and coins for each amount.

2nd Group the bills and coins of the same kind. Then count to find the total.

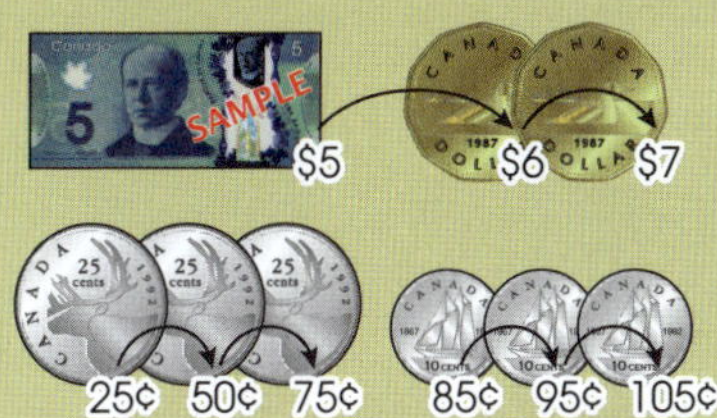

105¢: 1 dollar 5 cents

Total: 8 dollars 5 cents

Using Vertical Addition

e.g. Add 3 dollars 65 cents and 2 dollars 45 cents.

- Line up the "dollars" and "cents". Then add.
- Trade 100 cents for 1 dollar.

	dollars	cents
	3	6 5
+	2	4 5
	~~5~~ 6	~~1 1 0~~ 10

110 ← equals 1 dollar 10 cents

Total: 6 dollars 10 cents

Application

① *Phillip wants an ice cream cone that costs 3 dollars 50 cents. He wants to get one for his sister with sprinkles, which costs 75 cents extra. How much will he have to spend on both ice cream cones?*

Solution:

Phillip's sister's cone:

	dollars	cents
	3	50
+		75
	3	125

4 dollars 25 cents

Both cones:

	dollars	cents
	3	50
+	4	25
	7	75

7 dollars 75 cents

Phillip will have to spend 7 dollars 75 cents.

② *The prices of the toys are partly covered. At least how much is needed to pay for both toys?*

Solution:

Add the largest possible amounts.

	dollars	cents
	2	**9**0
+	3	**9**5
	5	185

At least 6 dollars 85 cents is needed to pay for both toys.

5.5 Subtracting Money Amounts

Before starting this unit, ensure that you have a solid understanding of trading coins and adding money amounts. Doing subtraction can be more challenging since it requires breaking bills and coins, as well as understanding the concept of borrowing dollars to make cents.

Crossing Out Coins

This method is the most direct way to introduce subtraction of money.

e.g. Take away 2 dollars 5 cents. How much is left?

Steps

1st Cross out the coins.

2nd Count the remaining coins.

Answer: 2 dollars 20 cents

There are times when coins need to be traded first.

e.g. Take away 2 dollars 5 cents. How much is left?

Steps

1st Break the money into smaller values.

2nd Cross out the coins.

3rd Count the remaining.

Answer: 3 dollars 20 cents

Counting Up

e.g. What is 5 dollars 25 cents – 3 dollars 75 cents?

1st Count up from the smaller amount to the nearest dollar.

2nd Count up to the "dollar" in the greater amount.

3rd Count up to the greater amount.

3 dollars 75 cents	→ 25 cents →	4 dollars	→ 1 dollar →	5 dollars	→ 25 cents →	**5 dollars 25 cents**

4th Add.

25 cents + 1 dollar + 25 cents

= 1 dollar 50 cents

Answer: 1 dollar 50 cents

Vertical Subtraction

e.g. What is 7 dollars 15 cents – 5 dollars 25 cents?

1st Line up the "dollars" and "cents".

	dollars	**cents**
	7	(15)
–	5	25

← Since 15 < 25, borrow 100¢ from $7.

2nd Subtract.

	dollars	**cents**
	6 ~~7~~	~~15~~ 115
–	5	25
	1	**90**

6 – 5 = 1   115 – 25 = 90

Answer: 1 dollar 90 cents

Application

I bought a jar of jam for 1 dollar 35 cents and a loaf of bread for 4 dollars 60 cents. I paid with a $10 bill and the cashier gave me back 2 toonies and 1 nickel.

Did he get the correct change?

Solution:

Find his change.

	dollars	cents			dollars	cents
	9	100			8	65
−	1	35	→	−	4	60
	8	65			4	5

2 toonies and 1 nickel = 4 dollars 5 cents

Yes, he got the correct change.

Chapter 6

Measurement

6.1 Measuring Length in "cm", "m", and "km"

Familiarize yourself with the uses of different measuring units. For instance, the width of a laptop should be measured in cm, whereas the distance between a house and an airport should be measured in km.

Centimetre (cm)

Many things around us are measured in centimetre (cm). We can find measurements in cm with a ruler.

e.g.

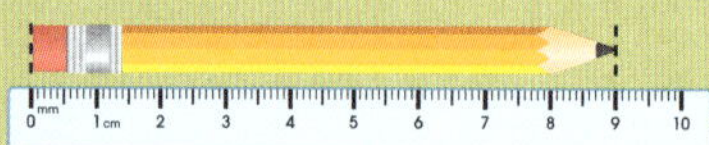

The pencil is 9 cm long.

Metre (m)

The metre (m) is a larger unit than the centimetre (cm).

e.g.

Kilometre (km)

The kilometre (km) is the most common unit used to measure long distances.

e.g.

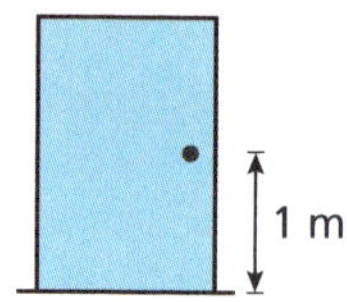

height from floor to doorknob

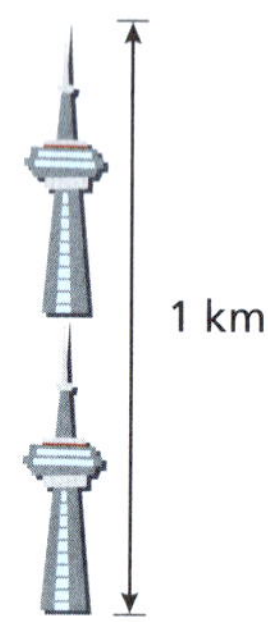

height of two CN Towers

Use these benchmarks to help estimate lengths and distances.

6.2 Measuring Capacity in "L"

The litre is the first unit you will use to describe capacity. You should understand that capacity is the amount of liquid (e.g. water, juice, milk, etc.) a container can hold, and can be measured in litres. Using a bottle to hold a litre of juice is a good way to learn how litres fit into your daily life.

Estimating Capacities

Familiarize yourself with the concept of 1 litre with containers from around the house. Being familiar with 1 L will help you make reasonable estimates.

Stage 1

Determine whether a container has a capacity of more or less than 1 L.

Stage 2

Make estimates that are more precise, such as a quarter of a litre, half a litre, etc.

Stage 3

Make estimates that are more than 1 L.

Describing Capacities

It is important that you are able to describe capacities. Try the activity below to reinforce your ability to describe given capacities.

1st Find a clear bottle that has a capacity of 1 L.

2nd Draw markings on the bottle to divide it into 4 equal parts.

3rd Fill the bottle with water to different levels. Describe the amount of water it contains.

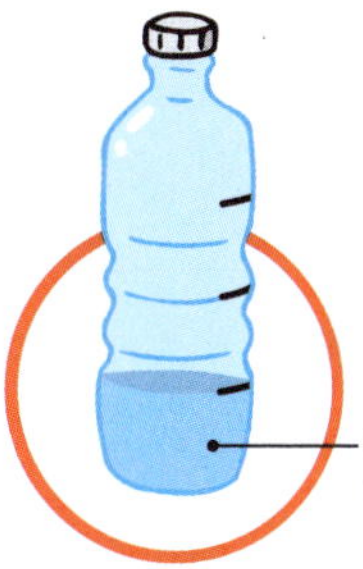

Application

A pot has a capacity of 8 L and a bowl has a capacity of half a litre. How many bowls of water are needed to fill half of the pot?

Solution:

Pot = 8 L
Half the pot = 4 L

Find the number of bowls needed to fill half of the pot, which is 4 L.

 = half a litre

2  = 1 L

8  = 4 L ← fills half of the pot

So, 8 bowls are needed.

6.3 Measuring Mass in "kg"

At this stage, you should have a good understanding of mass and should be able to use words such as "heavier" and "lighter" to compare mass. In this unit, you will learn to estimate and describe mass using a standard unit of measure: the kilogram.

Getting Familiar with 1 kg

Find things around the house that are 1 kg. Weigh the items in your hands to become familiar with a mass of 1 kg.

Suggested items:

Describing Mass in kg

Describe mass in kg. Try the activity below.

1st Gather a bag of 7 apples with a mass of about 1 kg.

2nd Take out 4 apples. Describe its mass.

3rd Think of another item that has about the same mass.

4th Repeat the activity with 3 apples and 6 apples.

Use these words:

- a quarter of a kilogram
- half a kilogram
- three quarters of a kilogram

Application

A bigger object must have a greater mass than a smaller object.

Is this true? Explain and give an example.

Solution:

No, it is not true. A bigger object does take up more space, but it is not necessarily heavier than a smaller object.

e.g. balloon tennis ball

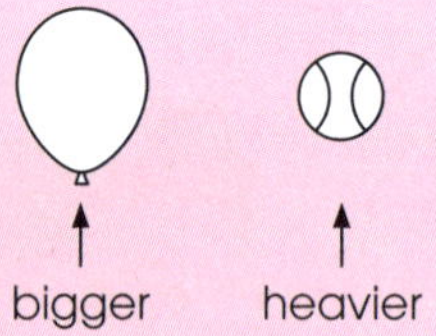

Even though a balloon is bigger, it does not have a greater mass than a tennis ball.

Chapter 7

Time and Temperature

7.1 Reading and Writing Time

In this unit, you will learn to tell time to the nearest five minutes. Therefore, it is important that you are able to count forward by 5's.

Reading an Analogue Clock

* Make sure you know that the hour hand is short and the minute hand is long.

- Hour: If the hour hand is between two numbers, pick the "earlier" hour.
- Minute: Count on by 5's from 12.

e.g. The clock shows 35 minutes after 12.

or

- Hour: If the hour hand is between two numbers, pick the "later" hour.
- Minute: Count on by 5's from the numbers to 12.

e.g. The clock shows 25 minutes before 1.

Writing Time in 12-hour Notation

a.m. denotes the time before noon.

p.m. denotes the time after noon.

e.g. 7:30 a.m. means 7:30 in the morning.

7:30 p.m. means 7:30 in the evening.

Note: Midnight is 12:00 a.m. Noon is 12:00 p.m.

Reading a Digital Clock

The clock shows 24 minutes after 10.

7.2 Relating Different Units of Time

You should be familiar with some relationships between units of time. In this unit, new relationships will be introduced. To understand them better, figure out the relationships using different tools, including clocks, monthly calendars, and yearly calendars.

Summary

1 hour = 60 minutes
1 day = 24 hours
1 week = 7 days
1 year = 52 weeks

Minutes and Hours

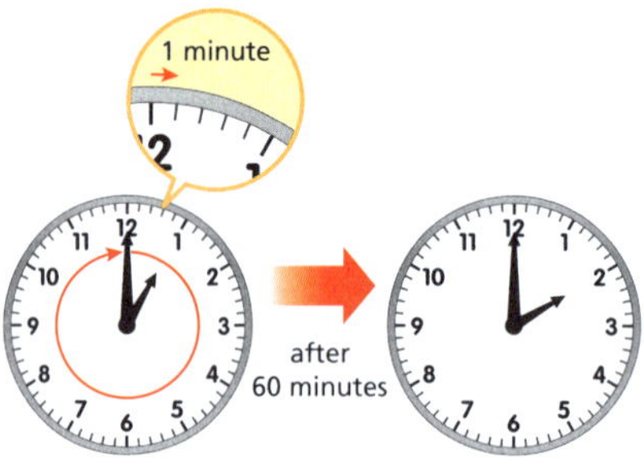

Count the number of minutes there are in one hour.

Hours and Days

Remember that a day starts at midnight (12:00 a.m.) and ends at 11:59 p.m. at night.

Days and Weeks

October						2015
S	M	T	W	T	F	S
27	28	29	30	1	2	3
4	5	6	7	8	9	10
11	12	13	14	15	16	17
18	19	20	21	22	23	24
25	26	27	28	29	30	31

← 7 days in a week

Count the number of days there are in a week.

Weeks and Years

Count the number of weeks there are in a year.

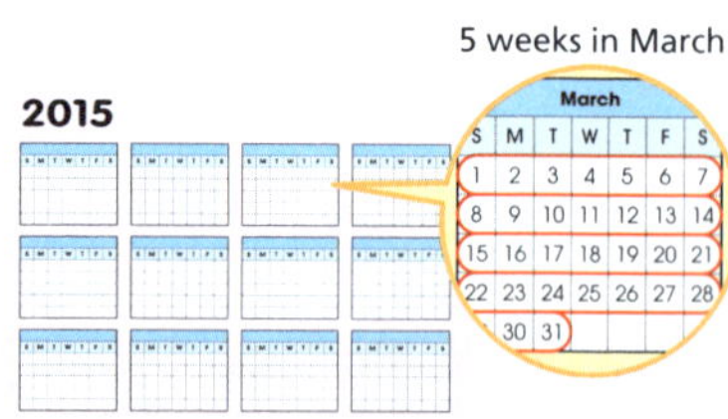

Application

Louise, Jacqueline, and Dominic were given an art project. It took Louise 3 days to finish it, more than 1 week for Jacqueline, and 48 hours for Dominic.

> Put the students in order from the one who spent the least time to the one who spent the most.

Solution:

Compare the amount of time in days.

Louise: 3 days
Jacqueline: 1 week = 7 days
Dominic: 48 hours = 2 days

$2 < 3 < 7$

The order is Dominic, Louise, and Jacqueline from the person who spent the least to the most time on the art project.

7.3 Recording and Describing Temperatures

At this point, you should be able to read temperatures on a thermometer. This unit focuses on identifying the benchmarks for different temperatures as they relate to water and air.

Do the following activities and record the temperatures in the chart.

Temperatures of Water

Use a thermometer to measure and record the temperatures of the things below.

- freezing

full bowl of ice

- cold

ice water

- cool

melted ice

- warm

add some hot water until it feels warm

- hot

add some hot water until it feels hot

- boiling

do not touch

Temperatures of Air

Use a thermometer to measure the temperature of air whenever possible. If this is not possible, think about the temperatures of the seasons and use them as reference.

- cold (winter: 1°C)
- cool (fall: 12°C)
- warm (spring: 20°C)
- hot (summer: 35°C)

Description	Water	Air
freezing		Air does not freeze.
cold		
cool		
warm		
hot		
boiling	100°C	Air does not boil.

Record in this chart for the activities.

Application

A glass of water is 40°C after being left on a countertop for half an hour. Do you think it was taken out of a fridge, or was it boiling half an hour ago? Explain.

Solution:

Fridge: about 3°C
Room temperature: about 20°C to 26°C
Boiling water: about 100°C

It is impossible for it to have been taken out of a fridge because room temperature cannot "heat up" water to 40°C.

The water must have been boiling and then cooled down at room temperature to 40°C.

Chapter 8

Perimeter and Area

8.1 Finding Perimeter

At this point, you should know what perimeter is and be able to find perimeters using non-standard units. In this unit, you will learn how to find perimeters in standard units, using a centimetre grid, a ruler, etc.

Using a Centimetre Grid

1st Identify the outline of the shape or object to be measured.

2nd Count.

Perimeter: 20 cm

Using a Ruler

1st Measure the sides and record them. (Estimate when needed.)

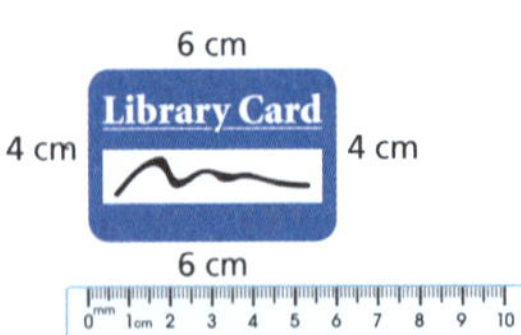

2nd Add up all sides.
Perimeter: 6 + 4 + 6 + 4 = 20

The perimeter is 20 cm.

Use this grid to find perimeters in cm.

Application

Katie wants to put a fence around the rectangular garden in her backyard. The garden has a length of 3 m and a width of 2 m. Will 8 m of fencing be enough?

Solution:

Draw a diagram of the garden and label its measurements.

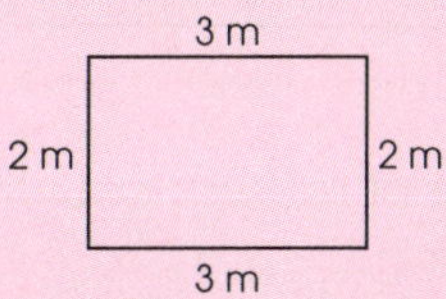

Finding the amount of fencing needed for the rectangular garden means finding the perimeter of the garden.

Perimeter = 3 + 2 + 3 + 2 = 10

The garden needs 10 m of fencing, so 8 m of fencing will not be enough.

8.2 Finding Area

You should be familiar with measuring area using different non-standard units. In this unit, you will compare the different number of units needed to cover the same area when the measuring units are different.

Finding Area on a Grid

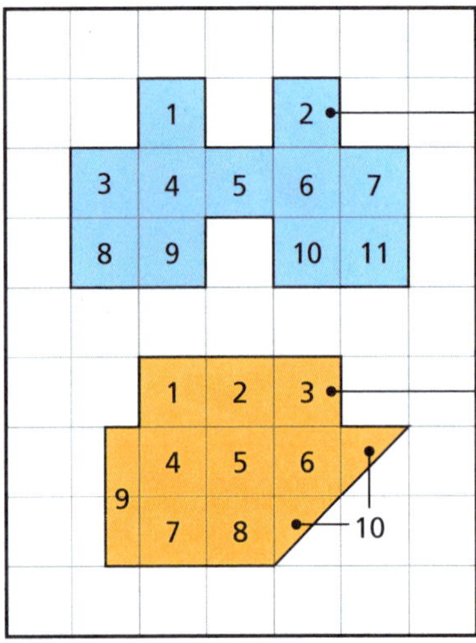

Write the number of squares counted as you are counting.

Area of 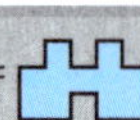 : 11 □

Count the complete squares first. Then count the half squares: ◺ or ▯ . Count 2 halves as 1 square.

Area of  : 10 □

Make some grids as a tool to explore the concept of area.

Make a 1-cm grid with a marker on a piece of wax paper. Make a 1.5-cm grid and a 2-cm grid as well.

Measure the area of an object (e.g. a library card, a notepad, etc.) using all three grids. Then think about the questions below:

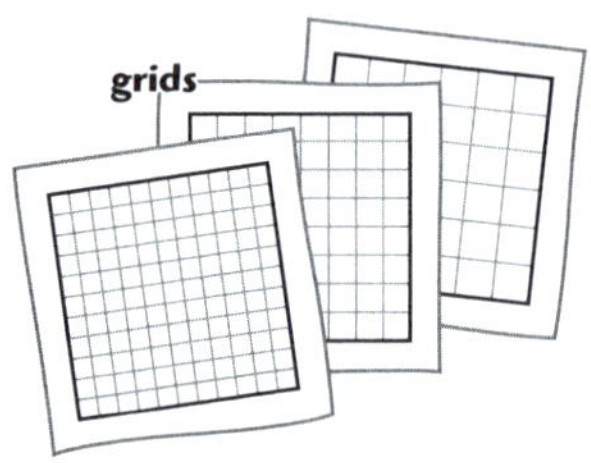

1. Does the area of the object change when different grids are used?
2. Is it more accurate to use a 1-cm grid or a 2-cm grid?

Chapter 9

Two-dimensional Shapes

9.1 Identifying and Describing Angles

Use tools such as pencils, Popsicle sticks, and chopsticks to create angles to help yourself understand how angles can be formed. Right angles can be used as a benchmark for comparing angles of different sizes.

Identifying Right Angles

Identify right angles on different objects.

e.g.

Using a tool to identify right angles:

1st Tear out a corner of a sheet of paper (a right angle) and use it as a tool.

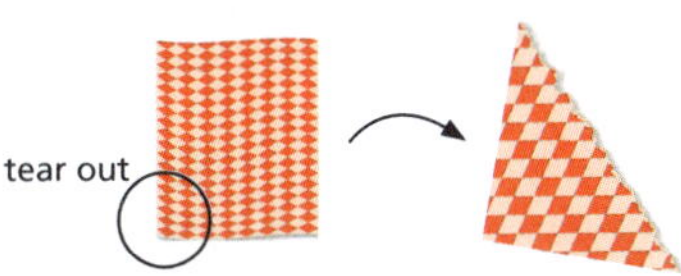

2nd Place the "tool" on the angles to be measured.

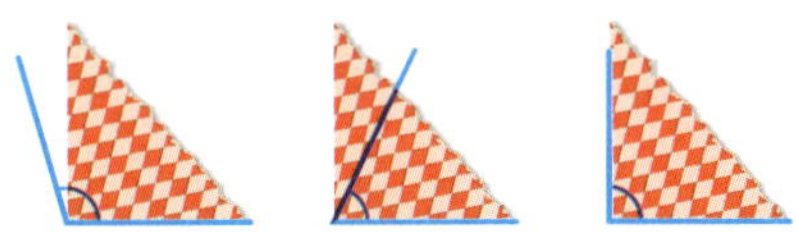

larger than a right angle | smaller than a right angle | a right angle

Comparing Angles

The farther apart the lines are, the larger the angle is.

e.g.

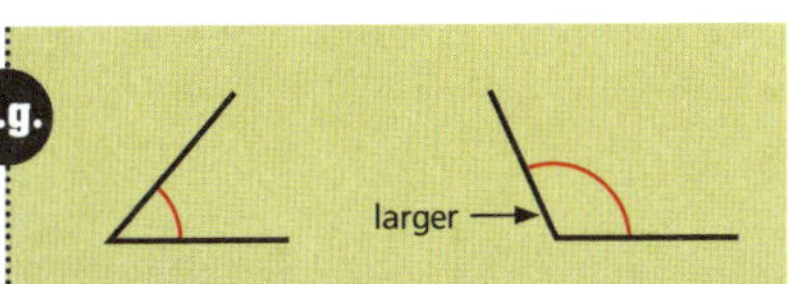

Make angles with your thumb and index fingers.

e.g.

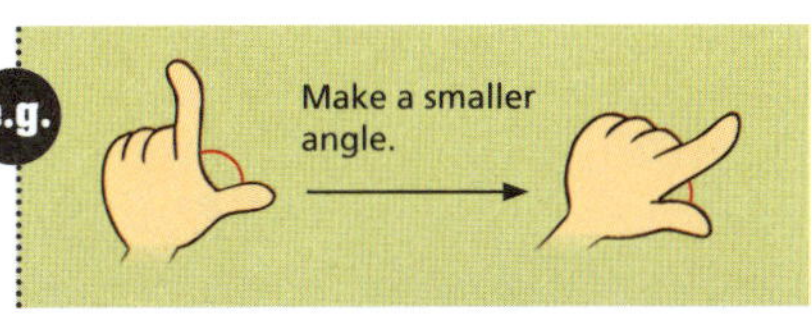

Application

The angle that the blue arms make must be bigger because the arms are longer.

Is what the girl says true? Explain.

Solution:

No, it is not true.

The size of an angle is not affected by the lengths of the arms. For example, the corner of a desk and the corner of a ruler are both right angles, even though the arms of the desk are longer.

9.2 Identifying and Composing Shapes

In this unit, you will learn the names of shapes based on the number of sides they have. You will also identify some properties of shapes including the number of angles they have. You will learn what congruent shapes are and how to compose shapes.

Naming Shapes

Shapes are named based on the number of sides they have:

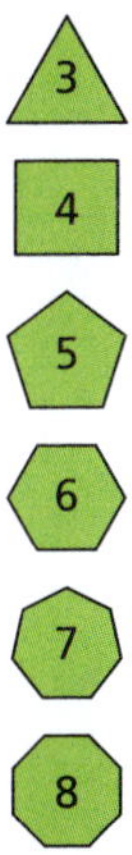

triangle

quadrilateral

pentagon

hexagon

heptagon

octagon

Identifying Congruent Shapes

Congruent shapes are shapes that are the exact same shape and size, even if they are reflected or rotated.

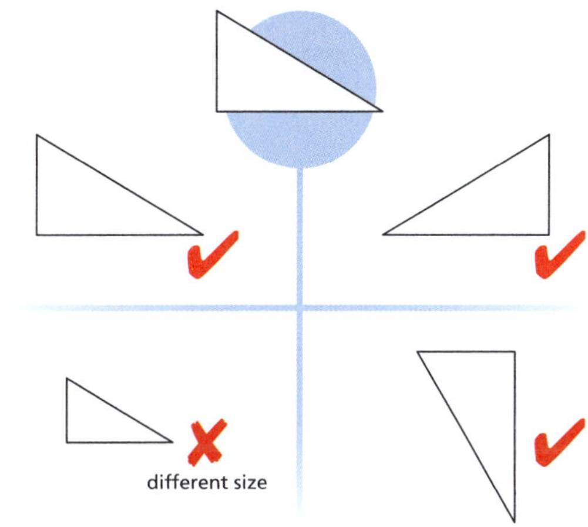

Composing Shapes

Many shapes can be composed to form other shapes.

e.g. Below are some shapes that are composed by triangles and squares.

hexagon: 6 triangles | pentagon: 1 triangle and 3 sqaures | trapezoid: 4 triangles and 2 squares | triangle: 4 triangles

Application

Jody made a pentagon with five triangles, but I can make one with only three triangles.

Is it possible? Describe how and make a sketch.

Solution:

Jody's pentagon Oscar's pentagon

made with 5 triangles made with 3 triangles

Yes, it is possible.

Chapter 10

Three-dimensional Figures

10.1 Naming 3-D Figures

You should be able to differentiate between prisms and pyramids. In this unit, the focus is on naming these prisms and pyramids by the shape of their bases.

Identifying Prisms and Pyramids

Prism: has 2 bases

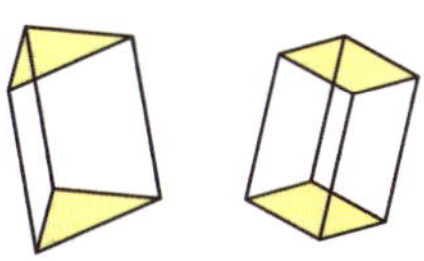

Pyramid: has 1 base

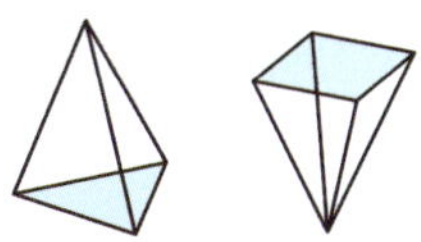

Note: The base is not always at the bottom.

Naming 3-D Figures

e.g.

1st Identify whether it is a prism or a pyramid.

a prism

2nd Name the prism or pyramid by the shape of its base(s).

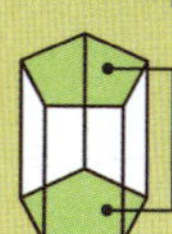

a pentagonal prism

Name these figures:

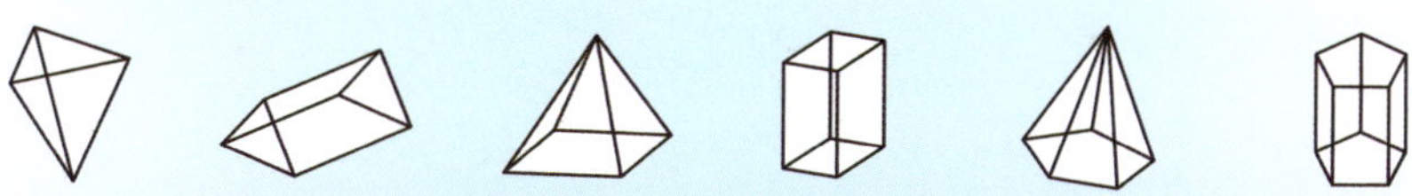

Application

Gordan wants to build this figure using triangular prisms. Is it possible? If so, how many prisms are needed? Show how the figure is built.

Solution:

Yes, it is possible.

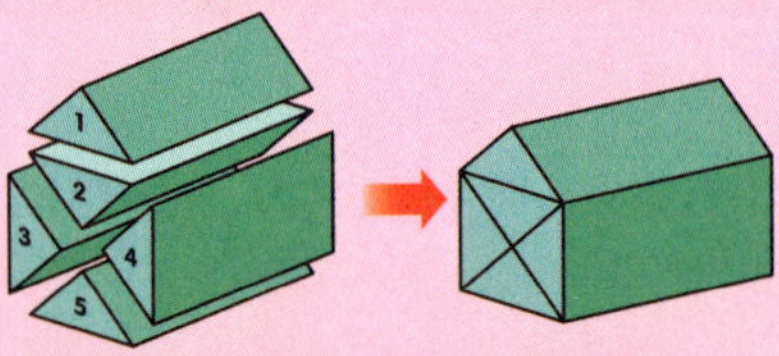

5 triangular prisms are needed.

10.2 Comparing and Sorting 3-D Figures

In this unit, you will identify the shapes of the faces of 3-D figures. You will also be introduced to vertices and edges. As you may find it difficult to visualize 3-D figures printed on paper, you may use real objects, such as a cereal box and a refrigerator, for rectangular prisms.

Describing the Faces of 3-D Figures

Learn to identify the shapes of the faces of 3-D figures.

e.g. Identify the faces.

2 triangles	1 pentagon
3 rectangles	5 triangles

You may find it difficult to identify the faces of drawn figures that are not transparent. It is helpful to visualize them by using real objects.

e.g.

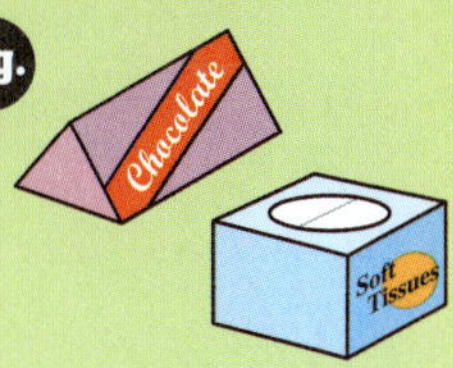

Identifying Vertices and Edges

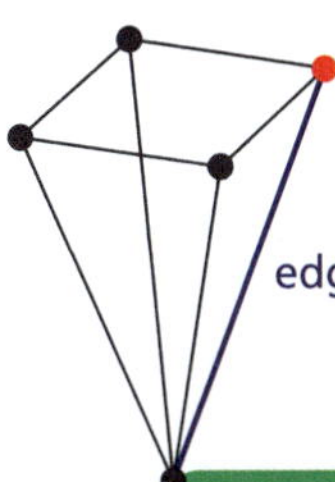

vertex: a corner

edge: joining two or more vertices

5 vertices
8 edges

Touch a vertex or an edge and identify it.

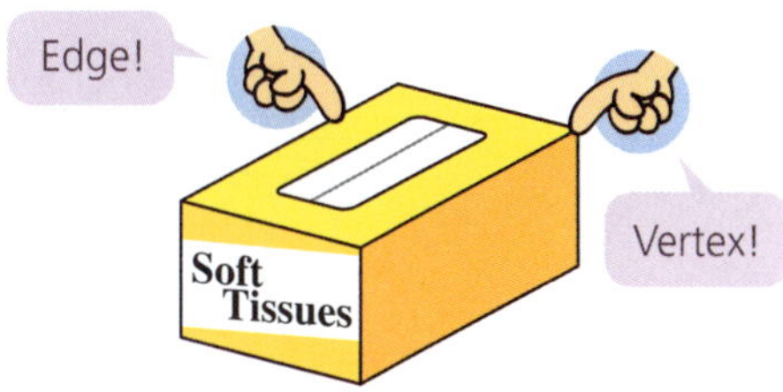

Application

Karen built some 3-D figures. All of these figures have one thing in common: the number of faces is the same as the number of vertices. Did she build pyramids or prisms? Explain and give examples.

Solution:

Randomly pick a pyramid and a prism and draw them.

prism

pyramid

5 faces
6 vertices ✘

4 faces
4 vertices ✔ same

Draw more pyramids to see if this applies to them as well.

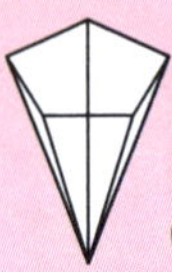
pyramid
✔

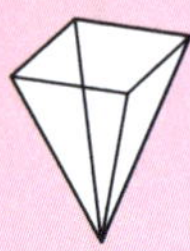
pyramid
✔

These pyramids have the same number of faces and vertices too.

So, Karen built pyramids.

10.3 Constructing 3-D Figures

Learning to construct 3-D figures will help you visualize them. Before building the figures, it is a good idea to make sketches on paper so that you have an idea of what you are building.

Building Figures

Way 1 Using marshmallows and uncooked spaghetti

1st Use marshmallows as vertices and spaghetti as edges.

2nd Break the spaghetti into shorter pieces if needed.

3rd Name the 3-D figures you have built. Then describe their properties.

Samples:

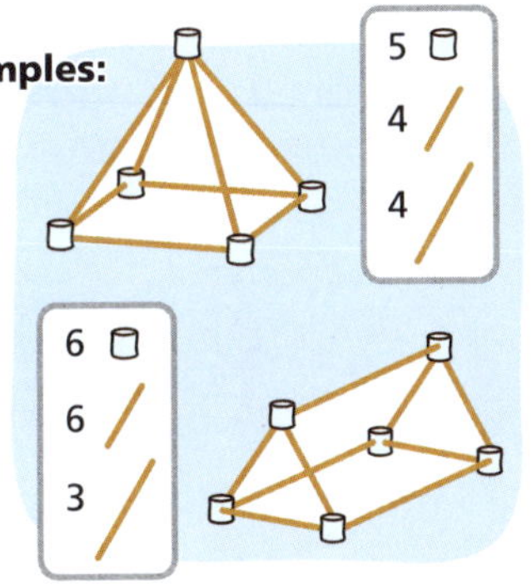

Way 2 Using paper nets

1st There are two templates on the next page. Trace each template onto a sheet of paper.

2nd Cut out each template.

3rd Fold the templates along the lines and glue the tabs.

4th Name the figures and describe them.

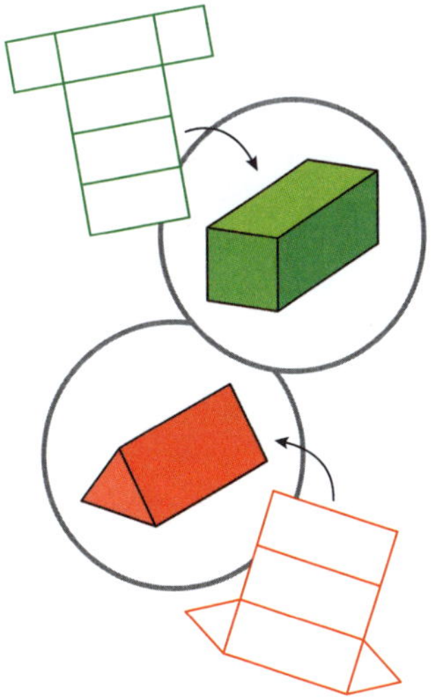

Application

I want to build a prism using 12 marshmallows and some sticks. What prism can I build? How many sticks do I need?

Solution:

12 marshmallows = 12 vertices

A prism must have 2 bases which have the same number of vertices. So, each base would have 6 vertices.

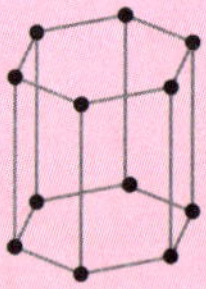

vertices: 12
edges: 18

So, she can build a hexagonal prism. She needs 18 sticks.

Chapter 11

Locations and Movements

11.1 Describing Movements on a Grid Map

In this unit, you will learn to describe movement from one location to another on a simple grid map. First, familiarize yourself with the four directions: up, down, left, and right. Then count squares to describe movements.

Giving Directions

Trace your finger on the map from the centre to "up", "down", "left", and "right". This will familiarize you with the 4 directions.

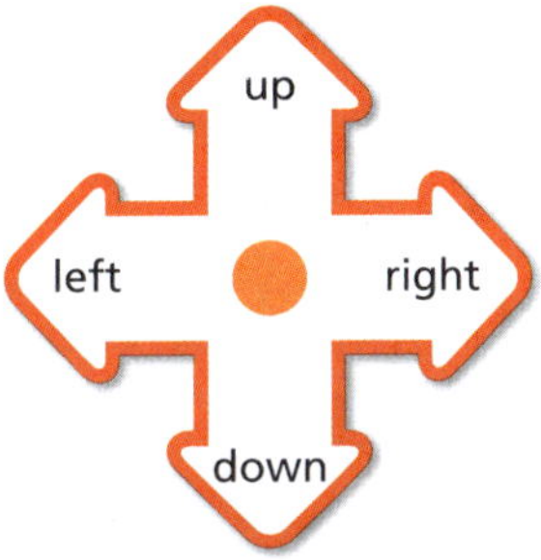

You may have trouble differentiating between left and right. If needed, you may make an "L" with your thumbs and fingers. The hand that makes the "L" is the "**L**eft" hand.

Try the following:

1st Point at .

2nd Go 2 squares right and 2 squares down.

3rd You should be pointing at .

Navigate the grid by following these directions: go ______ square(s) **left / right** and ______ square(s) **up / down** .

11.2 Identifying and Drawing Symmetrical Shapes

At this stage, you should be able to identify symmetrical figures and their lines of symmetry. In this unit, you will learn that some figures have more than one line of symmetry, and be able to identify them.

To help visualize that a figure can have more than one line of symmetry, you should make some figures. Try the following activities to understand the concept.

Folding and Cutting

1. 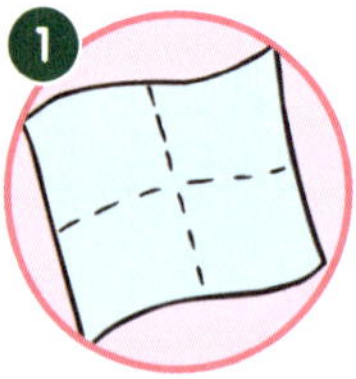
Fold a square piece of paper along the dotted lines.

2. 
Cut out a random shape.

3. 
Unfold the paper. Mark the folded lines. These are the lines of symmetry of the figure.

* To make more lines of symmetry, make more folds before cutting out a shape.

Mirroring

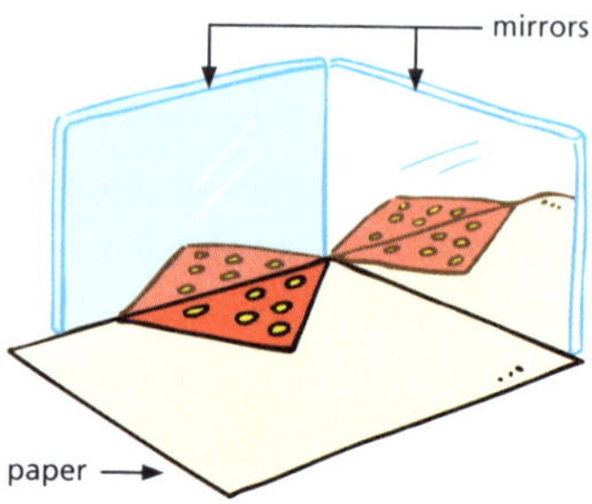

The images and the shape drawn make a figure that has 2 lines of symmetry.

1. Draw a shape on a sheet of paper.
2. Place two mirrors at the edges of the piece of paper.

Application

What shape has many, many lines of symmetry?

Name the shape and explain.

Solution:

The more sides a shape has, the more lines of symmetry it has:

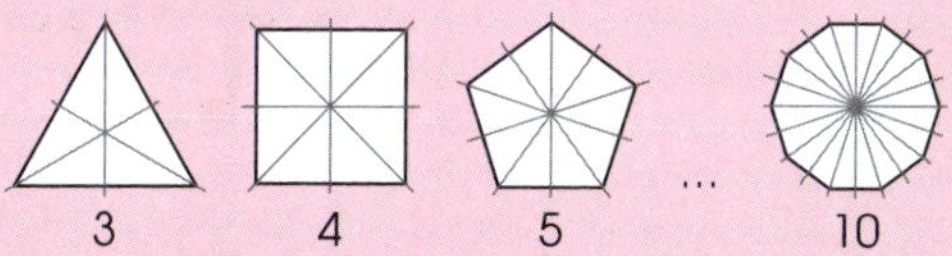

Notice that the more sides a shape has, the more it looks like a circle.

So, a circle has many, many lines of symmetry.

11.3 Identifying Transformations

When it comes to transformations, make sure you understand that a shape that is transformed is still the same shape, colour, and size; only its orientation and/or location has changed.

Translation (Slide)

- a figure sliding from one place to another

  e.g. a skater gliding on ice

Rotation (Turn)

- a figure making a turn

  e.g. a Ferris wheel turning

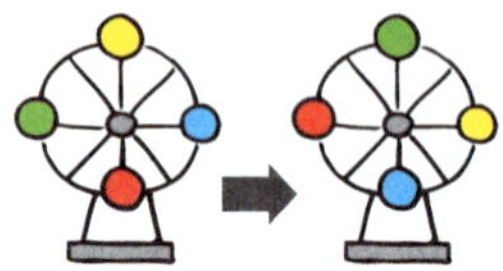

Reflection (Flip)

- a figure that is flipped

  e.g. the reflected image of yourself in a mirror

Note: After any of the transformations above, the figures are still the same size.

Chapter 12

Patterning and Algebra

12.1 Identifying and Extending Patterns

In this unit, you will explore patterns that have two changing attributes. More focus will be placed on number patterns at this level.

Extending Patterns

To extend a pattern, you must be able to identify the attributes first.

e.g. What comes next?

Colour	red	yellow	yellow	red	yellow	yellow	**red**
							+
Size	big	small	big	small	big	small	**big**

Attributes of the pattern:

- ✔ size
- ○ orientation
- ○ shape
- ✔ colour

The next fish must be red and big.

Identifying and Making Number Patterns

Three types of number patterns:

- **repeating**: repeating numbers
  e.g. 20, 5, 20, 5, 20, 5
- **growing**: numbers get larger
  e.g. 20, 22, 24, 26, 28
- **shrinking**: numbers get smaller
  e.g. 20, 16, 12, 8, 4

Make a pattern.

e.g. Start at 5. Add 3 each time.

+3 +3 +3

5 , 8 , 11 , 14

Try to make more patterns.

e.g. Start at 10. Subtract 2 each time.
Start at 20. Add 5 each time.

Application

Look at the growing pattern the boy is showing. Some numbers are covered with ink. Figure out the numbers and write a pattern rule.

Solution:

15, 2■, ■7, 33

1st ■ must be greater than 20 and smaller than 33:

27

15, 2■, 27, 33

2nd

27 →(+6) 33

So, the difference between this number and 27 must be 6.

21

15, →(+6) 21, →(+6) 27, →(+6) 33

The numbers are 21 and 27. The pattern rule is:
Start at 15. Add 6 each time.

12.2 Solving Equations and Identifying Properties

This unit requires you to have a good understanding of equality. You will be introduced to related facts, which is an essential concept for solving equations. You will also learn some basic properties of addition and multiplication.

Finding Related Facts

Related facts: addition and subtraction sentences that are related because they have the same numbers in them

e.g. Write the related facts of $1 + 2 = 3$.

$2 + 1 = 3$
$3 - 1 = 2$
$3 - 2 = 1$

Note that the numbers used in each number sentence are the same.

Activity

1. Make a set of cards with the numbers 1 to 10 and the signs "+", "–", and "=".
2. Make a number sentence.

   e.g. 4 + 2 = 6

3. Make the related facts.

This activity will help you understand that related facts are from the same three numbers. You should make correct number sentences using these three numbers.

e.g.

6 – 2 = 4 ✓

6 + 2 = 4 ✗

Finding Missing Numbers in Equations

Once you are familiar with related facts, you will be ready to find missing numbers in equations.

e.g. 12 – **?** = 7

Think Related fact: 7 + **?** = 12

7 + **5** = 12

So, 12 – **5** = 7. ← 5 is the missing number.

Properties of Addition and Subtraction

- When adding three or more numbers, the sum will be the same even if the order of the numbers being added is different.

Activity

1. Pick three numbers from your set of cards.
2. Arrange them horizontally and add them from left to right.

2	5	1

   sum: 8
3. Rearrange the cards and add again.

5	1	2

   sum: 8

- A number multiplied by 1 is always the number itself; a number multiplied by 0 is always 0.

Activity Use zip-lock bags and any small items, such as paper clips and candies, to learn the concept.

e.g. How many candies are there in total?

1. 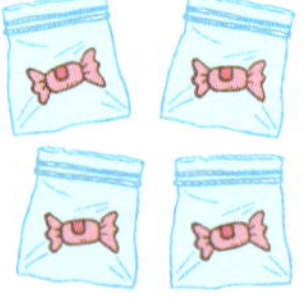

   4 groups of 1

2. 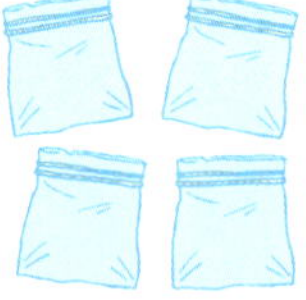

   4 groups of 0

Chapter 13

Data Management

13.1 Analyzing Graphs

You will analyze different types of graphs and learn the essential components of a graph. You will also learn to find the mode of a set of data.

A Tally Chart

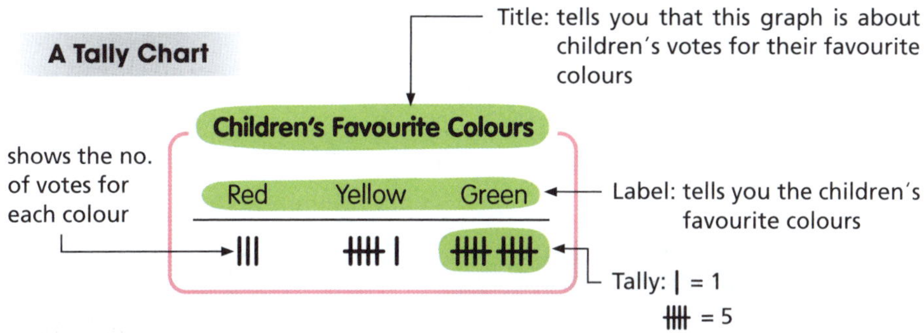

A Pictograph

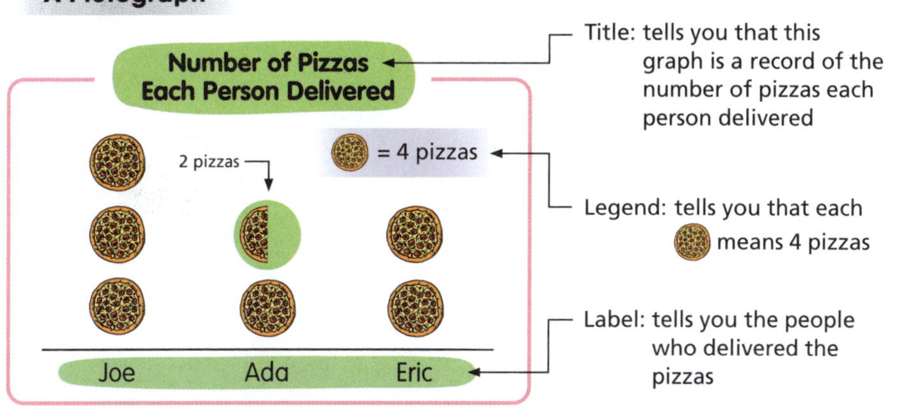

A Bar Graph

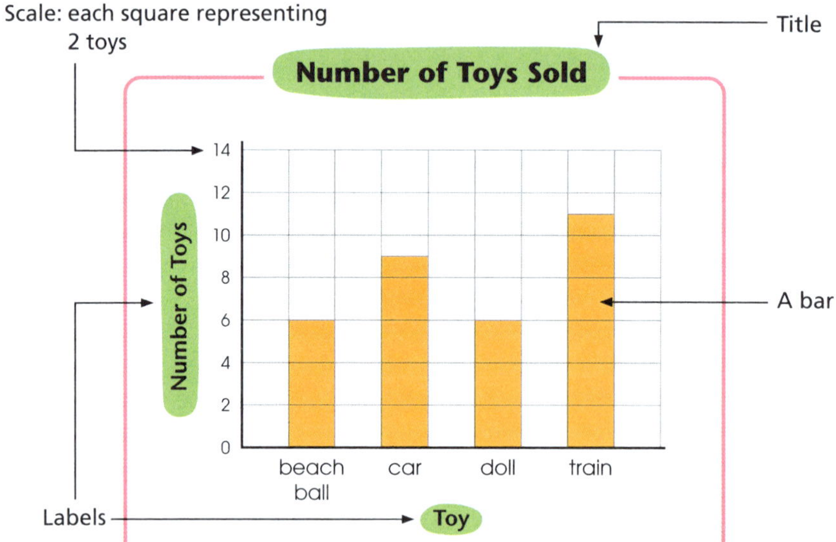

Think about the following questions:

- Summer starts next month. Do you think more beach balls will be sold?
- If you were the manager of the shop, would you stock up on more trains?

Finding the Mode of a Set of Data

Mode: the number that appears most often

e.g. What is the mode of the number of toys sold in the graph above?

Toy	Number
beach ball	6
car	9
doll	6
train	11

appears most often

The mode of the set of data is 6.

13.2 Drawing Graphs

In this unit, you will learn to organize data and present the data in graphs. You will need to make appropriate titles, labels, scales, and categories for the graphs.

When making a graph, make sure the following things are included:

Title A descriptive title gives people a good idea of what the graph is about.

○ Eye Colours ✔ Eye Colours of Students in My Class

Label Label the axes with precise and clear wording.

✔ Eye Colour
○ Colour of Eyes

and

○ Students
✔ Number of Students

Scale Decide on a good scale to represent the data.

✔ a scale from 0 to 12
○ a scale from 0 to 1000

Category Name the categories clearly.

○ bl br h g
✔ blue brown hazel green

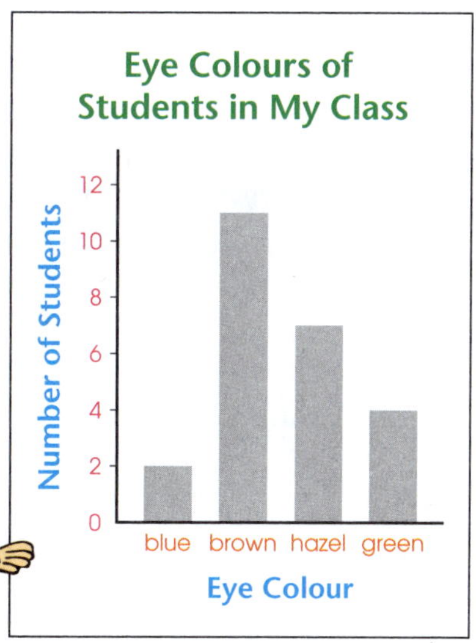

Make sure the widths of the bars are the same.

Chapter 14

Probability

14.1 Finding the Frequency of an Outcome

In this unit, you will learn to predict and describe an event more precisely. For example, you may be able to predict that if a dice is rolled 10 times, an odd number will come up 5 times. Try the activity below to understand the concept of frequency of an outcome.

Instructions

Materials:

- tissue paper
- a highlighter or marker
- a shopping bag

1. Crumple up 10 pieces of tissue paper. Colour 5 of them with a highlighter or a marker. Then put all 10 of them into a shopping bag.
2. Predict the number of times each kind of tissue paper will be drawn (coloured or uncoloured) if you draw 10 times.
3. Pick out a piece of tissue paper 10 times. Record the results. Put the tissue paper back each time.
4. Follow the description on the bag in the Record section below and change the combinations of tissue paper accordingly. Then repeat steps 2 and 3.

Record

		Prediction	Actual
A	5 coloured		
	5 uncoloured		
B	6 coloured		
	4 uncoloured		
C	8 coloured		
	2 uncoloured		

Questions

- If you draw a piece of tissue paper from A 5 times, will the number of each type of tissue paper picked be the same?
- If you want to pick an uncoloured piece of tissue paper, which combination should you use, A, B, or C?

Application

My brother, Luke, rolled the dice 15 times. It landed on an even number and an odd number the same number of times.

Is this possible? Explain.

Solution:

List the most possible cases.

	Case 1	Case 2	Case 3	Case 4
Odd	6	7	8	9
Even	9	8	7	6
Total	15	15	15	15

There is no case where the number of odd numbers and the number of even numbers are equal.

So, it is not possible.

14.2 Determining Fairness

Once you learn to find the frequency of an outcome, you will be able to understand the concept of fairness, which is the occurrence of equally likely outcomes.

To determine whether or not an event is fair, find out whether the occurrence of each outcome is the same.

Make sure you understand that the number of outcomes does not affect fairness. Rather, it is the likelihood of each outcome that determines fairness. For example, as shown above, the first and the last spinners are fair because the likelihood of getting each colour is exactly the same.

Application

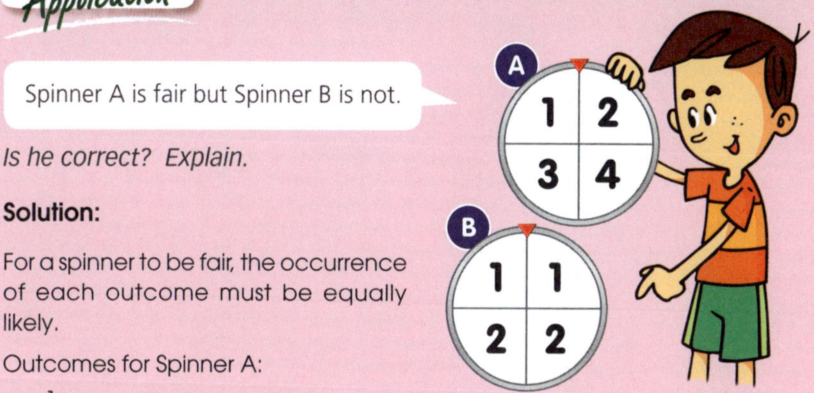

Is he correct? Explain.

Solution:

For a spinner to be fair, the occurrence of each outcome must be equally likely.

Outcomes for Spinner A:

1, 2, 3, 4 — one fourth for all; equally likely outcomes

Spinner A is fair.

Outcomes for Spinner B:

1, 2 — one half for all; equally likely outcomes

Spinner B is fair.

He is incorrect. Both spinners are fair.

Grade 4

Chapter 1

Whole Numbers to 10 000

1.1 Writing Numbers to 10 000

At this level, you are expected to be able to write numbers up to 1000. In this unit, you will learn to write numbers up to 10 000. You may use drawings to help yourself understand the value of thousands.

Writing Numbers in Different Forms

Place value chart: shows the positions of the digits in a number

Thousands	Hundreds	Tens	Ones
2	3	5	6
2000	300	50	6

Value of a digit

depends on its position in a number

e.g. 2 has a value of 2000.

Base-ten Blocks

= 1000

= 100

= 10

= 1

Standard form : 2356

Expanded form : 2000 + 300 + 50 + 6

"0" is a placeholder. Don't leave it out.

e.g. 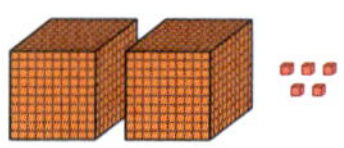 → 2005 (not 25)

placeholders

Writing Numbers in Words

Say the numbers that you find in words.

e.g. number of pages in a book
amount of juice in a bottle

Be extra careful when there are zeros in a number.

e.g. 405 → four hundred **five**
450 → four hundred **fifty**

1.2 Comparing and Ordering Numbers

In this unit, you will learn to represent and compare whole numbers up to 10 000 using base-ten blocks, number lines, and digit comparisons.

Way 1 Using Base-ten Blocks

1st Draw base-ten blocks to represent the numbers.

2nd Compare the number of blocks each number has. The number that has more blocks is greater.

e.g.

2310

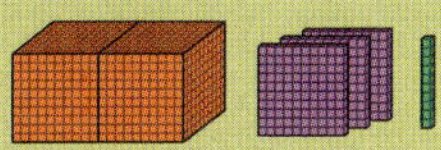

3105

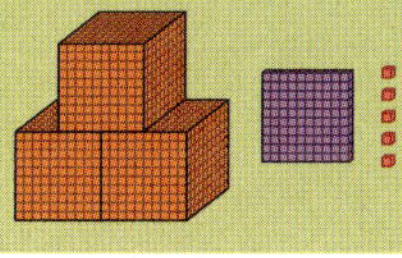

3105 has more blocks, so it is greater.

Way 2 Using a Number Line

1st Mark the numbers on a number line.

2nd The number that is farthest to the right is the greatest.

e.g.

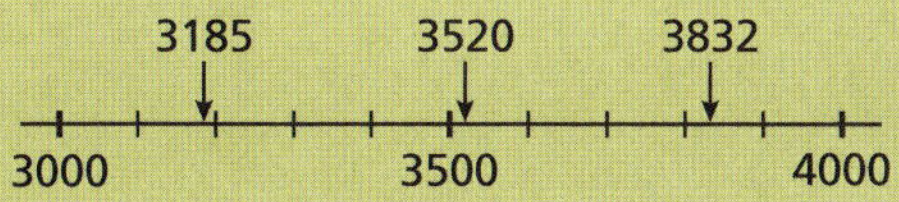

3832 is farthest to the right, so it is the greatest.

Way 3 Comparing Digits

1st Write the numbers on a place value chart.

2nd Compare the thousands. If the digits are the same, compare the hundreds, and so on, until the digits are different.

e.g.

Th	H	T	O
3	6	9	2
3	6	8	4
same	same	9 > 8	

3692 is greater.

Application

Which number is Ivy describing?

6598 6924 5426 6361 5648

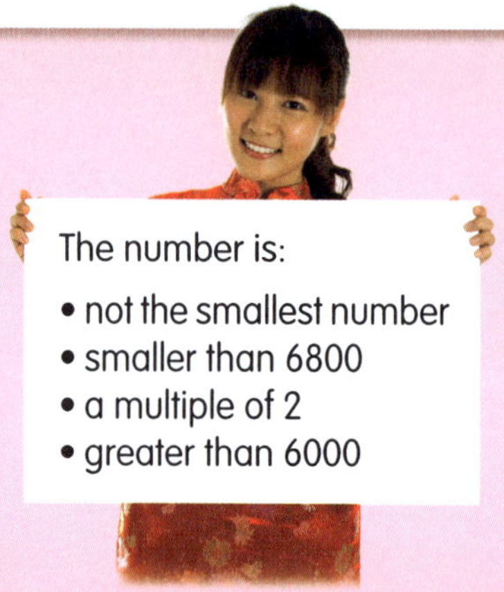

Solution:

5426 ✗ the smallest number

6924 ✗ greater than 6800

6361 ✗ not a multiple of 2

5648 ✗ smaller than 6000

6598 ✔

Ivy is describing 6598.

1.3 Rounding Numbers

You should be able to round numbers to the nearest ten. In this unit, you will use the same concept to round whole numbers to the nearest hundred and thousand.

Way 1 Using a Number Line

e.g. Round 1639 to the nearest hundred.

Think
nearest hundred:
1600 or **1700**

Draw a number line that includes 1600 and 1700. Locate 1639.

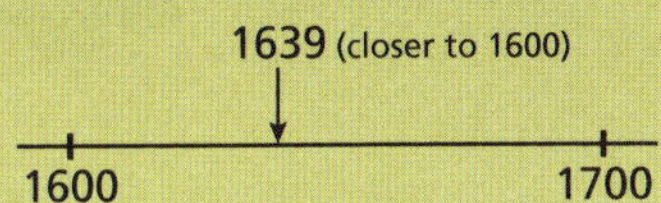

So, 1639 is rounded to <u>**1600**</u> .

e.g. Round 1639 to the nearest thousand.

Think
nearest thousand:
1000 or **2000**

Draw a number line that includes 1000 and 2000. Locate 1639.

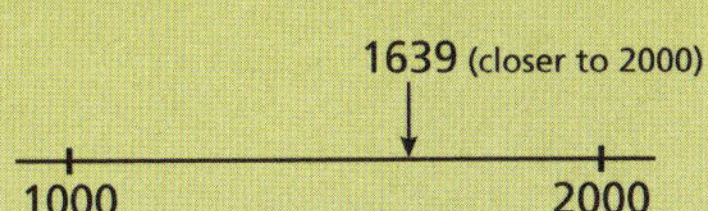

So, 1639 is rounded to <u>**2000**</u> .

Way 2 Rounding Up or Down

1st The digit you are rounding is the last digit to keep. This means all digits to its right will be "0".

2nd Round down: leave this digit the same if the digit to its right is smaller than 5.

Round up: add 1 to this digit if the digit to its right is 5 or greater.

e.g. Round 1639 to the nearest hundred.

1 6 3 9

6 ↑ keep this digit

3 ↑ smaller than 5; round down

So, 1639 is rounded to <u>**1600**</u> .

e.g. Round 1639 to the nearest thousand.

1 6 3 9

1 ↑ keep this digit

6 ↑ greater than 5; round up

So, 1639 is rounded to <u>**2000**</u> .

Application

It doesn't matter whether I round this 4-digit number to the nearest hundred or to the nearest thousand because the result will be 4000 for both.

What are the possible numbers?

Solution:

1st numbers that are 4000 when rounded to the nearest thousand

3500 4000 4400

2nd numbers that are 4000 when rounded to the nearest hundred

3950 4000 4049

The possible answers are any numbers from 3950 to 4049.

Chapter 2

Addition and Subtraction

2.1 Adding and Subtracting Using Mental Strategies

In this unit, you will learn various mental addition and subtraction strategies.

Mental Addition

Way 1 Splitting and Adding

1st Split the numbers into tens and ones.

54 + 49

50 + 4 → 54; 49 ← 40 + 9

2nd Add the tens. Then add the ones.

50 + 40 = **90**

4 + 9 = **13**

3rd Add the total tens and ones.

90 + 13 = 103

So, 54 + 49 = **103**.

Way 2 Making a Friendly Number

Make one of the numbers a friendly number, which is a multiple of 10. Then add.

54 + 49

−1 (54), +1 (49) — Make 49 friendly (add 1 to 49, so subtract 1 from 54).

53 + 50 = 103

So, 54 + 49 = **103**.

Mental Subtraction

Way 1 Counting Forward

e.g. 91 – 68 = ?

1st Count forward by 10's from 68 to 91.

68 →(10) 78 →(10) **88** — 98 (crossed out): over 91; stop at 88

Counted **20**

2nd Count forward by 1's.

88 →(1) 89 →(1) 90 →(1) 91

Counted **3**

3rd Add how much you counted.

20 + 3 = 23

So, 91 – 68 = **23**.

Way 2 Making a Friendly Number

Make the second number friendly. Then subtract.

91 – 68

+2 (91), +2 (68)

93 – 70 = 23

So, 91 – 68 = **23**.

Application

A toy truck is $24 and a teddy bear is $38. I bought both and got some change.

If she paid with $20 bills only, how many bills did she use? What was her change?

Solution:

Total cost: $24 + $38 = $62

Number of $20 Bills	Total Value	
1	20	
2	40	
3	60	
4	80	✔ enough to pay

Change: $80 – $62 = $18

She used 4 $20 bills and got $18 in change.

2.2 Adding and Subtracting Four-digit Numbers

This unit builds upon your existing knowledge of number lines, base-ten blocks, and vertical addition. You will apply these three approaches to add and subtract numbers up to 10 000.

Addition

e.g. 2958 + 1213 = ?

Using a Number Line

Think 1213 = 1000 + 100 + 100 + 10 + 1 + 1 + 1

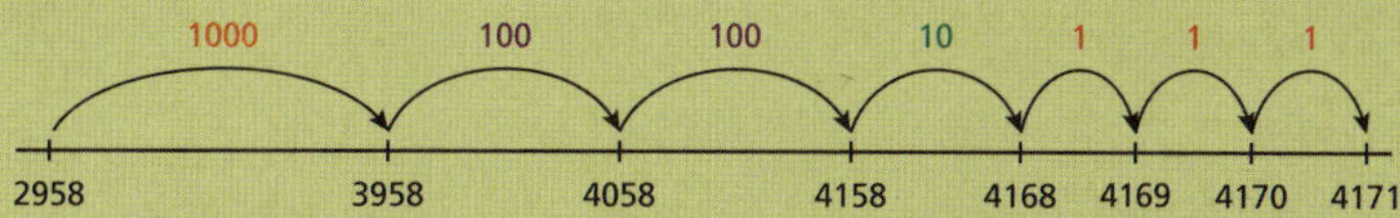

Using Base-ten Blocks

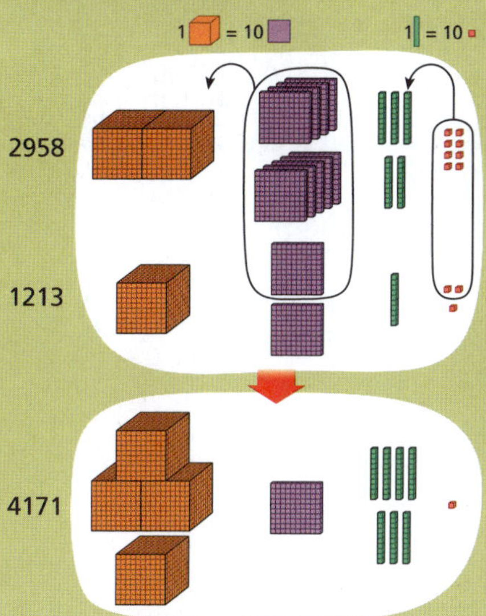

Using Vertical Addition

1st Align the digits.

2nd Add the ones, tens, hundreds, and then the thousands.

$$\begin{array}{r} \scriptsize{1}\scriptsize{1} \\ 2\,9\,5\,8 \\ +\,1\,2\,1\,3 \\ \hline 4\,1\,7\,1 \end{array}$$

9 + 2 = 11 carry 1 to thousands

8 + 3 = 11 carry 1 to tens

So, 2958 + 1213 = **4171**.

Subtraction

Using a Number Line

e.g. 3171 – 1948 = ?

Think Count from 1948 to 3171 by 1000's, 100's, 10's, and 1's.

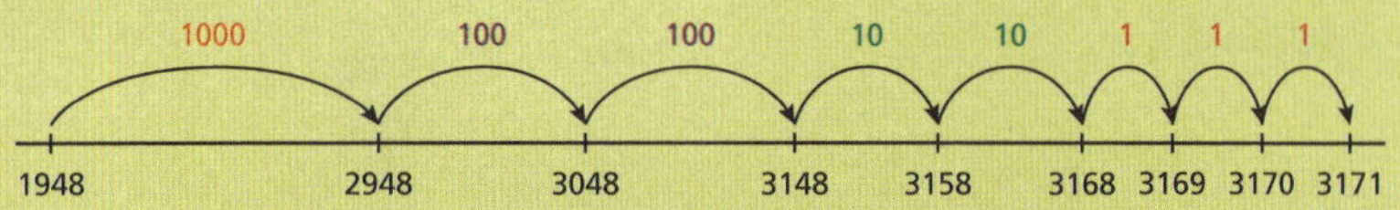

Total counted: 1223

Using Base-ten Blocks

e.g. 3171 – 1948 = ?

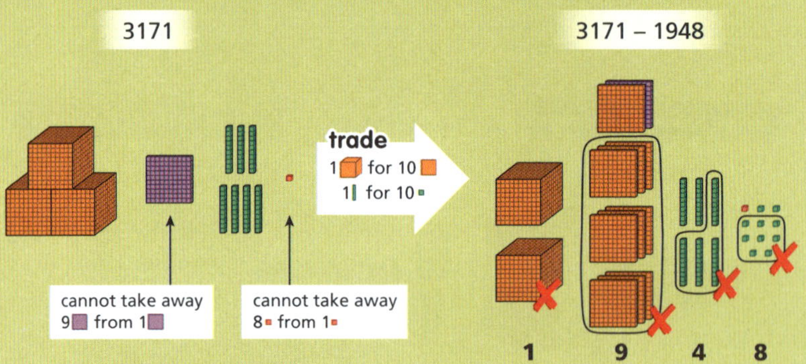

Using Vertical Subtraction

e.g. 3171 – 1948 = ?

1st Align the digits.

2nd Subtract the ones, tens, hundreds, and then the thousands.

$$\begin{array}{r} \overset{2}{\cancel{3}}\ 1\ \overset{6}{\cancel{7}}\ 1 \\ -\ 1\ 9\ 4\ 8 \\ \hline 1\ 2\ 2\ 3 \end{array}$$

borrow 1 from the thousands; 11 – 9 = 2

borrow 1 from the tens; 11 – 8 = 3

So, 3171 – 1948 = 1223.

Chapter 3

Multiplication and Division

3.1 Multiplying One-digit Numbers

This unit introduces various approaches to doing multiplication, such as using counters and skip counting.

Using Counters

The most basic and direct approach to doing multiplication is to use counters.

e.g. 5 x 3 = ?

Think 5 x 3 means 5 groups of 3.

Draw 5 groups of 3.

5 groups total = 15

So, 5 x 3 = **15**.

Using Skip Counting

e.g. 5 x 3 = ?

Think Start at 0. Count forward by 5 three times.

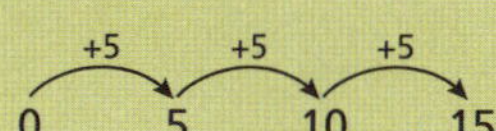

So, 5 x 3 = **15**.

Using Doubles

Use this method if you are good at finding doubles.

e.g. 5 x 3 = ?

double of 5 is 10

5 x 3 = 5 + 5 + 5
= 10 + 5
= 15

So, 5 x 3 = **15**.

Using Multiplication Facts

Use multiplication facts that you know to help find answers.

e.g. 5 x 3 = ?

You may know 5 x 2 = 10.

5 x 3 = 5 x 2 + 5
= 10 + 5
= 15

So, 5 x 3 = **15**.

Application

A set of books cost \$9. Joanna gets \$5 off for each purchase of 9 sets. How much does it cost her to buy 10 sets?

Solution:

Cost of 9 sets before discount:

+9 +9 +9 +9 +9 +9 +9 +9

9 18 27 36 45 54 63 72 81

Cost of 9 sets after discount: \$81 – \$5 = \$76
Cost of 10 sets: \$76 + \$9 = \$85

It costs her \$85 to buy 10 sets.

3.2 More Multiplying

In this unit, you will multiply numbers by 10, 100, and 1000, and be introduced to multiplication involving two-digit numbers.

Multiplying by 10, 100, and 1000

The key to multiplying numbers by 10, 100, and 1000 is to simply count the number of zeros.

e.g. 8 x 10 = ?

same

8 x 10 = 80

1 zero

So, 8 x 10 = **80**.

e.g. 8 x 100 = ?

same

8 x 100 = 800

2 zeros

So, 8 x 100 = **800**.

e.g. 8 x 1000 = ?

same

8 x 1000 = 8000

3 zeros

So, 8 x 1000 = **8000**.

Multiplying Two-digit Numbers

e.g. 37 x 6 = ?

1st Align the numbers.

$$\begin{array}{r} 3\ 7 \\ \times \quad 6 \\ \hline \end{array}$$

2nd Multiply the ones. If needed, carry every 10 ones to the tens column.

$$\begin{array}{r} ④ \\ 3\ 7 \\ \times \quad 6 \\ \hline 2 \end{array}$$

7 x 6 = 42

3rd Multiply the tens. If needed, add the tens that were carried over.

$$\begin{array}{r} ④ \\ 3\ 7 \\ \times \quad 6 \\ \hline 2\ 2\ 2 \end{array}$$

6 x 3 + 4 = 22

3.3 Dividing by One-digit Numbers

This unit further reinforces the concept of division that was introduced to you in the previous grade. You will learn to visualize division and use multiplication to find answers to division problems.

Using Counters

You may find it beneficial to visualize the math concept you are learning. Drawing counters and using concrete materials are two effective ways to help you do this.

e.g. What is $20 \div 4$?

You should understand that $20 \div 4$ means
- putting 20 into 4 groups, **or**
- putting 20 into groups of 4

$20 \div 4 = ?$

Put 20 into 4 groups.

1st Draw 4 boxes.

2nd Draw 20 circles in the boxes in the order shown by the arrow.

3rd Count the number of circles there are in each box.

Each box has 5 circles.

So, $20 \div 4 = \underline{5}$.

Put 20 into groups of 4.

1st Draw 4 counters. Circle them.

2nd Continue until there are 20 counters.

3rd Count the groups.

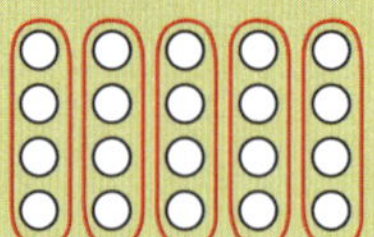

There are 5 groups.

So, $20 \div 4 = \underline{5}$.

Using Multiplication Facts

Division is closely related to multiplication. Hence, it is important to be able to apply the concept of multiplication when doing division.

e.g. What is $20 \div 4$?

Think $4 \times ? = 20$

$4 \times \mathbf{5} = 20$ ← related fact*

So, $20 \div 4 = \underline{5}$.

* Related facts in multiplication and division will be discussed further in unit 13.2.

Application

Box A holds 8 chocolates and Box B holds 9. I need to package 42 chocolates.

How many of each kind of box are needed?

Solution:

Total	Number of Box A	Number of Chocolates in Box A	Remaining Chocolates for Box B	
42	1	8 x 1 = 8	42 - 8 = 34	✘ not a multiple of 9
42	2	8 x 2 = 16	42 - 16 = 26	✘ not a multiple of 9
42	[3]	8 x 3 = 24	42 - 24 = [18]	✔ a multiple of 9
	3 of Box A		18 ÷ 9 = 2 2 of Box B	

She needs 3 of Box A and 2 of Box B for 42 chocolates.

3.4 More Dividing

This unit introduces a technique to quickly solve division by 10 and 100. You will also learn a systematic algorithm for doing division that involves two-digit numbers.

Dividing Numbers by 10 and 100

Use a calculator to find the answers.

600 ÷ 10 = ______

600 ÷ 100 = ______

6000 ÷ 10 = ______

6000 ÷ 100 = ______

Describe the pattern that you find.

- Which digits do the dividend and the answer have in common?
- Are there more or fewer zeros in the answer than in the dividend?
- Can you find a pattern in the equations?

Once you have completed the activity above, use this method to divide efficiently.

e.g. 80 ÷ 10 = ?

8~~0~~

1st Rewrite 80.

2nd 10 has 1 zero. So, cross out 1 zero.

So, 80 ÷ 10 = <u>8</u>.

e.g. 8000 ÷ 100 = ?

80~~00~~

1st Rewrite 8000.

2nd 100 has 2 zeros. So, cross out 2 zeros.

So, 8000 ÷ 100 = <u>80</u>.

Dividing Two-digit by One-digit Numbers

e.g. What is 72 ÷ 3?

1st Divide the tens.

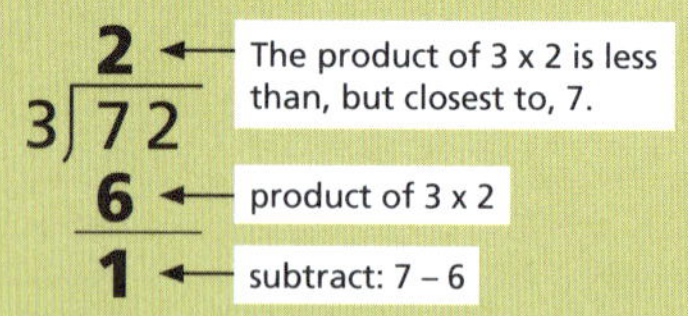

2nd Bring down and divide.

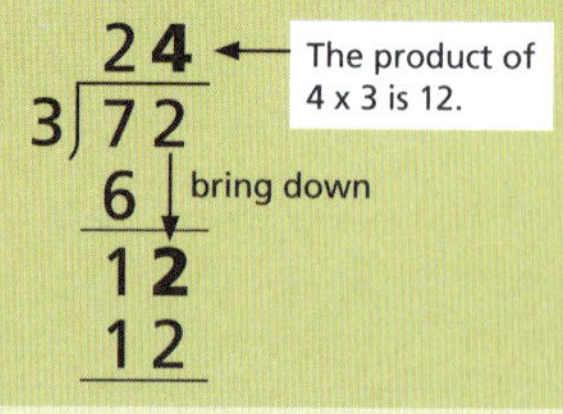

So, 72 ÷ 3 = <u>24</u>.

Application

A volunteer can look after at least 6 children and 8 children at most. If there are 96 children, what is the minimum number and the maximum number of volunteers needed?

Solution:

To find the minimum number of volunteers needed, have each volunteer look after 8 children.

Find 96 ÷ 8.

$$\begin{array}{r} 12 \\ 8\overline{)96} \\ \underline{8} \\ 16 \\ \underline{16} \end{array}$$

To find the maximum number of volunteers needed, have each volunteer look after 6 children.

Find 96 ÷ 6.

$$\begin{array}{r} 16 \\ 6\overline{)96} \\ \underline{6} \\ 36 \\ \underline{36} \end{array}$$

The minimum number of volunteers needed is 12 and the maximum is 16.

Chapter 4

Fractions

4.1 Describing Parts with Fractions

In this unit, you will learn to describe parts of a whole using fractions. You will also be introduced to the terms "numerator" and "denominator".

Describing Parts of a Whole Using Fractions

A fraction describes parts of a whole. It has two parts:

- Numerator: the number above the line showing the number of parts being considered
- Denominator: the number below the line showing the total number of parts

e.g. Describe the coloured part.

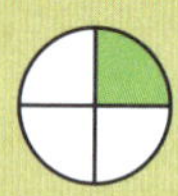

$\frac{1}{4}$

numerator: 1 part is coloured

denominator: 4 parts in total

Showing Fractions in Diagrams

You should already know how to represent fractional names in diagrams. So, understanding that fractions can be translated to fractional names will help you represent fractions using diagrams.

e.g. Show $\frac{3}{5}$ in a diagram.

Think $\frac{3}{5}$ is three fifths. →

three fifths

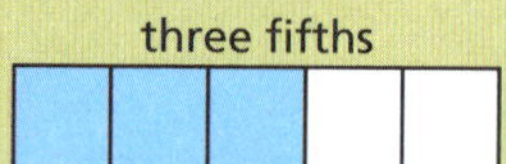

$\frac{3}{5}$ is coloured.

Application

Fold a piece of square paper in half three times. Colour half of it and then unfold it. How much of the piece of paper is coloured? Explain.

Solution:

Paper coloured and unfolded:

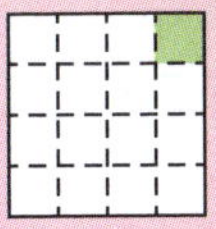

The folded lines "divided" the piece of paper into 16 equal parts and 1 part is coloured.

So, $\frac{1}{16}$ of the piece of paper is coloured.

4.2 Comparing and Ordering Fractions

This unit introduces basic fraction comparison. You need to be able to represent fractions in diagrams since the strategies that are introduced in this unit require this skill.

Comparing Fractions in Diagrams

Comparing fractions using diagrams is the best way to understand this concept.

e.g. Which fraction is greater: $\frac{1}{5}$ or $\frac{3}{5}$?

1st Draw 2 shapes of the same size.

2nd Draw to show both fractions.

3rd Compare.

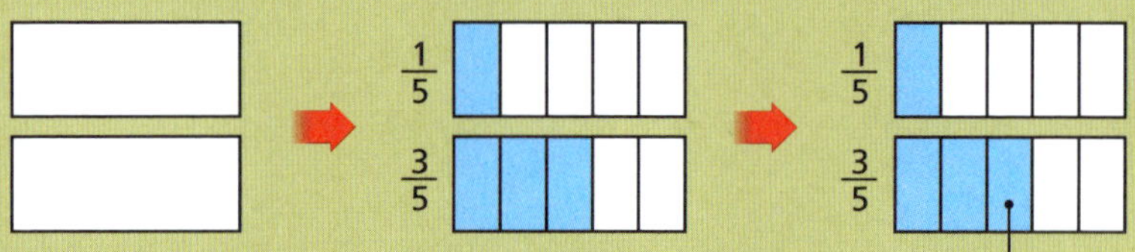

* Rectangles should be used as they are the easiest shapes to divide into equal parts.

* The shapes are aligned vertically to make it easier to compare them.

So, $\frac{3}{5}$ is greater.

Comparing Fractions by Numerators

Fractions that have the same denominator can be compared by their numerators. The fraction that has the greater numerator is greater.

e.g. Which fraction is greater: $\frac{1}{5}$ or $\frac{3}{5}$?

$\frac{1}{5}$ $\frac{3}{5}$ ← $3 > 1$

So, $\frac{3}{5}$ is greater.

Note that this method is only for fractions that have the same denominator.

Application

Lisa had $\frac{1}{8}$ of a pizza and her brother had $\frac{2}{8}$ of another pizza, but Lisa had a bigger slice of pizza than her brother. Explain how this is possible.

Solution:

It is possible if Lisa's slice is from a large pizza and her brother's is from a small pizza.

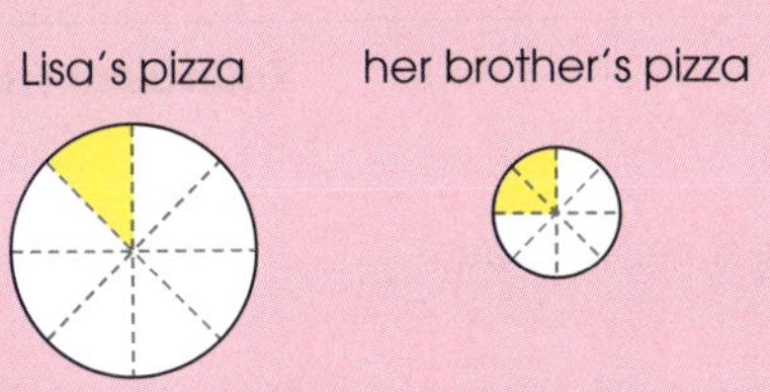

Even though Lisa's slice is $\frac{1}{8}$ and her brother's is $\frac{2}{8}$, Lisa's slice is still bigger.

4.3 More about Fractions

This unit introduces equivalent fractions and counting fractional parts beyond one whole. We strongly recommend that you go through the hands-on activities below as this concept can sometimes be difficult to understand.

Understanding Equivalent Fractions

Using fraction circles or fraction strips is a great way to learn the concept of equivalent fractions.

Equivalent Fractions

$\frac{\quad}{2}$ $\frac{\quad}{4}$ $\frac{\quad}{8}$

1st Trace the rectangle below onto a sheet of paper and cut it out.

2nd Fold the rectangle along the red line. Colour one part. Describe the coloured part in a fraction and write it in the chart.

3rd Fold along the blue line. Write the fraction. Fold along the green lines. Write the fraction.

After this activity, you will see that:

$\frac{1}{2} = \frac{2}{4}$ and $\frac{1}{2} = \frac{4}{8}$

Through this activity, you should understand that equivalent fractions are fractions that represent the same value.

You may use drawings to help yourself understand equivalent fractions.

e.g. $\frac{2}{3} = \frac{4}{6}$ and $\frac{2}{3} = \frac{8}{12}$

Colour 2 parts. | Add lines to make 6 parts. | Add a line to make 12 parts.

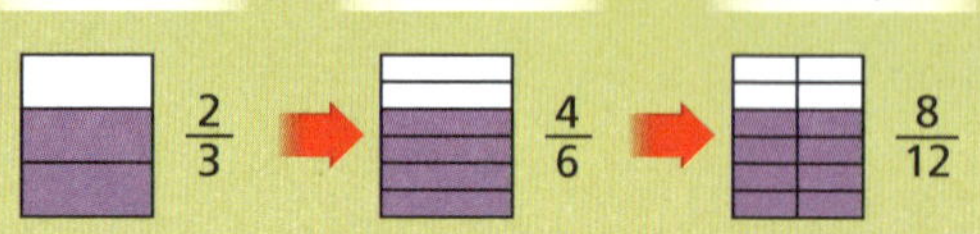

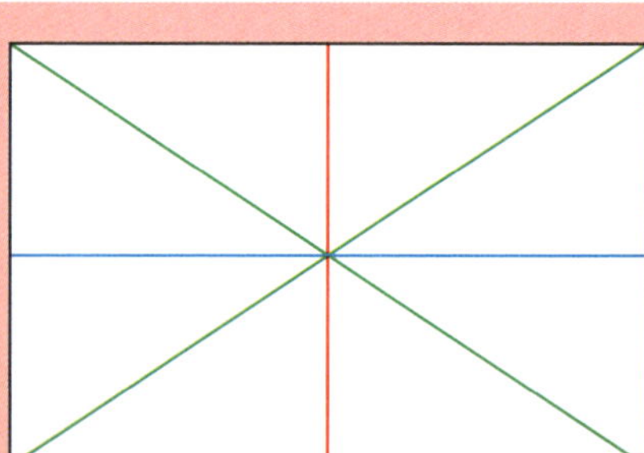

Counting Forward

At this stage, one of the main goals of learning to count forward (by halves, thirds, fourths, and tenths) is to develop the concept of making wholes with fractional parts.

Counting forward by fourths

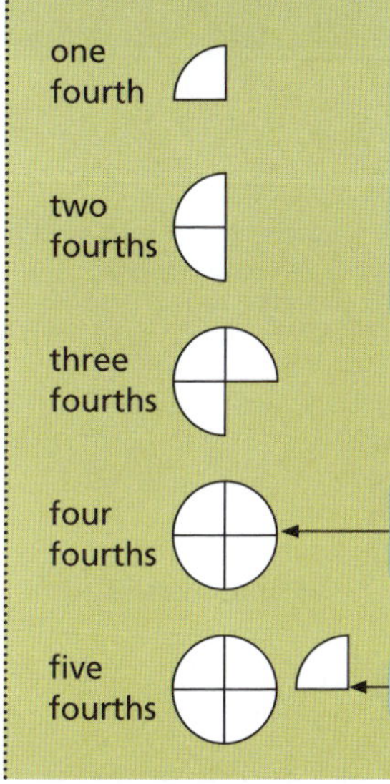

Activity

Trace the circles onto a piece of paper and cut them into fourths. Use the fourths to show the concept of counting forward.

Note that four fourths is the same as one whole.

Continue counting until you reach eight fourths.

Count forward by halves, thirds, and tenths beyond one whole using fraction circles and number lines.

At the end of this activity, you will understand that fractional parts can make wholes. This concept will help you understand the meaning of mixed numbers in the future.

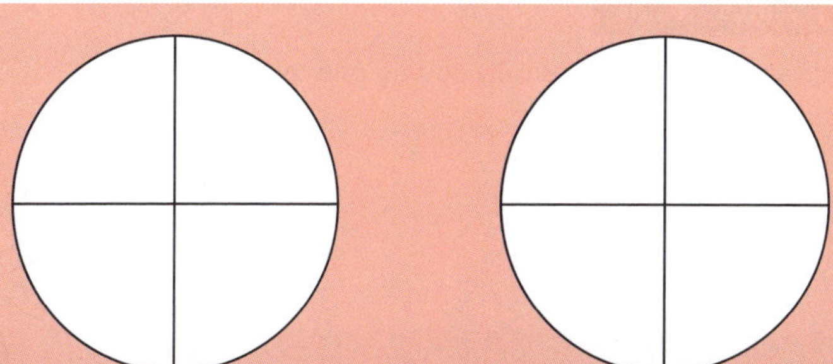

Chapter 5

Decimal Numbers to Tenths

5.1 Writing Decimal Numbers

In this unit, you will learn to use decimal numbers to describe parts of a whole. You will learn to count forward by tenths.

Representing Decimal Numbers to Tenths

First, describe the parts of a whole that is divided into 10 equal parts. Then describe the parts of a whole with decimal numbers.

e.g. four tenths

number of wholes: 0
number of parts: 4 → 0.4

one and four tenths

number of wholes: 1
number of parts: 4 → 1.4

Format of a Decimal Number

e.g.

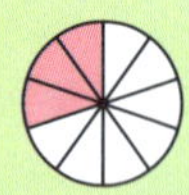

ones tenths

0.3

number of wholes — number of parts of a whole

Counting Forward by Tenths

Counting forward by tenths is basically adding one tenth each time.

e.g. Using a diagram

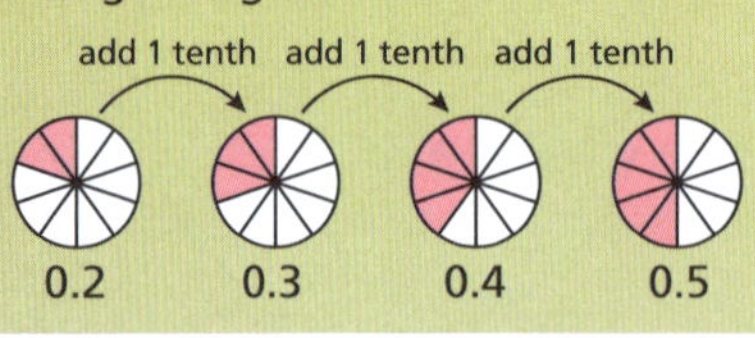

Find the relationship between mm and cm using the concept of tenths.

5.2 Comparing and Ordering Decimal Numbers

This unit introduces three strategies that you can use to compare decimal numbers. The approach is very similar to comparing whole numbers, including the use of diagrams and number lines.

Using Diagrams

Using diagrams is generally the first step in comparing decimals.

1st Draw diagrams to represent the decimals being compared. Divide them into 10 equal parts.

2nd Colour to show the decimals.

3rd Compare.

e.g. Which is greater, 0.7 or 0.3?

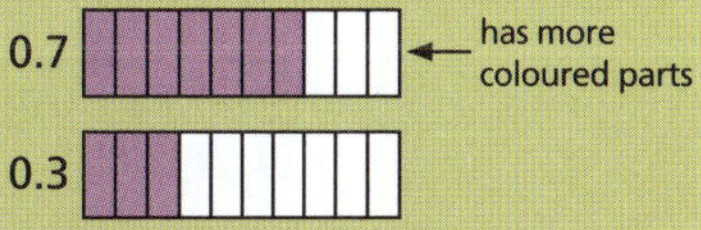

So, **0.7** is greater.

Using a Number Line

A number line can also help you find the relationship between the two numbers being compared.

1st Draw a number line.

2nd Locate the decimals being compared.

3rd The number to the right is greater.

e.g. Which is greater, 0.7 or 0.3?

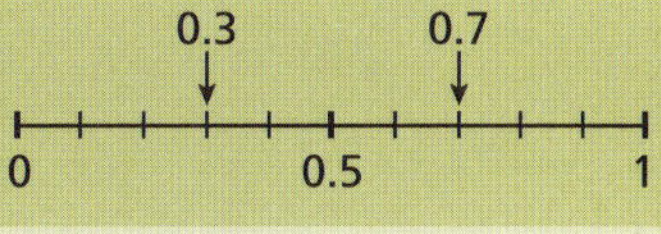

So, **0.7** is greater.

Comparing Digits

First, compare the ones digits of the decimals. If they are the same, compare the tenths digits.

e.g. Which is greater, 0.7 or 0.3?

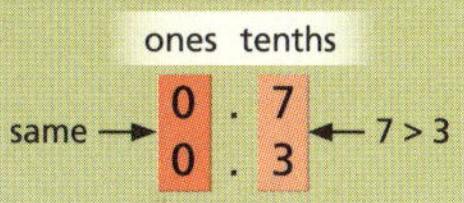

So, **0.7** is greater.

Application

The passing score of a contest is 5.5. Jason got 5.8 and his sister got a lower passing score. What are the possible scores Jason's sister got?

Solution:

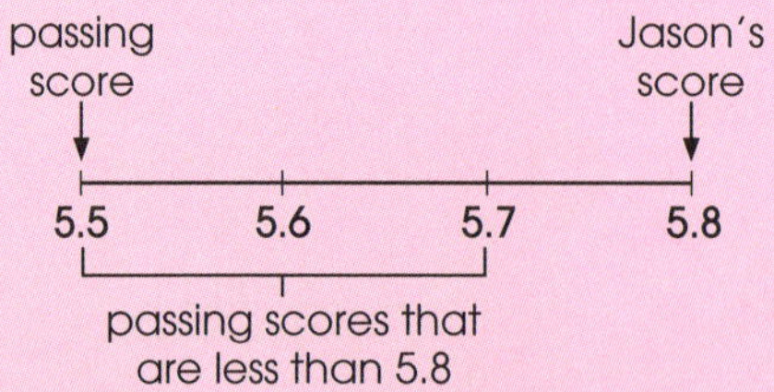

Jason's sister got a score of 5.5, 5.6, or 5.7.

5.3 Adding and Subtracting Decimal Numbers

Adding and subtracting decimal numbers is very similar to adding and subtracting whole numbers. Doing addition and subtraction first with diagrams will help you visualize the concepts.

Adding Decimals

Using Diagrams

1st Draw and colour a diagram to show the first decimal.

2nd Colour to add the second decimal to the diagram. The coloured part is the sum.

e.g. What is 1.4 + 0.7?

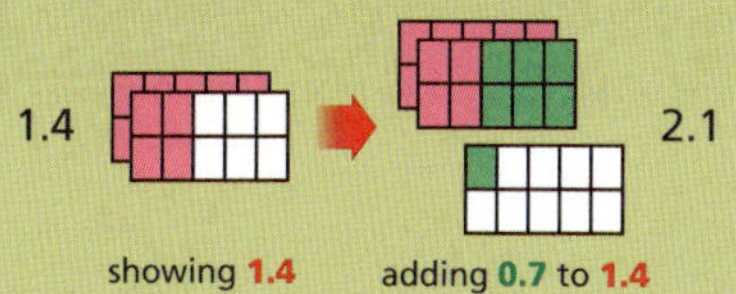

So, 1.4 + 0.7 = **2.1**.

Using Vertical Addition

1st Align the decimal points.

2nd Add the digits.

3rd Add a decimal point to the answer.

e.g. What is 1.4 + 0.7?

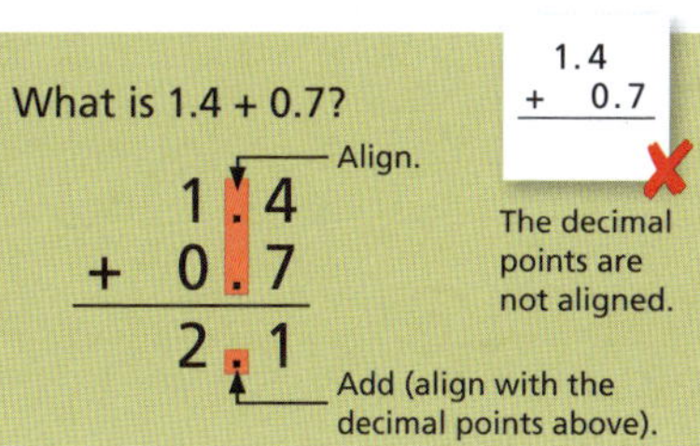

So, 1.4 + 0.7 = **2.1**.

Subtracting Decimals

Using Diagrams

1st Draw a diagram to show the first decimal.

2nd Cross out the second decimal.

3rd The remaining part is the difference.

e.g. What is 2.8 – 1.7?

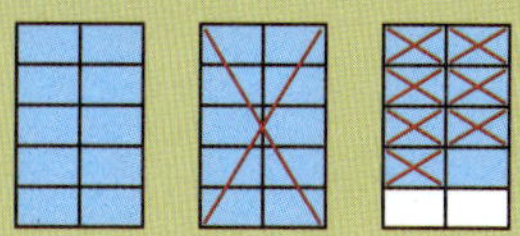

So, 2.8 – 1.7 = **1.1**.

Using Vertical Subtraction

1st Align the decimal points.

2nd Subtract the digits.

3rd Add a decimal point to the answer.

e.g. What is 2.8 – 1.7?

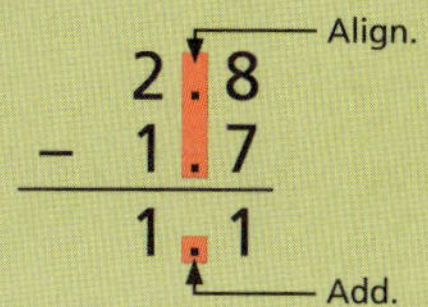

So, 2.8 – 1.7 = **1.1**.

Application

This is not drawn to scale.

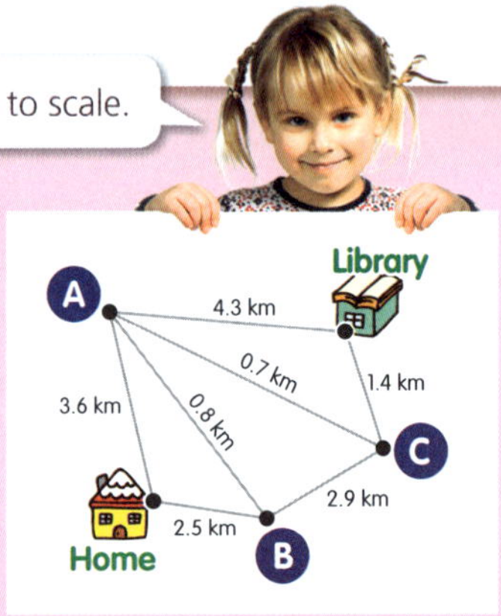

Which is the shortest route from home to the library? How long is the route?

Solution:

Choose the possible shortest routes. Then find the lengths and compare.

Home → A → Library: 3.6 + 4.3 = 7.9
Home → B → C → Library: 2.5 + 2.9 + 1.4 = 6.8
Home → B → A → C → Library: 2.5 + 0.8 + 0.7 + 1.4 = 5.4 ← shortest

The shortest route from home to the library is the one passing points B, A, and C. The route is 5.4 km long.

5.4 Fractions and Decimals

This unit introduces the concept of how fractions and decimal numbers are related. We strongly recommend using diagrams to help you visualize the concept. The goal is to help you understand that a fraction can be converted into a decimal and vice versa.

Relating Fractions and Decimals

Relating fractions and decimals can be a challenging task. At first glance, it may not seem obvious to you that $\frac{2}{5}$ and 0.4 are equivalent. Try the following examples to help yourself understand the concept.

e.g. Relate $\frac{2}{10}$ to 0.2.

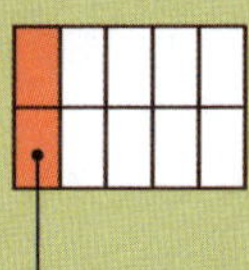

$\frac{2}{10}$ and 0.2 both describe the coloured parts.

e.g. Relate $\frac{1}{5}$ to 0.2.

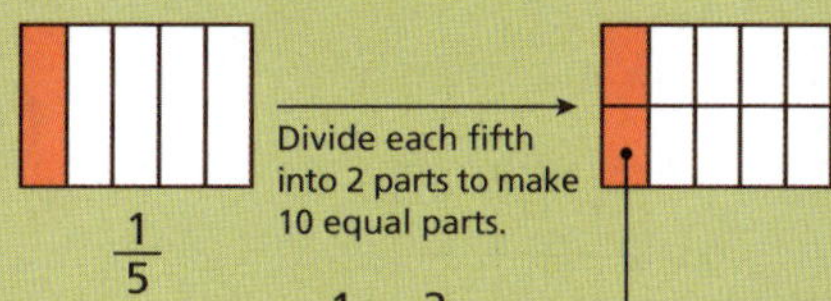

$\frac{1}{5}$, $\frac{2}{10}$, and 0.2 all describe the coloured parts.

Converting Fractions into Decimals

1st Draw the fraction in a diagram.

2nd Decompose the fraction so that it has 10 equal parts.

3rd Describe the diagram using decimals.

e.g. Write $\frac{1}{2}$ as a decimal.

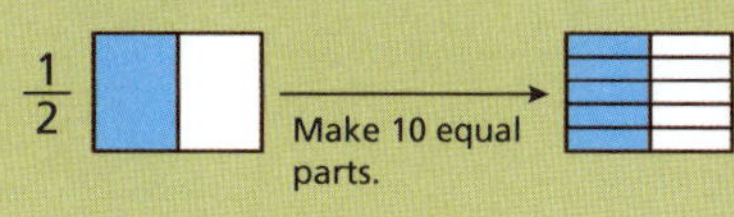

So, $\frac{1}{2}$ is **0.5**.

At this level, you will find it much easier to find the relationships between decimals and fractions that are in halves, fifths, and tenths since they can be represented in tenths.

You may also learn to use a calculator to convert a fraction into a decimal.

e.g. Write $\frac{1}{2}$ as a decimal.

> $\frac{1}{2}$ can be interpreted as $1 \div 2$.
> So press: 1 ÷ 2 =

So, $\frac{1}{2}$ is **0.5**.

Dividing the numerator by its denominator will give you the decimal form of the fraction.

Converting Decimals into Fractions

Use a diagram.

e.g. Write 0.6 as a fraction.

0.6

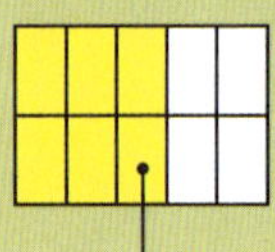

0.6 and $\frac{6}{10}$ both describe the coloured parts.

Rewrite the tenths digit as a numerator over 10.

e.g. Write 0.3 as a fraction.

$$0.3 = \frac{3}{10}$$

So, 0.3 is $\mathbf{\frac{3}{10}}$.

Application

I need to prepare 0.5 of a pot of soup. $\frac{1}{5}$ of the pot is filled with soup. How much of the pot still needs to be filled?

Solution:

To be filled: $0.5 = \frac{5}{10}$

Filled: $\frac{1}{5} = \frac{2}{10}$

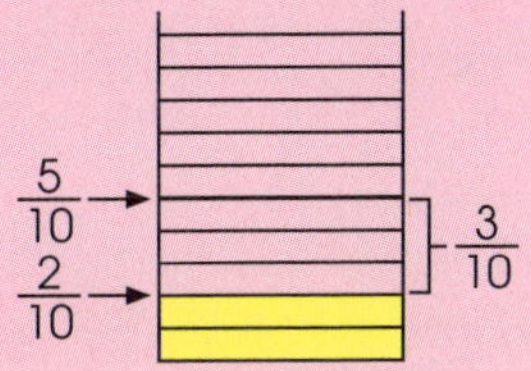

$\frac{3}{10}$ of the pot still needs to be filled.

Chapter 6
Money

6.1 Representing Money Amounts to $100

In this unit, you will learn to find and represent money amounts up to $100 with bills and coins.

Finding Money Amounts

e.g. Find the total amount of money.

The total amount of money is $91.30.

Steps

1st Group the bills and coins of the same kind together.

2nd Count the bills and coins starting with the one that has the highest value.

Showing Money Amounts

e.g. Use the fewest bills and coins to show $91.30.

Total: $91.30

Use the highest possible valued bill and coin each time.

6.2 Adding and Subtracting Money Amounts

In this unit, you will do addition and subtraction with money. This sets the foundation for money transactions later on.

Adding Money Amounts

Drawing and Counting Money

Steps

1st Draw the fewest bills and coins for each money amount to be added.

2nd Group the bills and coins.

3rd Count to find the total.

e.g. Add $24.85 and $42.35.

$24.85 $42.35

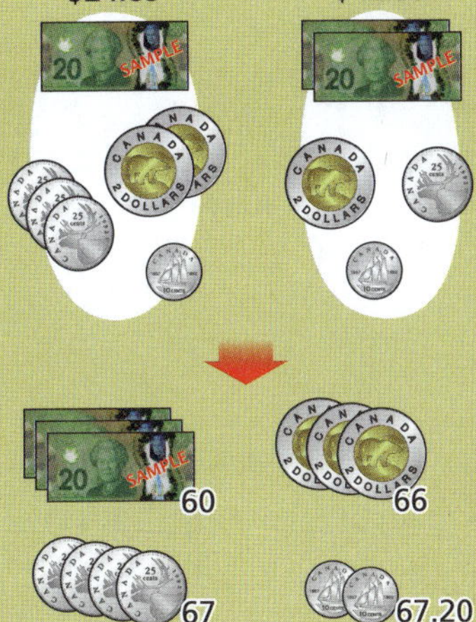

Total: $67.20

Using Vertical Addition

e.g. Add $24.85 and $42.35.

Line up the dollars and cents.

	dollars	cents	
	24	85	
+	42	35	
67	~~66~~	~~120~~	20

+ $1

Total: $67.20

Trade 100 cents for 1 dollar.

Subtracting Money Amounts

Crossing Out Bills and Coins

e.g. Subtract $14.75 from $62.50.

Answer: $47.75

Steps

1st Draw the bills and coins to show the money amount to be subtracted from.

2nd Cross out the bills and coins to subtract. (Break the bills or coins if needed.)

3rd Count the remaining bills and coins.

Counting Up

e.g. Subtract $14.75 from $62.50.

1st Count up to the nearest dollar.

2nd Count up in dollars.

3rd Count up in cents.

$14.75 —(25¢)→ $15.00 —($47)→ $62.00 —(50¢)→ $62.50

4th Add.
25¢ + $47 + 50¢ = $47.75

Answer: $47.75

Vertical Subtraction

e.g. Subtract $14.75 from $62.50.

Since 50¢ is less than 75¢, borrow 100¢ from $1.

	dollars	cents
	61	150
−	14	75
	47	75

Answer: $47.75

Application

A customer paid $30 for a meal and I gave him 6 bills in change.

Is this possible? Explain.

Solution:

The lowest valued bill is $5.

Least amount of money made up of 6 bills: $5 × 6 = $30

This is not possible because the customer paid $30, and the lowest total value of 6 bills is $30, so the customer could not get 6 bills back in change.

Chapter 7

Measurement

7.1 Measuring Length

In this unit, you will be introduced to more standard units of length, and learn which units are most appropriate for various situations and how to convert between them.

Using Millimetres and Decimetres

- A **millimetre (mm)** is a smaller measuring unit than a centimetre. It is used to describe small measurements (e.g. the width of a grain of rice).
- A **decimetre (dm)** is a larger measuring unit than a centimetre. It is suitable for describing relatively larger measurements (e.g. the height of a window).

smallest

millimetre (mm)
centimetre (cm)
decimetre (dm)
metre (m)
kilometre (km)

largest

Relationships between Units of Length

1 cm = 10 mm
1 dm = 10 cm
1 m = 100 cm or 10 dm
1 km = 1000 m

Use the benchmarks below for estimating lengths.

1 mm
thickness of a coin

1 cm
thickness of an eraser

1 dm
height of a cup

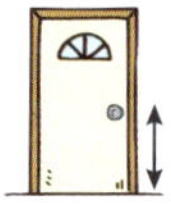

1 m
height from floor to doorknob

1 km
height of 2 CN Towers

Converting Measurements

e.g. 4 m = ? cm

1 m = 100 cm
4 m = 400 cm ← 100 x 4

So, 4 m = **400 cm**.

e.g. 4000 m = ? km

1000 m = 1 km
4000 m = 4 km ← 4000 ÷ 1000

So, 4000 m = **4 km**.

Application

James drew a map of his bedroom and recorded the measurements, but he forgot to include the measuring units. What should the units be? Explain.

Solution:

Possible lengths:

9000 mm = 900 cm = 9 m ← most reasonable
9000 cm = 90 m
9000 dm = 900 m
9000 m
9000 km

Possible widths:

70 mm
70 cm
70 dm = 7 m ← most reasonable
70 m
70 km

The units should be mm for 9000 and dm for 70.

7.2 Measuring Mass

This unit introduces two standard units of mass: the gram and the milligram. You will determine the most appropriate units for different measurements and do conversions between them to solve problems.

Using Milligrams and Grams

- A **milligram (mg)** is a very small measuring unit and is used for objects that are very light.

e.g.

about 500 mg

- A **gram (g)** is a small measuring unit and is used for light objects.

e.g.

about 15 g

Relationships between Units of Mass

smallest

milligram (mg)
gram (g)
kilogram (kg)

largest

1 g = 1000 mg
1 kg = 1000 g

Converting Measurements

e.g.

20 g = ? mg

1 g = 1000 mg
20 g = 20 000 mg (1000 x 20)

So, 20 g = **20 000 mg**.

How much does this watermelon weigh in kg?

1000 g = 1 kg
8000 g = 8 kg (8000 ÷ 1000)

So, it weighs **8 kg**.

Balancing Objects on a Scale

e.g.

Each ♥ has a mass of 500 g.

Draw the number of ♥ needed to balance a toy truck.

Think 2 kg = 2000 g

There are four 500 g in 2000 g, so draw 4 ♥.

7.3 Measuring Capacity

This unit introduces the millilitre. You will learn how it relates to the litre and how to convert between the two units.

Using Millilitres

Capacity is the maximum amount of liquid a container can hold. You should already know how to describe capacity in litres (L). For smaller measurements, millilitres are commonly used.

- A **millilitre (mL)** is a small measuring unit for capacity.

e.g.

capacity: 250 mL

1 L = 1000 mL

> The amount of water a 1 cm cube can hold is 1 mL. So its capacity is 1 mL.

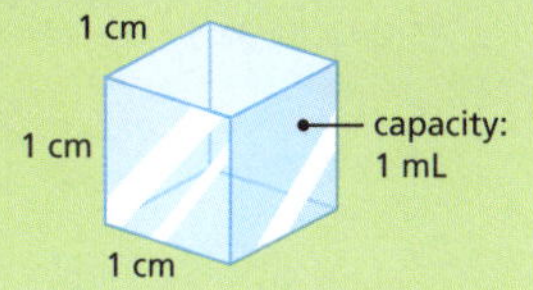

Converting between Units

e.g.

Convert 5 L to mL.

1 L = 1000 mL
5 L = 5000 mL

1000 x 5

So, 5 L = **5000 mL**.

How many litres of juice do I have?

1000 mL = 1 L
2000 mL = 2 L

2000 ÷ 1000

She has **2 L** of juice.

Find containers around the house with measurements in L with whole number values. Convert them from L to mL.

Application

3 red pots fill up 1 green pot with soil, and 2 green pots fill up 1 yellow pot. If the red pot has a capacity of 2 L, what is the capacity of the yellow pot?

Solution:

3  = 1 

2  = 1 

Capacity of 6  = 6 of 2 L = 12 L

Capacity of 1  = 12 L

The capacity of a yellow pot is 12 L.

7.4 Measuring Volume

In this unit, you will be introduced to the concept of volume. You will learn how to differentiate it from other concepts and how to describe volume through manipulatives and drawings.

Using Volume

Volume is defined as the amount of space an object takes up.

You may find it confusing to differentiate volume from mass or capacity. Use examples on the right to help yourself understand the differences.

Volume vs Mass vs Capacity

a question on volume
Does this fit in the fridge?

a question on mass
Is this heavy?

a question on capacity
How much water does this hold?

Describing Volume

Once you grasp the concept of volume, you are ready to describe volume. You may build structures using cubes (preferably 1 cm^3 if possible) and describe their volumes.

e.g.

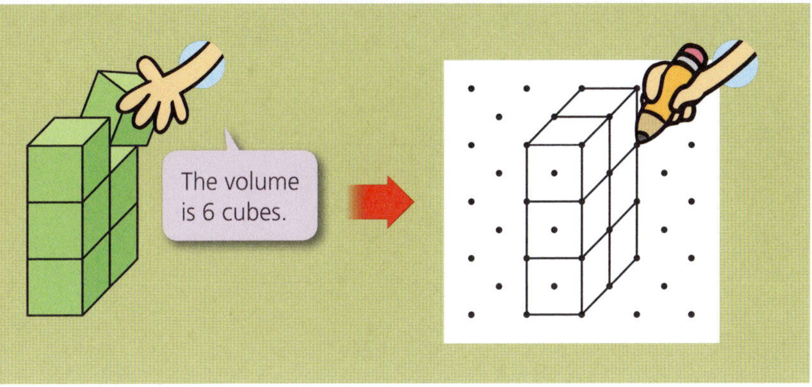

Application

Kayla made a prism with 3 centimetre cubes. What are the length, width, and height of the prism?

Solution:

Kayla can build a prism with 3 centimetre cubes in two ways.

Way 1

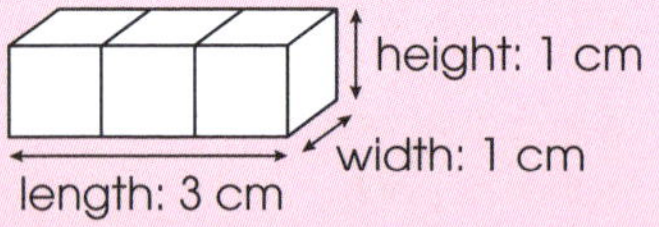

The prism has a length of 3 cm, a width of 1 cm, and a height of 1 cm.

Way 2

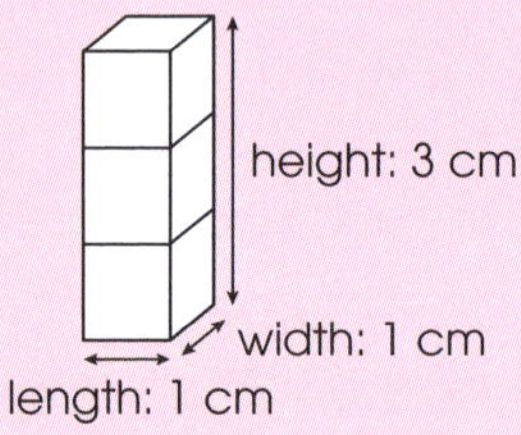

The prism has a length of 1 cm, a width of 1 cm, and a height of 3 cm.

Chapter 8

Time

8.1 Measuring Time

This section introduces the common units used to describe time. You will learn how they relate and how to convert between them.

Units of Time

longest

- century
- decade
- year
- month
- week
- day
- hour (h)
- minute (min)
- second (s)

shortest

- century – The light bulb was invented over 2 centuries ago.
- decade – The first handheld phone was made about 5 decades ago.

Relationships between Units of Time

1 minute	=	60 seconds
1 hour	=	60 minutes
1 day	=	24 hours
1 week	=	7 days
1 year	=	52 weeks
1 year	=	12 months
1 decade	=	10 years
1 century	=	100 years
1 century	=	10 decades

Converting between Units of Time

e.g. Convert 3 decades into years.

1 decade = 10 years
3 decades = 30 years ← 10 x 3

So, 3 decades is **30 years**.

You can also convert the time spent on day-to-day activities from one unit of time to another. For example, how long does it take you to brush your teeth?

Application

Jane is 8 years old and my son is 42 years old. I am half a century and half a decade older than Jane. How old was I when my son, Mr. Wood, was born?

Solution:

Half a century: 50 years
Half a decade: 5 years
Total: 50 years + 5 years = 55 years

Grandpa's age: Jane's age + 55 = 8 + 55 = 63
Mr. Wood's age: 42
Grandpa's age when Mr. Wood was born: 63 – 42 = 21

Grandpa was 21 years old when Mr. Wood was born.

8.2 Reading and Showing Time on Clocks

In this unit, you will learn to tell time shown on an analogue clock. You will also learn to draw clock hands on an analogue clock.

Writing Time

e.g. Write the time shown on the clock.

If the **hour** hand is between two numbers, pick the previous number.

Count forward to find out what the **minute** hand is pointing at.

If required, write "a.m." to denote time before noon and "p.m." for time after noon.

Drawing Clock Hands to Show Time

1st Locate the hour hand based on the position of the minute hand. For example, if the minute hand is pointing at 30, the hour hand should be halfway between two hours.

2nd Locate the minute hand.

Show 10:45.

Application

I placed the clock hands to show that I had breakfast at 8:06.

Did Andrea show the time correctly? If not, describe the mistake and draw to show the correct time.

Solution:

No, Andrea did not show the time correctly. She mistakenly switched the hour hand and the minute hand.

8.3 Finding Elapsed Time

This unit introduces strategies for finding elapsed time in weeks, days, hours, and minutes using calendars and analogue clocks.

Finding Elapsed Time

In days:

e.g. from May 26, 2016 to June 2, 2016

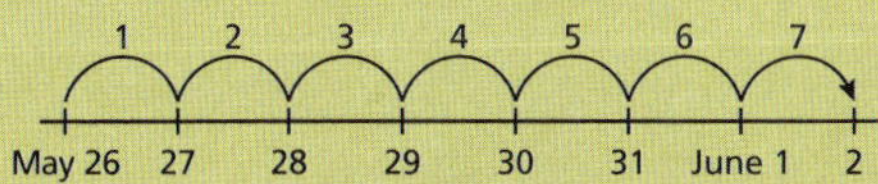

There are 7 days.

In weeks:

e.g. from May 3, 2016 to May 24, 2016

There are 3 weeks.

MAY 2016

S	M	T	W	T	F	S	
1	2	(3)	4	5	6	7	week 1
8	9	10	11	12	13	14	week 2
15	16	17	18	19	20	21	week 3
22	23	(24)	25	26	27	28	
29	30	31					

On clocks:

e.g. from 3:55 to 4:15

The elapsed time is 20 minutes.

e.g. It is now 8:25. What time will it be in 40 minutes?

1st Draw to show 8:25 on the clock.

2nd Count to 40 by 5's.

It will be 9:05.

Application

If I woke up at 8:00, and it took me 5 minutes to get dressed, 5 minutes to eat breakfast, and 15 minutes to get to school, would I make it to school by 8:20?

Solution:

5 minutes to get dressed — 5 minutes to eat breakfast — 15 minutes to get to school

← arrive at school at 8:25

No, he would not make it to school by 8:20.

Chapter 9

Perimeter and Area

9.1 Finding Perimeter

This unit introduces two strategies for finding the perimeter: counting the sides of a shape on a grid, and adding up all the side lengths of a shape.

Using a Centimetre Grid

1st Identify the edges of the shape or object being measured.

2nd Count.

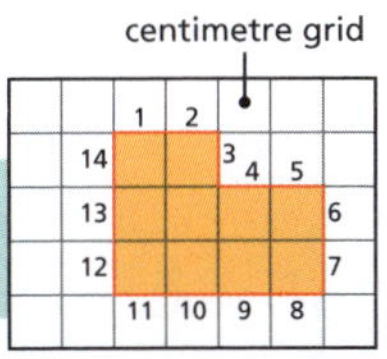

Perimeter: 14 cm

Using a Ruler

1st Measure the sides with a ruler and record the lengths.

2nd Add up the lengths.

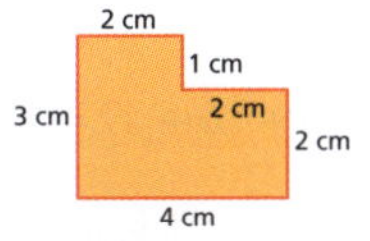

Perimeter:
2 + 1 + 2 + 2 + 4 + 3
= 14 (cm)

Use this grid to find the perimeter of an object. Then use a ruler to find its perimeter. Compare the results.

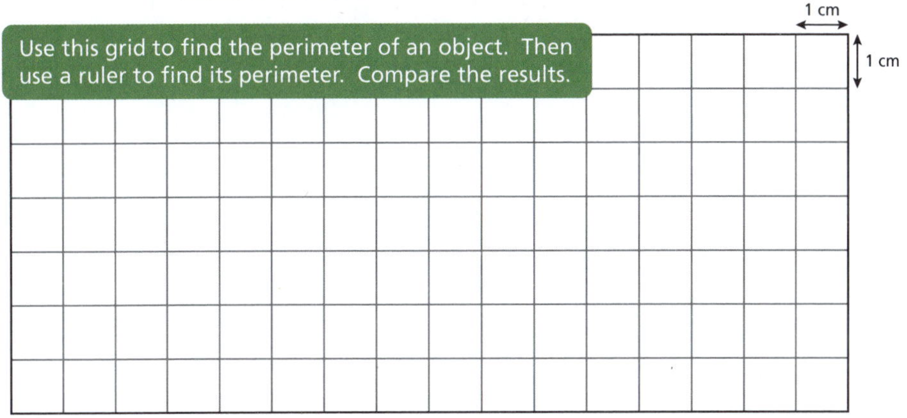

Application

How much trimming does she need?

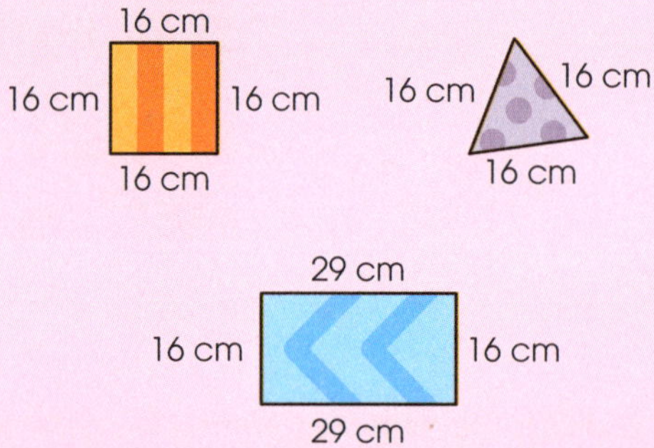

Solution:

Draw and label the fabric pieces.

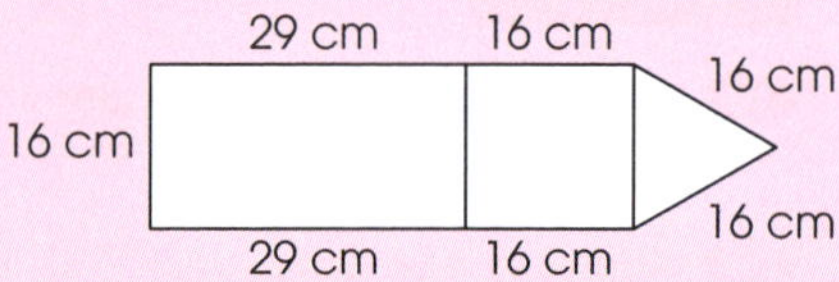

Add the side lengths:

16 + 29 + 16 + 16 + 16 + 16 + 29 = 138

She needs 138 cm of trimming.

9.2 Finding Area

In this unit, you will learn to find the area by multiplying the length and width for rectangles, and by counting squares for other shapes.

Counting Squares

Describe area in square centimetres. Each unit is a 1 cm by 1 cm square.

e.g. Find the area of the shape in square centimetres.

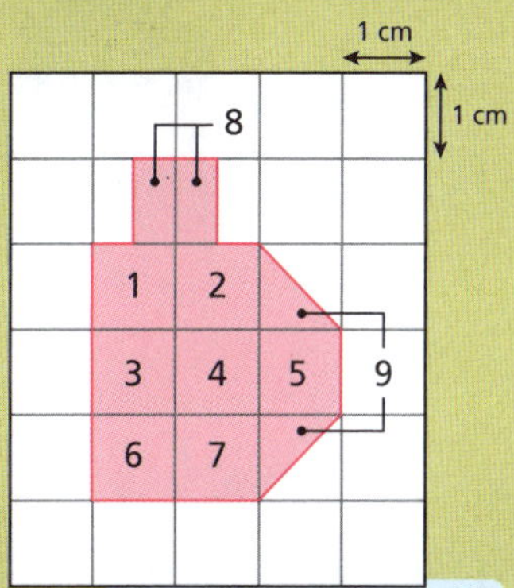

Count the complete squares first. Then count every 2 half squares as 1 square.

The area of the shape is **9 square centimetres**.

Multiplying Length and Width

At this stage, you are not required to memorize the formula for finding the area of a rectangle, but you should be familiar with this concept.

e.g. Find the area of the rectangle.

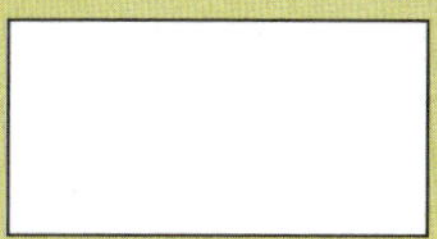

1st Measure the length and width.

2nd Draw lines to divide the rectangle into 1 cm by 1 cm squares.

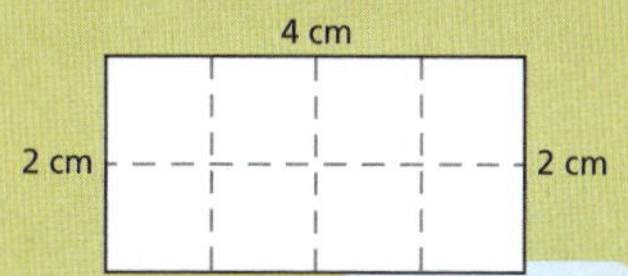

2 rows of 4 □

2 rows of 4
= 2 x 4 ← length and width of the rectangle
= 8

The area of the rectangle is **8 square centimetres**.

Application

Tony has 12 squares. How many different rectangles can he make? What are their lengths and widths?

Solution:

All possible rectangles:

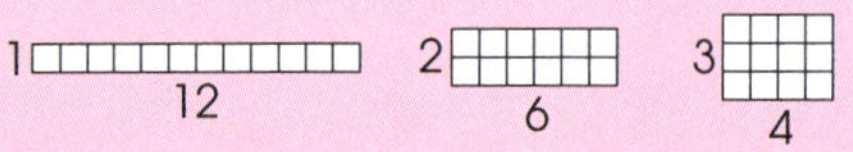

Tony can make 3 different rectangles.

The lengths and widths are: 12 cm and 1 cm, 6 cm and 2 cm, and 4 cm and 3 cm.

9.3 Relating Perimeter and Area

This unit focuses on comparing perimeter and area. You will learn how these two concepts relate to each other, as well as how they differ.

Distinguishing between Perimeter and Area Problems

When confronted with a word problem, you may find it challenging to determine whether it is a perimeter or an area problem. Refer to the definitions of perimeter and area.

Perimeter:
- the distance around an object

Area:
- the measure of an object's surface

e.g. Alan wants to find how many pieces of paper he needs to cover a bulletin board, and how much framing he needs for its border.

- pieces of paper needed (an area problem)
- amount of framing needed (a perimeter problem)

Identify whether each is a perimeter or an area problem:

- How many tiles are needed for a kitchen floor? (area problem)
- How much framing is needed for a picture? (perimeter problem)
- How much wall paper is needed for a wall? (area problem)
- How much fencing is needed for the backyard? (perimeter problem)

Finding the Relationship between Perimeter and Area

Try the following activity. Through this activity, you will understand that shapes with the same perimeter do not necessarily have the same area, and vice versa.

1st Cut 8 squares out of a piece of paper.

2nd Make two different rectangles with 8 squares.

3rd Compare their perimeters.

e.g.

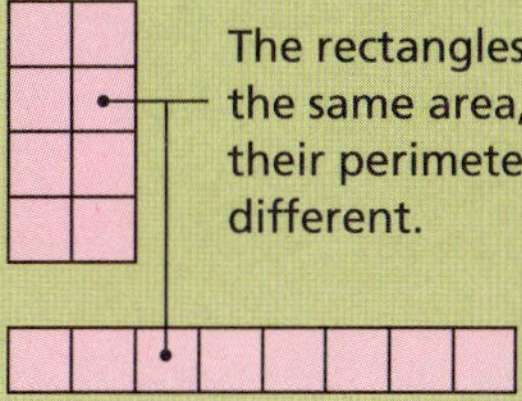

The rectangles have the same area, but their perimeters are different.

Application

Josh has enough materials for a fence that is 24 m in perimeter. What is the maximum area of his rectangular garden?

Solution:

a perimeter of 24 m = 24 m of fencing

All possible rectangles:

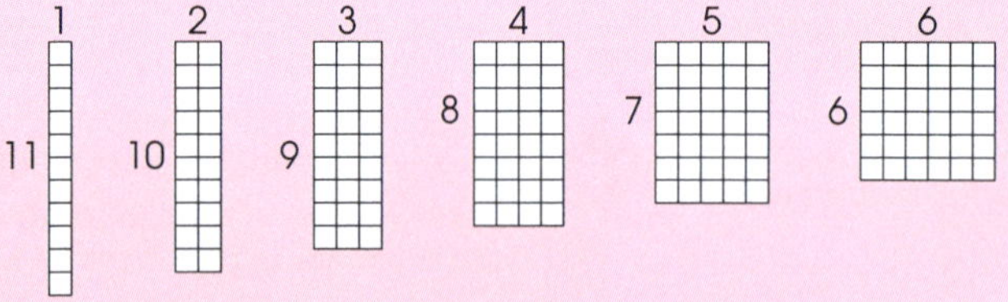

Area: 11□ 20□ 27□ 32□ 35□ 36□

The maximum area of the rectangular garden is 36 square metres.

Chapter 10
Two-dimensional Shapes

10.1 Identifying Angles

In this unit, you will study and be able to identify the three benchmark angles: right angle, half a right angle, and straight angle.

Identifying Degrees of Benchmark Angles

You should be able to identify right angles and angles that are smaller or larger than a right angle. At this stage, you will learn to describe angles in degrees.

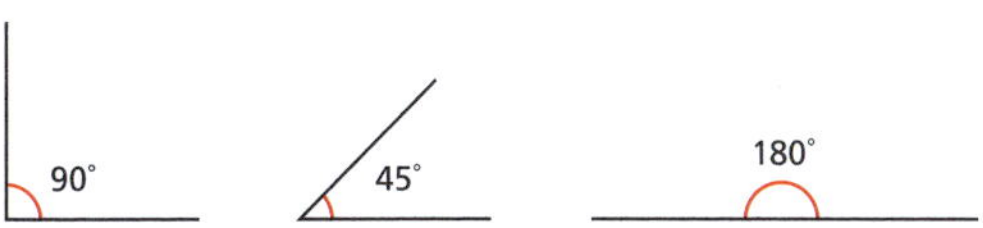

right angle | half a right angle | straight angle

Angles are measured in degrees, which are denoted by °. For example, a right angle is 90° (90 degrees).

Making Benchmark Angles

Practise making the benchmark angles. Think about how benchmark angles are related and the size of each angle in degrees.

Tear off the corner of a piece of paper. Colour the corner that makes a right angle. Then write 90°.

Tear off another corner. Fold the corner in half. Colour the corner that makes a 45° angle and write 45°.

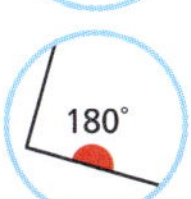

Tear off a part of the piece of paper that has a straight edge. Colour to show a straight angle. Then write 180°.

Use these cut-outs as tools to measure the angles of different objects.

Application

What is the measure of the angle that Joe made?

Solution:

greater than half a right angle = greater than 45°
smaller than a right angle = smaller than 90°

So, the angle is greater than 45° and smaller than 90°.

$$45^\circ < \text{size of angle} < 90^\circ$$

The size of the angle is from 46° to 89°.

10.2 Classifying Quadrilaterals

In this unit, you will learn the definition of a quadrilateral and the properties of different quadrilaterals.

Identifying Quadrilaterals

Quadrilateral: a shape with 4 sides

e.g.

Quadrilaterals | Not Quadrilaterals

Common Quadrilaterals

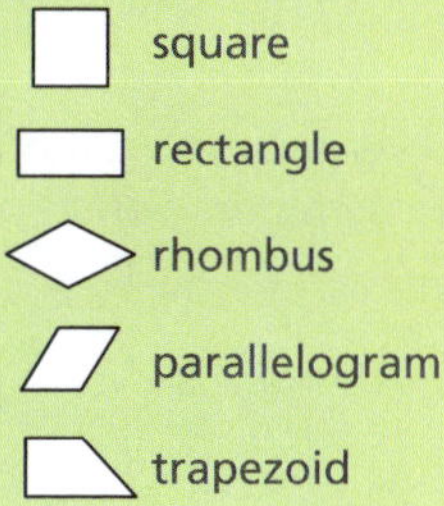

Properties of Quadrilaterals

Below are some properties of a quadrilateral that you need to be able to identify.

- lines of symmetry
- right angles
- equal sides
- parallel sides

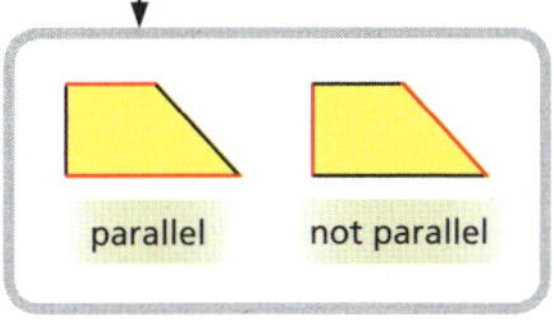

e.g. Identify the properties of the shapes.

square:

- 4 lines of symmetry
- 4 right angles
- 4 equal sides
- 2 pairs of parallel sides

trapezoid:

- no lines of symmetry
- 2 right angles
- not all sides are equal
- 1 pair of parallel sides

Application

I made a quadrilateral that has 2 pairs of parallel lines and more than 1 line of symmetry but no right angles.

Name the shape that she made.
Describe its side lengths.

Solution:

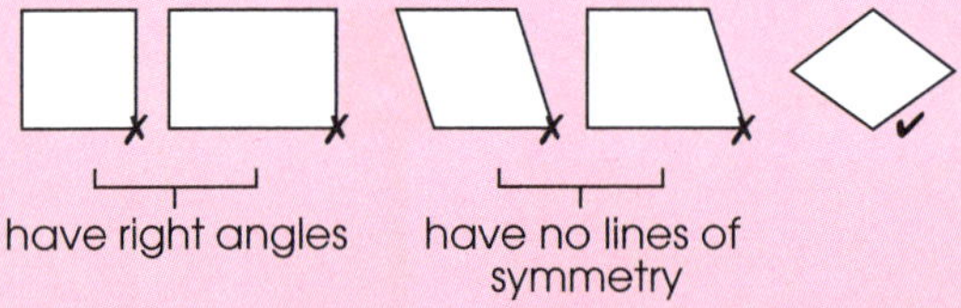

She made a rhombus. A rhombus has 2 pairs of parallel lines, 2 lines of symmetry, and no right angles. The side lengths of a rhombus are equal.

Chapter 11

Three-dimensional Figures

11.1 Naming and Describing 3-D Figures

This unit introduces the naming conventions and the properties of 3-D solids.

Naming 3-D Figures

You should be able to name 3-D figures.

To name a 3-D figure:

1st Identify the **shape** of its base(s).

2nd Determine whether it is a **prism** or **pyramid**.
(A prism has exactly 2 bases; a pyramid has only 1 base.)

Other 3-D Figures

 cylinder

 cone

 sphere

e.g. 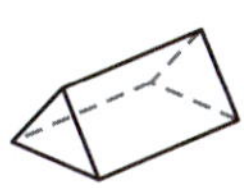 **triangular prism**  **rectangular pyramid**

Identifying Properties of 3-D Figures

Once you are able to identify 3-D figures, you should learn to identify their properties.

Properties of 3-D Figures:

- **faces:** the flat surfaces of a 3-D figure
- **vertices:** the corners of a 3-D figure
- **edges:** the sides that join the vertices

Think about these questions:

- Do all pyramids have triangular faces?
- Do all prisms have an even number of vertices?

e.g. Describe the faces, vertices, and edges.

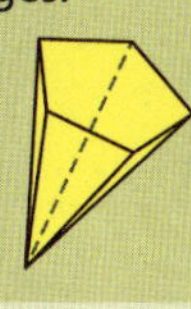

faces: 1 pentagonal face
5 triangular faces

vertices: 6 vertices

edges: 10 edges

Application

Colin is gluing two identical triangular prisms together to make a new prism. Is it possible that the new prism will have the same number of edges and vertices as each triangular prism? If so, name the prism.

Solution:

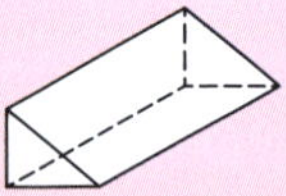

triangular prism:
9 edges and 6 vertices

Possible constructions:

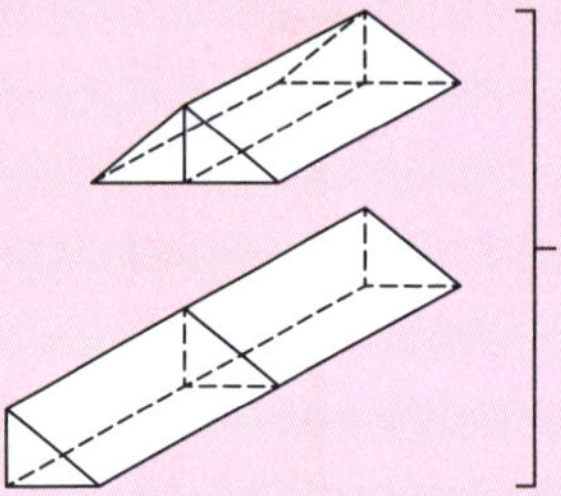

Both ways form a triangular prism, so it has 9 edges and 6 vertices.

Yes, it is possible.

11.2 Constructing 3-D Figures

In this unit, you will learn to construct 3-D solids with paper nets. You will also be required to identify 3-D solids mentally from nets and skeletons.

Nets of 3-D Figures

You should be able to visualize 3-D figures from a given net. You should also be able to draw nets of 3-D figures.

All nets of prisms have rectangular faces.

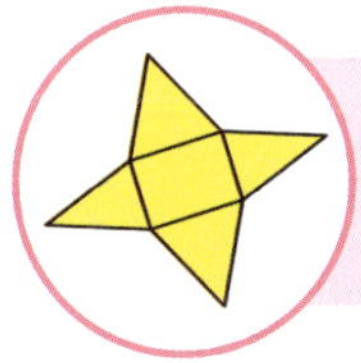

All nets of pyramids have triangular faces.

You should also be able to identify nets that cannot form 3-D figures. Have a look at the nets on the next page and identify which nets can form cubes. Describe why two of the nets cannot form cubes and how they can be fixed. Through this activity, you will learn to draw nets of 3-D figures.

Skeletons of 3-D Figures

Make skeletons using marshmallows and uncooked spaghetti noodles to learn how to identify 3-D figures from skeletons.

no. of marshmallows needed = no. of vertices of the 3-D figure

no. of noodles needed = no. of edges of the 3-D figure

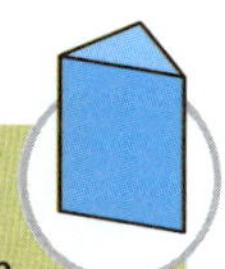

e.g. Make the skeleton of a triangular prism.

no. of marshmallows: 6
no. of noodles: 9

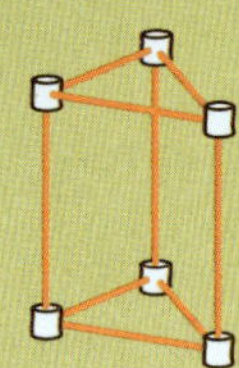

A

B

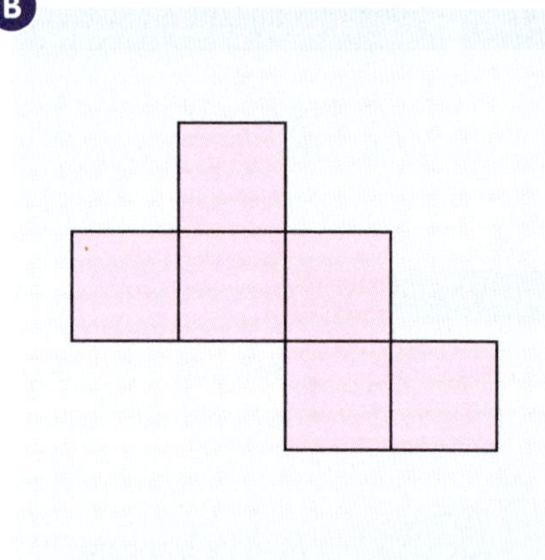

C

D

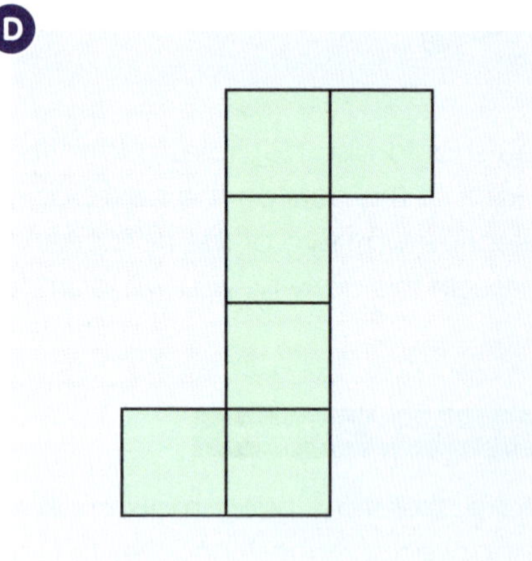

*Only B and D can form cubes.

Application

Jill made two identical pyramids, one with 7 pieces of modelling clay and 12 sticks, and the other with a net. Name the pyramid. Draw the skeleton and the net of the pyramid.

Solution:

Since it is a pyramid, there must be a pointy top which needs 1 piece of modelling clay. The remaining 6 pieces of modelling clay are for the base, so the base must have 6 vertices – a hexagon.

Jill made a hexagonal pyramid, which has 7 vertices and 12 edges.

skeleton:

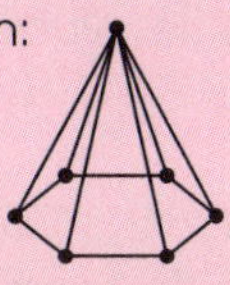

net:

Chapter 12

Locations and Movements

12.1 Locations and Movements on a Grid Map

In this unit, you will learn to locate and describe objects on a grid map using coordinates. You will also use directional words to describe movements.

Writing Coordinates

A grid map has its columns labelled with letters starting with A, and its rows labelled with numbers starting with 1.

To use coordinates to describe a location, write the letter first, and then the number.

e.g. Write the coordinates.

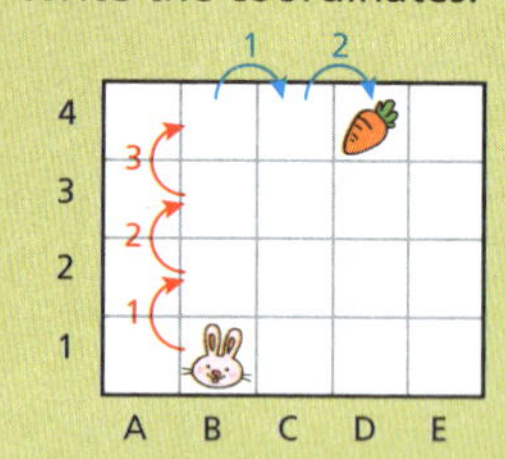

B1 D4

Describing Movements

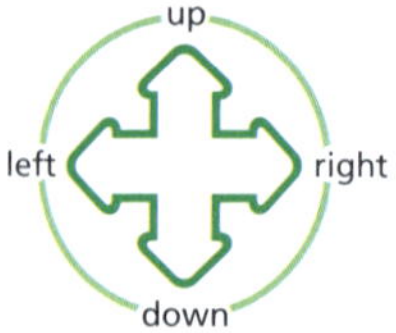

This diagram helps you identify the directions of movements on a grid map.

e.g. Describe the 's route to the .

Move 3 squares up and 2 squares to the right.

You can tell between left and right using this strategy. Hold your thumbs and index fingers as shown. The hand that makes the "L" is the left side.

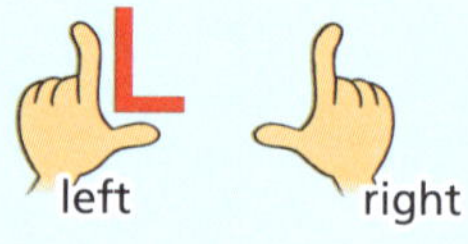

12.2 Making and Describing Reflections

In this unit, you will learn about reflections and how to draw them correctly on a grid.

Identifying Reflections

A reflection is a transformation in which a shape is flipped and a mirrored image of the original shape is formed. Stand in front of a mirror. The image in the mirror is your reflection.

e.g.

Description
The shape is reflected over line P.

Drawing Reflections

You should learn to draw reflected images on grids.

To draw a reflected image on a grid:

1st Identify the line the shape is to be reflected over.

2nd Draw the part of the image that is closest to the line.

3rd Draw the rest of the image.

e.g. Do the reflections and label the images.

Image A: Reflect the shape over line X.

Image B: Reflect the shape over line Y.

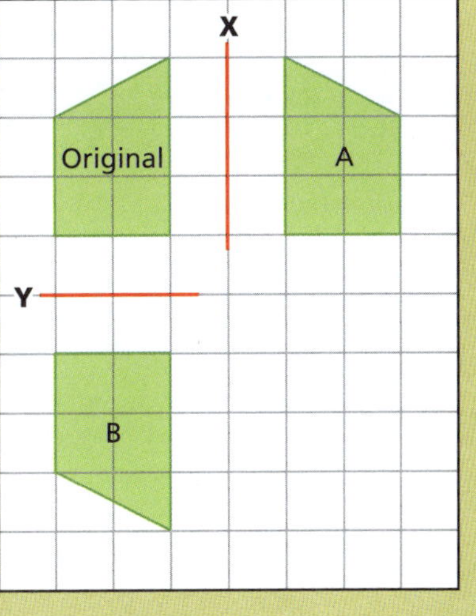

Application

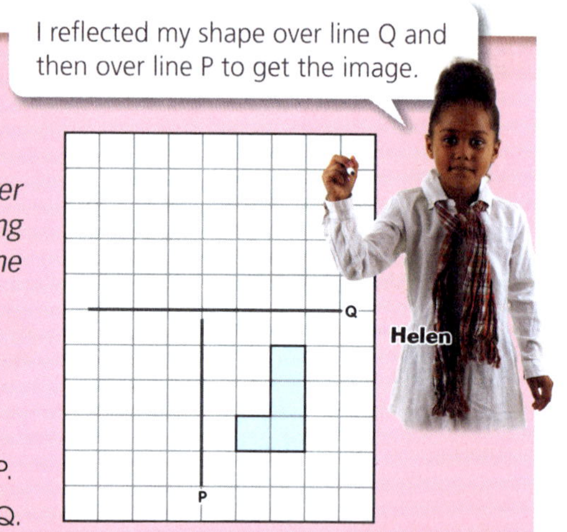

Draw Helen's original shape.

Is there a way to transform her shape to the image without doing a reflection? If so, name the transformation.

Solution:

To get the original shape:

1st Reflect the image over line P.

2nd Reflect the image over line Q.

To transform Helen's original shape to the image, make a rotation.

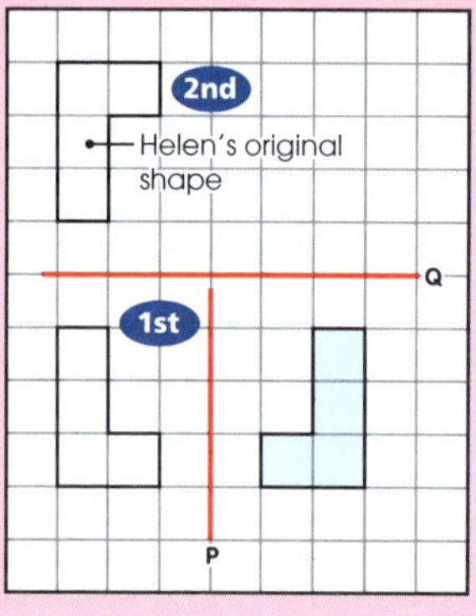

Chapter 13

Patterning

13.1 Describing Numeric and Geometric Patterns

In this unit, you will investigate number patterns and geometric patterns.

Number Patterns

Identify and describe pattern rules.

e.g. Describe the number pattern.

Find the relationship between the terms. Addition, subtraction, and multiplication might be involved.

×2 −1 ×2 −1 ×2 −1

2 4 3 6 5 10 9

Pattern rule: Start at 2. Multiply by 2. Then subtract 1.

e.g. Find the 11th term of the pattern.

The last term in the given pattern is the 7th term. Extend the pattern from the 7th to the 11th term.

×2 −1 ×2 −1

9 18 17 34 33

7th term (9) … 11th term (33)

The 11th term is **33**.

Geometric Patterns

Convert geometric patterns into number patterns.

Geometric Pattern

e.g. How many sticks are needed to make Frame 5?

1st Show the pattern in a chart and find the pattern rule.

2nd Find the term with the given term number.

Frame No.	No. of Sticks
1	3
2	7
3	11
4	15
5	19

+4 +4 +4 +4

Pattern rule: Add 4 each time.

So, **19 sticks** are needed for Frame 5.

13.2 Solving Equations

In this unit, you will learn about related facts and how to apply them in solving equations.

Finding Related Facts

Related facts: a set of addition and subtraction sentences or multiplication and division sentences that are related and have the same numbers

e.g. Write the related facts of 2 x 3 = 6.

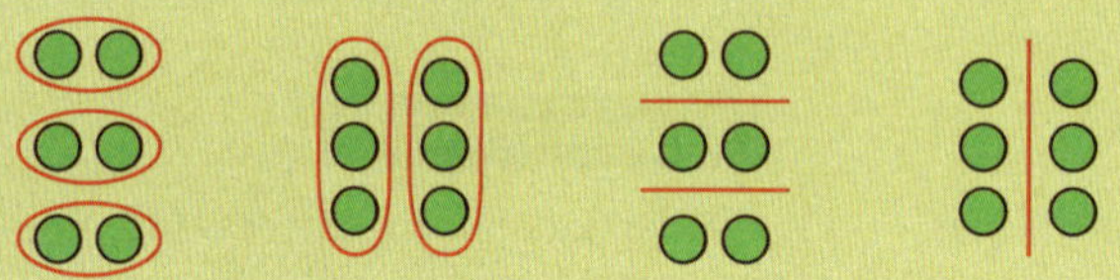

2 x 3 = 6   3 x 2 = 6   6 ÷ 3 = 2   6 ÷ 2 = 3

The numbers in each number sentence in a set of related facts are the same.

Finding Missing Numbers

Before finding missing numbers in equations, you must be familiar with finding related facts.

e.g. 36 ÷ ? = 9

Think a related fact:

9 × ? = 36

Since 9 x 4 = 36,

36 ÷ **4** = 9.

↑

4 is the missing number.

e.g. 4 x ? = 36

Think a related fact:

36 ÷ 4 = ?

Since 36 ÷ 4 = 9,

4 x **9** = 36.

↑

9 is the missing number.

Application

Write an equation to show what Kelly says. Find the number of candies on each cupcake.

There were 7 cupcakes and each had 5 candies on it. I got 14 more candies and I put the same number of candies on each cupcake.

Solution:

Before adding candies:

$5 \times 7 = 35$

↑ 7 — number of cupcakes

↑ 5 — number of candies on each cupcake

After adding candies:

$? \times 7 = 35 + 14$

$? \times 7 = 49$

$7 \times 7 = 49$

So, there are 7 candies on each cupcake.

13.3 Using Properties of Multiplication

This unit introduces the commutative and distributive properties of multiplication. You will learn to apply these properties to simplify the multiplication process.

Commutative Property of Multiplication

This property states that changing the order of the numbers when multiplying will not change the product. Use blocks, such as the set below, to demonstrate this concept.

Rearranging a set of blocks in different ways does not change the number of blocks in the set.

4 pieces of 2 x 3
= 4 x 2 x 3
= 24

3 pieces of 2 x 4
= 3 x 2 x 4
= 24

2 pieces of 4 x 3
= 2 x 4 x 3
= 24

Apply this property to make multiplication easier.

e.g. 18 x 7 x 5 = ?

Way 1 Without applying the property:

18 x 7 x 5
= 126 x 5
= 630

Way 2 Applying the property:

18 x 7 x 5
= 18 x 5 x 7 ← 18 x 5 = 90; 90 is a friendly number.
= 90 x 7
= 630

Doing multiplication with or without using the property will give the same answer, but applying the property when applicable can make the process easier.

Distributive Property of Multiplication

This property states that in multiplication, numbers can be broken down, multiplied, and then added to get the product. Use the example below to understand the concept.

Using counters

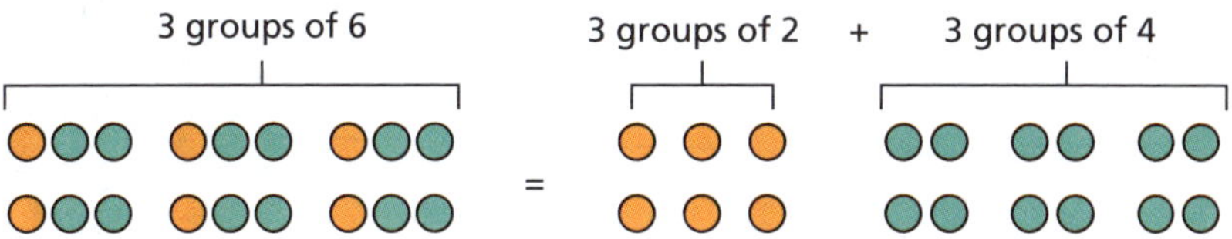

3 x **6** = 3 x **2** + 3 x **4** (breaking 6 into 2 and 4)

18   18

Using rectangles

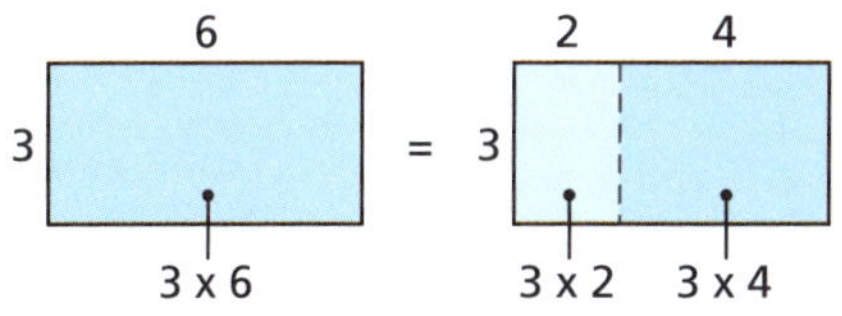

3 x 6 = 3 x 2 + 3 x 4

Once you understand this property, you can use it to do multiplication.

e.g.

73 x 4 = ? ← If the distributive property is not used, vertical multiplication will be used, which can be difficult to do mentally.

73 x 4

= 70 x 4 + 3 x 4 ← Break 73 into 70 and 3 because 70 is a friendly number.

= 280 + 12 ← Add.

= 292

Application

Can you use the distributive property of multiplication to find the answer to 47 x 18? Explain.

Solution:

You have not learned to multiply numbers by 2-digit numbers yet, but you can use the distributive property to find the answer.

47 x 18
= 47 x 10 + 47 x 8 ← applying the property
= 470 + 376
= 846

Chapter 14

Data Management and Probability

14.1 Analyzing and Displaying Data

In this unit, you will review the concept of mode and learn about median. You will also be introduced to stem-and-leaf plots.

Understanding Median and Mode

Median – the middle number in a set of data that is ordered from least to greatest

Mode – the number that appears most frequently in a set of data

Consider the data below as an example to help you understand how the median and mode are found.

Ages of Children in a Library

9 11 10 9 10 8 10

Finding the Median

1st Order the data from least to greatest.

2nd Find the middle value. This value is the median.

median

8 9 9 (10) 10 10 11

* If there are two middle values, add both values up and divide the sum by 2. The answer is the median.

Finding the Mode

Find the number of times each value appears. The value that appears most often is the mode.

appears most often; 10 is the mode

8 9 9 10 10 10 11

* There can be more than one mode. If there were one more 9 in the set of data in the example, both 9 and 10 would be the modes of the data.

Stem-and-Leaf Plots

A stem-and-leaf plot is a tool that is used to organize a set of data. Each data value is split into a "stem" (the first digit) and a "leaf" (usually the last digit).

e.g. Organize the set of data using a stem-and-leaf plot.

1st Determine the "stems" of the plot. (In our example, the stems are 1, 2, and 3.)

2nd Group the data values that have the same stem. Then write them in the plot from least to greatest.

A set of data

18	25	27	36	19
24	15	32	11	18
21	26	34	18	25

Stem	Leaf
1	1 5 8 8 8 9
2	1 4 5 5 6 7
3	2 4 6

Cross out the data values that you have put into the plot.

14.2 Finding the Frequency of an Outcome

In this unit, you will learn to determine the frequency of an outcome. In addition, you will learn how repetition affects conclusions drawn in experiments.

Predicting the Frequency of an Outcome

You should be able to find the probability of an outcome and apply the concept to find the frequency of an outcome.

e.g. Predict the number of times the spinner will land on red if the spinner is spun 20 times.

Think The probability of the spinner landing on red is one half. If the spinner is spun 20 times, it will land on red one half of the times. One half of 20 is 10.

So, the spinner will land on red **10 times**.

How Repetition Affects Conclusions Drawn

You will need to understand that the more repetitions there are in an experiment, the closer the result will be to the predicted frequency. Try the simple activity below.

1st Get a coin. In each trial, toss the coin 10 times and record the number of times heads comes up. Do 5 trials.

2nd Combine the results of the 5 trials.

3rd Compare the individual results and the combined results.

Trial	1	2	3	4	5
No. of Heads					

All Trials

______ heads

Grade 5

Chapter 1

Whole Numbers to 100 000

1.1 Writing Numbers to 100 000

In this unit, you will learn the concept of place value in whole numbers up to 100 000. You will then be required to solve problems related to whole numbers up to 100 000.

At the beginning, you should use a place value chart to display a number. Using a place value chart can help you see clearly the value of each digit in a number. After that, you can learn how to represent a number in three other ways.

Place Value Chart

When writing a five-digit number, remember to leave a space between the hundreds and the thousands digits.

e.g. Write 25 368.

Thousands					
Hundred	Ten	One	Hundreds	Tens	Ones
	3	2	0	8	0

8 in the ones place means **8**.

6 in the tens place means **60**.

3 in the hundreds place means **300**.

5 in the thousands place means **5000**.

2 in the ten thousands place means **20 000**.

Writing Numbers in Three Ways

In standard form : 25 368

In expanded form : 20 000 + 5000 + 300 + 60 + 8

In words : twenty-five thousand three hundred sixty-eight

Writing numbers in expanded form shows the value of each digit.

e.g. Write the number that is in the place value chart in three ways.

Thousands					
Hundred	Ten	One	Hundreds	Tens	Ones
	3	2	0	8	0

In standard form : 32 080

In expanded form : 30 000 + 2000 + 80

In words : thirty-two thousand eighty

Application

Look at the 5 digits that Julia wrote on the board. Using each digit only once, form as many 5-digit numbers as possible. Describe the strategy you used to find all the possible numbers.

Solution:

Numbers cannot start with 0, so start with 2 and 3.

1st Start with 2 followed by 3 and move 3 back one digit at a time.

2**3** 000
20 **3**00
20 0**3**0
20 00**3**

— 4 possible numbers

2nd Start with 3 followed by 2 and move 2 back one digit at a time.

3**2** 000
30 **2**00
30 0**2**0
30 00**2**

— 4 possible numbers

There are 8 possible 5-digit numbers that can be formed using Julia's digits.

1.2 Comparing, Ordering, and Rounding Numbers

You may find it easier to compare and order whole numbers using a number line or a place value chart.

e.g. Which one is greater, 28 036 or 23 998?

Using a Number Line

- Place the 2 numbers on a number line marked with multiples of 10 000.
- The number to the right is greater.

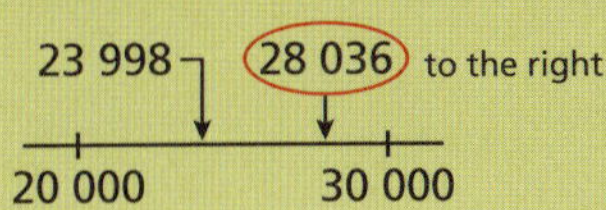

28 036 is greater.

Using a Place Value Chart

- Write the 2 numbers in a place value chart.

Thousands					
H	T	O	H	T	O
	2	8	0	3	6
	2	3	9	9	8

the same — Compare these two digits. 8 > 3, so 28 036 is greater.

28 036 is greater.

You can follow the steps below to round a whole number to a specified place value.

Rounding a Number

e.g. Round 57 981 to the nearest thousand.

1st Locate the digit* in the thousands place.

57 981 ← 7 is in the thousands place.

2nd Look at the digit to the right of **7**.

57 981 — 9 is greater than 5, so round up.

Round 7 up to 8 and replace all the digits to its right with zeros.

57 981 is rounded to **58 000**.

* Be careful if this digit is 9.

e.g. Round 49 653 to the nearest thousand.

49 653 → 50 000

Round up.

9 becomes 10, so 49 → 50.

Application

Use the given digits to form 5-digit numbers that are 50 000 when rounded to the nearest thousand.

Solution:

Think: numbers that are 50 000 when rounded to the nearest thousand

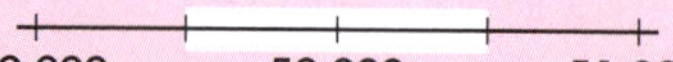

The numbers must be from 49 500 to 50 499.

The given digits: 3, 2, 8, 4, 9

- The digit in the ten thousands place must be 4.
- The digit in the thousands place must be 9.

Thousands						
	4	9	8	3	2	> 49 500
	4	9	8	2	3	> 49 500

49 832 and 49 823 are the numbers that can be formed.

1.3 Multiplying Two-digit Numbers

You should be able to multiply two-digit numbers by one-digit numbers (e.g. 45 x 6 = ____).

If not, you should practise more before beginning this unit. In this unit, you will learn how to multiply two-digit numbers by two-digit numbers.

It takes 3 steps to multiply.

Multiplying by a Two-digit Number

e.g. 39 x 27 = ______

1st Multiply by the ones.

```
  6          6
  39         39
x 27   →   x 27
   3        273
```

2nd Multiply by the tens.

```
  1          1
  39         39
x 27   →   x 27
 273        273
  80        780
```

Remember to put a "0" in the ones column.

3rd Add.

```
   39
x  27
  273
  780
 1053
```

So, 39 x 27 = **1053**.

Tricks for Two-digit Numbers x Two-digit Numbers

e.g.

31 x 25 = 6	Multiply the two numbers in the tens column.
31 x 25 = 6_5	Multiply the two numbers in the ones column.
31 x 25 = ~~6~~75 (7 written above; 15 + 2 = 17)	Do 3 x 5 and 1 x 2 separately. Then add.

So, 31 x 25 = **775**.

Application

Use the clues to find the two 2-digit numbers. Then find their product.

- *The sum of the two numbers is 81.*
- *Their difference is 11.*

Solution:

This is a guess-and-check question. Start with numbers that are halfway between 0 and 81 (which are 41 and 40).

If the sum of two numbers is an odd number, it means that one of the numbers is odd and the other is even.

First Number	Second Number	Difference	Is the Difference 11?
41	40	1	✗
42	39	3	✗
43	38	5	✗
44	37	7	✗
45	36	9	✗
46	35	11	✔

$46 + 35 = 81$
$46 - 35 = 11$

So, the two numbers are 46 and 35.

$46 \times 35 = 1610$

The product of 46 and 35 is 1610.

1.4 Dividing Three-digit Numbers

In this unit, you will learn to divide three-digit numbers by one-digit numbers. At the beginning, you can do the division on grid paper. This can help you understand how to align the numbers when doing division.

Three-digit Numbers ÷ One-digit Numbers

Below are three typical division problems:

- quotient: a three-digit number

e.g.

	1	7	8	R	1
2	3	5	7		
	2				
	1	5			
	1	4			
		1	7		
		1	6		
			1		

3 > 2; start the division in the hundreds place.

357 ÷ 2 = **178R1**

Terms Used in Division

e.g.

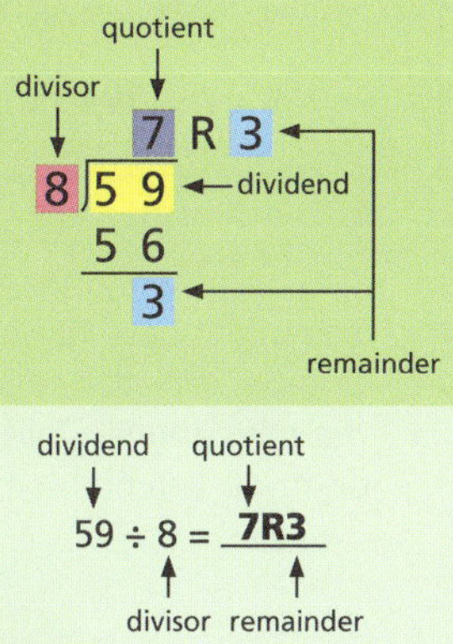

- quotient: a two-digit number

e.g.

		8	2	R	3
6	4	9	5		
	4	8			
		1	5		
		1	2		
			3		

4 < 6; so consider one more digit to make it "49 ÷ 6".

495 ÷ 6 = **82R3**

- quotient: with "0"

e.g.

Put a "0" in the tens column.

	1	**0**	7	R	4
7	7	5	3		
	7				
		5	3		
		4	9		
			4		

753 ÷ 7 = **107R4**

Put a "0" in the ones column.

		3	**0**	R	5
9	2	7	5		
	2	7			
			5		

275 ÷ 9 = **30R5**

You might have difficulty doing division, especially questions like the ones above. Try the questions on my left to practise more.

Try these!

- 634 ÷ 6
- 567 ÷ 8
- 734 ÷ 7
- 481 ÷ 6
- 524 ÷ 5
- 419 ÷ 4

Checking Answers

After doing the division, you should use multiplication and addition to check the answers.

e.g. Is 307 ÷ 5 = **61R4** correct?

Check

61 x 5 = 305 (61: quotient; 5: divisor)

305 + 4 = 309 (4: remainder; 309: not the same as dividend)

So, 307 ÷ 5 = **61R4** . ✗

e.g. Is 453 ÷ 6 = **75R3** correct?

Check

75 x 6 = 450 (75: quotient; 6: divisor)

450 + 3 = 453 (3: remainder; 453: same as dividend)

So, 453 ÷ 6 = **75R3** . ✓

Application

Use the given digits to form a division sentence to get the greatest quotient. Find the quotient and explain your thinking.

Solution:

a very large dividend ↓ ↓ a very small divisor

☐☐☐ ÷ ☐ = the greatest quotient

1st Select the smallest number to be the divisor. In this case, 2 is the smallest.

④⑧②⑤

☐☐☐ ÷ ☐

2nd Form the largest 3-digit number with the remaining numbers 4, 8, and 5. The largest 3-digit number is 854.

8 5 4 ÷ 2 = 427

The greatest quotient is 427.

Chapter 2

Decimal Numbers to Hundredths

2.1 Writing Decimal Numbers

In this unit, you will learn to write decimal numbers to hundredths. You will then learn how to use a place value chart to write decimal numbers.

Representing Decimal Numbers

= 1 one = 1 tenth = 1 hundredth

e.g.

2 ones
(2)

5 tenths
(0.5)

6 hundredths
(0.06)

Writing Decimal Numbers

Ones	Tenths	Hundredths
2 .	5	6

= 2 + 0.5 + 0.06

=

1 tenth = 10 hundredths

So, 5 tenths = 50 hundredths.

Reading Decimal Numbers

For 2.56, we say "two and fifty-six hundredths".

2.2 Comparing Decimal Numbers

When we compare numbers, we should always start with the left-most digits. Comparing decimal numbers is the same as comparing whole numbers. Compare the whole numbers first. If they are the same, compare the tenths. If the tenths are the same, compare the hundredths to determine which decimal is greater.

Before doing comparisons, make sure you understand the meaning of equivalent decimals.

Equivalent Decimals

0.4
(4 tenths)

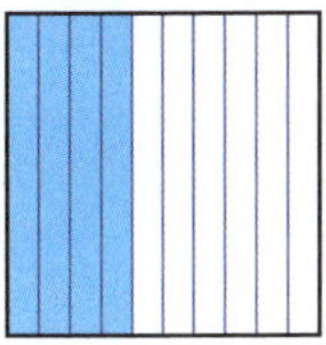

0.40
(40 hundredths)

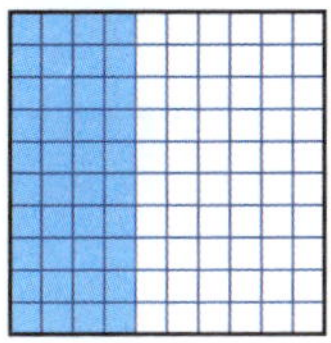

> **Equivalent Decimals**
>
> decimals that represent the same amount
>
> **e.g.** 0.2 = 0.20
>
> 0.2 and 0.20 are equivalent decimals.

From the diagram, we can see that 0.4 and 0.40 represent the same amount. So, 0.4 and 0.40 are equivalent decimals.

Comparing Decimals

You may use a place value chart or a number line to help compare decimals.

e.g. Compare: 3.24 and 3.42

Using a Place Value Chart

Ones	Tenths	Hundredths
3 .	2	4
3 .	4	2

the same (Ones) — Compare: 2 < 4. (Tenths)

So, **3.42** is greater.

Using a Number Line

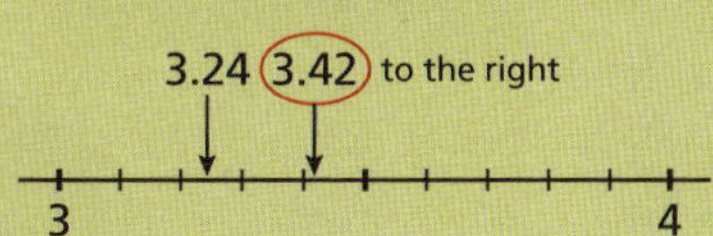

So, **3.42** is greater.

2.3 Rounding Decimal Numbers

You should be able to round decimals to the nearest whole number. In this unit, you will learn to round decimals to the nearest tenth. This method shortens a decimal number so that it has one digit after the decimal point. You may practise the following ways to help yourself do the rounding.

Rounding to the Nearest Tenth

Way 1 Using a Number Line

e.g. 12.76

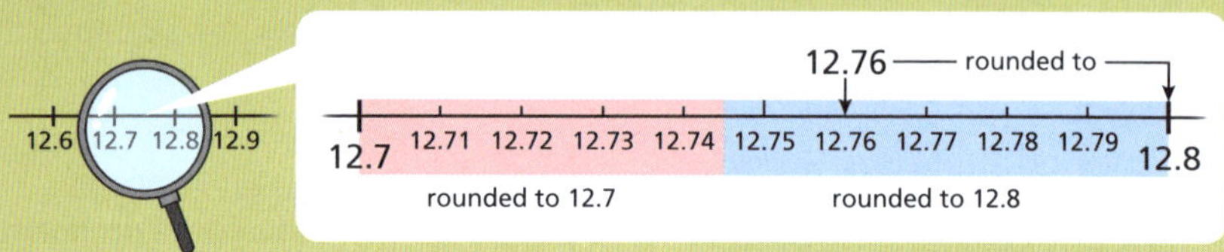

12.76 $\xrightarrow{\text{rounded to}}$ **12.8**

Way 2 Checking the Digit in the Hundredths Place

If it is 5 or more, add 1 to the digit in the tenths place (round up).
If it is less than 5, leave the digit in the tenths place the same (round down).

Don't forget to drop the digit in the hundredths place after rounding.

e.g.

5.27 $\xrightarrow{\text{rounded to}}$ **5.3**

7 > 5; round up.

3.62 $\xrightarrow{\text{rounded to}}$ **3.6**

2 < 5; round down.

Application

The decimal I wrote is smaller than 16. When rounded to the nearest tenth, it is 16.0. Write all the possible decimals and explain your thoughts.

Solution:

Since it is smaller than 16, it must start with 15. 15 . □□

For it to round to 16.0, it must have a 9 in its tenths place. 15 . 9 □ (Tenths)

For the tenths to round up, it must have either a 5, 6, 7, 8, or 9 in its hundredths place. 15 . 9 9/8/7/6/5

The possible answers are 15.95, 15.96, 15.97, 15.98, and 15.99.

2.4 Adding and Subtracting Decimal Numbers

When adding and subtracting decimals, you should try to estimate answers before calculating. Estimating answers is a good way to get a rough idea of what the correct answers are.

Estimating can help you find an answer that is fairly close to the actual answer.

Estimate by Rounding

1st Round each decimal to the nearest whole number.

2nd Add or subtract the rounded numbers to get the estimated answer.

Adding and Subtracting Decimals

1st Align the decimal points.

2nd Add/Subtract the same way as we do whole numbers.

3rd Put the decimal point in the answer.

e.g. 2.3 + 6.85 = ______

$$\begin{array}{r} {}^{1} \\ 2.30 \\ +\ 6.85 \\ \hline 9.15 \end{array}$$

Align the decimal points.

Add "0" to fill the empty place value.

Put the decimal point in the answer.

Remember to fill empty place values with zeros so that the two numbers have the same number of decimal places.

e.g. 6 − 2.47 = ______

$$\begin{array}{r} {}^{5}\ \ {}^{9}\,{}^{10} \\ \not{6}.\not{0}\not{0} \\ -\ 2.47 \\ \hline 3.53 \end{array}$$

Add two "0"'s to fill the empty place values.

Put the decimal point in the answer.

Application

Max and Julia are 5.64 m apart. If Max steps back 0.88 m and Julia walks 1.27 m toward Max, how far away will they be from each other?

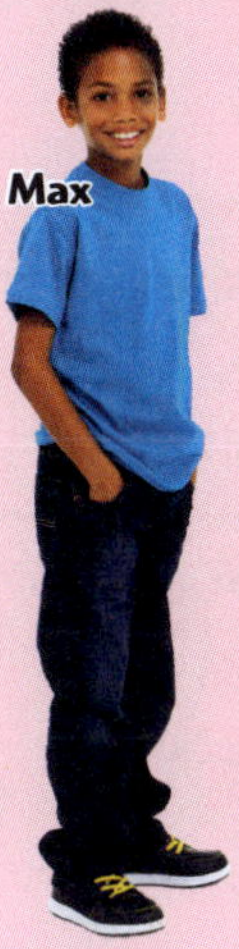

Solution:

You should draw pictures to illustrate the question.

1st

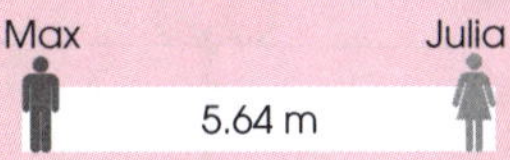

2nd

distance apart: 0.88 + 5.64 = 6.52 (m)

3rd

distance apart: 6.52 – 1.27 = 5.25 (m)

So, Max and Julia will be 5.25 m away from each other.

2.5 Multiplying and Dividing Decimal Numbers by 10, 100, and 1000

At this level, you will learn to use mental math to multiply and divide decimals by 10, 100, and 1000. The trick is to move the decimal point as many places as there are zeros in the number 10, 100, or 1000.

Multiplying by 10, 100, and 1000

e.g. 2.53 x 100 = ____
2 zeros

Move "." 2 places to the right.

2.53.
1 place → 2 places

2.53 x 100 = **253**

A Decimal ✖ 10, 100, or 1000

Move the decimal point 1, 2, or 3 places to the **RIGHT**.

A Decimal ÷ 10, 100, or 1000

Move the decimal point 1, 2, or 3 places to the **LEFT**.

Dividing by 10, 100, and 1000

e.g. 2.53 ÷ 1000 = ________
3 zeros

Move "." 3 places to the left. Add zeros if needed.

0.002.53
1 place
2 places
3 places

2.53 ÷ 1000 = **0.00253**

Challenge!

When a decimal is multiplied by 10 000, where should we move the decimal point?

2.8 x 10 000
= ____________

Once you understand the concept of using mental math to find answers, you can try the questions below to consolidate the concept and have a better understanding of multiplying and dividing decimals by 10, 100, and 1000.

Finding the Correct Operations (x or ÷)

e.g. 52.9 ◯ 100 = **0.529**

Think 5 2 . 9 (division)

52.9 (÷) 100 = **0.529**

The answer is smaller than the decimal 52.9, which means that it is a division sentence.

Filling in the Correct Numbers 10, 100, or 1000

e.g. 82.4 x ______ = 82 400

Line up the two numbers to figure out the answer.

8	2.	4		
8	2	4	0	0

(Move 3 places to the right.)

So, 82.4 x **1000** = 82 400.

Application

The cost of 10 pizzas is $89.50. How much will I collect if 1000 pizzas are sold?

Solution:

10 pizzas = $89.50

↓ Multiply 10 by 100 to get 1000.

↓ Multiply 89.50 by 100 to get the answer. (Move the decimal point 2 places to the right.)

1000 pizzas $8950

If 1000 pizzas are sold, he will collect $8950.

Chapter 3

Fractions and Decimals

3.1 Identifying Fractions and Mixed Numbers

You should be able to use standard fractional notation to represent fractions and understand the terms denominator (the bottom number) and numerator (the top number). In this unit, you will learn how to identify the three types of fractions and convert between improper fractions and mixed numbers.

Three Types of Fractions

Proper Fraction (numerator < denominator)	Improper Fraction (numerator ≥ denominator)	Mixed Number (a whole number + a proper fraction)
e.g. 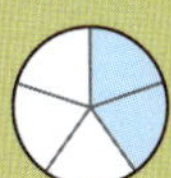	e.g. 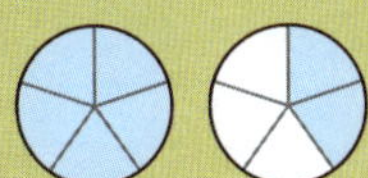	e.g. 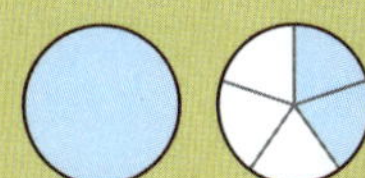
$\frac{2}{5}$	$\frac{7}{5}$	$1\frac{2}{5}$

A proper fraction is the only type of fraction that describes amounts that are less than 1.

Improper Fractions ⟳ Mixed Numbers

Improper fractions and mixed numbers are 2 different ways to represent the same number.

Improper Fractions → Mixed Numbers

- using division

e.g. $\frac{7}{3}$

$$3\overline{)7}$$

2 – whole number; 3 – denominator; 6; 1 – numerator

$= 2\frac{1}{3}$

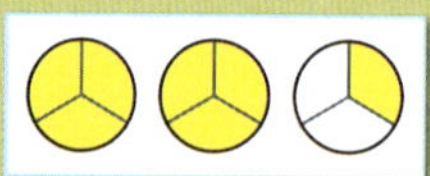

Mixed Numbers → Improper Fractions

- using multiplication and addition

e.g. $3\frac{1}{4} = \frac{3 \times 4 + 1}{4}$ (3: whole number; 4: denominator; 3 x 4 + 1: numerator)

$= \frac{12 + 1}{4}$

$= \frac{13}{4}$

Application

Help Jason fill in the missing numbers for each pair consisting of a mixed number and an improper fraction.

Solution:

Mixed numbers and improper fractions share the same denominator.

1st Pair

$\square\frac{5}{6}$ and $\frac{11}{\blacksquare}$

same denominator, $\blacksquare = 6$

$\square\frac{5}{6}$ and $\frac{11}{6}$

$6 \times \square + 5$

Try $\square = 1$

So, $6 \times 1 + 5 = 11$. ✔

The first pair is $1\frac{5}{6}$ and $\frac{11}{6}$.

2nd Pair

$3\frac{4}{\blacksquare}$ and $\frac{\blacksquare}{5}$

same denominator, $\blacksquare = 5$

$3\frac{4}{5}$ and $\frac{\blacksquare}{5}$

$3 \times 5 + 4 = 19$

So, $\blacksquare$ 19. ✔

The second pair is $3\frac{4}{5}$ and $\frac{19}{5}$.

3.2 Finding Equivalent Fractions

Equivalent fractions are fractions that represent the same parts of a whole or group. You can use pictures to "visualize" the concept initially. Once you grasp the idea, you can try to make equivalent fractions using multiplication and division.

Finding Equivalent Fractions in Three Ways

- by drawing

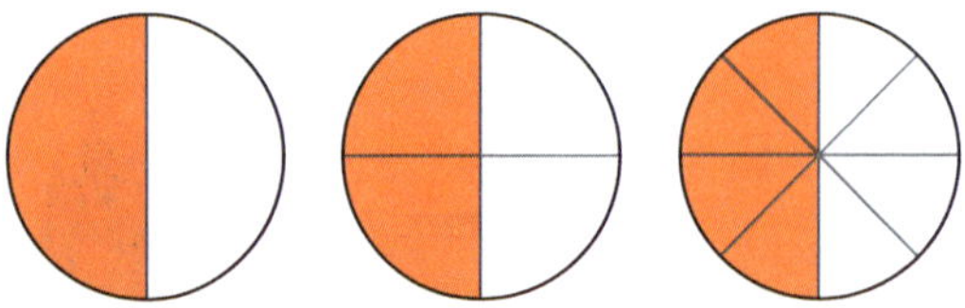

$\frac{1}{2}$ $\frac{2}{4}$ $\frac{4}{8}$ ← These are all equivalent fractions.

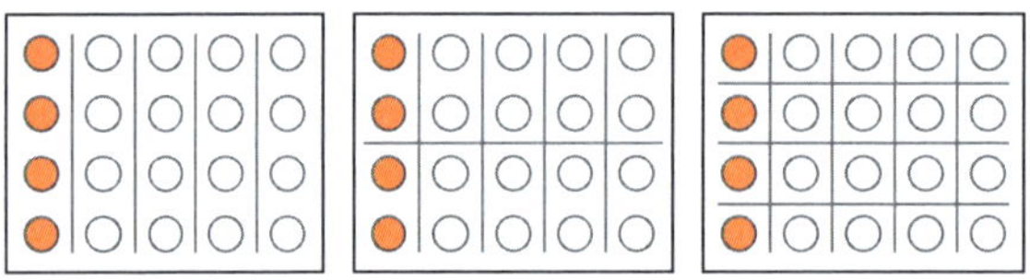

$\frac{1}{5}$ $\frac{2}{10}$ $\frac{4}{20}$ ← These are all equivalent fractions.

- using fraction strips

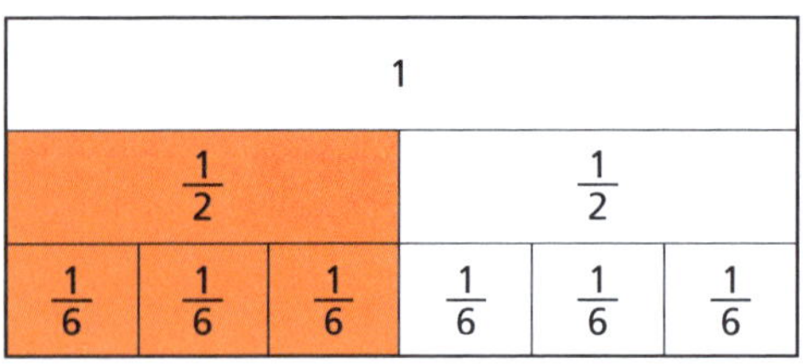

← $\frac{1}{2}$

← $\frac{3}{6}$

$\frac{1}{2}$ and $\frac{3}{6}$ are equivalent fractions.

• using multiplication or division

You can multiply or divide both the numerator and the denominator by the same number to get an equivalent fraction.

Multiply

$$\frac{4}{5} \overset{\times 2}{=} \frac{8}{10}$$

$\frac{4}{5}$ and $\frac{8}{10}$ are equivalent fractions.

Divide

$$\frac{9}{18} \overset{\div 3}{=} \frac{3}{6}$$

$\frac{9}{18}$ and $\frac{3}{6}$ are equivalent fractions.

Be careful!

Remember to use only whole numbers when multiplying or dividing to get an equivalent fraction.

Application

The Bettan family has 2 pizzas of the same size. The pepperoni pizza is cut into 8 slices and the cheese pizza is cut into 12 slices.

If each family member has 2 slices of pepperoni pizza and 3 slices of cheese pizza, does each person have more cheese pizza or pepperoni pizza?

Solution:

pepperoni pizza

$\frac{2}{8}$ of a circle

cheese pizza

$\frac{3}{12}$ of a circle

From the pictures, we can see that $\frac{2}{8}$ and $\frac{3}{12}$ represent the same portion.

This means that they are equivalent fractions.

So, each person has the same amount of cheese and pepperoni pizza.

3.3 Relating Fractions and Decimals

You should understand that fractions and decimals both represent parts of a whole. So, we can write fractions with denominators of 10 and 100 as decimals.

Fractions and Decimals

Fractions and decimals are two different ways of representing the same number.

e.g.

Fraction		Decimal
$\frac{7}{10}$	=	0.7

They both represent seven tenths.

Fraction		Decimal
$\frac{45}{100}$	=	0.45

They both represent 45 hundredths.

Converting Fractions into Decimals

If a fraction does not have a denominator of 10 or 100, you should find an equivalent fraction that does before converting it into a decimal.

e.g. $\frac{2}{5}$

Equivalent Fraction

$$\frac{2}{5} \xrightarrow{\times 2} \frac{4}{10}$$

$$\frac{2}{5} = \frac{4}{10}$$

So, $\frac{2}{5} =$ **0.4**.

The denominator should only contain the following numbers: 2, 4, 5, 20, 25, or 50 so that it can be multiplied or divided by a whole number to get either 10 or 100.

Application

Read what Kevin thinks. Explain whether he is correct or not.

There are no ways to write the mixed number $2\frac{1}{4}$ as a decimal.

$2\frac{1}{4}$

Solution:

Kevin is not correct. A mixed number is formed by a whole number and a proper fraction.

whole number → 2 | $\frac{1}{4}$ ← proper fraction

Write $\frac{1}{4}$ as a decimal.

$$\frac{1}{4} = \frac{1 \times 25}{4 \times 25} = \frac{25}{100} = 0.25$$

$$2\frac{1}{4} = 2 \text{ and } 0.25$$
$$= 2.25$$

So, $2\frac{1}{4}$ can be written as 2.25.

Chapter 4

Money

4.1 Writing Money Amounts

In this unit, you will learn to read and write money amounts up to $1000 in words and decimals.

Finding the Amount of a Collection of Money

1st Sort the bills and coins into groups.

2nd Find the amount of each group.

3rd Add up the amounts of the groups to find the total.

It will be easier to find the total if you organize all the bills and coins from the ones of the highest value to the least.

e.g. Organize the bills and coins.

$100

$50

$20

$10

$5

$2

$1

25¢

10¢

5¢

e.g.

1st

2nd	\$200	\$150	\$1	75¢

3rd Total: **\$351.75**

In words:

Three hundred fifty-one dollars and seventy-five cents

* Add "and" between the dollars and cents.

Application

Mrs. Green had 2 \$100 bills, 1 \$50 bill, 3 \$5 bills, 4 toonies, 5 quarters, and 3 dimes. She gave 1 \$50 bill and 1 quarter to the cashier and got 1 loonie back. How much does Mrs. Green have now? Write the answer in decimals and in words.

Solution:

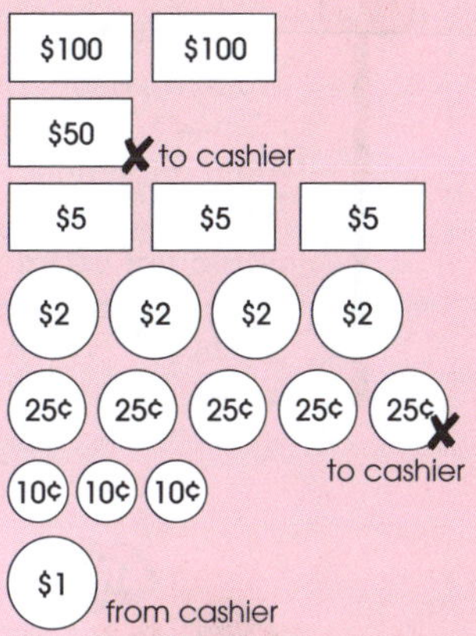

\$200

\$15

\$8

\$1

\$0.30

\$1

Total: \$225.30

Mrs. Green now has \$225.30 or two hundred twenty-five dollars and thirty cents.

4.2 Solving Problems with Money

At this level, you will deal with problems involving money amounts up to \$1000. You should try to estimate the answer to a question before doing the calculation so that you would have a rough idea of the actual answer.

Identifying key words in word problems is the first step to take to determine the correct operations. Below are some key words for your reference:

- finding the total ← using "+"
- finding money saved ← using "–"
- making change ← using "–"
- how much more needed ← using "–"

> At this level, word problems about money involve addition and subtraction only. The multiplication and division of decimals will be introduced in Grade 6.

e.g. Jason buys 2 pairs of running shoes and 1 cap. How much does he need to pay?

finding the total (using "+")

Estimate (Round to the nearest ten.)

$$\begin{array}{r} 90 \\ 90 \\ +\ 20 \\ \hline 200 \end{array}$$

(The answer should be close to 200.)

Actual

$$\begin{array}{r} 89.29 \\ 89.29 \\ +\ 17.89 \\ \hline 196.47 \end{array}$$

Jason needs to pay \$196.47.

e.g. Tim pays for a laptop with 5 $100 bills. What is his change? Give Tim his change using the fewest bills and coins.

making change (using "–")

Payment : 5 $100 bills = $500

Price : $469.55

Change : $500 – $469.55

= **$30.45**

Show $30.45 using the fewest bills and coins.

Organizing Your Thoughts

Remember to include a short description of each step that you take in your calculation. It helps organize your thoughts.

Checking Answers

You can check the answer by counting up from the price of the purchased item to the amount that the person pays with.

Referring to the example above:

Counting up from $469.55

$469.55 → (10¢) → $469.65 → (10¢) → $469.75 → (25¢) → $470 → ($10) → $480 → ($20) → **$500** (amount Tim pays)

So, $30.45 is the correct amount of change.

Application

Lisa bought two items for her dog for $208.40 after getting a $29.77 discount. Which two items did she buy?

Pet Shop

Pet Bed	**$129.39**	Cat Bowl	**$12.88**
Dog Mat	**$28.78**	Cat Scratcher	**$36.77**
Dog Carrier	**$108.78**	Bird Cage	**$119.45**
Dog Crate	**$165.85**		

Solution:

Before the discount, the two items cost:

$208.40 + $29.77 = $238.17

Look at the cost of each item.

Pet Bed	$129.39 ⟶ $129.39
Dog Mat	$28.78 ✘ too small
Dog Carrier	$108.78 ⟶ $108.78
Dog Crate	$165.85 ⟶ $165.85
Cat Bowl	$12.88 ✘ too small
Cat Scratcher	$36.77 ✘ too small
Bird Cage	$119.45 ⟶ $119.45

4 items are left to be considered.
The total cost of two of the items is **$238.17**.

Think: Which two numbers need to be added up to get 7 in the hundredths place?

The two numbers are $129.39 and $108.78.

Check:
$$\begin{array}{r} 129.39 \\ +\ 108.78 \\ \hline 238.17 \end{array}$$

So, Lisa bought the pet bed and the dog carrier.

Chapter 5

Time and Temperature

5.1 Telling Time to the Nearest Second

In Grade 4, you learned to tell the time to the nearest minute. At this level, you will learn to tell and write the time to the nearest second. Drawing clock hands to show given times is a way to learn the concept of telling the time.

Analogue Clock

When we write the time, we write the "hour" first, and then the "minute", followed by the "second". This clock shows 09:25:12.

Telling Time

e.g.

hour	minute	second
09	25	12

25 minutes 12 seconds after 9 o'clock

e.g. 10:45:26
45 minutes 26 seconds after 10 o'clock

Steps to Drawing Clock Hands

1st Draw the hour hand.

2nd Draw the minute hand.

3rd Draw the second hand.

* The hour hand points between 10 and 11, but closer to 11.

5.2 Finding Elapsed Time

You will learn to determine the elapsed time, given the start and end times of an event expressed in minutes, hours, days, weeks, months, or years. Before solving problems related to time, you should make sure you understand the relationship among units of time and 24-h notation.

Units of Time

1 hour = 60 minutes

1 day = 24 hours

1 week = 7 days

1 month = about 4 weeks / 28 days / 29 days / 30 days / 31 days

1 year = 12 months / 365 days / 366 days

12-h Clock and 24-h Clock

	12-h Clock	24-h Clock
midnight to noon	a.m.	0:00, 1:00, 2:00, ..., 12:00
noon to midnight	p.m.	12:00, 13:00, 14:00, ..., 0:00

Converting 12-h Clock to 24-h Clock

- midnight to noon: no change
  e.g. 9:00 a.m. = 9:00
- noon to midnight: Add 12 hours to any hour after noon.
  e.g. 4:00 p.m. = 16:00

Finding Elapsed Time

Use subtraction to find the elapsed time.

Elapsed Time = End Time – Start Time

Have the times in 24-h notation when doing calculations.

e.g. From 8:49 (start time) to 15:24 (end time)

```
   14  84
   1̸5̸:2̸4̸   ←  24 < 49, so trade 1h for 60 min; 24 + 60 = 84.
 –  8:49
    6:35
```

The elapsed time is 6 h 35 min.

Application

Linda goes grocery shopping at noon. It takes her 1 h 12 min to finish shopping and 54 min to drive home. What time does Linda arrive home?

Solution:

Start

$\xrightarrow{+\,1\text{ h }12\text{ min}}$

Finish Shopping

$$\begin{array}{r} \text{h} \quad \text{min} \\ 0 : 0\,0 \\ +\ 1 : 1\,2 \\ \hline 1 : 1\,2 \end{array}$$

$\xrightarrow{+\,54\text{ min}}$

Arrive Home

$$\begin{array}{r} \text{h} \quad \text{min} \\ \overset{1}{1} : 1\,2 \\ +\ 0 : 5\,4 \\ \hline 2 : 0\,6 \end{array}$$

Linda arrives home at 2:06 p.m.

5.3 Measuring and Recording Temperatures

You should be able to read and record positive temperature values to the nearest degree Celsius using a thermometer. At this level, you will learn to record negative temperature values and temperature changes. To describe negative temperature values, we use the words "below 0°C" instead of integers, for example, -10°C.

Recording Temperatures

In our daily lives, we say "-10°C" as "minus 10 degrees Celsius", but in math, we say "10°C below 0°C" to indicate the negative value.

-10°C = 10°C below 0°C

Temperature Changes

You should remember that we can find temperature changes by counting.

e.g. morning temperature : 2°C
evening temperature : 12°C below 0°C

From the morning to the evening, the temperature dropped by 14°C.

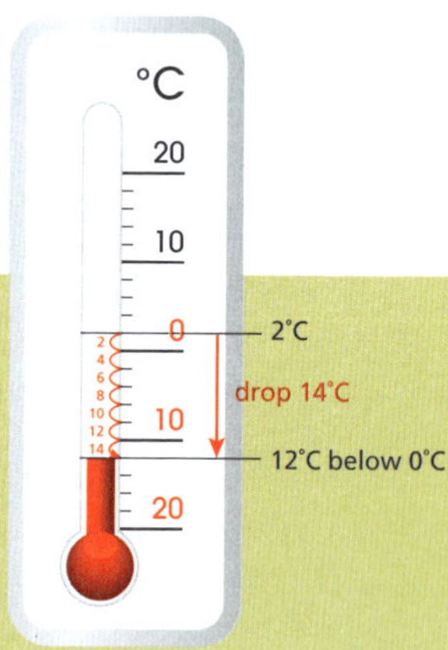

Chapter 6

Measurement

6.1 Measuring Length Using Standard Units

In this unit, you will learn to select and justify the most appropriate unit to perform a measurement.

You can learn to measure by using measurement benchmarks in daily life so that you know the different units of measurement to use.

For example:

- the thickness of a coin (mm)
- the length of a book (cm)
- the height of a door (m)
- the length of a highway (km)

small unit

millimetre (mm)
centimetre (cm)
decimetre (dm)*
metre (m)
kilometre (km)

big unit

* The decimetre is a less commonly used unit.

In addition, you should be able to do unit conversions, such as metres to centimetres and kilometres to metres.

When converting big units to small units, we multiply. When converting small units to big units, we divide.

e.g.

0.68 m = **68** cm

x 100 (Move the decimal point 2 places to the right.)

3542 m = **3.542** km

÷ 1000 (Move the decimal point 3 places to the left.)

Application

Mrs. Bernard measured a window that is 1.68 m wide. Write the width of the window using 3 other units. Explain which unit is the most appropriate to record the measurement.

Solution:

$$1.68\text{ m} \xrightarrow{\times 100} \underline{168\text{ cm}} \xrightarrow{\times 10} \underline{1680\text{ mm}}$$

1.68 m = 168 cm = 1680 mm

$$1.68\text{ m} \xrightarrow{\div 1000} \underline{0.00168\text{ km}}$$

1.68 m = 0.00168 km

1.68 m can be written as 1680 mm, 168 cm, and 0.00168 km. The centimetre is the most appropriate unit to use because the number 168 is not too big (like 1680) or too small (like 0.00168). Also, 168 cm is a whole number and is easier to work with than decimals (like 1.68). So, it is best to use 168 cm to represent the width of the window.

6.2 Finding Perimeter of Polygons

By now you should know how to find the perimeters of simple shapes using grid paper or adding up the lengths of all sides. At this level, you will learn to find the perimeters of more complicated shapes using grid paper, and use formulae to find the perimeters of rectangles.

Finding Perimeter Using Grid Paper

You may find the perimeter of a figure by counting the units along the outside of the figure.

e.g. Each side of every square on this grid is 1 cm long.

The perimeter is **18 cm**.

Finding Perimeter Using Formulae

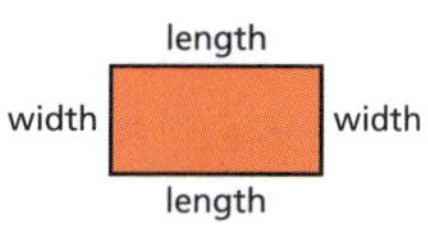

Perimeter of a Rectangle
= 2 x length + 2 x width

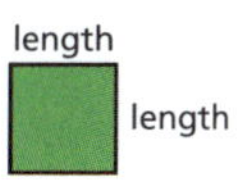

Perimeter of a Square
= 4 x length

You should multiply the length and width by 2 separately and then add the products to find the perimeter.

e.g.

Perimeter
= 2 x 9 + 2 x 5 ← Do "2 x 9" and "2 x 5" first.
= 18 + 10 ← Then add.
= 28

The perimeter is **28 cm**.

Application

Farmer George wants to build a rectangular pen for his pigs. If the fence is 180 m long, what dimensions will the pen be? Give George two possible suggestions.

Solution:

If the fence is 180 m long, the perimeter of the pen will be 180 m.

1st Suggestion

Assume the length of the pen is 50 m.

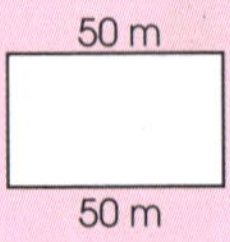

2 widths = 180 – 50 – 50 = 80

1 width = 80 ÷ 2 = 40

The dimensions of the pen are 40 m by 50 m.

2nd Suggestion

Assume the length of the pen is 45 m.

2 widths = 180 – 45 – 45 = 90

1 width = 90 ÷ 2 = 45

The dimensions of the pen are 45 m by 45 m.

6.3 Finding Area of Polygons

In previous years, you learned to estimate and measure different shapes using grid paper. This year, you will learn to use grid paper to find the areas of more complicated shapes, and apply formulae to find the areas of rectangles and squares.

Finding Area Using Grid Paper

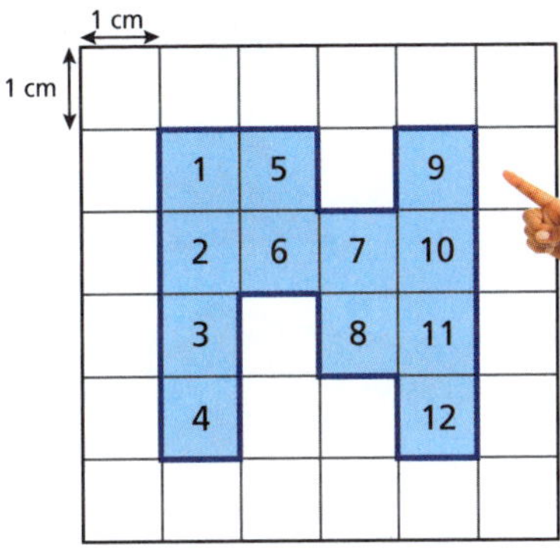

The area of the shape is **12 cm²**.

Area measurements always contain the word square, such as square metres and square centimetres.

e.g. 12 cm^2 = 12 square centimetres

Finding Area Using Formulae

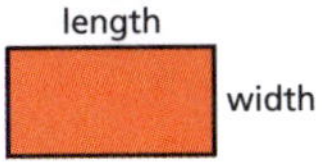

Area of a Rectangle
= length x width

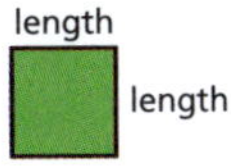

Area of a Square
= length x length

e.g. The side length of a square is 6 cm. What is its area?

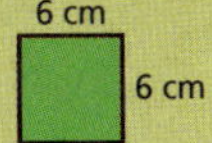

Area = 6 x 6
= 36

The area of the square is **36 cm^2**.

Application

Jennifer has cut a square into 9 identical strips. Each strip has a length of 18 cm. What are the dimensions of each strip? What is its area?

Solution:

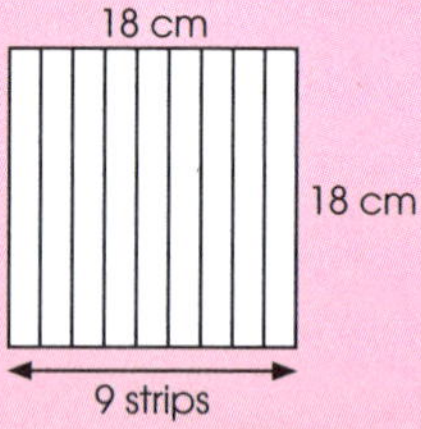

The width of each strip = 18 ÷ 9 = 2

The dimensions of each strip are 18 cm by 2 cm.

Area = 18 × 2 = 36

The area of each strip is 36 cm^2.

6.4 Solving Problems Involving Perimeter and Area

Before solving problems involving perimeter and area, make sure you have grasped the concepts of perimeter and area and are able to apply the formulae to find the perimeter and area of rectangles and squares.

Perimeter

the distance around the outside of a shape

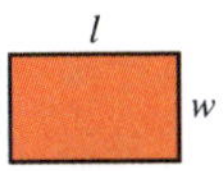

Perimeter of a Rectangle
$= 2 \times l + 2 \times w$

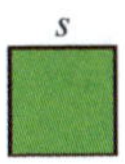

Perimeter of a Square
$= 4 \times s$

Area

the amount of surface within a closed shape

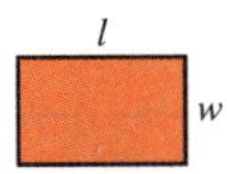

Area of a Rectangle
$= l \times w$

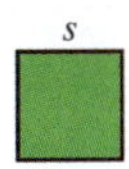

Area of a Square
$= s \times s$

You can follow the following steps to solve word problems.

4 Steps to Solving Word Problems

- **1st** Read the whole question and underline the key words.
- **2nd** Draw the figure and label the dimensions if they are available.
- **3rd** Determine whether the question is about perimeter or area.
- **4th** Determine the correct formula to find the answer.

It is important to take the second step. Drawing can help illustrate the problem and give you a better understanding of it.

Application

Jenny has a rectangular sheet that is 36 cm long and 12 cm wide. If she cuts the sheet and gets 2 identical rectangles and 2 identical squares, what will the perimeters and areas of the rectangles and the squares be?

Solution:

(Suggested answer)

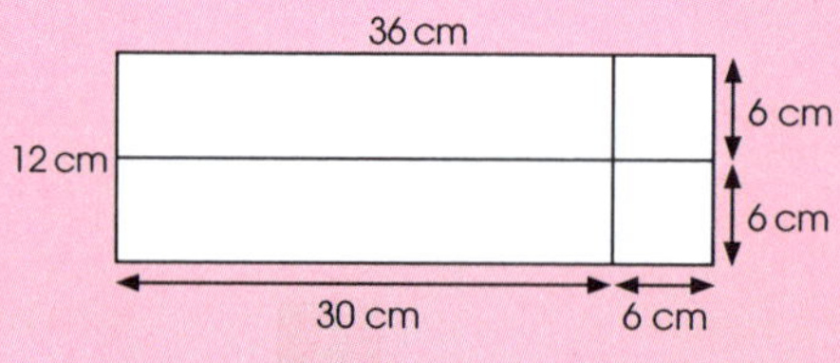

	Rectangle	**Square**
Perimeter	$30 \times 2 + 6 \times 2 = 72$ (cm)	$6 \times 4 = 24$ (cm)
Area	$30 \times 6 = 180$ (cm^2)	$6 \times 6 = 36$ (cm^2)

Think: 2 squares have a side length of 12 cm in total.

2 squares = 12 cm

1 square = 6 cm

The dimensions of each rectangle are 30 cm by 6 cm.

6.5 Finding Volume of Rectangular Prisms

In this unit, you will learn to use a formula to find the volume of rectangular prisms. Before learning the formula, you can use centimetre cubes* to build a prism. So, the volume of the prism can be found by counting the total number of centimetre cubes that have been used.

If you don't have centimetre cubes at home, you can use building blocks or dice instead to build prisms, but you have to assume that each item has a volume of 1 cm^3.

***a centimetre cube**

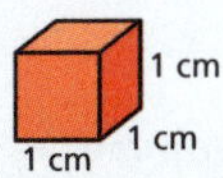

volume = 1 cm^3

1 cm^3 is read as "one cubic centimetre".

Volume of a Rectangular Prism

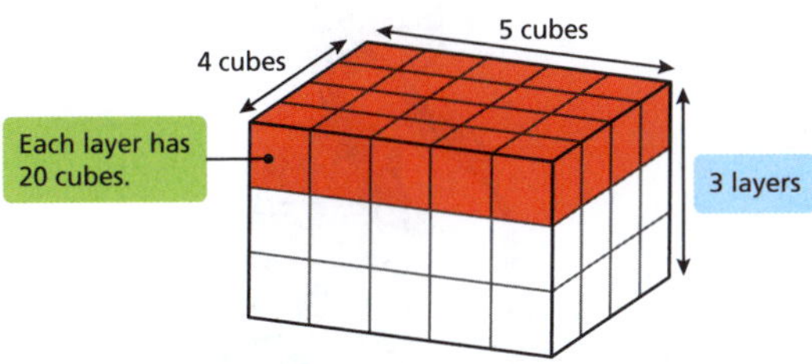

Volume = no. of cubes in each layer x no. of layers

= 20 x 3

= 60 (cubes)

= 60 (cm^3)

The volume of the prism is **60 cm^3**.

Volume of a Rectangular Prism

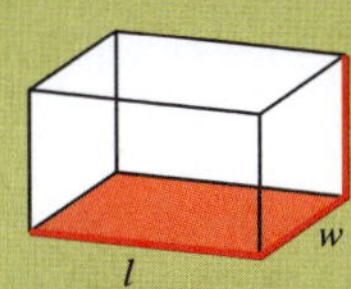

V = area of base x height

$= l \times w \times h$

Volume of the prism in the example

= 4 x 5 x 3

= 60 (cm^3)

In addition to finding the volume of rectangular prisms, you should understand the relationship between volume and capacity.

Volume and Capacity

Volume		Capacity
1 cm³	=	1 mL
1000 cm³	=	1000 mL = 1 L

a container

Volume: the amount of space it takes up

Capacity: the amount of liquid it can hold

e.g.

Volume $= 3 \text{ cm} \times 5 \text{ cm} \times 12 \text{ cm}$
$= 180 \text{ cm}^3$

Capacity $= 180 \text{ mL}$
$= 0.18 \text{ L}$

You can find the volume and capacity of a cardboard box by measuring its side lengths. This will help you grasp the concept of measurement.

Application

Jason is helping his dad make a small staircase for their backyard. What is the volume of the staircase?

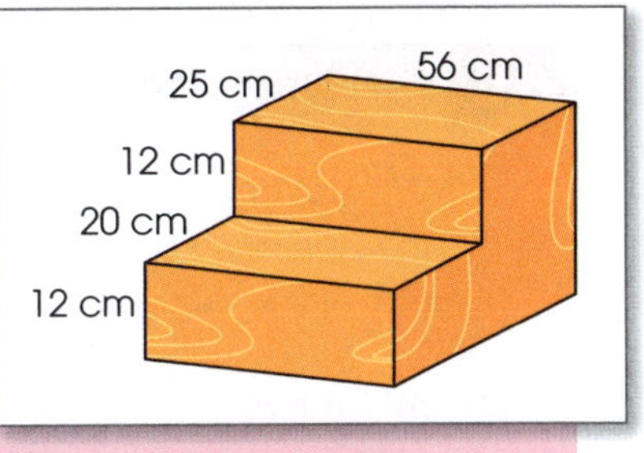

Solution:

Draw a line in the picture as shown to cut the staircase into two prisms.

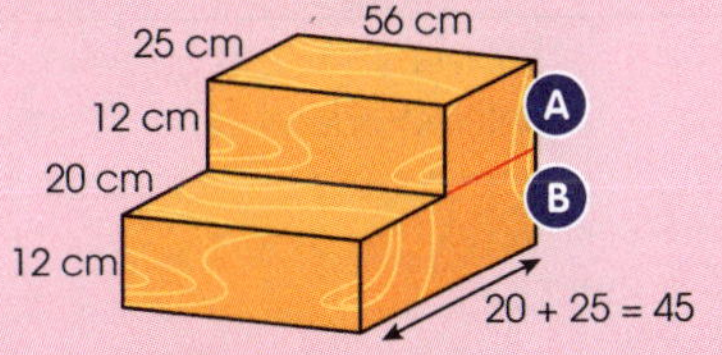

Volume of A = 12 × 25 × 56 = 16 800

Volume of B = 12 × 45 × 56 = 30 240

Total volume = 16 800 + 30 240 = 47 040

The volume of the staircase is 47 040 cm³.

6.6 Measuring Mass

We use milligrams (mg), grams (g), kilograms (kg), and tonnes (t) to measure mass.

Milligram – for very light objects

e.g.  weighs about 50 mg

Gram – for light objects

e.g.  weighs about 35 g

Kilogram – for heavy objects

e.g. 

weighs about 5 kg

Tonne – for very heavy objects

e.g.  weighs about 10 t

You should use these benchmarks for mass. These guidelines will help you determine the most appropriate units to measure the masses of different objects.

Relationships among Units of Mass

1 t = 1000 kg
1 kg = 1000 g
1 g = 1000 mg

Unit Conversion

big unit —×→ small unit
small unit —÷→ big unit

e.g. 2.8 kg = **2800** g (× 1000)

Application

A delivery service charges \$2 per kilogram. About how much money will Kevin make for this delivery?

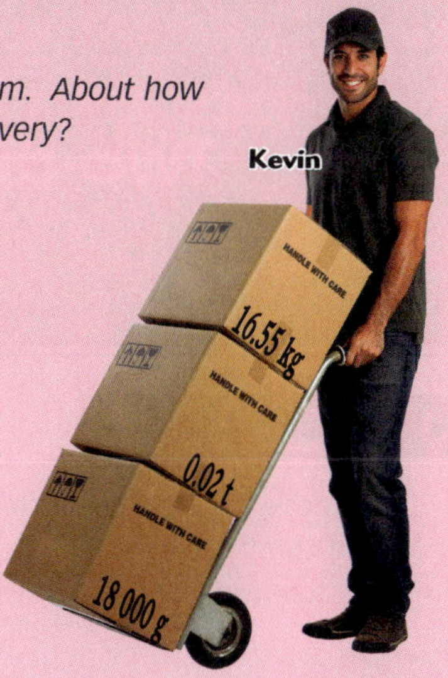

Solution:

1st Find the total weight in kilograms.

16.55 kg →	16.55 kg
0.02 t →	20 kg
18 000 g →	18 kg
Total:	54.55 kg

2nd Find the service charge.

Charge = 54.55 × 2 = 109.10

Kevin will make \$109.10 for this delivery.

Chapter 7

Two-dimensional Shapes

7.1 Identifying Polygons

In Grade 5, you are expected to be able to identify and describe polygons and compare them with non-polygonal figures. You should understand the following key words when talking about polygons.

Key Words:

- **angle:**
  the space between two line segments with a common end point
- **line of symmetry:**
  a line that divides a shape into two congruent parts that can overlap perfectly when folded along this line
- **polygon:**
  a closed shape formed by three or more line segments
- **quadrilateral:**
  a polygon with 4 straight sides
- **regular polygon:**
  a closed shape in which all sides and angles are equal
- **side:**
  one of the lines that makes up a shape

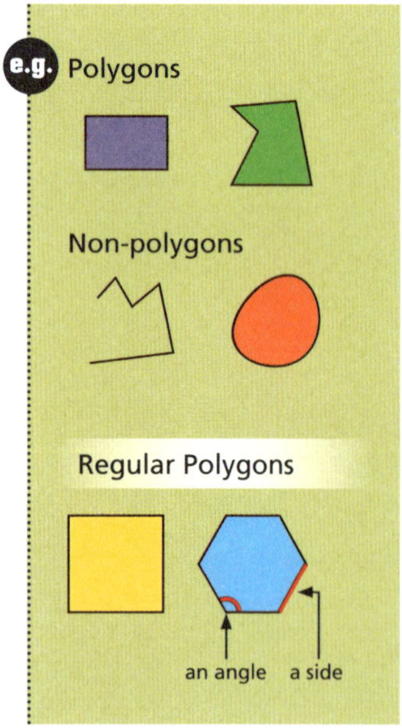

e.g.

This shape has

- 5 straight sides
- 5 equal sides
- 5 equal angles
- 5 lines of symmetry

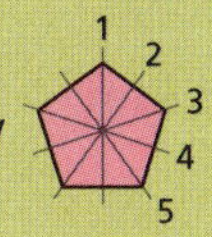

It is a regular pentagon because all of its sides and all of its angles are equal.

Regular polygons can be a challenge to draw. Use the template below when examining regular polygons.

Common Regular Polygons

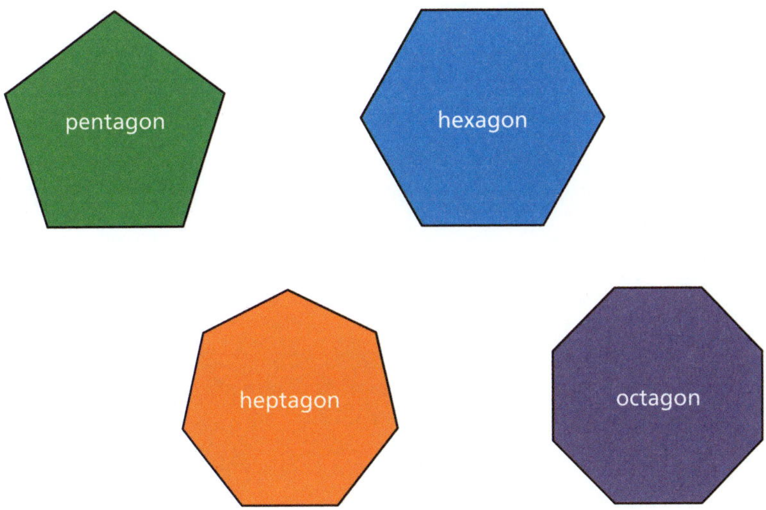

Application

What shape is Jason describing? Draw and name the shape.

It is a quadrilateral, but it is not a regular polygon. It has 1 line of symmetry and it can be formed by 3 identical triangles.

Solution:

guessing shapes

- a quadrilateral
  ↳ a polygon with 4 sides
- not a regular polygon
  ↳ not a square (✗)
  not a rhombus (✗)
- 1 line of symmetry
  ↳ not a rectangle (✗)
  not a parallelogram (✗)

It is a trapezoid, which can be formed by 3 identical triangles.

7.2 Measuring and Naming Angles

Angles are named according to their sizes. There are four types of angles that you will learn about at this level. They are as follows:

Types of Angles

Acute Angle
less than 90°

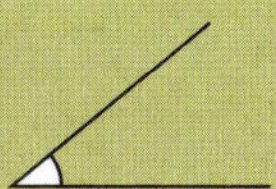

Right Angle
90°

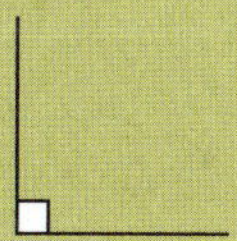

Obtuse Angle
between 90° and 180°

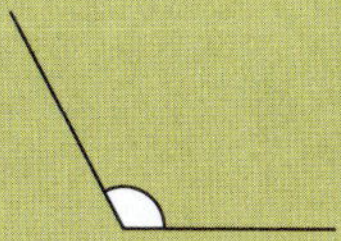

Straight Angle
180°

You may have no problem identifying angles, but you may find it difficult to measure or construct an angle using a protractor.

Constructing an Angle

Steps to Constructing an Angle

1st Draw one arm of an angle.

2nd Place the centre of the protractor at one end of the arm.

3rd Mark the angle at the edge of the protractor.

4th Remove the protractor. Draw the arm by joining the mark and the end of the arm.

e.g. Construct $\angle ABC = 35°$.

1st

2nd

protractor

3rd

4th

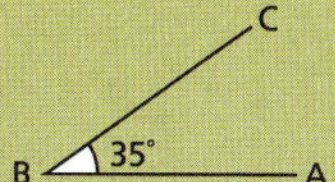

Application

Determine whether the statement is true or false. Give an example or a counter-example to support your answer.

Combining two acute angles always gives you an acute angle.

Solution:

The statement is false. Combining two acute angles sometimes gives you an obtuse angle.

e.g. acute angle + acute angle = obtuse angle

7.3 Classifying Triangles

Triangles can be classified according to their angles and sides. You should have prior knowledge of angle types (acute, obtuse, and right) and experience measuring angles with a protractor before beginning this unit. You can draw different triangles on grid paper to grasp the concept.

Classifying Triangles

by Angles

- **Acute Triangle**
  - has three angles that are less than 90°

- **Right Triangle**
  - has one right angle

- **Obtuse Triangle**
  - has one angle that is greater than 90°

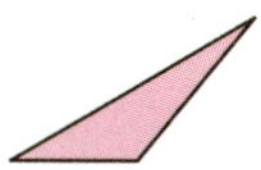

by Sides

- **Scalene Triangle**
  - has three sides of different lengths

- **Isosceles Triangle**
  - has two sides of the same length

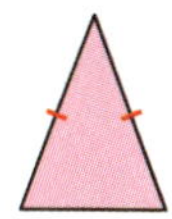

- **Equilateral Triangle**
  - has three sides of the same length

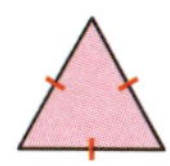

e.g.

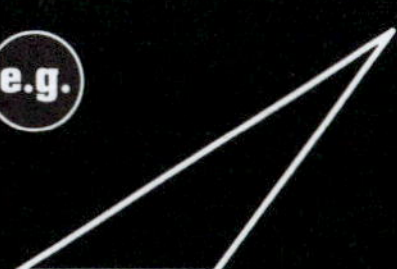

- **obtuse triangle**
- **scalene triangle**

All triangles can be named in 2 ways.

Application

Draw the trapezoid to show how Natalie formed it. Then name the triangles according to their angles and sides.

Solution:

Draw a trapezoid with two right angles and different side lengths. Then cut it into two triangles. (Suggested answers)

Way 1

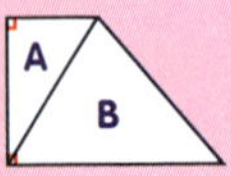

or

Way 2

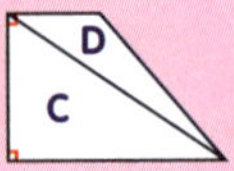

	Name by Angles	Name by Sides
A	right triangle	scalene triangle
B	acute triangle	scalene triangle
C	right triangle	scalene triangle
D	obtuse triangle	scalene triangle

Different triangles can be created by varying the side lengths of a trapezoid. Therefore, you may come up with a different answer.

7.4 Constructing Triangles

You are expected to be able to construct triangles using a ruler and a protractor when given acute or right angles and side measurements. You should remember to label the measurements of the angles and sides you have drawn when constructing triangles. This can help you gain a better understanding of the triangle that you have constructed.

Constructing a Triangle

At this level, you will only learn to draw acute and right triangles.

The minimum information needed to construct a triangle:

- 2 sides and 1 angle
- 1 side and 2 angles

e.g. Construct triangle ABC.

Side AB is 8 cm long.
Angle B is 60°.
Side BC is 5 cm long.

4 Steps to Constructing a Triangle:

1st Draw an 8 cm long line. Label the ends of the line A and B, and label the length of the line 8 cm.

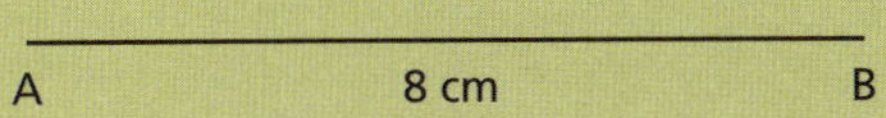

You can also label the line the other way around.

2nd Place the centre of the protractor at the end labelled B. Mark 60° at the edge of the protractor.

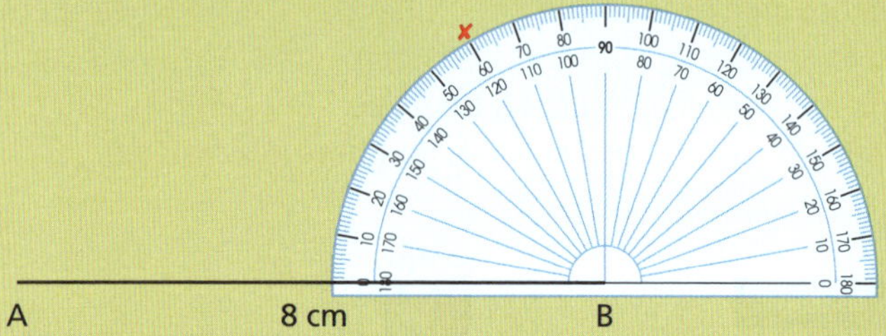

3rd Remove the protractor. Place a ruler with the 0 cm mark at B and line it up with the 60° mark. Draw a 5 cm long line. Then label the end of the line C.

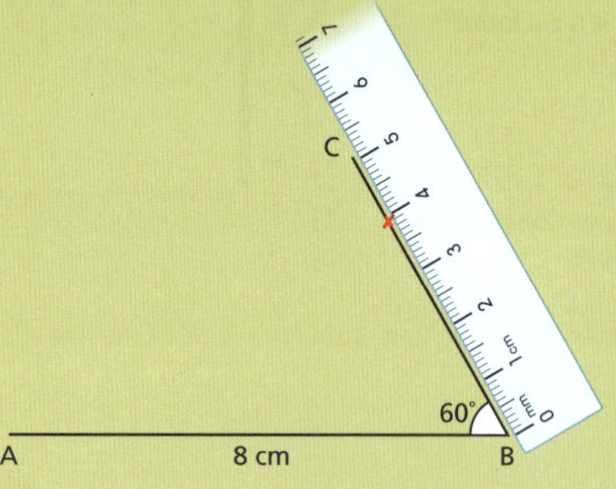

4th

AC = 7.1 cm
∠A = 39°
∠C = 81°

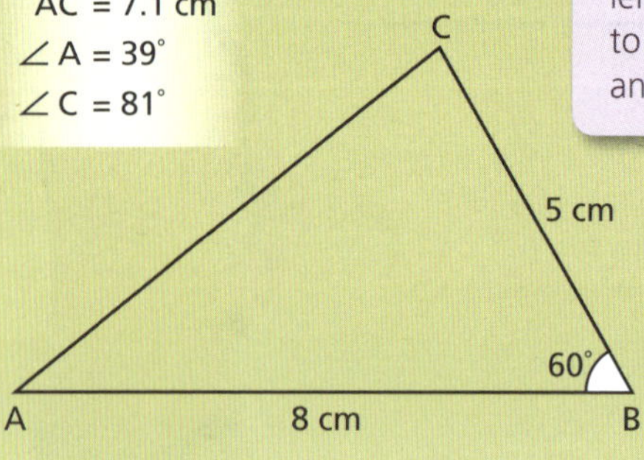

You can use a ruler to find the length of AC and a protractor to find the measurements of angles A and C.

Application

Read what Yvonne says. Draw two triangles that match her description. Then name the triangles according to their sides and label the sides with their measurements.

Solution:

1st Suggestion

Draw a 4-cm vertical line and a 5.7-cm horizontal line to create a right angle. Connect the two straight lines to form a triangle.

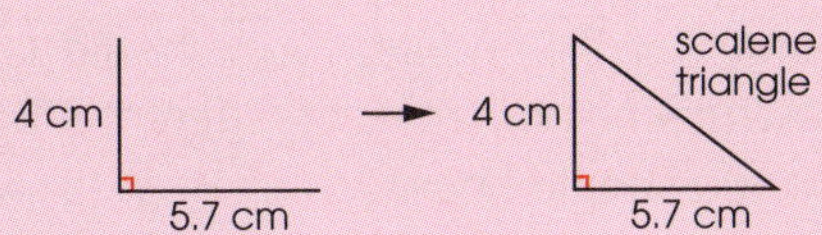

2nd Suggestion

Draw a 4-cm vertical line and a long horizontal line to create a right angle. Then use a ruler to measure 5.7 cm from the top of the vertical line down to the horizontal line.

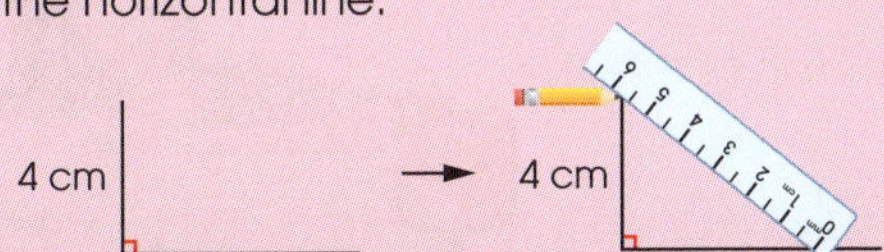

Measure the horizontal line.

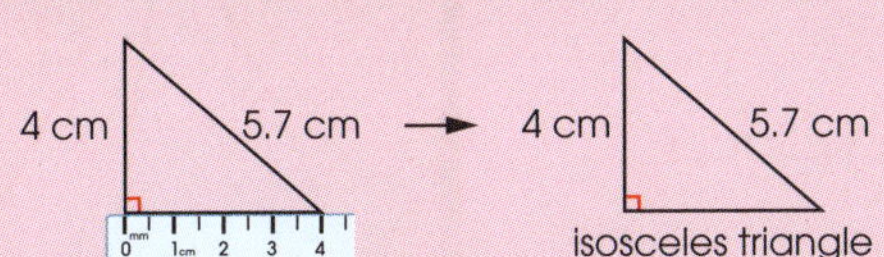

Chapter 8

Three-dimensional Figures

8.1 Identifying Prisms and Pyramids

Apart from knowing the names of 3-D figures, you should learn the mathematical language to describe the properties of different 3-D figures. Below are the key words that you should know.

Key Words:

- **edge:**
  the line segment where two surfaces meet in a 3-D figure
- **face:**
  one of the polygons that make up a polyhedron
- **polyhedron:**
  a 3-D figure that has polygons as faces
- **prism:**
  a 3-D figure with two parallel and congruent bases
- **pyramid:**
  a 3-D figure with a polygon base and triangular faces that meet at a common vertex
- **vertex:**
  the common end point of two or more line segments

This is a rectangular pyramid.

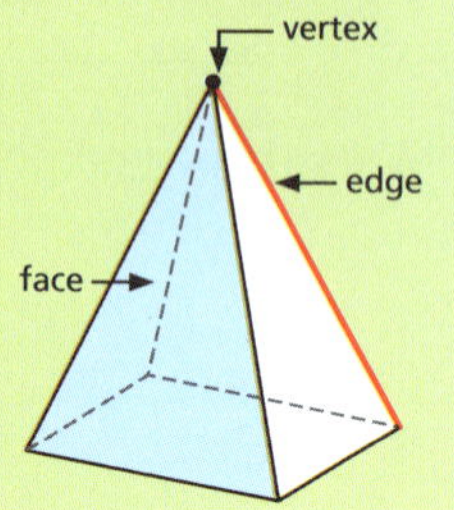

- 5 vertices
- 8 edges
- 4 triangular faces
- 1 rectangular face

Cylinders are **not** prisms.

Below are the common prisms and pyramids that you should know.

Prisms

triangular prism

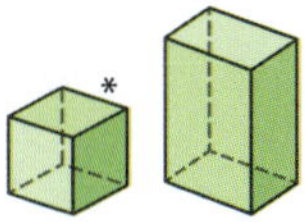

rectangular prisms

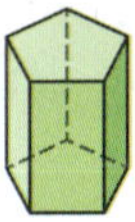

pentagonal prism

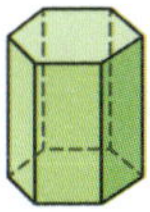

hexagonal prism

* A cube is a rectangular prism.

Pyramids

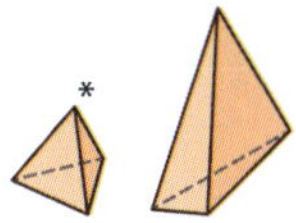

triangular pyramids

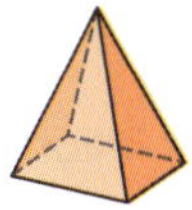

rectangular pyramid

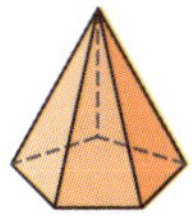

pentagonal pyramid

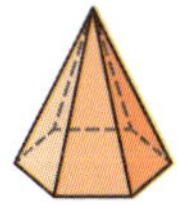

hexagonal pyramid

* A triangular pyramid that has 4 congruent faces in the shape of an equilateral triangle is called a tetrahedron.

Drawing Prisms and Pyramids

You can follow the steps below to draw 3-D figures easily.

e.g. Draw a rectangular prism.

1st Draw one end.

2nd Draw the other end to the right and up a bit.

3rd Join the matching vertices.

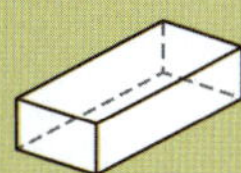

e.g. Draw a rectangular pyramid.

1st Draw the base.
(Tilt the rectangle a bit.)

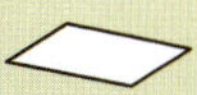

2nd Draw a point above the base.

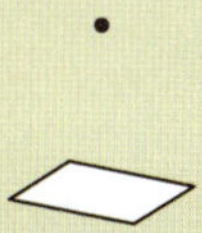

3rd Join each vertex of the base to the point.

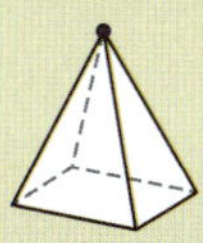

Application

Write about this 3-D figure using geometric vocabulary.

Solution:

Remember to use the geometric vocabulary that you have learned to write about the tetrahedron. Below is a list of the features of a tetrahedron.

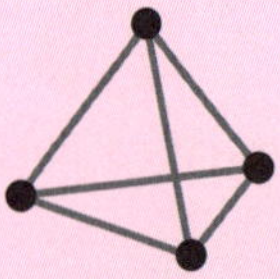

Tetrahedron features

- a polyhedron
- a triangular pyramid
- has 4 congruent faces that are equilateral triangles
- has 6 edges that are equal in length
- has 4 vertices
- none of its faces are parallel to each other
- has 3 faces meeting at each vertex

8.2 Identifying and Constructing Nets

A net shows all the faces of a 3-D figure joined together in one piece. It can be folded to form the 3-D figure. There are many ways to construct a net. The best way to understand nets is to learn from hands-on activities. You can unfold cereal boxes in different ways and draw the nets on grid paper. This can help you develop visual-spatial skills and determine the correct arrangement of the faces to build the 3-D figure.

Before drawing a net, you should identify the number and the shapes of the faces of a 3-D figure.

e.g. Draw a net of a triangular prism.

triangular prism ⟵ 3 rectangular faces and 2 triangular faces

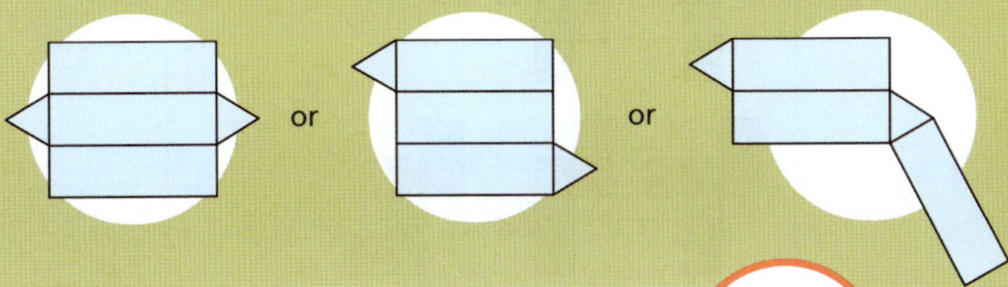

There are many ways to draw the net of a triangular prism. Can you draw one more?

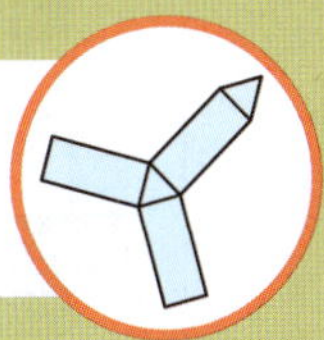

Application

Read what Tim says. Draw all the nets that form a cube and colour parallel faces the same colour.

Solution:

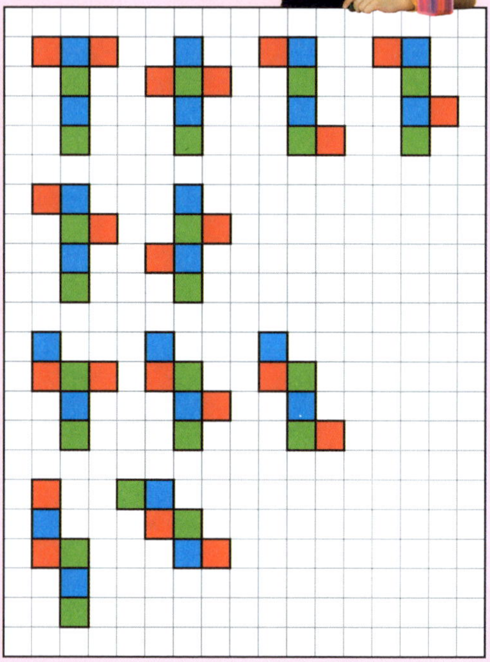

A very high geometrical spatial sense is required to find all eleven nets of a cube. If you are not able to draw all eleven nets, it is not a problem. Try to draw different nets on grid paper and then cut them out to see if they can be folded into a cube to figure out the different nets. Through this hands-on activity, your spatial sense will improve.

Chapter 9

Locations and Movements

9.1 Coordinate Systems

There are two different ways you will learn to locate and describe an object on a grid map.

Using Cardinal Directions

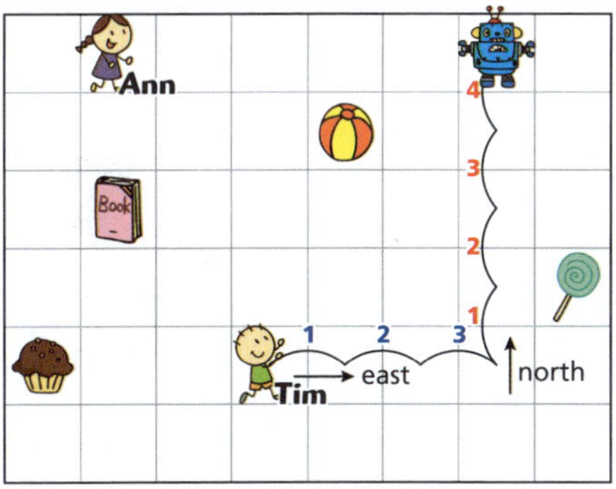

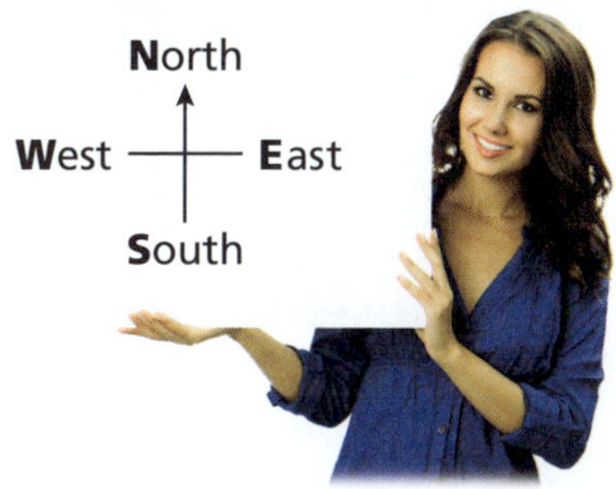

How does Tim get to the robot?

He goes <u>3 blocks east</u> and <u>4 blocks north</u>.

Using Grid Systems

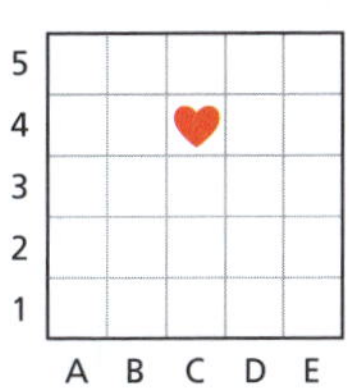

Grid

a system of numbered squares on a map to show the exact position of an object or a place

Coordinates

a number and letter used to locate a place or an object on a map (the format of a coordinate is letter number)

9.2 Performing Transformations

Reflections, translations, and rotations are all transformations. In Grade 4, you learned to identify and describe reflections using grids. At this level, you are expected to be able to identify and describe translations of two-dimensional shapes.

Translation

To do a translation, slide a figure along a straight line. The way that we describe a translation is " ____ units left/right and ____ units up/down".

e.g. Describe the translation.

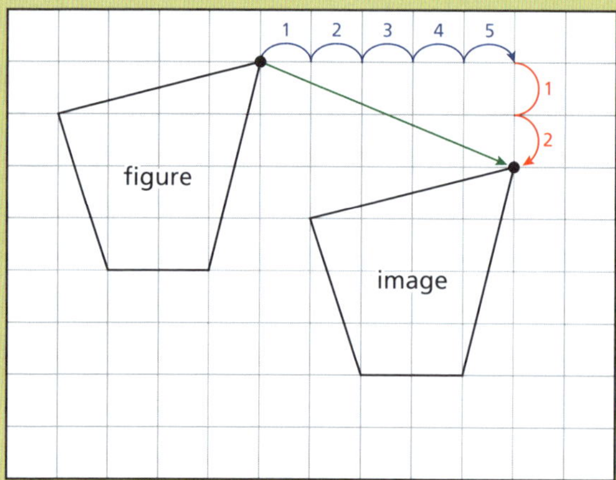

Translate the figure **5** units **right** and **2** units **down** to get the image.

e.g. Describe the translation.

Translate the figure 4 units left and 5 units down.

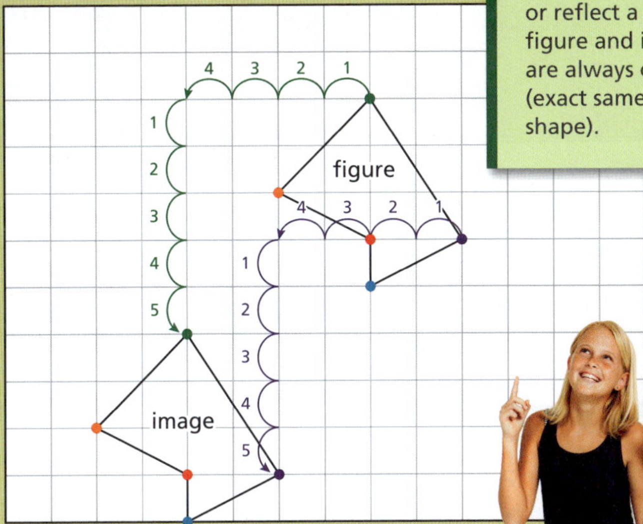

Pay Attention!

When you translate or reflect a figure, the figure and its image are always congruent (exact same size and shape).

You should translate each and every vertex using the same description. Then join the new vertices to get the image.

Chapter 10

Patterning

10.1 Identifying and Extending Patterns

At this level, you will learn to identify, extend, and describe more complex numeric and geometric patterns. You can follow the steps below to make sure you grasp the concept.

Numeric and Geometric Patterns

1st Determine whether the pattern is growing or shrinking.

2nd Find the pattern rule. If the pattern is growing, the rule involves addition or multiplication. If the pattern is shrinking, the rule involves subtraction or division.

3rd Extend the pattern to create the next term.

Numeric Pattern

e.g. 3, 6, 12, 24, 48...

- The numbers are getting bigger, so it is a growing pattern.
- Use addition or multiplication.

x2 x2 x2 x2

3 6 12 24 48

Pattern rule: x2
(Multiply by 2 each time.)

- The next term is __96__ (48 x 2).

Geometric Pattern

e.g.

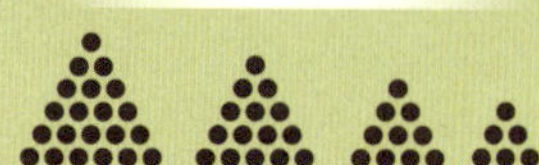

- The number of circles is getting smaller, so it is a shrinking pattern.
- Use subtraction or division.

-6 -5 -4

21 15 10 6

Pattern rule: -6, -5, -4
(Subtract by 6. Then subtract one less each time.)

- The next term is  (3 circles).

Application

See how Eric creates a pattern with marbles. Draw the one that comes next and write the matching number sentence.

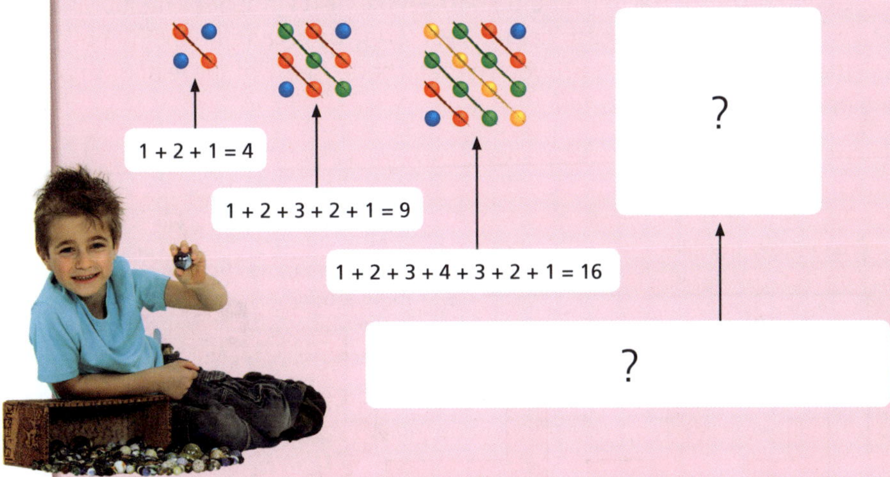

Solution:

You should note that the number of rows and the number of columns increase by 1 each time.

Pattern: 2 by 2, 3 by 3, 4 by 4...

So, the dimensions of the next array of marbles should be 5 by 5.

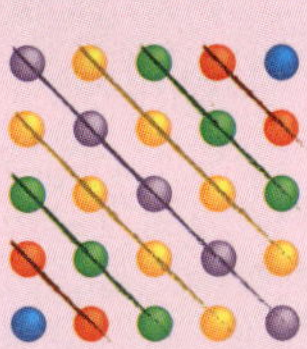

From the diagram, we can find the number sentence by grouping the coloured marbles diagonally and summing all groups of marbles. Below is the number sentence.

1 + 2 + 3 + 4 + 5 + 4 + 3 + 2 + 1 = 25

10.2 Representing Number Patterns

You will learn to represent, analyze, and generalize a variety of patterns using tables. You will make a table of values for a pattern that is generated by adding or subtracting a number to get the next term, or by multiplying or dividing by a number to get the next term. By organizing the numbers that you get from a pattern, you will get a better sense of the relationships between the numbers.

e.g. Create L's using tiles.

How many tiles will be needed to build the 7th L in this pattern?

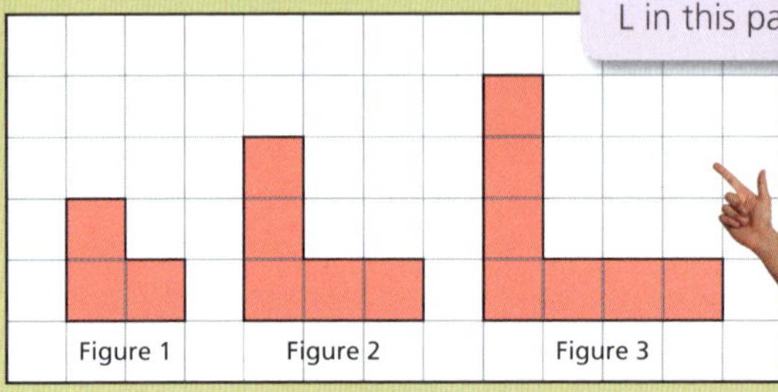

Figure	No. of Tiles
1	3
2	5
3	7
4	9
5	11
6	13
7	15

(+2 between each consecutive number of tiles)

Pattern in the number of tiles: increase by 2 with each figure

Continue with this pattern to figure out the number of tiles in Figure 7.

Attention!

Remember to label each column in a table.

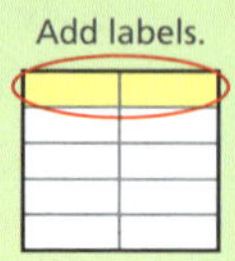

<u>15</u> tiles will be needed to build the 7th L.

10.3 Finding Missing Numbers in Equations

This is the first time that you will learn to write an expression or a number sentence using symbols and letters. You should start with simple and straightforward questions. This will make it easier for you to grasp the concept of using symbols and letters to represent changing quantities.

e.g.

Each combo costs \$5. What will be the total cost (C) of n combos?

Think

total cost **combo** **n combos**

\$5

It is a multiplication problem. ← Identify what kind of problem it is.

Total cost = unit cost x no. of combos

$\underline{\boldsymbol{C = 5 \times n}}$

If you find it difficult to determine if it is a multiplication problem, you can use an exact number, such as 5 combos or 9 combos. This will remind you that multiplication is needed to find the total.

After being introduced to writing an expression, you will learn to determine the missing number in equations involving addition, subtraction, multiplication, or division with one- or two-digit numbers.

e.g. 16 × □ = 64

You should use the "guess-and-check" method to find the unknown.

□ = 1, 16 x 1 = 16

□ = 2, 16 x 2 = 32

□ = 3, 16 x 3 = 48

□ = 4, 16 x 4 = 64 ✔

Guess □	Check	
1	16	(not 64) ✘
2	32	(not 64) ✘
3	48	(not 64) ✘
4	64	✔

So, **□ = 4**

You should use tables to do your work. This can help you organize your thoughts.

Application

If the total cost of 2 balls equals the total cost of a bear and a bunny, how much does one ball cost?

Solution:

1st Find the total cost of a bear and a bunny.

13 + 9 = 22

2nd Come up with an equation for 2 balls which equals $22.

 × 2 = $22

 = $22 ÷ 2 = $11

A ball costs $11.

Chapter 11

Data Management

11.1 Finding the Mean of a Set of Data

In this unit, you will learn to calculate the mean of a set of data and apply it to describe the shape of a set of data across its range of values using tables and graphs, which will be covered in the following units.

Mean

the sum of a set of numbers divided by the total number of addends

$$\text{Mean} = \frac{\text{the sum of a set of numbers}}{\text{the total no. of addends}}$$

Finding the Mean

e.g. The weights of the apples

The mean weight:

$$\frac{86 + 72.5 + 85.5 + 79 + 87}{5}$$

← the total weight of the apples

↑ 5 apples in this group

$$= \frac{410}{5}$$

$$= 82$$

The mean weight is **82 g**.

Look at the example again. Put the apples in order from lightest to heaviest.

72.5 79 85.5 86 87

↑ This is the middle value.

The median weight is **85.5 g**.

You already learned to find the median of a set of data in Grade 4. You may be confused by the word "mean". You can review the definition of median to better understand these two terms.

Median: the middle value of a set of data arranged in order

Application

Write two sets of data with 3 numbers each and with a mean of 30. Explain.

Solution:

The mean of 3 numbers is 30. So, the sum of the three numbers must be 90 (30 × 3). As long as you can come up with a set of numbers that has a total of 90, your answer is correct.

Below are some suggested answers:

30, 30, 30   20, 30, 40   5, 10, 75

11.2 Identifying Discrete and Continuous Data

It is important for you to understand the difference between discrete and continuous data. This concept can help you display data using appropriate graphs and scales to suit the range and distribution of the data.

Discrete Data

Discrete data includes certain values that are countable. The data values are often whole numbers.

e.g. the number of students absent

the number of times a word is used

Continuous Data

Continuous data includes any measurable values.

e.g. the amount of money George earns by working various hours per week

the distance travelled by a car in 2 hours

Marbles	Number
green	4
red	5
yellow	10
blue	6

Grade	Height
2	1.21 m
3	1.26 m
4	1.3 m
5	1.38 m

Application

Give one example of each type of data. Then list the possible values that each set of data may have.

Discrete Data

Continuous Data

Solution:

(Suggested answer)

Discrete Data

Examples with data that include only whole numbers

Number of days it rained each month

No. of Days	Month
3	March
7	April
5	May
12	June

Continuous Data

Examples with data that include any numerical value

Amount of rainfall each month

Amount	Month
10.3 mm	March
80.5 mm	April
60.9 mm	May
165.2 mm	June

11.3 Interpreting and Making Graphs

You are expected to organize and display collected data in tables and graphs. In tables, labels for rows and columns must be included. You will then learn to interpret and draw conclusions from different types of graphs. Below are the features and examples of four different types of graphs that you should know at this level.

Four Different Types of Graphs

- **Pictograph:** using pictures to display information
- **Bar Graph:** using bars to compare data
- **Line Graph:** showing how the data changes over time
- **Circle Graph:** showing parts of a whole

Examples:

Pictograph

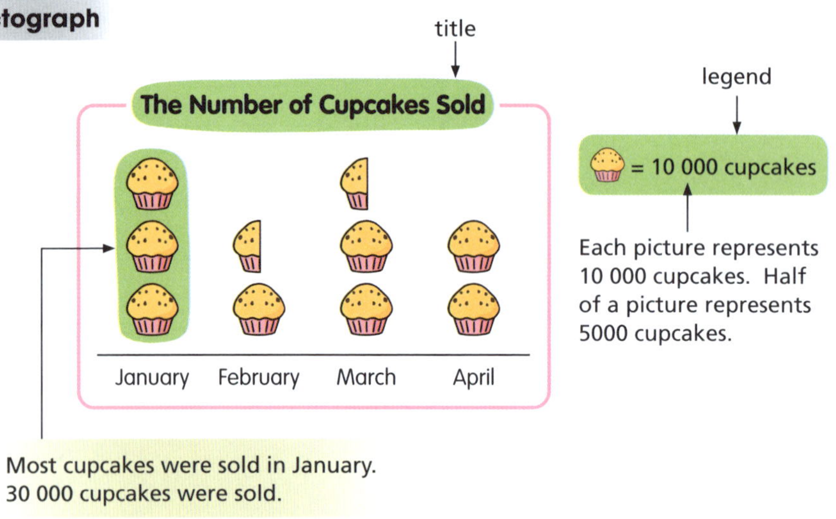

Bar Graph

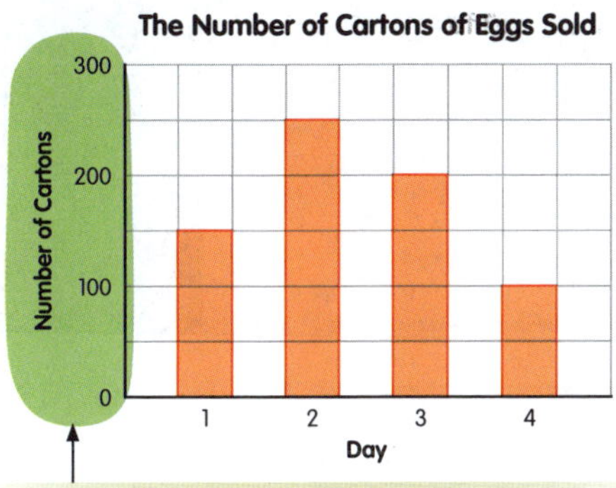

The number of cartons ranging from 0 to 300; a scale of 50 is used for each unit

Steps to Making a Bar or Line Graph

1st Give the graph a title.

2nd Label the axes.

3rd Draw the bars or plot the data points.

4th Label the bars or connect the points.

Tip!

Look for the intervals of a bar or line graph. Figure out the number of units between each pair of lines before you interpret it.

Line Graph

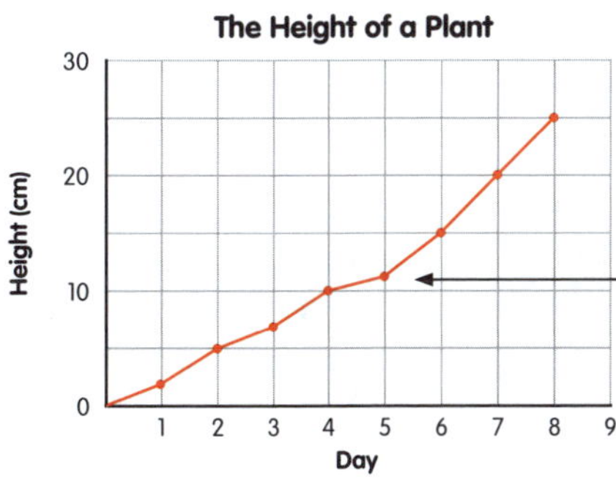

Join the plotted points with straight lines.

Circle Graph

$\frac{1}{4}$ of the children like hockey. If 20 children are asked, there will be **5** children who like hockey.

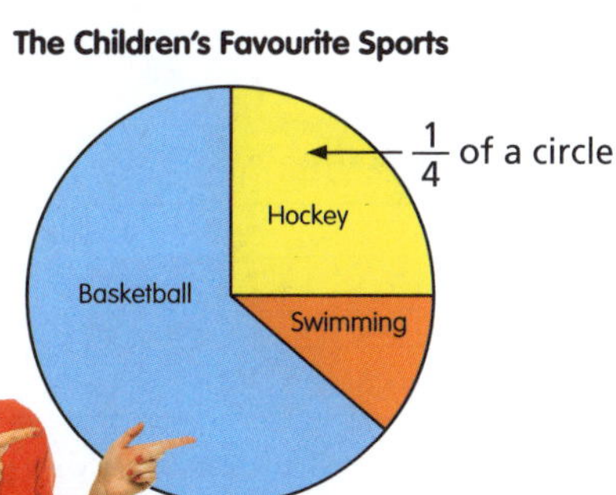

Chapter 12

Probability

12.1 Determining the Possible Outcomes of an Event

In this unit, you will learn to determine and represent all the possible outcomes of a simple probability experiment in an organized way using tables, charts, and tree diagrams.

You may already know how to list all the possible outcomes of a simple probability experiment.

With a question like the example below, you can show the possible outcomes by making an organized list and then drawing a tree diagram or a chart.

e.g. Jason spins the pointers of these spinners. What are the possible outcomes?

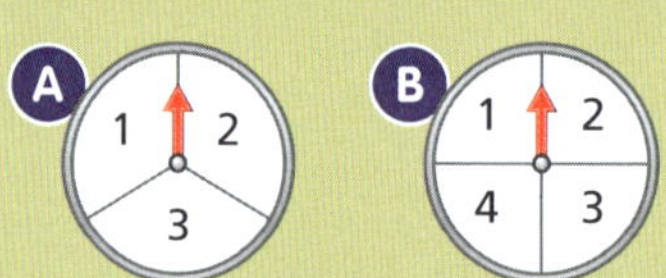

Using a Chart

A \ B	1	2	3	4
1	1, 1	1, 2	1, 3	1, 4
2	2, 1	2, 2	2, 3	2, 4
3	3, 1	3, 2	3, 3	3, 4

12 possible outcomes

Using a Tree Diagram

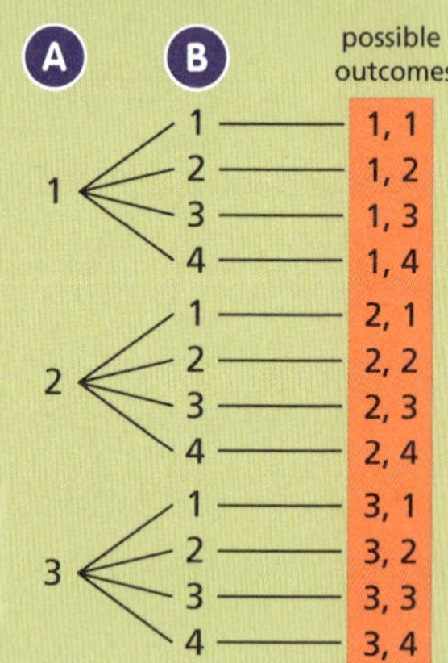

12 in all

Application

If we wish to have 2 girls and 1 boy, which outcomes would match our wish? What is the difference among those outcomes?

Solution:

1st child	2nd child	3rd child	Possible Outcomes
G	G	G	GGG
		B	GGB ✔
	B	G	GBG ✔
		B	GBB
B	G	G	BGG ✔
		B	BGB
	B	G	BBG
		B	BBB

There are 3 outcomes (GGB, GBG, BGG) that match their wish. The difference is in the order of the children born. For example, for the outcome GGB, it means Mr. and Mrs. Jones get 2 girls followed by a boy.

12.2 Determining the Probability of an Event with Fractions

In the previous unit, you learned to list all possible outcomes of an event. Now you will learn to describe the probability of a particular outcome as a fraction of all possible outcomes.

Probability

- a number showing how likely it is that an event will happen

$$\textbf{Probability} = \frac{\text{No. of outcomes of a particular event}}{\text{Total no. of outcomes}}$$

* The more probable the event, the greater the fraction.

If it has no chance of happening, the probability is 0. If it is certain to happen, the probability is 1.

e.g.

The probability of landing
on red = 1
on yellow = 0

e.g. Spin this spinner once.

- 4 equal sections
- 4 possible outcomes – green, orange, blue, and red

The probability of landing on red is **1 out of 4** or $\frac{1}{4}$.

The spinner will land on red once for every 4 times you spin.

Grade 6

Chapter 1

Whole Numbers to 1 000 000

1.1 Writing Numbers to 1 000 000

In this unit, you will be expected to demonstrate an understanding of reading, writing, and representing whole numbers to 1 000 000 in different forms. In order to grasp the concept of the numerical system, you should use a place value chart to represent large numbers so that you can visualize the value of each digit and read numbers in groups of three digits.

Numbers in Three Different Forms

Place Value Chart

Millions			Thousands					
H	T	O	H	T	O	H	T	O
			4	2	5	0	9	8

H = hundreds
T = tens
O = ones

4 is in the hundred thousands place; it means 400 000.

There are no "hundreds" in this number. So, "0" is used as a placeholder.

e.g. 425 098

- in **Standard Form:** 425 098

  Leave a space for every three digits.

- in **Written Form:**

  four hundred twenty-five thousand ninety-eight

To write in expanded form, you can expand the place value chart as shown here to see the value of each digit in the number 425 098.

- in **Expanded Form:**

  425 098
  = 4 hundred thousands + 2 ten thousands + 5 thousands + 9 tens + 8 ones
  = 400 000 + 20 000 + 5000 + 90 + 8

	Thousands					
	H	T	O	H	T	O
	4	0	0	0	0	0
		2	0	0	0	0
			5	0	0	0
					9	0
+						8
	4	2	5	0	9	8

* You should be able to convert among the 3 forms.

Application

Using the digits 6, 7, 3, and three zeros, find all the possible 6-digit odd numbers.

Solution:

The numbers must be odd numbers, so the digits in the ones must be either 3 or 7.

Odd numbers with 3 in the ones place:

600 073   700 063
600 703   700 603
607 003   706 003
670 003   760 003

Odd numbers with 7 in the ones place:

300 067   600 037
300 607   600 307
306 007   603 007
360 007   630 007

1.2 Comparing and Ordering Whole Numbers

In this unit, you will learn to use two different methods to compare numbers up to 1 000 000. Make sure you are confident in applying the concepts learned in the previous unit because this unit builds upon what you previously learned.

Using a Number Line

1st Mark the numbers on a number line.

2nd The number farthest to the left is the least, while the one farthest to the right is the greatest.

345 397 is farthest to the left and 346 980 is farthest to the right.

e.g. Order the numbers from least to greatest.

345 397   346 980   346 253

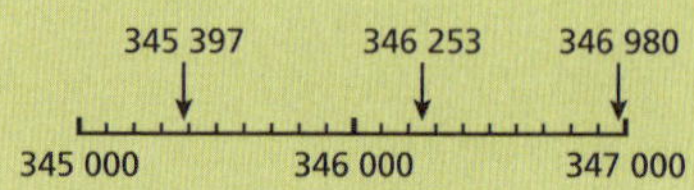

345 397 < 346 253 < 346 980

Using a Place Value Chart

1st Write the numbers in the place value chart.

2nd Compare the digits farthest to the left. If they are the same, move on to the next digit to the right until they are different.

e.g.

Thousands					
H	T	O	H	T	O
3	4	5	3	9	7
3	4	6	9	8	0
3	4	6	2	5	3

same same

5 is the least, so 345 397 is the least number.

9 is the greatest, so 346 980 is the greatest number.

For numbers that do not have the same number of digits, make sure they are aligned at the ones when comparing.

Thousands					
H	T	O	H	T	O
1	7	2	5	0	4
	2	5	9	4	8

✓

Thousands					
H	T	O	H	T	O
1	7	2	5	0	4
2	5	9	4	8	

✗

1.3 Prime and Composite Numbers

This unit introduces the concepts of prime and composite numbers and the properties that each type of number has. A solid understanding of the decomposition of numbers through multiplication and division is vital.

Identifying Prime and Composite Numbers

Prime number : a number that has only 1 and itself as factors

Composite number : a number that has more than two factors

You should remember that there is no pattern for finding prime numbers. However, any number that is under 100 and is not divisible by 2, 3, 5, or 7 is a prime number.

There are 25 prime numbers that are smaller than 100.

e.g. Is 21 a prime number?

No, 21 is not a prime number because it is divisible by 3 and 7.

e.g. Is 41 a prime number?

Yes, 41 is a prime number because it is not divisible by 2, 3, 5, or 7.

The First 25 Prime Numbers

2 3 5 7 11 13 17
19 23 29 31 37 41 43
47 53 59 61 67 71 73
79 83 89 97

Note: 1 is neither a prime nor a composite number.

1	2	3	~~4~~	5	~~6~~	7	~~8~~	~~9~~	~~10~~
11	~~12~~	13	~~14~~	~~15~~	~~16~~	17	~~18~~	19	~~20~~
~~21~~	~~22~~	23	~~24~~	~~25~~	~~26~~	~~27~~	~~28~~	29	~~30~~
31	~~32~~	~~33~~	~~34~~	~~35~~	~~36~~	37	~~38~~	~~39~~	~~40~~
41	~~42~~	43	~~44~~	~~45~~	~~46~~	47	~~48~~	~~49~~	~~50~~
~~51~~	~~52~~	53	~~54~~	~~55~~	~~56~~	~~57~~	~~58~~	59	~~60~~
61	~~62~~	~~63~~	~~64~~	~~65~~	~~66~~	67	~~68~~	~~69~~	~~70~~
71	~~72~~	73	~~74~~	~~75~~	~~76~~	~~77~~	~~78~~	79	~~80~~
~~81~~	~~82~~	83	~~84~~	~~85~~	~~86~~	~~87~~	~~88~~	89	~~90~~
~~91~~	~~92~~	~~93~~	~~94~~	~~95~~	~~96~~	97	~~98~~	~~99~~	~~100~~

All the multiples of 2, 3, 5, and 7 are crossed out (except for 2, 3, 5, and 7).

Application

Grace wants to make a prime number by multiplying three numbers (excluding 1). Is this possible? Explain.

Solution:

No, this is not possible. For a number to be a prime number, it must have only two factors: 1 and the number itself.

If a number is a product of three different numbers, it implies that this number has three factors, and therefore, cannot be a prime number.

1.4 Order of Operations

This unit introduces the order of operations. You should be familiar with these rules as they set the foundation for more complex mathematical computation.

Order of Operations

1st ( ) Do operations in brackets.

2nd x ÷ Do multiplication or division.

3rd + − Do addition or subtraction.

You should understand the importance of applying the order of operations by going through the examples below.

The Importance of the Order of Operations

e.g. 5 + 4 x 3 = ____

without the rule	with the rule
5 + 4 x 3	5 + 4 x 3
= 9 x 3	= 5 + 12
= 27 ✗	= 17 ✓

e.g. 3 x (2 + 5) = ____

without the rule	with the rule
3 x (2 + 5)	3 x (2 + 5)
= 6 + 5	= 3 x 7
= 11 ✗	= 21 ✓

You will see that not applying the order of operations will result in different answers. Therefore, it is important that you follow the order of operations whenever applicable.

Application

Solve the expression.

(26 ÷ (4 + 9)) x (28 – 6)

Solve the expression from the inside out.

Solution:

Solve the innermost brackets first. Then solve the remaining brackets.

$(26 \div (4 + 9)) \times (28 - 6)$ ← Solve (4 + 9) first.
$= (26 \div 13) \times (28 - 6)$ ← Solve the remaining brackets.
$= 2 \times 22$
$= 44$

1.5 Multiplying by Two-digit Numbers

This unit introduces the steps involved in multiplying by two-digit numbers. Additionally, you will learn about the commutative and distributive properties of multiplication and how to apply them to make multiplication easier.

Multiplying by Two-digit Numbers

e.g. 283 x 38 = ______

1st Multiply by the ones.

```
   6 2
   2 8 3
x    3 8
--------
   2264
```

2nd Multiply by the tens.

```
   2
   2 8 3
x    3 8
--------
   2 2 6 4
   8 4 9 0  ← Don't forget the placeholder.
```

3 x 2 + 2 → 8; 8 x 3 → 4; 3 x 3 → 9

3rd Add.

```
    2 8 3
x     3 8
---------
  2 2 6 4
  8 4 9 0
---------
  10754
```

So, 283 x 38 = **10 754**.

Estimate

283 → 300
38 → 40

300 x 40
= 12 000

10 754 is close to 12 000, so the answer is reasonable.

Try to estimate to determine if your answers are reasonable. This practice will help improve your computational skills.

It is important that you understand the commutative and distributive properties of multiplication.

Commutative Property of Multiplication

This property states that changing the order of the numbers will not change the product.

e.g. 2 x 3 x 5 = 3 x 5 x 2

↓ 30 ↓ 30

As you can see, even though the order of the numbers is different, the answers are still the same.

Distributive Property of Multiplication

This property allows you to break one of the numbers into two numbers, which are then multiplied separately and added to reach the answer.

e.g. 6 x 5
= (2 x 5) + (4 x 5) ← Break 6 into 2 and 4.
= 10 + 20
= 30

Sometimes, breaking a number into smaller numbers to multiply makes calculations simpler.

Once you understand both properties, introduce the methods below to help you multiply more efficiently.

Strategy 1 Split and Multiply

e.g. 44 x 25 = ______

1st 25 is an easier number to multiply, so split 44.

44 = 22 x 2

2nd Replace 44 with 22 x 2 and multiply.

44 x 25
= 22 x 2 x 25 ← easy to multiply
= 22 x 50
= 1100

Strategy 2 Expand and Add

e.g. 44 x 25 = ______

1st 25 is an easy number to multiply, so expand 44.

44 = 40 + 4

2nd Apply the distributive property. Then add.

44 x 25
= 40 x 25 + 4 x 25
= 1000 + 100
= 1100

So, 44 x 25 = **1100**.

Application

An ice cream machine makes 455 L of ice cream per hour. If the owner upgrades the machine, it will make 35 L more per hour. How many litres of ice cream will the machine make in 24 hours after it is upgraded?

Solution:

Amount of ice cream made after upgrade:

$$\begin{array}{r} 455 \\ +\quad 35 \\ \hline 490 \end{array}$$

455 ← before upgrade; 490 ← after upgrade

Amount of ice cream made in 24 hours:

$$\begin{array}{r} 490 \\ \times\quad 24 \\ \hline 1960 \\ 9800 \\ \hline 11760 \end{array}$$

490 ← after upgrade; 24 ← 24 hours

The amount of ice cream made in 24 hours will be 11 760 L after upgrading.

1.6 Dividing by Two-digit Numbers

In this unit, you will learn to do division involving two-digit numbers. You will also learn to check answers using multiplication and addition, and to apply the distributive property to division.

Dividing Using Different Strategies

e.g. 3709 ÷ 23 = ______

```
     1               16              161 R 6
23 ) 3709       23 ) 3709       23 ) 3709
     23              23              23
     140             140             140
                     138             138
                      29              29
                                      23
                                       6
```

(161: quotient; 23: divisor; 3709: dividend; 6: remainder)

So, 3709 ÷ 23 = **161R6** .

You should use multiplication and addition to check answers.

To check answers:

1st Multiply the quotient and divisor.

2nd Add the remainder to the product. If the sum is the same as the dividend, the answer is correct; otherwise, it is incorrect.

e.g. 2348 ÷ 32 = **73R12** .

1st 73 x 32 = 2336

2nd 2336 + 12 = 2348 (same as dividend)

So, 2348 ÷ 32 = **73R12** . ✔

You should be familiar with applying the distributive property to multiplication. You should also keep in mind that it can be applied to division.

This property allows you to break one of the numbers into two numbers, which are then divided and added to reach the answer.

e.g.

$35 \div 5$
$= (30 + 5) \div 5$
$= (30 \div 5) + (5 \div 5)$
$= 6 + 1$
$= 7$

Use this property to help with mental division.

e.g.

$735 \div 7 =$ ______

$735 \div 7$
$= (700 + 35) \div 7$ ← $735 = 700 + 35$
$= (700 \div 7) + (35 \div 7)$ ← Divide.
$= 100 + 5$ ← Add.
$= 105$

So, $735 \div 7 =$ **105** .

1st Break 735 into 700 and 35, as both numbers can easily be divided by 7.

2nd Do the division separately. Then add to find the answer.

Once you grasp the concept, do the division below mentally.

Try These!

$428 \div 4 =$ ________ $2149 \div 7 =$ ________

$321 \div 3 =$ ________ $1585 \div 5 =$ ________

$189 \div 9 =$ ________ $7212 \div 6 =$ ________

Chapter 2
Decimal Numbers to Thousandths

2.1 Writing Decimal Numbers

This unit introduces decimal numbers to the thousandths. You will also learn how to round decimal numbers to the hundredths place.

Writing Decimal Numbers

e.g. Describe the diagram in a decimal and in words.

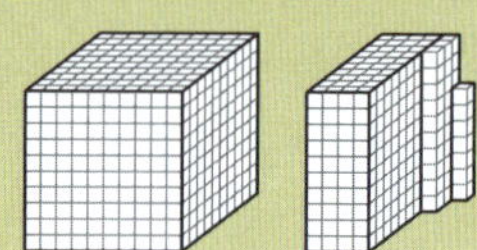

In a decimal: 1.437
In words: 1 and 437 thousandths

Finding the Value of a Digit

To start, you should write decimals in a place value chart to identify the values of their digits.

e.g. What is the value of each digit in 2.457?

ones	tenths	hundredths	thousandths
2.	4	5	7

2 means 2.
4 means 0.4.
5 means 0.05.
7 means 0.007.

Rounding Decimal Numbers

To round a decimal to the nearest hundredth, look at the digit in the thousandths place.

e.g. Round 2.457 to the nearest hundredth.

2.457 ← Thousandths: 7 > 5; round up.

So, 2.457 is rounded to **2.46**.

Application

Kyle put some sand into 3 buckets. Round the weights to the nearest kg.

Bucket A: 995 g
Bucket B: 6250 g
Bucket C: 1103 g

Solution:

Rounding the weights to the nearest kg means rounding them to the nearest thousand in g and then converting them from g into kg.

1st Round to the nearest thousand in g.

Bucket A: 995 g → 1000 g
Bucket B: 6250 g → 6000 g
Bucket C: 1103 g → 1000 g

2nd Convert g into kg.

Bucket A: 1000 g = 1 kg
Bucket B: 6000 g = 6 kg
Bucket C: 1000 g = 1 kg

The weights of Bucket A, Bucket B, and Bucket C rounded to the nearest kg is 1 kg, 6 kg, and 1 kg respectively.

2.2 Comparing and Ordering Decimal Numbers

In this unit, you will learn about the concept of equivalent decimals and how to compare decimal numbers using different strategies.

Before comparing decimal numbers, you must understand the concept of equivalent decimals.

Identifying Equivalent Decimals

Equivalent decimals are decimal numbers that represent the same value.

e.g.

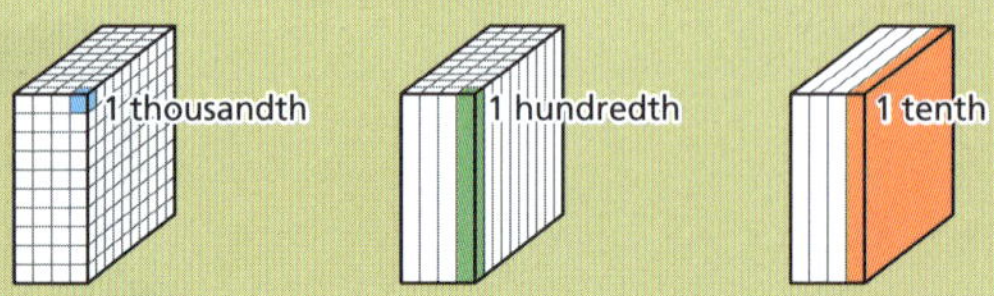

0.400 (400 thousandths) | 0.40 (40 hundredths) | 0.4 (4 tenths)

0.400 = 0.40 = 0.4

From the diagram, you should see that even though 0.400, 0.40, and 0.4 look different, they are equivalent.

Comparing Decimals

Using a Number Line

1st Locate the decimals on a number line.

2nd The number farthest to the right is the greatest.

e.g. Order 2.536, 2.653, and 2.563 from least to greatest.

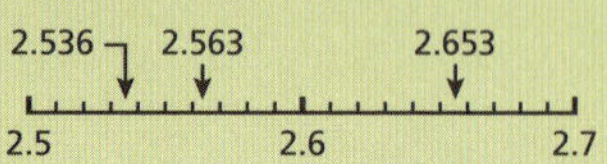

So, **2.536 < 2.563 < 2.653**.

Comparing Digits

Compare the digits farthest to the left. If they are the same, move on to the next digit to the right. Repeat until the digits are different.

e.g. Which is greater: 5.039 or 5.093?

Ones	Tenths	Hundredths	Thousandths
5 .	0	3	9
5 .	0	9	3
same	same	9 > 3	

So, **5.093** is greater.

Application

Some digits of the boys' weights are covered. If Joe is the lightest and Ken is the heaviest, what are the boys' weights?

Solution:

Joe:35.9__8 kg → lightest;
must be lighter than Eric, so the digit must be 0

Ken:35.__86 kg → heaviest;
must be heavier than Eric, so the digit must be 9

Eric: 35.90__ kg → heavier than Joe;
so the digit must be greater than 8, which is 9

So, Joe is 35.908 kg, Ken is 35.986 kg, and Eric is 35.909 kg.

2.3 Adding and Subtracting Decimal Numbers

This unit introduces addition and subtraction of decimal numbers. You will also learn to round decimal numbers to estimate and determine the reasonableness of your answers.

Adding and Subtracting Decimals

1st Align the decimal numbers by their decimal points.

2nd Add or subtract the same way we do whole numbers.

3rd Put a decimal point in the answer.

Remember to add "0" as a placeholder when needed.

e.g. 2.395 + 0.84 = ______

```
  1 1
  2.395
+ 0.840  ← Add "0" as a placeholder.
  3.235
```

Align the decimal points.

Put a decimal point in the answer.

e.g. 8 − 4.592 = ______

```
  7  9 9 10
  8.0 0 0  ← Three "0"s are added as placeholders.
− 4.5 9 2
  3.4 0 8
```

Estimating Sums and Differences

It is important for you to make estimations. It is helpful in daily life (e.g. estimating the total cost of items) and it also helps you determine if the answers are reasonable.

1st Round each decimal to the nearest one.

2nd Add or subtract the rounded numbers to find the estimate.

e.g. Is 2.395 + 0.84 = 3.235 reasonable?

2.395 —rounded to→ 2

0.84 —rounded to→ 1

2 + 1 = 3

3.235 is close to 3, so the answer is reasonable.

Application

A glass bottle floated 5.463 km away from the shore in the morning, 2.09 km toward the shore in the afternoon, and 1.971 km away from the shore at night. How far away is it from the shore now?

Solution:

Use a simple diagram to represent the distances.

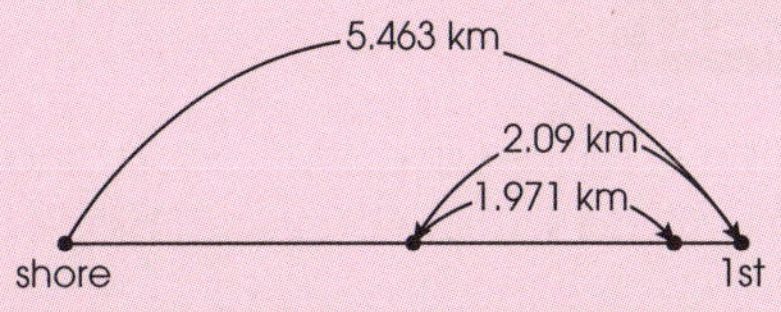

Distance away from shore:

5.463 – 2.09 + 1.971
= 3.373 + 1.971
= 5.344 (km)

The glass bottle is 5.344 km away from the shore.

2.4 Multiplying Decimal Numbers

In this unit, you will learn to multiply decimal numbers by one-digit numbers. You will first be introduced to the concept through diagrams. Additionally, you will learn strategies for multiplying decimal numbers by 10, 100, 1000, and 10 000, and by 0.1, 0.01, and 0.001 mentally.

Multiplying Decimal Numbers by One-digit Numbers

Before doing multiplication using algorithms, make sure you understand the concept of multiplying decimal numbers. To do so, use base-ten blocks.

e.g. 1.5 x 3 = _____

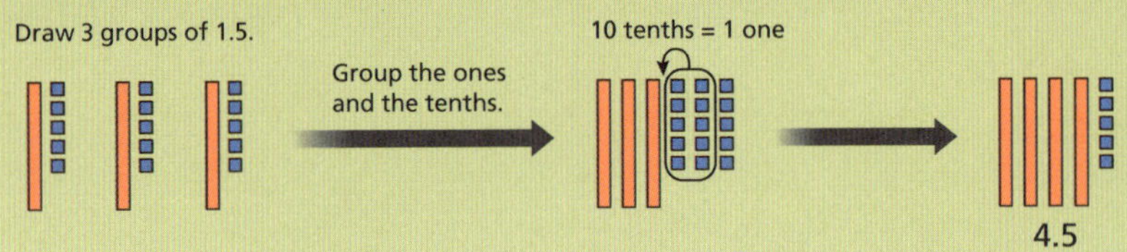

So, 1.5 x 3 = **4.5** .

Once you grasp this concept, you can learn how to find the same answer using algorithms.

1st Multiply the numbers as if there were no decimal points.

2nd Put a decimal point in the answer.

The number of decimal places in the answer is equal to the total number of decimal places in the multiplied numbers.

e.g. 1.5 x 3 = _____

```
   1
  1.5
x   3
-----
  4.5
```

Don't forget to add a decimal point.

So, 1.5 x 3 = **4.5** .

You also need to be able to multiply decimal numbers by 10, 100, 1000, and 10 000, and by 0.1, 0.01, and 0.001 mentally.

Multiplying by 10, 100, 1000, and 10 000

Move the decimal point to the **right**. The answer will be **greater** than the decimal number.

x 10	1 zero; **1** decimal place to the **right**
x 100	2 zeros; **2** decimal places to the **right**
x 1000	3 zeros; **3** decimal places to the **right**
x 10 000	4 zeros; **4** decimal places to the **right**

e.g.

2.0 8 7 x 10 = 20.87 (1)

2.0 8 7 x 100 = 208.7 (1 2)

2.0 8 7 x 1000 = 2087 (1 2 3)

2.0 8 7 x 10 000 = 20 87**0** (1 2 3 4) ← placeholder

Multiplying by 0.1, 0.01, and 0.001

Move the decimal point to the **left**. The answer will be **smaller** than the decimal number.

x 0.1	1 decimal place; **1** place to the **left**
x 0.01	2 decimal places; **2** places to the **left**
x 0.001	3 decimal places; **3** places to the **left**

e.g.

8 7. x 0.1 = 8.7 (1)

8 7. x 0.01 = 0.87 (2 1)

8 7. x 0.001 = 0.**0**87 (3 2 1) ← placeholder

Add "0" as a placeholder.

2.5 Dividing Decimal Numbers

In this unit, you will learn to divide decimal numbers by one-digit numbers. You will also learn strategies for dividing decimal numbers by 10, 100, 1000, and 10 000, and by 0.1, 0.01, and 0.001 mentally.

Dividing Decimal Numbers by Whole Numbers

1st Do the division as if there were no decimal points.

2nd Align and put a decimal point in the answer.

e.g. 3.6 ÷ 2 = ____

$$\begin{array}{r} 1.8 \\ 2\overline{)3.6} \\ \underline{2} \\ 16 \\ \underline{16} \end{array}$$

Align and put a decimal point in the answer.

So, 3.6 ÷ 2 = **1.8**.

e.g. 2.7 ÷ 9 = ____

$$\begin{array}{r} \mathbf{0}.3 \\ 9\overline{)2.7} \\ \underline{27} \end{array}$$

So, 2.7 ÷ 9 = **0.3**.

Once you understand that dividing decimal numbers is similar to dividing whole numbers, with the exception of adding a decimal point in the appropriate place, you can try to solve simple division questions mentally.

Dividing Decimal Numbers by 10, 100, 1000, and 10 000

To divide decimal numbers by 10, 100, 1000, and 10 000, move the decimal point to the **left**.

		e.g.
÷ 10	**1** decimal place to the **left**	$15 \div 10 = 1.5$
÷ 100	**2** decimal places to the **left**	$15 \div 100 = 0.15$
÷ 1000	**3** decimal places to the **left**	$15 \div 1000 = 0.\mathbf{0}15$
÷ 10 000	**4** decimal places to the **left**	$15 \div 10\,000 = 0.\mathbf{00}15$

Dividing Decimal Numbers by 0.1, 0.01, and 0.001

To divide decimal numbers by 0.1, 0.01, and 0.001, move the decimal point to the **right**.

		e.g.
÷ 0.1	**1** decimal place to the **right**	$0.15 \div 0.1 = 1.5$
÷ 0.01	**2** decimal places to the **right**	$0.15 \div 0.01 = 15$
÷ 0.001	**3** decimal places to the **right**	$0.15 \div 0.001 = 15\mathbf{0}$

You may find it difficult to know when a decimal point should be moved to the left or to the right when doing both multiplication and division. One way to solve this problem is to determine whether the answer to a multiplication or division question will be greater or smaller. If it will be greater, move the decimal point to the right; if it will be smaller, move it to the left.

Application

The cost of 9 m^2 of carpet is \$3600. What is the cost of 1 cm^2 of carpet?

Solution:

Cost of 1 m^2 of carpet:

$$\$3600 \div 9 = \$400$$

$$9\overline{)3600} = 400$$

Cost of 1 cm^2 of carpet:

$1\ m^2 = 1\ m \times 1\ m$
$= 100\ cm \times 100\ cm$ ← 1 m = 100 cm
$= 10\,000\ cm^2$

$1\ m^2 = 10\,000\ cm^2$

1 m^2 of carpet costs \$400 means 10 000 cm^2 of carpet costs \$400.

$$\$400 \div 10\,000 = \$0.04$$

So, 1 cm^2 of carpet costs \$0.04.

Chapter 3

Fractions and Percents

3.1 Comparing and Ordering Fractions

In this unit, you will learn to compare fractions with different denominators using diagrams and the concept of equivalent fractions.

Comparing Fractions in Diagrams

Use diagrams to learn the concept of comparing fractions with different denominators.

e.g. Which fraction is greater: $\frac{2}{3}$ or $\frac{3}{4}$?

1st Draw 2 shapes of the same size.

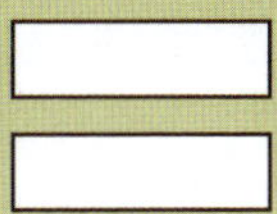

2nd Show both fractions.

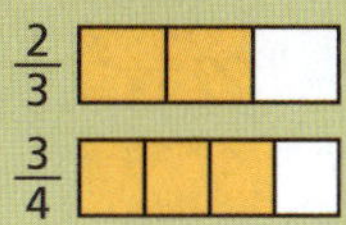

3rd Compare.

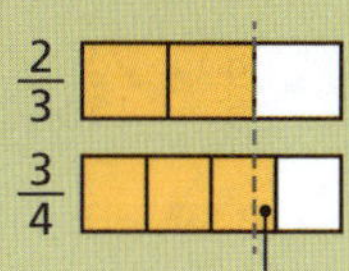

So, $\frac{3}{4}$ is greater.

Rewriting and Comparing Fractions

Rewrite the fractions being compared so that they have the same denominator. (You must be able to find equivalent fractions to do so.)

e.g. Which fraction is greater: $\frac{2}{3}$ or $\frac{3}{4}$?

$\frac{2}{3} = \frac{8}{12}$

$\frac{3}{4} = \frac{9}{12}$

same denominator (a product of 3 and 4)

$\frac{9}{12} > \frac{8}{12}$, so $\frac{3}{4} > \frac{2}{3}$

So, $\frac{3}{4}$ is greater than $\frac{2}{3}$.

Application

Eric got a cake for completing the laps. Read his description about his cake and circle the correct cake.

It is not the lightest cake and is lighter than $\frac{25}{15}$ kg.

$1\frac{2}{3}$ kg

$\frac{3}{2}$ kg

$1\frac{3}{5}$ kg

Solution:

Use a diagram to find the lightest cake and eliminate it.

$1\frac{2}{3}$

$\frac{3}{2}$ ✗ $\frac{3}{2}$ is less than $1\frac{2}{3}$ and $1\frac{3}{5}$.

$1\frac{3}{5}$

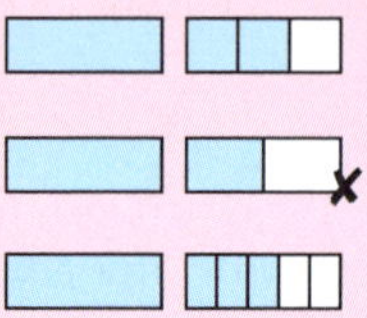

To find the fraction that is less than $\frac{25}{15}$, convert both $1\frac{2}{3}$ and $1\frac{3}{5}$ into improper fractions with denominators of 15.

$1\frac{2}{3} = \frac{5}{3} = \frac{25}{15}$

$1\frac{3}{5} = \frac{8}{5} = \frac{24}{15}$ ✔ $\frac{24}{15}$ is less than $\frac{25}{15}$.

So, Eric got the cake that weighs $1\frac{3}{5}$ kg.

3.2 Percents

In this unit, you will be introduced to percents. You will learn to describe parts of a whole with percents and recognize benchmark percents.

Understanding Percents

Percent (%): describes the number of parts out of 100 equal parts

"%" is read as "percent".

e.g.

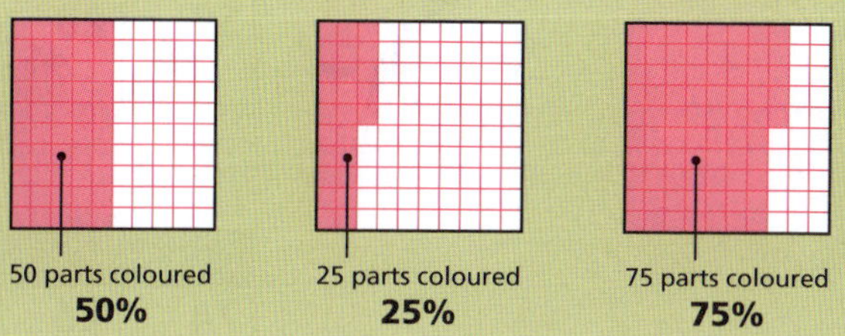

Benchmarks

25%	one quarter
50%	one half
75%	three quarters
100%	one whole

It is important for you to be familiar with these benchmarks. To reinforce your understanding of these benchmarks, fill a glass with water and estimate in percents how full the glass is.

e.g.

Application

See how many red and green apples the children picked. One of them says, "About 50% of my apples are red". Name that child.

Solution:

Find the quantity of red apples each child picked in percent.

Kenny

Red apples: 24
Total: 50
Percent: 48%

Carol

Red apples: 52
Total: 80
Percent: 65%

Andy

Red apples: 74
Total: 100
Percent: 74%

48% is about 50%, so the child must be Kenny.

3.3 Fractions, Decimals, and Percents

In this unit, you will learn how fractions, decimals, and percents are related. You will then convert among the three forms and compare quantities that are represented in different forms.

Relating Fractions, Decimals, and Percents

At this stage, you should be able to describe parts of a whole with fractions and decimals. Now you will learn to do so with percents.

You should be able to describe parts of a whole in all three forms.

e.g. Describe the coloured parts in fractions, decimals, and percents.

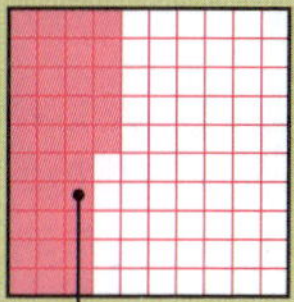

$\frac{35}{100}$

0.35

35%

35 parts out of 100 parts are coloured.

$\frac{1}{4}$

0.25

25%

1 part out of 4 parts is coloured.

Once you have a good understanding of how to describe parts of a whole in all three forms, you are ready to do conversions among them.

Writing Percents as Fractions

Write percents as fractions with denominators of 100.

e.g. Write 42% as a fraction.

$$42\% = \frac{42}{100}$$

$42\% = \underline{\frac{42}{100}}$

Writing Fractions as Percents

Write the equivalent fraction with 100 as its denominator. Then write it as a percent.

e.g. Write $\frac{1}{5}$ as a percent.

$$\frac{1}{5} = \frac{20}{100} = 20\% \quad (\times 20)$$

$\frac{1}{5} = \underline{20\%}$

Writing Percents as Decimals

1st Drop the "%".

2nd Move the decimal point 2 places to the left.

e.g. Write 15% as a decimal.

$$15.\not\%=0.15$$

(the decimal point moves 2 places to the left: 1, 2)

15% = **0.15**

Writing Decimals as Percents

1st Move the decimal point 2 places to the right.

2nd Add the "%".

e.g. Write 0.7 as a percent.

$$0.7\ \ = 70\%$$

(the decimal point moves 2 places to the right: 1, 2)

0.7 = **70%**

Comparing Fractions, Decimals, and Percents

e.g. Put 0.02, $\frac{1}{5}$, and 5% in order from least to greatest.

1st Convert the numbers into decimals. (You may also convert them all into fractions or percents.)

$0.02 \longrightarrow 0.02$

$\frac{1}{5} \longrightarrow 0.2$

$5\% \longrightarrow 0.05$

2nd Compare and put them in order.

$0.02 < 0.05 < 0.2$

↓

$0.02 < 5\% < \frac{1}{5}$

It doesn't matter which form the numbers are converted into as long as they are all in the same form.

Application

Chris, Anne, and Paul share the cost of renting a video game.

- *Chris pays 0.35 of the cost.*
- *Anne pays 20% of it.*
- *Paul pays the remaining cost.*

What fraction of the cost does Paul pay?

Solution:

You may find that calculations in whole numbers are easier to work with than decimals or fractions. So, convert the values into percents first.

Chris: 0.35 → 35%
Anne: 20%
Paul: 100% – 35% – 20% = 45%

$45\% = \frac{45}{100}$

So, Paul pays $\frac{45}{100}$ of the cost.

Chapter 4

Ratios and Rates

4.1 Ratios

In this unit, you will be introduced to the concept of ratios. You will learn the definition of a ratio, and how to write and represent ratios in basic comparisons.

Writing Ratios

Ratio: a comparison between two or more quantities of the same unit

e.g. What is the ratio of ● to ● ?
Write the ratio in three ways.

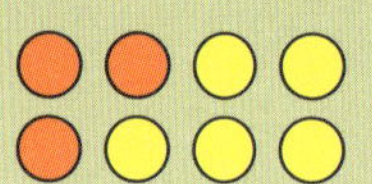

The ratio is **3:5**, **3 to 5**, or $\frac{3}{5}$.

The order of the quantities matters in a ratio. In the example above, if the answer was written as 5:3, it would be incorrect.

You may use ratios to describe quantities to consolidate your understanding of them.

- What is the ratio of apples to oranges in the fridge?
- What is the ratio of apples to all other fruits in the fridge?
- What is the ratio of cups to mugs in the cabinet?

Application

Natasha is 12 years old and her mother is 38 years old. In 4 years, what will be the ratio of Natasha's age to her mother's age?

Solution:

After 4 years

Natasha's age: $12 + 4 = 16$
Her mom's age: $38 + 4 = 42$

So, the ratio of Natasha's age to her mom's age will be 16:42, 16 to 42, or $\frac{16}{42}$.

4.2 Rates

This unit introduces the concept of rates. You will learn to find unit rates and apply the concept of unit rates to find speeds and unit prices.

Finding Unit Rates

Rate: a comparison between quantities of different units

e.g. 90 children/3 buses

The units in rates are separated by a "/" which is read as "per".

Unit rate: a special type of rate in which a quantity is compared to one unit of another quantity

e.g. 30 children/bus ⟵ 1 bus

e.g. Find the unit rate of selling 25 toys in 5 hours.

$25 \div 5 = 5$

So, the unit rate is **5 toys/hour**.

Finding Speeds

Speed: a unit rate that describes how fast someone or something is moving

A speed is found by dividing distance by time.

e.g. Ashton runs 275 m in 5 mins. What is his speed?

$275 \div 5 = 55$

Ashton's speed is **55 m/min**.

Finding Unit Prices

Unit price: a unit rate that describes the cost of an item

e.g. 6 cans of juice are sold for $12.

$12 \div 6 = 2$

The unit price is **$2/can** .

Unit prices are often used to determine whether or not an item in one store is a better buy than the same item in another store.

e.g. Store A sells 3 boxes of cereal for $9 and Store B sells 5 boxes of the same cereal for $10. Which store offers a better buy?

Store A: $9 \div 3 = 3$ ← $3/box

Store B: $10 \div 5 = 2$ ← $2/box ✓ better buy

So, **Store B** offers a better buy.

Chapter 5

Measurement

5.1 Area of Rectangles

In this unit, you will review the methodology of finding the area of a rectangle. You will also learn how to convert between squared units.

Finding Area of Rectangles and Squares

You should be familiar with finding the area of a rectangle using the formula below.

Area of a rectangle = length x width

A square is a special type of rectangle that has all sides equal.

Area of a square = length x length

e.g. Find the area of the rectangle.

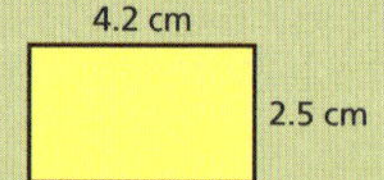

4.2 x 2.5 = 10.5

The area of the rectangle is **10.5 cm²**.

Converting m² into cm²

To understand the relationship between m² and cm², consider a square with side lengths of 1 m (or 100 cm).

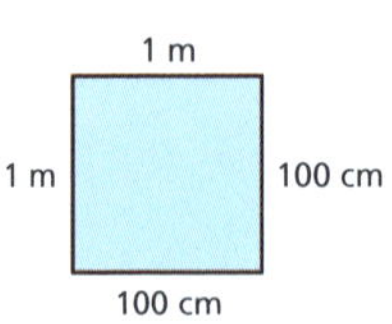

Area in m² = 1 m x 1 m
= **1 m²**

Area in cm² = 100 cm x 100 cm
= **10 000 cm²**

1 m² = 10 000 cm²

e.g. Convert 0.2 m² into cm².

0.2 (1 2 3 4) = 2000

So, 0.2 m² = **2000 cm²**.

Application

The perimeter of this board is 292 cm and its width is 52 cm. What is the area of the board?

Solution:

To find the area of a rectangle, both length and width are needed. The width is given, but the length needs to be found. Find the length of the rectangle using its perimeter and width.

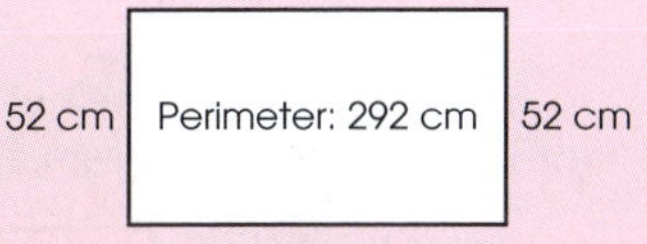

perimeter, width

$$\text{Length} = (292 - 52 - 52) \div 2$$
$$= 188 \div 2$$
$$= 94 \text{ (cm)}$$

$$\text{Area} = 94 \times 52$$
$$= 4888 \text{ (cm}^2\text{)}$$

So, the area of the board is 4888 cm^2.

5.2 Area of Parallelograms

In this unit, you will relate the area of rectangles to the area of parallelograms. You will learn how the formula for the area of a parallelogram is derived from the formula for the area of rectangles.

Finding Area of a Parallelogram

To understand how to find the area of a parallelogram, you should consider the area of a rectangle.

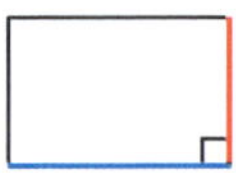

Area of □ = length x width

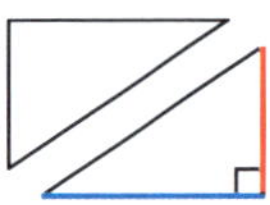

Cut the □ into 2 identical ◺.

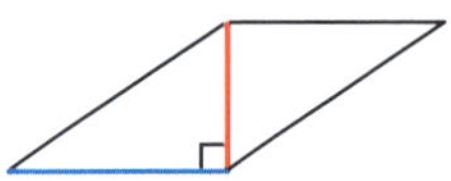

Combine them to form a ▱. Note that the total area stays the same.

The area of the ▱ is the same as the area of the original □. However, instead of length and width, the two sides are called base and height in a parallelogram.

Area of a parallelogram = base x height

e.g. Find the area of the parallelogram.

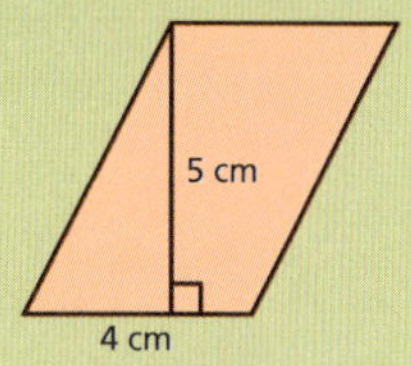

4 x 5 = 20

The area is **20 cm²** .

Sometimes the height needs to be measured outside of the parallelogram.

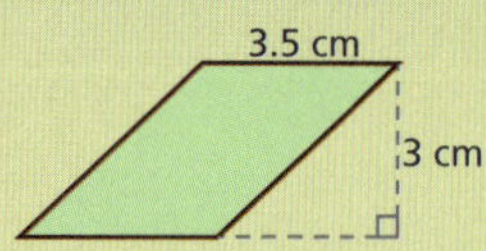

3.5 x 3 = 10.5

The area is **10.5 cm²** .

Application

The parallelogram is made up of two identical triangles and a square with a side length of 3 m. What is the area of the parallelogram?

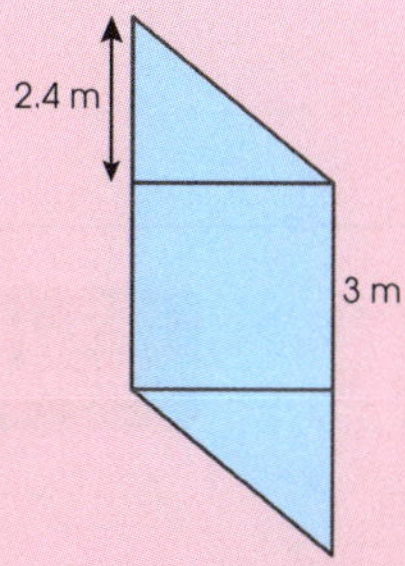

Solution:

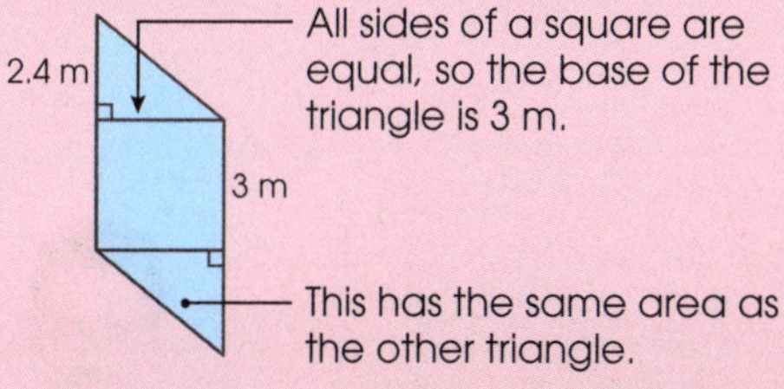

Area of two triangles:

$(3 \times 2.4 \div 2) \times 2$

$= 3.6 \times 2$

$= 7.2\ (m^2)$

Area of square:

3×3

$= 9\ (m^2)$

Total area:

$7.2 + 9$

$= 16.2\ (m^2)$

The area of the parallelogram is $16.2\ m^2$.

5.3 Area of Triangles

In this unit, you will relate the area of rectangles to the area of triangles. You will learn how the formula for the area of a triangle is derived, and how to identify the height and the base used in calculating the area of a triangle.

Finding Area of a Triangle

To understand how the area of a triangle is found, consider the area of a rectangle.

Area of a Triangle = base x height ÷ 2

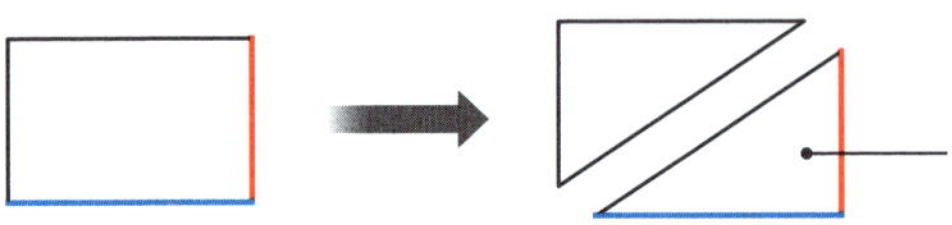

Area of ⊿ = Area of □ ÷ 2
base x height ÷ 2

Cut the □ into 2 identical ⊿. The total area of the ⊿ stays the same.

Be careful when identifying the base and height of a triangle. Remember that the base and height always make a 90° angle.

e.g. Find the area.

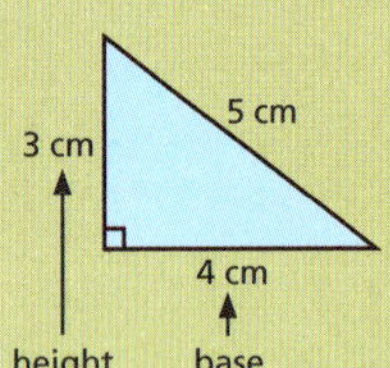

5 cm x 3 cm ÷ 2 ✗
= 7.5 cm²

5 cm is neither the base nor the height.

4 cm x 3 cm ÷ 2
= 6 cm² ✓

The area is **6 cm²**.

Application

What is the area of the big triangle?

Solution:

To find the area of the big triangle, its base needs to be found. To do so, find the base of the small triangle first because its base is the same as the big triangle's.

Base of the small triangle:

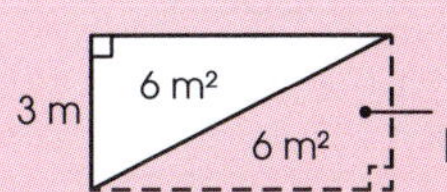

Area of ▭ : $6 + 6 = 12$ (m²)
Length of ▭ : $12 \div 3 = 4$ (m)
↑ base of small triangle

So, the base of the small triangle, which is also the base of the big triangle, is 4 m.

Area of the big triangle:

$4 \times 8 \div 2$
$= 32 \div 2$
$= 16$ (m²)

So, the area of the big triangle is 16 m².

5.4 Mass and Capacity

In this unit, you will review unit conversion among different units of mass and different units of capacity. You will learn a simple strategy to quickly convert between two units and apply unit conversion to real life situations.

You will learn to convert between two units to solve word problems.

Converting between Units of Mass

Mass

1 kg = 1000 g

1 g = 1000 mg

e.g. An apple pie is 1.6 kg and is cut into 8 equal slices. How many grams is each slice?

1st Convert 1.6 kg into g.

1.6 x 1000 = 1600

1.6 kg = 1600 g

2nd Divide 1600 g by 8.

1600 ÷ 8 = 200

Each slice is **200 g**.

Converting between Units of Capacity

Capacity

1 L = 1000 mL

e.g. A jar has 2.4 L of juice and is poured into 8 cups. How much juice does each cup have in mL?

1st Convert 2.4 L into mL.

2.4 x 1000 = 2400

2.4 L = 2400 mL

2nd Divide 2400 mL by 8.

2400 ÷ 8 = 300

Each cup has **300 mL** of juice.

In the problems above, division can be done before doing the conversions instead. However, you may find it easier to work with whole numbers when dividing.

Application

I have a vase that has a mass of 0.56 L more than this vase, and a bouquet of flowers that has a capacity of 0.2 kg less than this one.

Find the errors in what the girl says. Find the mass and capacity of her items in mL and g.

Solution:

The litre is a unit of capacity, not mass. The kilogram is a unit of mass, not capacity. Therefore, the girl should have compared the vases by capacity and the bouquets of flowers by mass.

Capacity of her vase: 5.8 L + 0.56 L = 6.36 L
Mass of her bouquet of flowers: 1.75 kg – 0.2 kg = 1.55 kg

So, her vase has a capacity of 6.36 L and her bouquet of flowers has a mass of 1.55 kg.

5.5 Volume and Surface Area

In this unit, you will relate your previous knowledge of area and volume to find the surface area and volume of rectangular and triangular prisms.

Finding Volume

Volume of a rectangular prism $= l \times w \times h$

You should be familiar with finding the volume of a rectangular prism.

e.g. Find the volume.

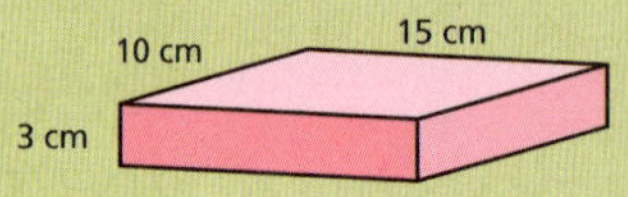

$15 \times 10 \times 3$
$= 150 \times 3$
$= 450$

The volume is **450 cm³**.

You will learn to find the volume of a triangular prism. This concept is built upon your understanding of calculating the volume of rectangular prisms.

A rectangular prism can be decomposed into two identical triangular prisms. Therefore, the volume of one triangular prism is half the volume of the rectangular prism.

Once you grasp the concept, remember that the volume of a triangular prism can also be found by multiplying the area of its base by its height.

Volume of a triangular prism = area of base x height

e.g. Find the volume.

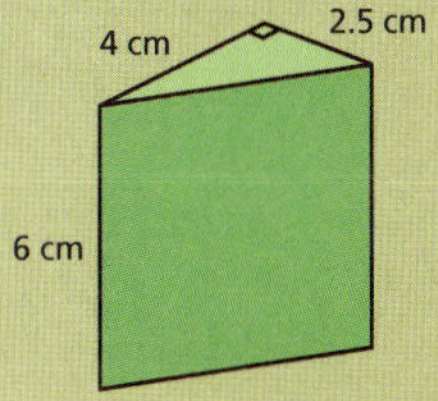

$4 \times 2.5 \div 2 \times 6$
$= 10 \div 2 \times 6$
$= 5 \times 6$
$= 30$

The volume is **30 cm³**.

Area of triangle:
$b \times h \div 2$

Finding Surface Area

Surface area: the total area of all the faces on a 3-D figure

Finding the surface area requires a good visualization of 3-D figures.

Visualizing a Rectangular Prism

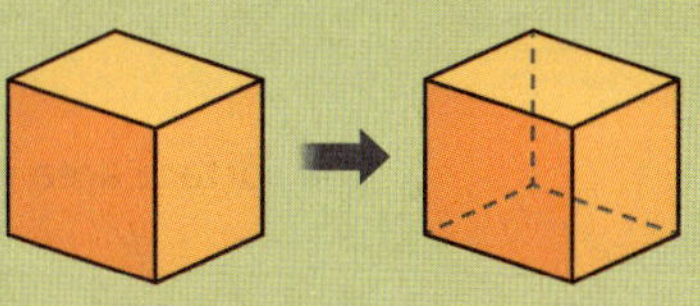

There can be up to 3 different sized rectangular faces on a rectangular prism. There are always at least 2 faces for each size which add up to 6 sides in total.

Surface area of a rectangular prism $= (l \times w + w \times h + l \times h) \times 2$

e.g. Find the surface area.

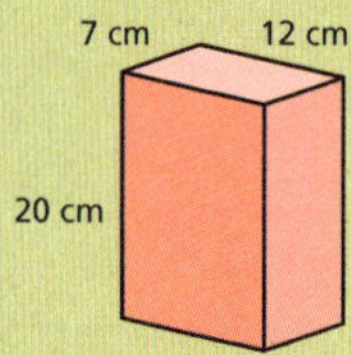

$(12 \times 7 + 7 \times 20 + 12 \times 20) \times 2$
$= (84 + 140 + 240) \times 2$
$= 464 \times 2$
$= 928$

The surface area is **928 cm²**.

Surface area of a triangular prism = (area of base x 2) + (area of 3 rectangular faces)

e.g. Find the surface area.

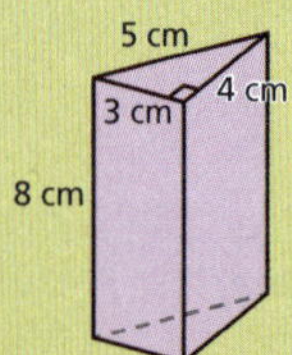

$(4 \times 3 \div 2 \times 2) + (8 \times 3 + 8 \times 4 + 8 \times 5)$
$= 12 + 96$
$= 108$

The surface area is **108 cm²**.

Application

Any triangular prism that is cut from a rectangular prism must be half the volume and half the surface area of the rectangular prism.

Is she correct? Explain.

Solution:

She is correct for volume. The two triangular prisms take up the same amount of space, which is the volume, as the original rectangular prism.

She is not correct for surface area. Consider the diagram below.

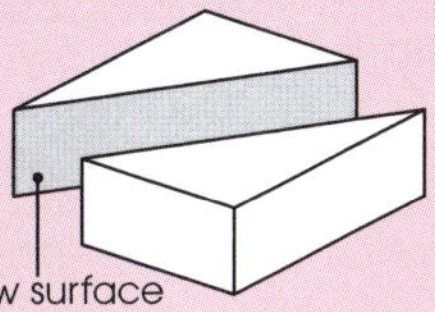

Two new surfaces are created when a rectangular prism is split into two triangular prisms. Therefore, the surface area of the triangular prism will not be half of the rectangular prism's.

Chapter 6
Geometry

6.1 Geometric Properties of Quadrilaterals

In this unit, you will analyze common quadrilaterals and identify and compare their various properties. You will also learn the symbols used to represent parallel sides and sides of equal length.

Properties of Quadrilaterals

A quadrilateral is any polygon that has 4 sides. Below are some common quadrilaterals and their properties.

square

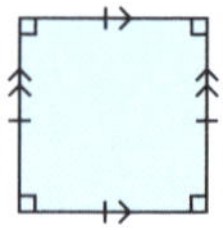

- 4 equal sides
- 2 pairs of parallel sides
- 4 right angles

rectangle

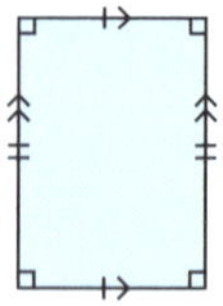

- 2 pairs of equal sides
- 2 pairs of parallel sides
- 4 right angles

parallelogram

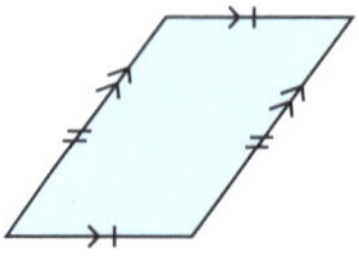

- 2 pairs of equal sides
- 2 pairs of parallel sides
- no right angles

| indicates sides that are equal in length

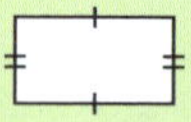

2 pairs of equal sides

> indicates sides that are parallel

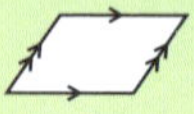

2 pairs of parallel sides

There are more properties than the ones mentioned above, for example, the number of lines of symmetry.

rhombus

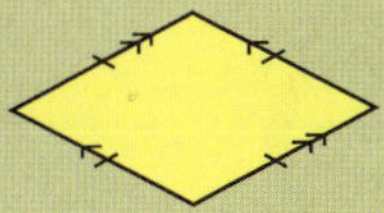

- 4 equal sides
- 2 pairs of parallel sides
- no right angles

kite

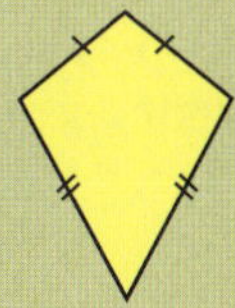

- 2 pairs of equal sides
- no parallel sides
- no right angles

trapezoid

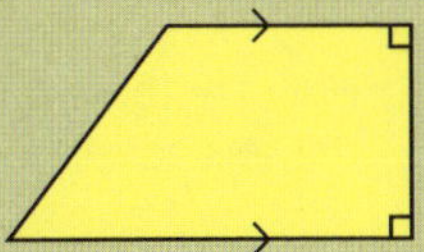

- not all sides are equal
- 1 pair of parallel sides
- may have right angles

Even though these shapes do not have special properties, they all have four sides, so they are all quadrilaterals.

Application

How are these quadrilaterals sorted? Identify the sorting rules.

Solution:

Find out the common attributes each group has (including the overlapping part).

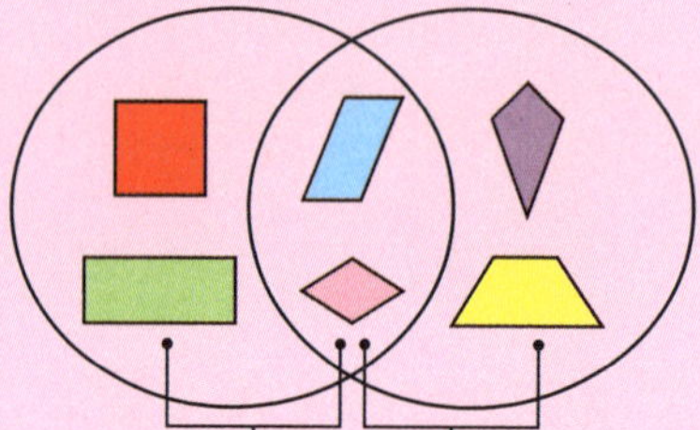

So, the sorting rules are: has 2 pairs of parallel sides and has no right angles.

6.2 Line of Symmetry and Rotational Symmetry

This unit introduces the concept of rotational symmetry. You will learn how to distinguish rotational symmetry from line of symmetry, identify rotational symmetry, and determine the order of rotational symmetry a shape has.

Identifying Line of Symmetry and Rotational Symmetry

You have learned that a line of symmetry cuts a shape into two equal halves. At this level, you will also learn to identify rotational symmetry.

e.g. Identifying figures that have rotational symmetry

A figure has rotational symmetry if it fits onto itself in one complete rotation.

If you have difficulty differentiating between line of symmetry and rotational symmetry, remember that a line of symmetry is formed by "folding" a shape into halves, whereas rotational symmetry is found by "rotating" a shape. Consider the shape below.

e.g.

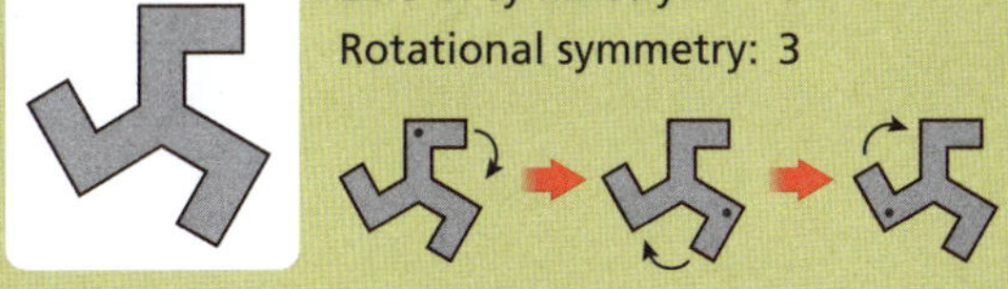

Line of symmetry: 0

Rotational symmetry: 3

The shape has no line of symmetry but has rotational symmetry of order 3.

The number of lines of symmetry has no correlation with the order of rotational symmetry.

Application

The number of lines of symmetry must be greater than the order of rotational symmetry.

Is she correct? Give examples.

Solution:

No, she is not correct.

Consider these letters.

N S Z

These three letters have rotational symmetry of order 2, but have no lines of symmetry.

So, the number of lines of symmetry is not always greater than the order of rotational symmetry.

6.3 Measuring and Constructing Angles

In this unit, you will review benchmark angles and construct angles of varying size using a protractor.

Types of Angles

Acute angle
- less than 90°

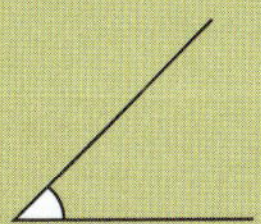

Right angle
- 90°

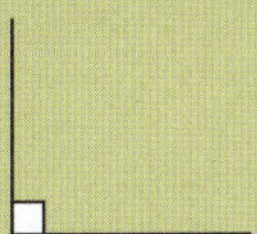

Obtuse angle
- between 90° and 180°

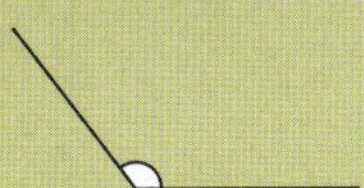

Straight angle
- 180°

Constructing Angles

Draw a 115° angle.

1st Draw one arm of the angle.

2nd Place the centre of the protractor at one end of the arm and mark the angle.

3rd Draw the second arm by joining the mark to the end of the first arm.

Tip 1 Use a sharp pencil to make the angle as precise as possible.

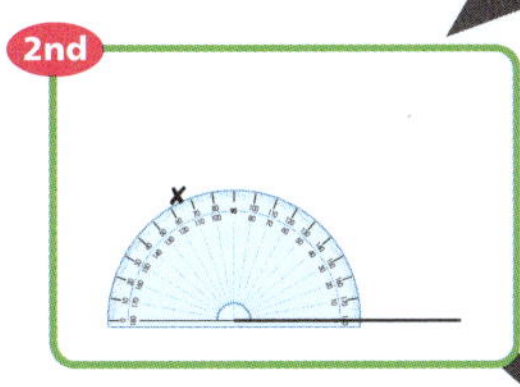

Tip 2 Before using the protractor, determine whether the angle is acute or obtuse. This will prevent you from using the wrong scale.

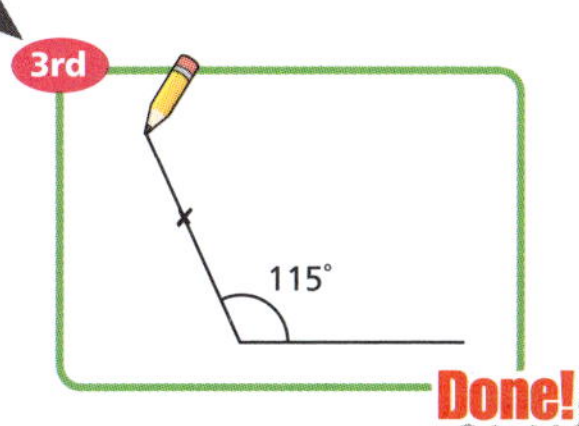

Tip 3 Measure the angle again to ensure a precise measurement.

Application

Do you think she is correct? If not, what could be the reason for the mistake?

Solution:

No, she did not do the reading correctly. It is obvious by inspection that the angle is an obtuse angle, but 75° is an acute angle.

She could have read the wrong scale on the protractor. 75° and 105° align on the same line; however, 75° is on the outer scale and 105° is on the inner scale.

6.4 Constructing Polygons

In this unit, you will learn how to construct polygons using a ruler and a protractor. Make sure you are comfortable using a protractor before starting this unit. We recommend that you go through the example below to see how to use a protractor in conjunction with a ruler.

To construct a polygon, remember that you need to make precise measurements with the correct tools including a sharpened pencil, a ruler, and a protractor.

e.g. Construct quadrilateral ABCD with these measurements.

line AB = 7 cm
angle B = 105°
line BC = 4 cm
angle C = 85°
line CD = 6.5 cm

1st Draw a line that is 7 cm long. Label the ends A and B.

2nd Place the centre of the protractor at B. Mark 105° at the edge of the protractor.

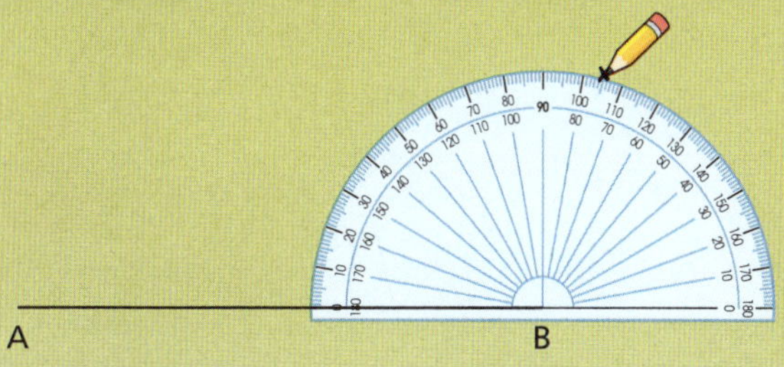

3rd Use a ruler to draw a 4-cm line that starts at B and intersects the mark. Label the new end C.

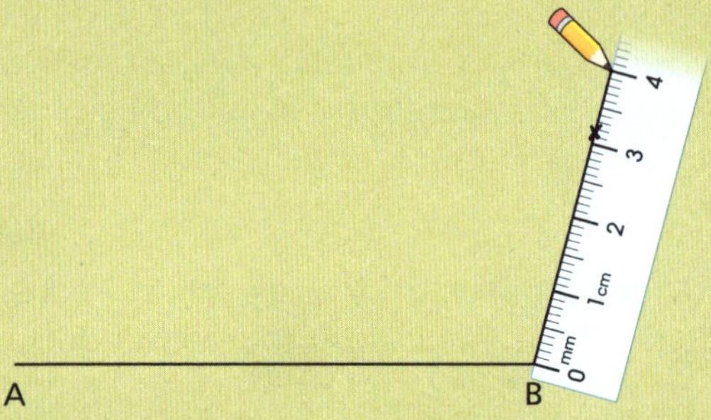

4th Place the centre of the protractor at C. Mark 85° at the edge of the protractor.

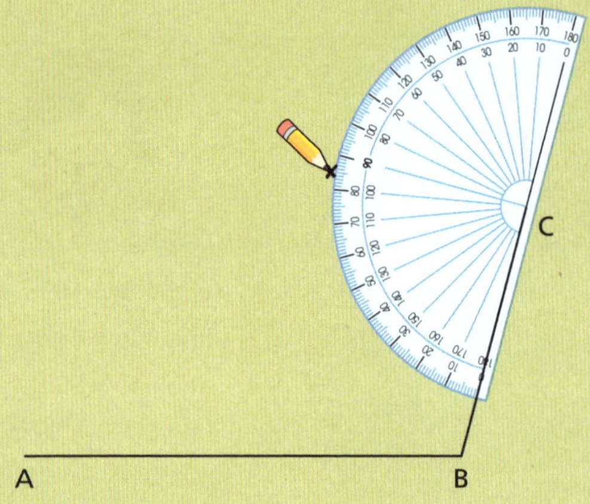

5th Use a ruler to draw a 6.5-cm line that starts at C and intersects the mark. Label the new end D.

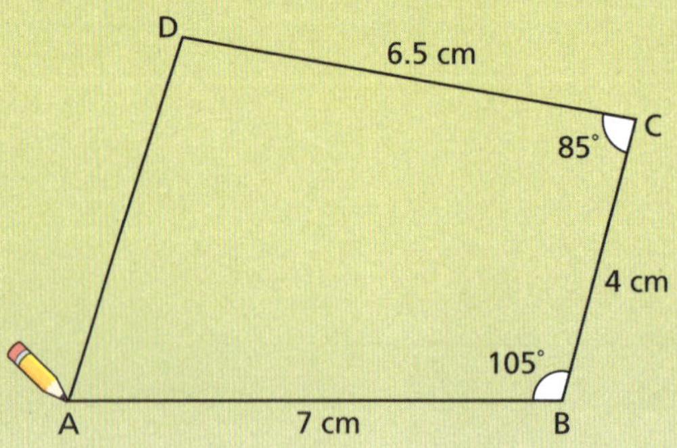

Since this is a quadrilateral, it has 4 sides. Connect A and D to complete the shape.

6.5 Different Views of Solids

This unit focuses on visualizing 3-D solids from different points of view. We recommend using real blocks to construct various structures and observing the structure from different angles.

Identifying and Drawing Views of Solids

To identify the different views of a solid, the ability to visualize 3-D solids is required. If you have difficulties visualizing 3-D solids, use connecting cubes or other manipulatives (such as dice).

You need to identify the top view, front view, and side view of a solid.

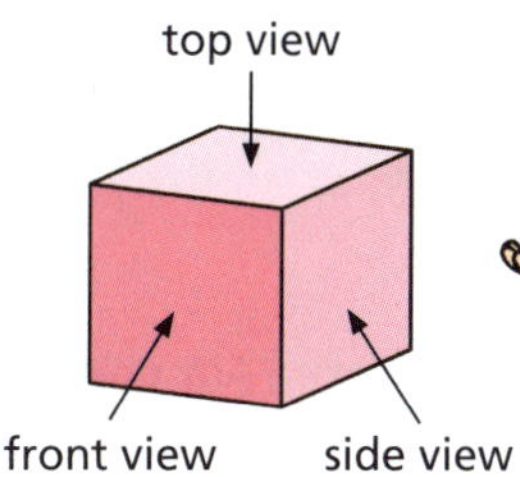

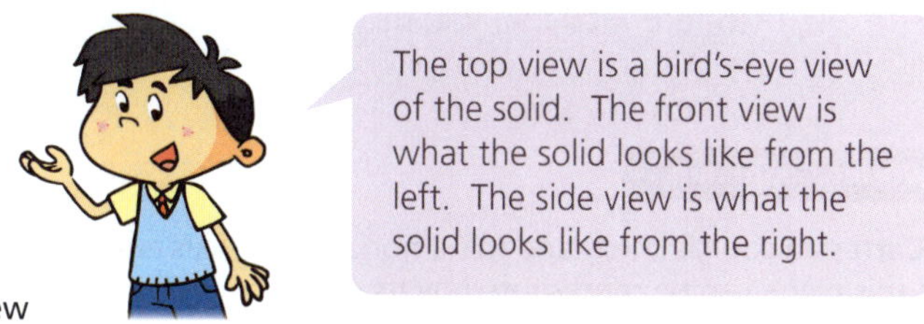

e.g. Draw the top, front, and side views of the solid.

The two most important components when drawing the views of a solid are the number of squares and their orientation.

Chapter 7

Locations and Movements

7.1 Coordinates on a Cartesian Coordinate Plane

This unit introduces plotting on a Cartesian coordinate plane. This topic is foundational for higher level math as the Cartesian coordinate plane system is an important aspect in geometry and algebra. It is, therefore, vital that you fully understand the concepts in this unit.

Writing Coordinates

A Cartesian coordinate plane has a horizontal x-axis and a vertical y-axis. Any point on this plane can be represented by its coordinates in the form of (x,y).

Coordinates are always written in this format.

(x, y)

↑ no. of units across the x-axis ↑ no. of units up the y-axis

Steps to finding coordinates:

1st Find the x-coordinate (the first number) on the x-axis.

2nd Find the y-coordinate (the second number) on the y-axis.

3rd Write the coordinates in the form of (x,y).

e.g.

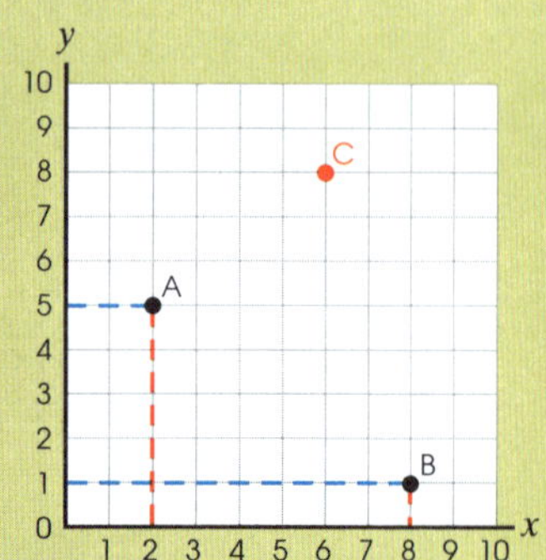

1. Find the coordinates of points A and B.

   A (2,5) B (8,1)

2. Plot (6,8) on the grid and label it C.

Application

What are the areas of the triangles on the grid?

Solution:

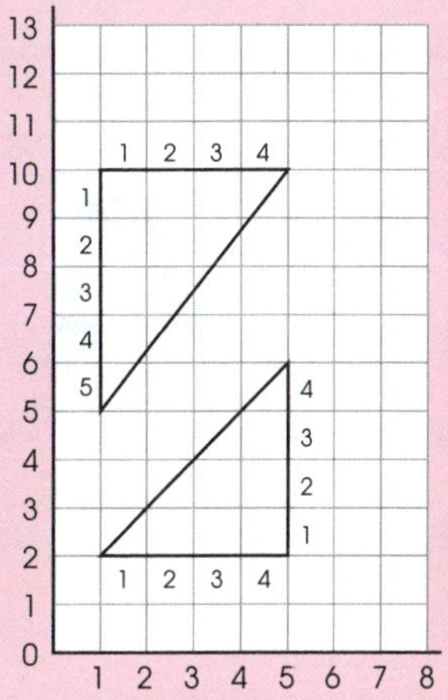

Find the area of ◸.

Base: 4 cm

Height: 5 cm

Area: $4 \times 5 \div 2 = 10$ (cm^2)

Find the area of ◢.

Base: 4 cm

Height: 4 cm

Area: $4 \times 4 \div 2 = 8$ (cm^2)

So, the areas of the triangles are 10 cm^2 and 8 cm^2.

7.2 Describing Rotations

You should be familiar with rotational transformations at this point. In this unit, you will build upon previous knowledge of rotations and learn to describe the direction and degree of a rotation.

Clockwise and Counterclockwise Rotations

Rotation

- a transformation in which a figure is turned about a fixed point, which is called a centre of rotation or a turn centre
- can be a clockwise or counterclockwise turn
- can be described in degrees

You must be familiar with identifying and performing rotations. At this level, you will learn to describe rotations based on the direction and degree of a turn.

Clockwise describes the direction that the hands on a clock turn. Counterclockwise is the opposite direction.

90° turn clockwise

180°

90° turn counterclockwise

Try this activity to learn how to describe and perform rotations.

Place a paper clip on a piece of paper and hold it in place with a pencil.

Pick and mark a starting point. Rotate the paper clip from the starting point and describe the rotation.

It is a 90° turn counterclockwise.

Make a 180° turn clockwise and a 180° turn counterclockwise. Think about why they are both the same as a 180° turn.

7.3 Creating Tiling Patterns Using Transformations

In this unit, you will apply your knowledge of transformations to describe and construct tiling patterns. Make sure that you are proficient in the different types of transformations first.

Identifying Transformations in Tiling Patterns

Tiling pattern: a pattern that is created by translating, reflecting, and rotating shape(s), resulting in a design that has no gaps and does not overlap

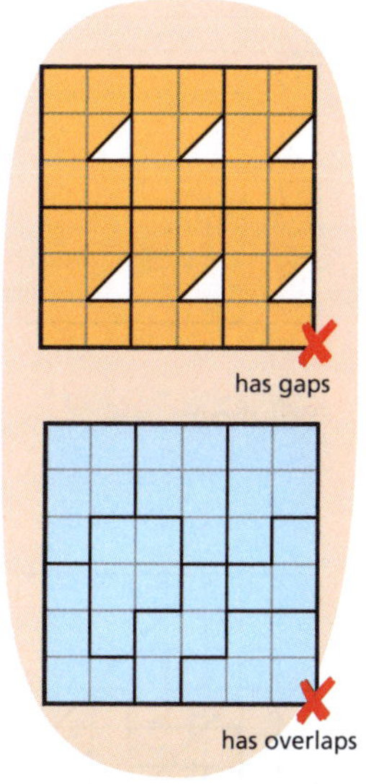

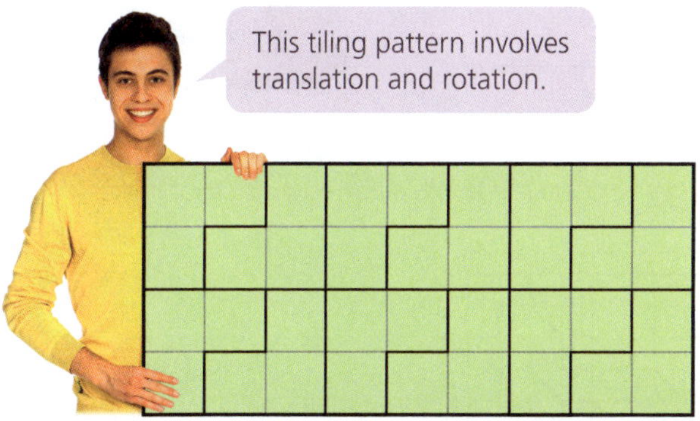

e.g. Name the transformations involved in the tiling pattern.

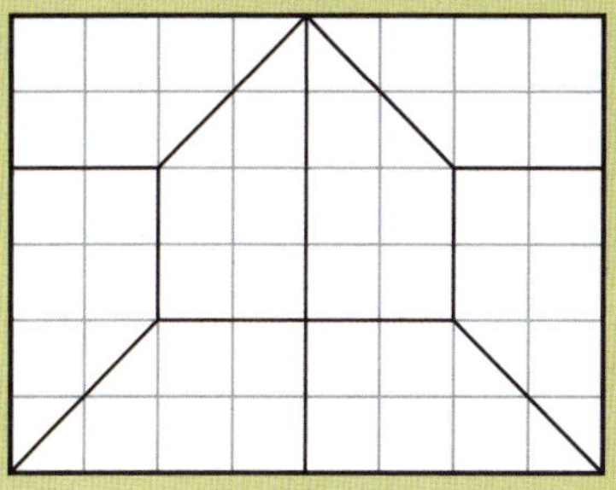

- reflection

  e.g. 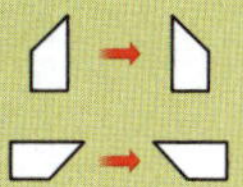

- rotation

  e.g. 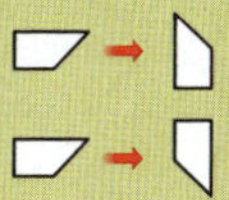

So, the transformations involved are **reflection** and **rotation**.

Application

Answer Jessica's question.

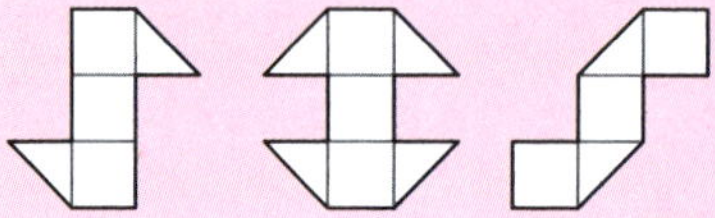

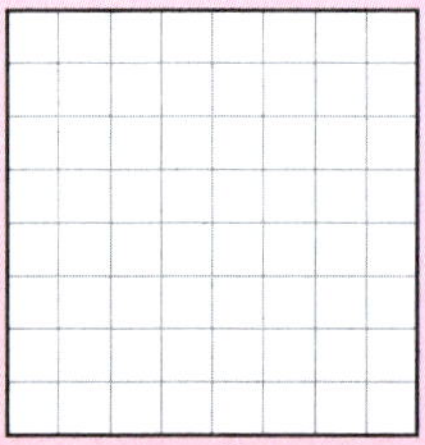

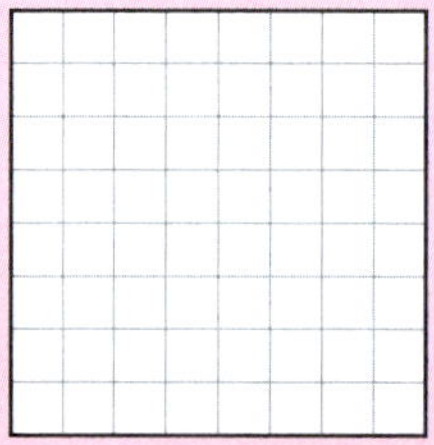

Solution:

To find the answer, try making tiling patterns with each figure so that there are no gaps or overlaps.

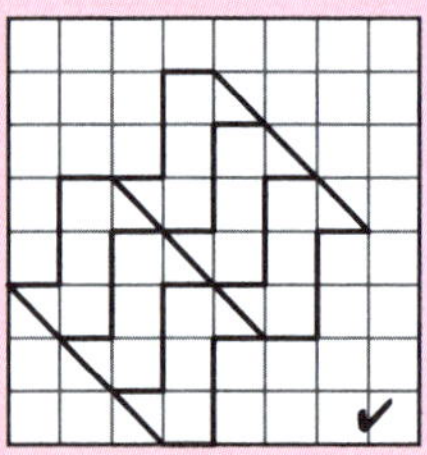

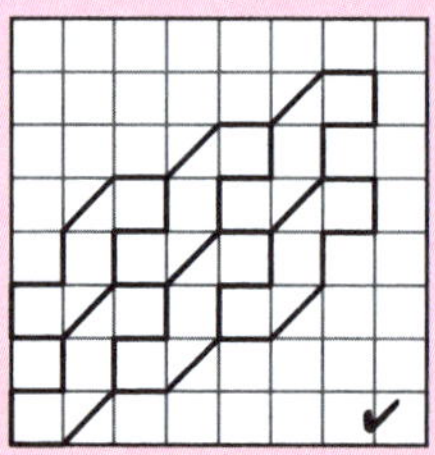

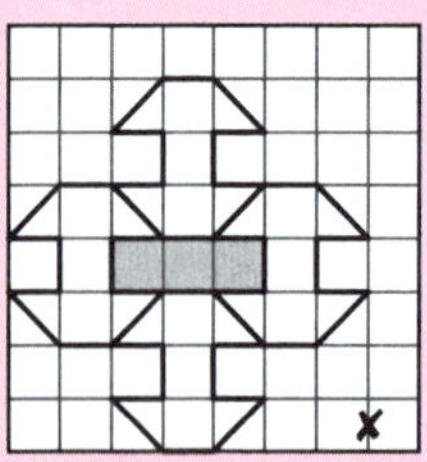

has gaps

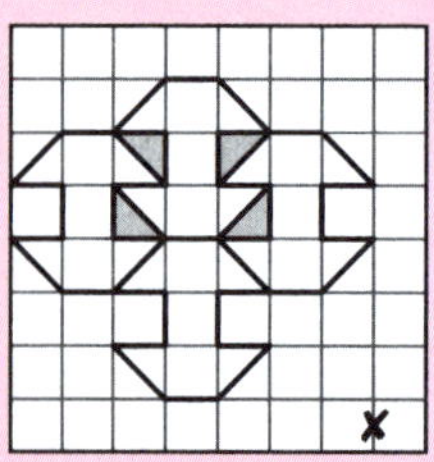

has gaps

Each of  and  forms a tiling pattern, but not 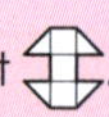.

Chapter 8

Patterning

8.1 Identifying, Extending, and Creating Patterns

In this unit, you will begin to incorporate term numbers into your descriptions of number patterns.

You should be familiar with identifying the pattern rules of patterns that involve addition, subtraction, multiplication, and division.

e.g. Describe the pattern.

Think Since the terms are decreasing, it must involve subtraction and/or division.

94 $\xrightarrow{\div 2}$ 47 $\xrightarrow{-1}$ 46 $\xrightarrow{\div 2}$ 23 $\xrightarrow{-1}$ 22 $\xrightarrow{\div 2}$ 11

Pattern rule: Start at 94. Divide by 2 and subtract 1 alternately.

e.g. Find the 8th term.

Think The last given term, 11, is the 6th term.

11 (6th term) $\xrightarrow{-1}$ 10 $\xrightarrow{\div 2}$ 5 (8th term)

The 8th term is **5**.

At this stage, you will learn to describe terms by referring to their term numbers.

Term Number	Term	
1	3	← 1 x 2 + 1
2	5	← 2 x 2 + 1
3	7	← 3 x 2 + 1
4	9	← 4 x 2 + 1

Pattern rule: Double the term number and add 1.

6th term: **6** x 2 + 1 = 13

Generally, it is much easier to determine the term once the pattern rule that involves term numbers is identified.

8.2 Graphing Patterns

In this unit, you will learn to model number patterns involving term numbers in graphs. This sets the foundation for higher level math when you will be required to model functions. It is, therefore, vital that you fully understand this concept.

You will learn to determine the term of a given term number and vice versa, using a graph.

You may extend the graph to help yourself answer questions about the graph.

e.g.

Pattern A

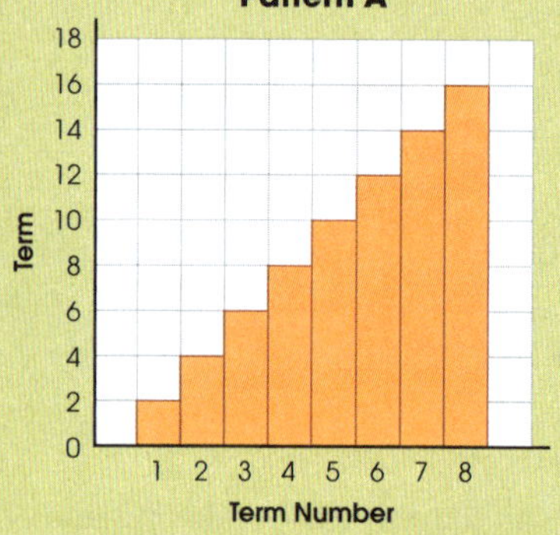

Find the term of the
- 5th term: 10
- 8th term: 16

Find the term number of
- 6: 3rd term
- 12: 6th term

The pattern may also be represented by a Cartesian coordinate plane.

Represent the term numbers using the x-coordinates and terms using the y-coordinates to get the coordinates.

Coordinates: (1,2), (2,4), (3,6), (4,8), (5,10), (6,12), (7,14), (8,16)

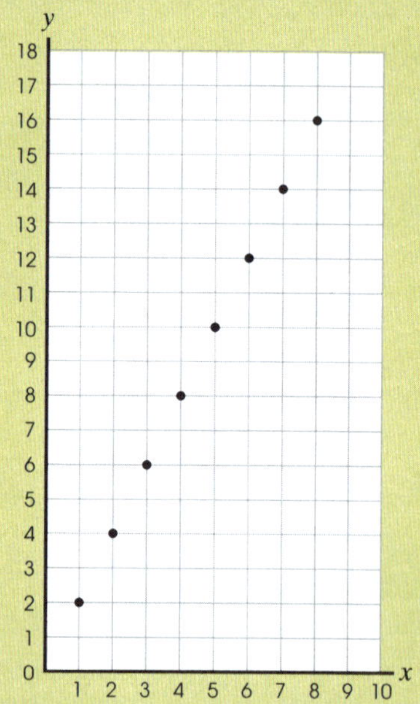

Chapter 9

Equations

9.1 Solving Equations

In this unit, you will learn to identify constants and variables in equations. This concept is important in mathematics. Additionally, you will be introduced to the concept of substitution which is essential for algebra.

Quantities in an Equation

Constant: a quantity that remains unchanged (e.g. 2, 99, 16)

Variable: a quantity that may change (e.g. l, w, A)

An equation can contain constants and/or variables.

e.g. Perimeter of a rectangle $= (l + w) \times 2$

variables (l, w) constant (2)

The length and width of the rectangle may change, but to find its perimeter, the sum of the length and width will always be multiplied by 2.

Solving Equations with One Variable

Way 1 Using the Guess-and-check Method

e.g. $2 + 12 \div a = 6$

Guess		Check
$a = 1$	$2 + 12 \div 1 = 14$	✗
$a = 2$	$2 + 12 \div 2 = 8$	✗
$a = 3$	$2 + 12 \div 3 = 6$	✓

So, $a =$ **3**.

Way 2 Using Counters

e.g. $2 + 12 \div a = 6$

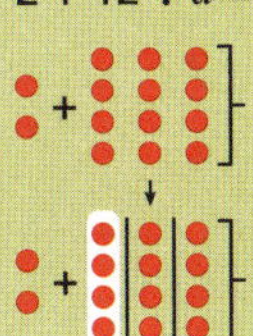

Think how to divide the group of 12 so that its quotient plus 2 is 6

Divide 12 into **3** groups of 4.
2 + 4 = 6.

So, $a =$ **3**.

Solving Equations with Two Variables

e.g. Given: $a + 2 = 5$

$a + 2 + b = 8$

Find: b

You may solve for b in two ways.

Way 1

$a + 2 + b = 8$

$5 + b = 8$ ← Replace $a + 2$ with 5 as given.

Now solve the equation in any way you prefer including guess-and-check, counters, or by inspection.

Since $5 + 3 = 8$, $b =$ __3__.

Way 2

1st Solve for a.

$a + 2 = 5$

$a = 3$

2nd Substitute the value of a into the 2nd equation.

$a + 2 + b = 8$

$3 + 2 + b = 8$

$5 + b = 8$

$b = 3$

So, $b =$ __3__.

Learn to solve equations in both ways since both ways require a thorough understanding of substitution, which is one of the most fundamental concepts in algebra.

Application

Write all the possible solutions for this equation:

$$2 \times m + n = 8$$

Solution:

At this level, you should only consider positive integers for the values of m and n. Start with $m = 0$.

Value of m	Substituting m into the Equation	Value of n
0	$2 \times 0 + n = 8 \rightarrow 0 + n = 8$	8
1	$2 \times 1 + n = 8 \rightarrow 2 + n = 8$	6
2	$2 \times 2 + n = 8 \rightarrow 4 + n = 8$	4
3	$2 \times 3 + n = 8 \rightarrow 6 + n = 8$	2
4	$2 \times 4 + n = 8 \rightarrow 8 + n = 8$	0
5	$2 \times 5 + n = 8 \rightarrow 10 + n = 8$	

↑ no positive integer can make the equation true

So, the possible values of m and n are 0 and 8, 1 and 6, 2 and 4, 3 and 2, and 4 and 0.

9.2 Formulating Equations

In this unit, you will learn to derive equations from word problems. You will also learn more about what letters and symbols represent in equations.

Try this example to learn how to formulate equations.

e.g.

Angie is 25 years old and her age is 2 times Tim's age plus 5. Find Tim's age.

1st Let Tim's age be t.

2nd Angie's age: 25

$2 \times t + 5$
(2 times Tim's age plus 5)

3rd $2 \times t + 5 = 25$

So, Tim's age is <u>10</u>.

Formulating an Equation

1st Identify the unknown quantity and assign a symbol or a letter to it.

2nd Find out how the other quantities relate to the unknown quantity.

3rd Write an equation to represent the word problem.

You may use any method you have learned to solve equations.

You should also be able to recognize that variables are not only used as unknown quantities but also as changing quantities.

The t in the example is an unknown quantity; whereas the variables A, l, and w in $A = l \times w$ are changing quantities because they describe the relationship among a rectangle's area, length, and width.

Application

Jake is 3 years older than Sean. The sum of their ages is 25. How old is Sean? Write two equations and find the answer.

Solution:

1st Jake is 3 years older than Sean.

$$j = s + 3$$

2nd The sum of the ages of Jake and Sean is 25.

$$j + s = 25$$

3rd Substitute j for $s + 3$ in $j + s = 25$.

$$\mathbf{j} + s = 25$$
$$\mathbf{s + 3} + s = 25$$
$$s + s + 3 = 25$$
$$2 \times s + 3 = 25$$

4th Find the answer using any method your child prefers, including the guess-and-check method.

Guess	Check (✔ or ✘)
10	$2 \times 10 + 3 = 23$ ✘
11	$2 \times 11 + 3 = 25$ ✔

So, Sean is 11 years old.

Chapter 10

Data Management

10.1 Mean, Median, and Mode

In Grade 6, you are expected to demonstrate a complete understanding of mean, median, and mode, and be able to apply them in analyzing different sets of data.

The weights of the cookies

80 g 88.6 g 79.3 g 80 g 82.5 g 81.6 g

Mean

the sum of a set of data values divided by the total number of data values

Median

the middle value in a set of data that are ordered from least to greatest (if there is an even number of values, the median is the mean of the two middle values.)

Put the data in order:

79.3 g 80 g (80 g 81.6 g) 82.5 g 88.6 g

The median is the mean of these two values.

Mode

the value(s) in a set of data that occur(s) most often

mean weight

total weight = 80 + 88.6 + 79.3 + 80 + 82.5 + 81.6

= 492

mean = 492 ÷ 6 = 82

mean weight = **82 g**

median weight

median = (80 + 81.6) ÷ 2

= 80.8

median weight = **80.8 g**

mode weight

mode = 80 (the most common value)

mode weight = **80 g**

Application

Find the mean, median, and mode scores for Jenny. Write about her overall performance.

Jenny Dion

Quiz	Scores
1	82
2	98
3	85
4	20
5	80
6	79

Solution:

To find the mean, add to find the total score and divide the sum by the number of quizzes.

Mean: $(82 + 98 + 85 + 20 + 80 + 79) \div 6$
$= 444 \div 6$
$= 74$

The mean is 74.

To find the median, put the scores in order from least to greatest. The middle value is the median.

20 79 80 82 85 98

median: $(80 + 82) \div 2 = 81$

The median is 81.

To find the mode, look for the data value that appears most often. Since all scores appear once, there is no mode in this set of data.

Jenny's scores started off in the 80s and 90s, and dropped to 20 on her 4th quiz but climbed back up in the 5th and 6th quizzes.

Jenny's overall performance is in the 70s and 80s.

10.2 Interpreting Graphs

In order to understand how to interpret information shown in graphs, you must learn how to read them correctly. Below are the key points that you should remember when reading graphs.

Interpreting Graphs

1. Identify what the graph represents based on
   - the title
   - the label on the x-axis
   - the label on the y-axis

2. Check the scale for each graph element.
   - pictographs – Check the legend to see how many units each picture represents.
   - bar graphs / line graphs – Check the increments along the y-axis to see the scale that is applied.

3. Locate the information that you need in graphs. For bar graphs, use a ruler and draw a line from the top of a bar to the scale. If needed, create a table or chart to organize the information. These techniques help prevent misreading information in graphs.

e.g. Compare the scales of the bar graphs.

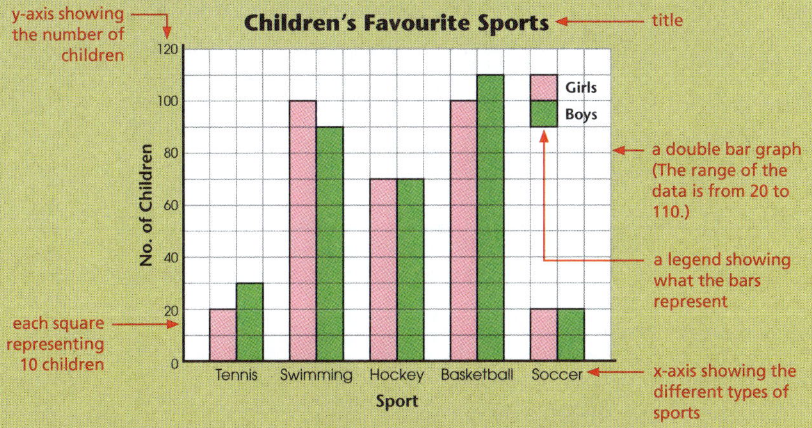

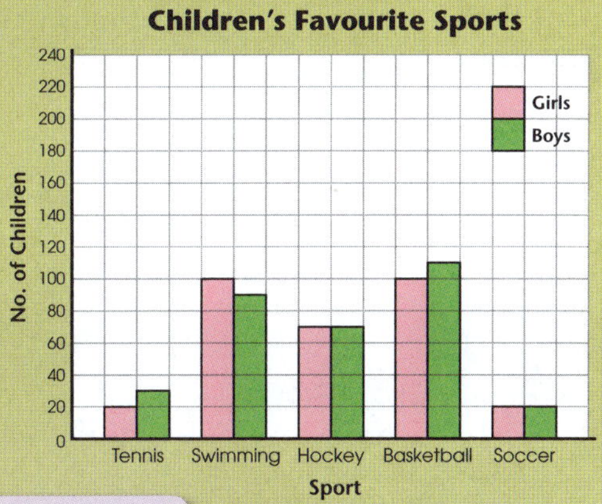

These two graphs represent the same set of data using different scales. You can clearly see in the first graph that a lot more children like basketball than tennis. This difference, however, is not as obvious in the second graph. Therefore, someone using the second graph may conclude that the difference between the number of children who like basketball and those who like tennis is smaller than it actually is.

Differences in scale can influence conclusions drawn from a graph.

Pay attention to the scale to ensure that it conveys the information the way you want it to.

10.3 Making Graphs

To present data graphically, you have to decide which type of graph is appropriate. Below are some guidelines to help you make this decision.

Choosing Which Type of Graph to Use:

- **Pictograph:**
  uses symbols to display data; suitable for showing data values that are multiples of a number

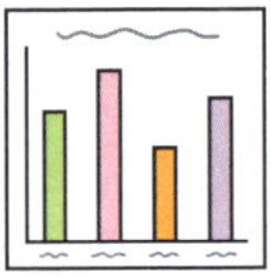

- **Bar Graph:**
  uses bars to display categories; suitable for making comparisons among data

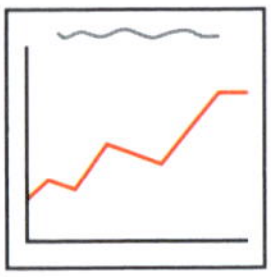

- **Line Graph:**
  useful for showing the trend that the data follows over time

- **Circle Graph:**
  suitable for showing data that are parts of a whole

No matter which type of graph you use, don't forget to give it a title, labels, and a legend.

Chapter 11
Probability

11.1 Finding Probability

This unit focuses on identifying the possible outcomes of a probability experiment and determining the probability of an outcome. You are expected to be able to express the probability of an event as a fraction and understand that the probability must have a value from 0 (impossible) to 1 (certain).

$$\text{Probability of an Event} = \frac{\text{No. of Favourable Outcomes}}{\text{Total No. of Possible Outcomes}}$$

Probability

0	$\frac{1}{2}$	1
impossible	equal	certain

The more likely an event will occur, the greater the fraction is.

e.g. Roll a dice numbered from 1 to 6. What is the probability of rolling an odd number?

Possible outcomes:
1, 2, 3, 4, 5, 6 ← 6 in total

Favourable outcomes (odd numbers):
1, 3, 5

Probability of rolling an odd number: $\frac{3}{6}$ (3 ← 3 favourable outcomes; 6 ← 6 possible outcomes)

In some cases, you will need to make use of a tree diagram or a chart to find all the possible outcomes. You should practise drawing tree diagrams or charts if you have difficulty creating them.

e.g. Flip a coin three times. What is the probability of getting 2 heads and 1 tail?

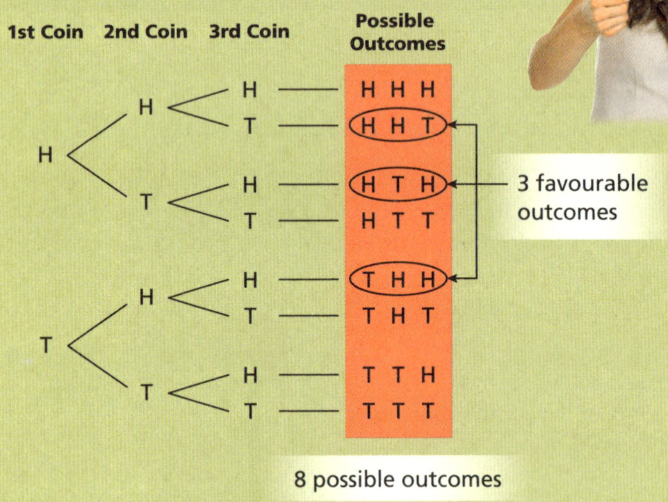

The probability of getting 2 heads and 1 tail is $\frac{3}{8}$.

Application

Eva has a box of 20 balls. The balls are red, green, blue, and yellow. If Eva draws a ball from the box, the probability of getting a red ball is $\frac{1}{10}$, a green ball is $\frac{2}{5}$, and a blue ball is $\frac{1}{4}$. What is the probability of getting a yellow ball?

Solution:

(The probability of getting a yellow ball is simply $1 - \frac{1}{4} - \frac{1}{10} - \frac{2}{5}$, which is $\frac{1}{4}$. However, this concept can be difficult. So, follow the steps below to derive the answer.)

1st Find the number of balls there are in each colour.

Number of red balls: $\frac{1}{4} = \frac{\boxed{5}}{20}$ (× 5) ← no. of red balls

Number of green balls: $\frac{1}{10} = \frac{\boxed{2}}{20}$ (× 2) ← no. of green balls

Number of blue balls: $\frac{2}{5} = \frac{\boxed{8}}{20}$ (× 4) ← no. of blue balls

Number of yellow balls: $20 - 5 - 2 - 8 = 5$

So, there are 5 yellow balls.

2nd Find the probability of getting a yellow ball.

Probability: $\frac{5}{20} = \frac{1}{4}$

So, the probability of getting a yellow ball is $\frac{1}{4}$.

11.2 Predicting the Frequency of an Outcome

In this unit, you will learn to predict the frequency of an outcome in a probability experiment using the probability of that outcome. You can apply the concept of equivalent fractions to find the frequency of an outcome.

Predicting the Frequency of an Outcome

1st Find the probability of an outcome.

2nd Find the frequency of the outcome using equivalent fractions.

e.g. How many times do you think the pointer will land on red?

The probability of landing on red is $\frac{2}{5}$.

For every 5 spins, 2 of them will land on red.

$$\frac{2}{5} = \frac{\boxed{40}}{100} \quad (\times 20 \text{ numerator and denominator})$$

5 equal sections;
2 sections are red

If the spinner is spun 100 times, the pointer will land on red about **40** times.

Grade 7

Chapter 1

Multiples and Factors

1.1 Multiples

In this unit, you will learn what a multiple is and determine the multiples of a given integer using different approaches.

Finding Multiples

A multiple of an integer is the product of the integer and another integer.

e.g. Find the first 5 multiples of 2.

Think Multiply 2 by the numbers 1 to 5.

2 x 1 = 2
2 x 2 = 4
2 x 3 = 6 ← multiples of 2
2 x 4 = 8
2 x 5 = 10

Multiples of 2: **2, 4, 6, 8, 10**

You should realize that multiples of 2 are basically products of 2 and other integers.

2 x 0.5 = 1 ← not a multiple of 2

Even though 1 is the product of 2 and 0.5, it is not a multiple of 2 because 0.5 is not an integer.

A hundreds chart is a useful tool for finding multiples by identifying the patterns they make. Try the activity below and do the questions to consolidate your understanding of multiples.

1	2	3	4	5	6	7	8	9	10
11	12	13	14	15	16	17	18	19	20
21	22	23	24	25	26	27	28	29	30
31	32	33	34	35	36	37	38	39	40
41	42	43	44	45	46	47	48	49	50
51	52	53	54	55	56	57	58	59	60
61	62	63	64	65	66	67	68	69	70
71	72	73	74	75	76	77	78	79	80
81	82	83	84	85	86	87	88	89	90
91	92	93	94	95	96	97	98	99	100

Activity Colour the multiples of 3 and 5 with the specified colours.

multiples of 3

multiples of 5

Try to identify a pattern when finding multiples. This will help you find multiples more efficiently as the numbers get bigger.

Questions

1. Describe the pattern each set of multiples forms.
2. Are there any multiples that are common to both 3 and 5? If so, what are they?

The multiples that are common to both numbers are called common multiples. The common multiples of 3 and 5 are 15, 30, 45, 60, 75, and 90. The concept and usage of common multiples will be further discussed in Grade 8.

Application

Gate A is opened every 6 minutes for visitors to Merryland and Gate B is opened every 8 minutes to Dreamland.

If both gates are opened at noon, what time are both gates opened at the same time again?

Solution:

For Gate A, find multiples of 6. For Gate B, find multiples of 8.

Open times for Gate A:

12 : 00 12 : 06 12 : 12 12 : 18 12 : 24 12 : 30

multiples of 6

Open times for Gate B:

12 : 00 12 : 08 12 : 16 12 : 24 12 : 32 12 : 40

multiples of 8

24 is a common multiple of 6 and 8. So, both gates are opened at the same time again at 12:24 p.m.

1.2 Factors

In this unit, you will be introduced to factors and learn to find them using different strategies.

Finding Factors

Factors are integers that form a product when multiplied. So, factors of a number are integers that, when multiplied, form the original number.

Once you grasp this concept, you can try the strategy below. This strategy allows you to skip the process of writing all the multiplication sentences.

e.g. Find the factors of 12.

1st Write down the multiplication sentences that have products of 12. Start from 1.

2nd Stop when the factors repeat.

3rd List the factors from least to greatest.

12 = **1** x **12**
12 = **2** x **6**
12 = **3** x **4**
12 = 4 x 3 ← same as 3 x 4; stop

Factors of 12: **1, 2, 3, 4, 6, 12**

e.g. Find the factors of 15.

Think 1 x 15 = 15
Write 1 and 15; space them out.
↓
Think 3 x 5 = 15
Write 3 and 5.
↓
Think 5 x 3 = 15 (same as 3 x 5; stop)

Factors of 15: **1, 3, 5, 15**

Remember, every number has at least two factors: 1 and itself.

Application

Carol is putting 15 red crayons and 20 blue crayons into separate boxes. The boxes hold the same number of crayons. How many crayons does each box hold? How many boxes are needed for the crayons in each colour?

Solution:

Since each box holds the same number of crayons, the number of crayons in each box must be a common factor of 15 and 20.

Factors of 15: 1, 3, 5, 15
Factors of 20: 1, 2, 4, 5, 10, 20

Common factors of 15 and 20: 1, 5

Each box holds more than 1 crayon, so there must be 5 crayons in each box.

Number of boxes for red crayons: $15 \div 5 = 3$
Number of boxes for blue crayons: $20 \div 5 = 4$

3 boxes are needed for red crayons and 4 boxes are needed for blue crayons.

Chapter 2

Perfect Squares and Square Roots

2.1 Perfect Squares

In this unit, you will learn various ways of understanding perfect squares and also strategies to evaluate whether or not a given number is a perfect square.

Finding Squares of Numbers

A perfect square is the product of a number that multiplies itself, or in other words, the square of a number.

e.g. Find the square of 3.

Square of 3 $= 3^2$
$= 3 \times 3$
$= 9$

The square of 3 is written as 3^2. The "2" is an exponent, which denotes that the "3" multiplies itself "2" times.

3^2 is read as 3 squared or 3 to the power of 2.

You may find it beneficial to relate a perfect square with the area of a square.

Try interpreting this as "find the area of a square with a side length of 3 units".

Area = 3 units x 3 units
= 9 units squared

Once you grasp the concept, you can investigate the relationship between a number and its square using the table below.

What is the relationship between each number and its square?

Perfect Squares

$11^2 = 121$

$12^2 = 144$

$13^2 = 169$

$14^2 = 196$

$15^2 = 225$

$16^2 = 256$

$17^2 = 289$

$18^2 = 324$

$19^2 = 361$

$20^2 = 400$

$21^2 = 441$

$22^2 = 484$

$23^2 = 529$

$24^2 = 576$

$25^2 = 625$

Hint 1 Compare the ones digits.

Hint 2 $3^2 = 9$ and $13^2 = 169$

The relationship between a number and its square lies in their ones digits. See the example below.

e.g.

$14^2 = 196$

$4 \times 4 = 16$

$24^2 = 576$

$4 \times 4 = 16$

Understanding this relationship will help you judge whether or not an answer is reasonable. It will also help you determine the square root of a number (as introduced in the next unit).

Although not necessary, it is beneficial for you to be familiar with perfect squares, meaning that you would be able to identify whether or not a number is a perfect square without doing any calculations.

2.2 Square Roots

This unit introduces the concept of square roots. You will learn to find square roots using different strategies.

Finding Square Roots

The number that multiplies itself to get a squared number is a square root.

e.g. Find the square root of 9.

Square root of 9 = $\sqrt{9}$ ← $\sqrt{\ }$ denotes "square root of".

= 3 ← 3 x 3 = 9, so 3 is the square root of 9.

You may find it difficult to find square roots. Below are two methods that may help you.

For small perfect squares:

1st Draw a square with an area equal to the squared number.

2nd Find its side length. The side length is the square root of the squared number.

e.g. Find $\sqrt{25}$.

Area:
25 units squared

Side Length:
5 units

So, $\sqrt{25}$ = **5** .

For large perfect squares:

- Refer to the strategy you learned on p. 336. The strategy helps narrow down the number of possible square roots.

e.g. Find $\sqrt{225}$.

Think The ones digit of the square root must be 5. So, the possible square roots are 5, 15, and 25. 5^2 is too small and 25^2 is too big, so try 15^2.

$15^2 = 225$

So, $\sqrt{225}$ = **15** .

Application

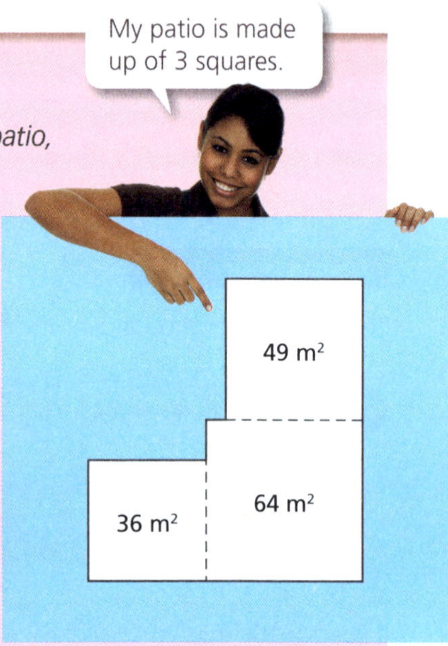

If Tracy wants to put a fence around the patio, how much fencing is needed?

Solution:

First, find the side length of each square.

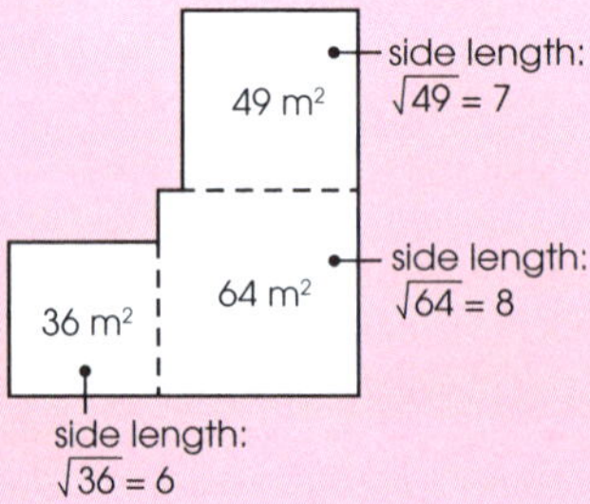

Add the measurements.

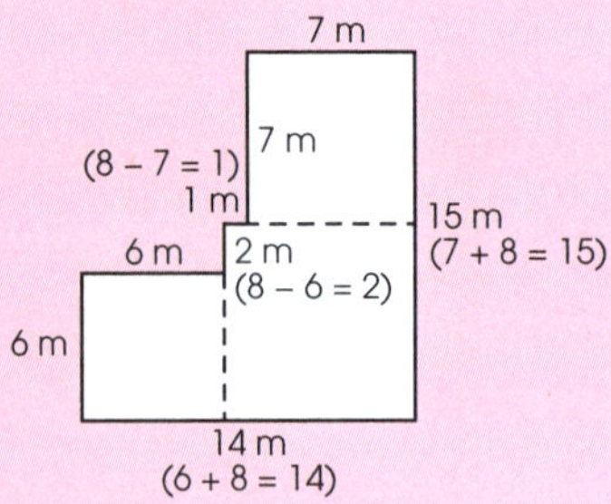

Perimeter: $7 + 15 + 14 + 6 + 6 + 2 + 1 + 7 = 58$

58 m of fencing is needed.

Chapter 3

Integers

3.1 Identifying and Comparing Integers

In this unit, you will learn about the properties of integers and the various strategies to compare them.

Positive numbers are denoted by "+", which is often omitted. Negative numbers are denoted by "–", which must always be included.

Identifying Integers

Properties of Integers

- a number that has no fractional parts

e.g. $\frac{1}{2}$ ✗ 0.27 ✗ 9 ✓

- can be either a positive or a negative number

e.g. 3 (positive) -2 (negative)

Comparing Integers

A number line is a useful tool for you to use when comparing both positive and negative integers.

1st Draw a number line that includes all the integers to be compared.

2nd Mark the integers being compared on the number line.

3rd The integer to the far left is the least; the one to the far right is the greatest.

e.g. Put -2, -4, and 3 in order from least to greatest.

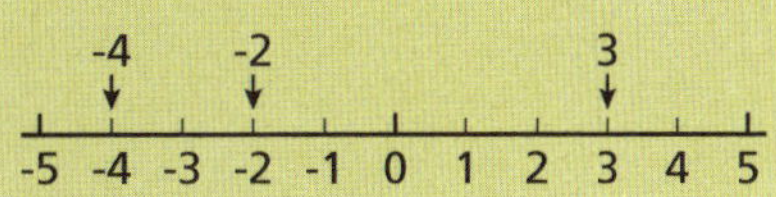

So, **-4 < -2 < 3**.

You may compare integers by inspection. To do so, familiarize yourself with the facts and suggestions listed below.

1. Positive integers are always greater than negative integers. So, compare them separately in two groups.
2. For negative integers, the integer that is closer to 0 is greater (which is the opposite for positive integers).

e.g. Put 5, -2, 2, and -5 in order from greatest to least.

Think Compare the positive integers first.

$5 > 2$

↑ greater

Think Compare the negative integers.

$-2 > -5$

↑ greater (-2 is closer to 0 than -5.)

So, $5 > 2 > -2 > -5$.

Application

Clara, Dad, and I are walking to the campsite. I am 6 m ahead of Dad, and Clara is 2 m behind Dad. How far apart are Clara and I?

Solution:

Draw a number line and locate the three people.

1st Locate Dad at 0.

2nd Locate the boy at 6 for being 6 m ahead.

3rd Locate Clara at -2 for being 2 m behind.

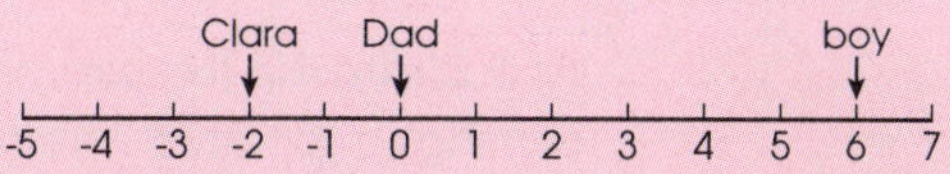

There are 8 units between -2 and 6. So, Clara and the boy are 8 m apart.

3.2 Adding and Subtracting Integers

This unit introduces you to addition and subtraction of positive and negative integers. We highly recommend that you do the examples as the concepts may be difficult to understand. Once you understand the concepts, learn the rules for accurate calculations.

Adding an Integer

Use a number line to illustrate the difference between adding a positive integer and adding a negative integer.

e.g. $1 + 3 = ?$

$1 + (-3) = ?$

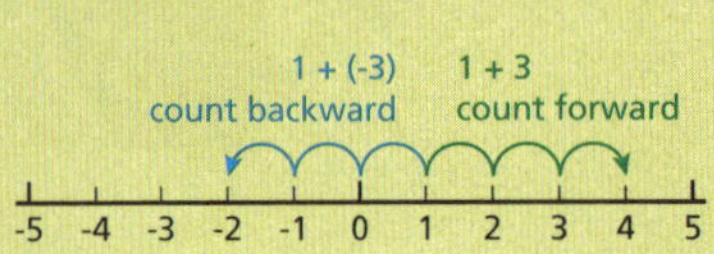

$1 + 3 = \underline{4}$

$1 + (-3) = \underline{-2}$

Does $1 - 3 = 1 + (-3)$?

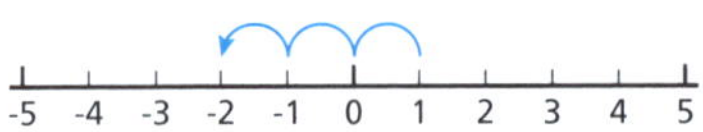

Yes, $1 - 3 = 1 + (-3)$.

As illustrated in the example, when adding a positive integer, count forward; when adding a negative integer, count backward.

Adding a negative number is subtraction. By comparing $1 + (-3)$ with $1 - 3$, you'll realize that even though they look different, they are actually the same.

Once you understand that adding a negative number is simply subtraction, you may try adding integers without using number lines.

e.g.
$8 + (-6)$
$= 8 - 6$
$= 2$

e.g.
$-4 + (-2)$
$= -4 - 2$
$= -6$

Subtracting an Integer

Subtraction works differently from addition. When subtracting a positive integer, count backward; when subtracting a negative integer, count forward.

e.g. $1 - 3 = ?$

$1 - (-3) = ?$

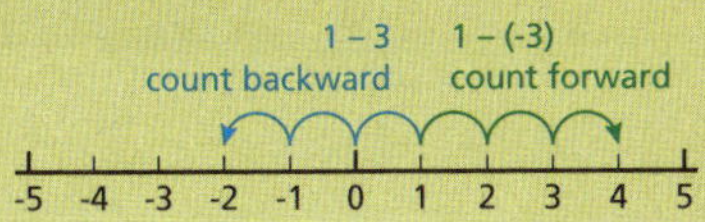

$1 - 3 = \underline{-2}$

$1 - (-3) = \underline{4}$

Does $1 - (-3) = 1 + 3$?

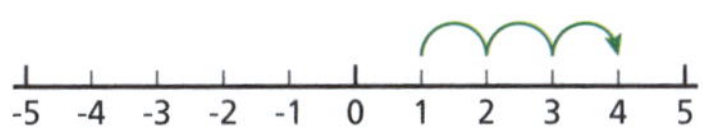

Yes, $1 - (-3) = 1 + 3$.

Remember these themes rules:

Rules

\+ \+ ➡ \+

− − ➡ \+

\+ − ➡ −

− \+ ➡ −

Two like signs yield a positive sign (addition).

e.g.

$-4 + (+2)$
$= -4 + 2$
$= -2$

$-4 - (-2)$
$= -4 + 2$
$= -2$

Two unlike signs yield a negative sign (subtraction).

e.g.

$-4 + (-2)$
$= -4 - 2$
$= -6$

$-4 - (+2)$
$= -4 - 2$
$= -6$

Chapter 4

Fractions

4.1 Representing and Comparing Fractions

In this unit, you will apply your knowledge of equivalent fractions to compare fractions with different denominators. Make sure you are confident in finding equivalent fractions before learning to compare fractions with different denominators.

Finding Equivalent Fractions

Before comparing fractions, you must be able to find equivalent fractions.

To find an equivalent fraction, multiply or divide both the numerator and the denominator by the same number.

e.g. Find two equivalent fractions of $\frac{4}{12}$.

$$\frac{4}{12} \overset{\times 2}{=} \frac{8}{24} \qquad \frac{4}{12} \overset{\div 2}{=} \frac{2}{6}$$

So, $\frac{8}{24}$ **and** $\frac{2}{6}$ are equivalent to $\frac{4}{12}$.

In this example, $\frac{2}{6}$ is a simplified form of $\frac{4}{12}$.

e.g. Simplify $\frac{2}{6}$.

$$\frac{2}{6} \overset{\div 2}{=} \frac{1}{3}$$

To simplify a fraction, divide both the numerator and the denominator by the same number.

In this example, $\frac{1}{3}$ is not only a simplified form of $\frac{2}{6}$, but it is also the simplest form because the numerator and the denominator cannot be further divided.

Now that you are able to find equivalent fractions, you are ready to compare fractions with different denominators.

Comparing Fractions with Different Denominators

1st Rewrite the fractions so that they have the same denominator.

2nd Compare the numerators. The fraction that has the greatest numerator is the greatest.

e.g. Put the fractions in order from least to greatest.

$\frac{7}{8}$ $\frac{2}{3}$ $\frac{3}{4}$

Think 24 is divisible by all three denominators (i.e. 3, 4, and 8). So, find each equivalent fraction with a denominator of 24.

$$\frac{7}{8} = \frac{21}{24} \ (\times 3) \qquad \frac{2}{3} = \frac{16}{24} \ (\times 8) \qquad \frac{3}{4} = \frac{18}{24} \ (\times 6)$$

Since $\frac{16}{24} < \frac{18}{24} < \frac{21}{24}$, so $\mathbf{\frac{2}{3} < \frac{3}{4} < \frac{7}{8}}$.

If two fractions have different denominators but the same numerator, then the fraction with the smaller denominator is greater.

e.g. Compare $\frac{2}{5}$ and $\frac{2}{6}$.

$\frac{2}{5}$ $\frac{2}{6}$

$5 < 6$

So, **$\frac{2}{5}$ is greater than $\frac{2}{6}$**.

Application

Eva ate $\frac{2}{4}$ of her pizza and Max ate $\frac{12}{16}$ of his. If Joanna cut her pizza into 8 slices and she ate more pizza than Eva but less than Max, how much of her pizza did she eat?

Solution:

To determine how many of the 8 slices of pizza Joanna ate, convert Eva's and Max's amounts to fractions with a denominator of 8.

Eva: $\frac{2}{4} = \frac{4}{\mathbf{8}}$ (× 2 numerator and denominator)   Max: $\frac{12}{16} = \frac{6}{\mathbf{8}}$ (÷ 2 numerator and denominator)

Since Joanna ate more than Eva ($\frac{4}{8}$) but less than Max ($\frac{6}{8}$), she must have eaten $\frac{5}{8}$ of her pizza.

4.2 Adding Fractions

In this unit, you will learn to add fractions with the same and different denominators. Both this unit and the next unit rely heavily upon the concepts of equivalent fractions and comparing fractions with different denominators. Make sure that you are able to apply these two concepts before proceeding.

Adding Fractions with Common Denominators

Use diagrams to learn the concept of adding fractions. Follow the steps below.

1st Draw and colour to show the first fraction.

2nd Colour the second fraction in the same diagram.

3rd The coloured part is the sum.

e.g. $\frac{1}{5} + \frac{2}{5} = ?$

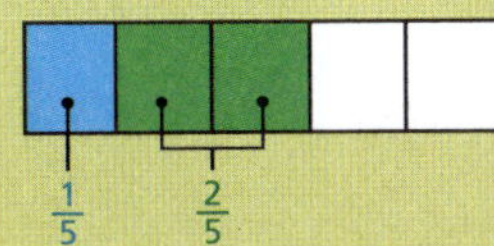

$\frac{3}{5}$ is coloured.

So, $\frac{1}{5} + \frac{2}{5} = \underline{\mathbf{\frac{3}{5}}}$.

Once you grasp the concept, try adding fractions without the use of diagrams.

To add fractions with like denominators, keep the denominators the same and add the numerators.

e.g.

$$\frac{1}{5} + \frac{2}{5}$$

$$= \frac{1+2}{5}$$ ← Add the numerators. ← Keep the denominator the same.

$$= \frac{3}{5}$$ ← the sum of 1 and 2

So, $\frac{1}{5} + \frac{2}{5} = \underline{\mathbf{\frac{3}{5}}}$.

Adding Fractions with Different Denominators

Before starting this section, make sure you are able to add fractions that have common denominators. To add fractions with different denominators, follow these steps.

1st Find a multiple that is common to the denominators of both fractions.

2nd Find the equivalent fraction of each fraction with the common multiple as the denominator.

3rd Add the numerators.

It is good practice to write the answers in simplest form. Some questions may require answers to be written in simplest form. So, remember to read questions carefully.

e.g. $\frac{1}{3} + \frac{1}{4} = ?$

1st 12 is a common multiple of 3 and 4.

2nd $\frac{1}{3} = \frac{4}{12}$ and $\frac{1}{4} = \frac{3}{12}$

3rd $\frac{4}{12} + \frac{3}{12}$

$= \frac{4+3}{12}$

$= \frac{7}{12}$

So, $\frac{1}{3} + \frac{1}{4} = \underline{\mathbf{\frac{7}{12}}}$.

Application

Joseph eats $\frac{1}{2}$ of a pizza and my sister and I each eat $\frac{1}{8}$ more than he does. At least how many pizzas need to be ordered for us?

Solution:

Joseph: $\frac{1}{2}$; girl: $\frac{1}{2} + \frac{1}{8}$; sister: $\frac{1}{2} + \frac{1}{8}$

$$\text{Total amount: } \frac{1}{2} + \frac{1}{2} + \frac{1}{8} + \frac{1}{2} + \frac{1}{8}$$

$$= \frac{4}{8} + \frac{4}{8} + \frac{1}{8} + \frac{4}{8} + \frac{1}{8}$$

$$= \frac{4+4+1+4+1}{8}$$

$$= \frac{14}{8}$$

$$= 1\frac{3}{4}$$

$1\frac{3}{4}$ of pizzas are needed, but $\frac{3}{4}$ of a pizza cannot be ordered.
So, at least 2 pizzas need to be ordered.

4.3 Subtracting Fractions

In this unit, you will learn to subtract fractions with the same and different denominators. The concepts and strategies applied are similar to the addition of fractions. You should not have trouble if you are comfortable with the previous unit.

Subtracting Fractions with Common Denominators

Follow the steps below to learn the concept of subtracting fractions using diagrams.

e.g. $\frac{3}{4} - \frac{1}{4} = ?$

1st Show the fraction to be subtracted in a diagram.

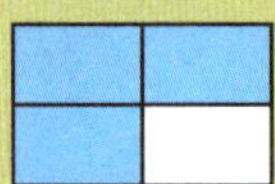

$\frac{3}{4}$

2nd Cross out the number of parts to be subtracted.

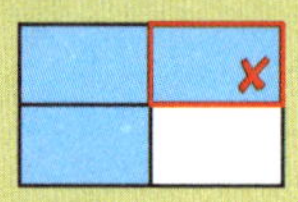

$\frac{1}{4}$ is crossed out.

3rd The remaining part is the difference.

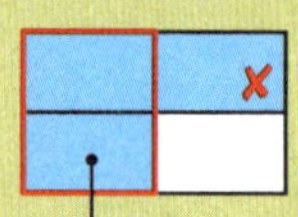

$\frac{2}{4}$, which is $\frac{1}{2}$, is remaining.

So, $\frac{3}{4} - \frac{1}{4} = \underline{\mathbf{\frac{1}{2}}}$.

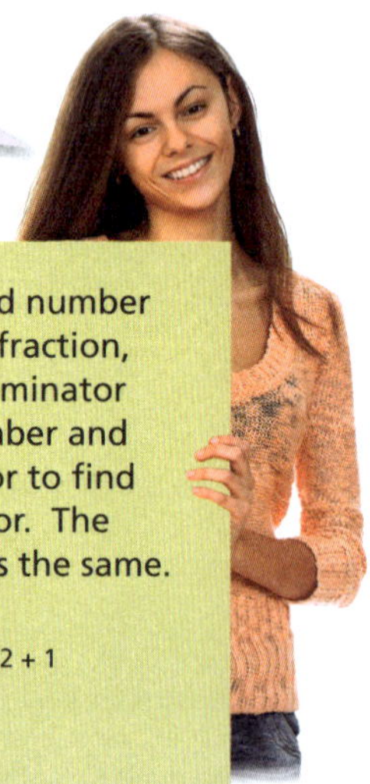

If there are mixed numbers in a subtraction, convert them into improper fractions first.

e.g. $2\frac{1}{4} - 1\frac{3}{4}$

$= \frac{9}{4} - \frac{7}{4}$ ← Convert the mixed numbers into improper fractions.

$= \frac{9-7}{4}$ ← Subtract the numerators.

$= \frac{2}{4}$

$= \frac{1}{2}$

So, $2\frac{1}{4} - 1\frac{3}{4} = \underline{\mathbf{\frac{1}{2}}}$.

To convert a mixed number into an improper fraction, multiply the denominator by the whole number and add the numerator to find the new numerator. The denominator stays the same.

e.g. $2\frac{1}{4} = \frac{9}{4}$ ← $4 \times 2 + 1$

Subtracting Fractions with Different Denominators

Similar to addition, if the fractions in a subtraction have different denominators, find their equivalent fractions that share the same denominator.

1st Find a common multiple of the denominators.

2nd Find the equivalent fraction of each fraction with the common multiple as the denominator.

3rd Subtract the numerators.

e.g. $3\frac{2}{5} - \frac{5}{6}$

$= \frac{17}{5} - \frac{5}{6}$ ← Convert the mixed number into an improper fraction.

$= \frac{102}{30} - \frac{25}{30}$ ← equivalent fractions with a common denominator

$= \frac{77}{30}$

$= 2\frac{17}{30}$ ← simplest form

In the example, $3\frac{2}{5}$ is converted into an improper fraction, and then to its equivalent fraction. Alternatively, you may find the equivalent fraction of $3\frac{2}{5}$ first, and then convert that into an improper fraction.

Application

For what fraction of an hour will Carly practise tomorrow if she practised for $\frac{7}{8}$ of an hour today?

Solution:

There are 60 minutes in an hour. 15 minutes of 60 minutes can be written as $\frac{15}{60}$. To do the calculation, simplify $\frac{15}{60}$ first.

$$\frac{15}{60} \underset{\div 15}{\overset{\div 15}{=}} \frac{1}{4}$$

Fraction of Carly's practice tomorrow: $\frac{7}{8} - \frac{1}{4}$

$$= \frac{7}{8} - \frac{2}{8}$$

$$= \frac{7-2}{8}$$

$$= \frac{5}{8}$$

Carly will practise for $\frac{5}{8}$ of an hour tomorrow.

4.4 Multiplying Fractions

This unit introduces the concept of multiplication with fractions. You will learn to multiply fractions with integers and other fractions.

Relating Multiplication to Addition

As you have learned, multiplication is simply repeated addition. Use this relationship to learn the concept of multiplication of fractions.

e.g. $\frac{1}{6}+\frac{1}{6}+\frac{1}{6}=?$

$\frac{1}{6}+\frac{1}{6}+\frac{1}{6}$

$=\frac{1}{6}\times 3$

$=\frac{3}{6}$

$=\frac{1}{2}$

Adding $\frac{1}{6}$ three times is the same as $\frac{1}{6}\times 3$.

To find the product of fractions, multiply the numerators and the denominators separately.

e.g. $\frac{2}{5}\times\frac{1}{4}$

$=\frac{2\times 1}{5\times 4}$ ← Multiply the numerators. ← Multiply the denominators.

$=\frac{2}{20}$ ← product of 2 and 1 ← product of 5 and 4

$=\frac{1}{10}$

e.g. $\frac{3}{7}\times 2$

$=\frac{3}{7}\times\frac{2}{1}$ ← 2 is the same as $\frac{2}{1}$.

$=\frac{3\times 2}{7\times 1}$

$=\frac{6}{7}$

Once the concept is understood, it is generally quite simple to multiply fractions because there is no need to find equivalent fractions as in addition and subtraction.

Application

I will eat $\frac{3}{8}$ of this pumpkin pie today and $\frac{1}{3}$ of the remaining pie tomorrow.

How much of the pie will be left?

Solution:

Pie remaining after today: $1 - \frac{3}{8}$

$$= \frac{8}{8} - \frac{3}{8}$$
$$= \frac{8-3}{8}$$
$$= \frac{5}{8}$$

Pie eaten tomorrow: $\frac{5}{8} \times \frac{1}{3}$

$$= \frac{5 \times 1}{8 \times 3}$$
$$= \frac{5}{24}$$

Pie remaining after tomorrow: $\frac{5}{8} - \frac{5}{24}$

$$= \frac{15}{24} - \frac{5}{24}$$
$$= \frac{15-5}{24}$$
$$= \frac{10}{24}$$
$$= \frac{5}{12}$$

$\frac{5}{12}$ of the pie will be left.

4.5 Dividing Fractions

This unit introduces the concept of division with fractions. You will first visualize the concept through simple examples and activities. You will then learn to apply reciprocals and use multiplication to solve division problems involving fractions.

Dividing Fractions Using Diagrams

You may be familiar with the concept of division with whole numbers. However, you may still find it difficult to understand how fractional parts are divided. Go through the example below to reinforce this concept.

e.g. $1 \div \frac{1}{2} = ?$

$1 \div \frac{1}{2}$ is the same as saying,

"How many ◖ are there in ● ?"

You should be able to tell that the answer is 2.

So, $1 \div \frac{1}{2} = \underline{\mathbf{2}}$.

Do the division below with the given diagrams.

- $1\frac{1}{2} \div \frac{1}{2} = ?$

Think How many $\frac{1}{2}$s are there in $1\frac{1}{2}$?

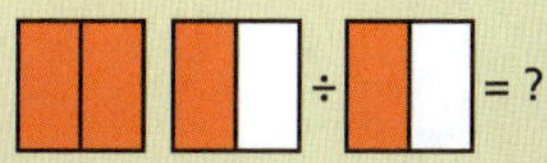

Not all division problems can be done using diagrams. The purpose of the example and activity above is to show you what it means to divide fractional parts. Follow the algorithm on the next page to divide fractions efficiently.

Before learning to divide fractions, make sure you know how to multiply fractions first.

To divide fractions:

1st Change "÷" to "x".

2nd Change the divisor to its reciprocal by swapping its numerator and denominator.

3rd Do the multiplication.

e.g.

$$\frac{2}{3} \div \frac{1}{3}$$

$$= \frac{2}{3} \times \frac{\mathbf{3}}{\mathbf{1}} \longleftarrow \text{reciprocal } \frac{1}{3} \rightarrow \frac{3}{1}$$

$$= \frac{2 \times 3}{3 \times 1}$$

$$= \frac{6}{3}$$

$$= 2$$

Do not forget to find the reciprocals of divisors that are whole numbers. In general, the reciprocal of a whole number is 1 over itself.

Find the reciprocal of 11.

$$11 = \frac{11}{1} \xrightarrow{\text{swap}} \frac{1}{11}$$

So, the reciprocal of 11 is $\frac{\mathbf{1}}{\mathbf{11}}$.

e.g.

$$4\frac{2}{5} \div 11$$

$$= \frac{22}{5} \div 11 \longleftarrow$$ Convert the mixed number into an improper fraction.

$$= \frac{22}{5} \times \frac{1}{11} \longleftarrow$$ Multiply by the reciprocal of 11.

$$= \frac{22 \times 1}{5 \times 11}$$

$$= \frac{22}{55}$$

$$= \frac{2}{5}$$

Application

Carlos has $\frac{4}{5}$ of a tank of fuel in his car. He uses $\frac{1}{10}$ of a tank each trip and he takes 2 trips each day. How many days will the fuel last?

Solution:

Amount of fuel used each day: $\frac{1}{10} \times 2$

$$= \frac{1}{10} \times \frac{2}{1}$$

$$= \frac{1 \times 2}{10 \times 1}$$

$$= \frac{2}{10}$$

$$= \frac{1}{5}$$

Number of days the fuel will last: $\frac{4}{5} \div \frac{1}{5}$

$$= \frac{4}{5} \times \frac{5}{1}$$

$$= \frac{4 \times 5}{5}$$

$$= \frac{20}{5}$$

$$= 4$$

The fuel will last 4 days.

Chapter 5
Decimals

5.1 Adding and Subtracting Decimals

In this unit, you will learn to add and subtract decimals. You will learn how the process of adding and subtracting decimals differs from the addition and subtraction of integers, and how to use placeholders to ensure accurate calculations.

When adding and subtracting numbers, you are used to aligning numbers to the right. However, when adding and subtracting decimals, the decimals must be aligned by their decimal points.

Adding Decimals

e.g. 23.045 + 6.72 = ?

$$\begin{array}{r} 23.045 \\ +\ \ 6.720 \\ \hline 29.765 \end{array}$$

Align the decimal points.

Add "0" as a placeholder.

Put the decimal point in the answer.

So, 23.045 + 6.72 = **29.765** .

Once the decimal points are aligned, the other place values will automatically be aligned correctly.

Subtracting Decimals

e.g. 40 – 9.731 = ?

$$\begin{array}{r} 40.\mathbf{000} \\ -\ \ 9.731 \\ \hline 30.269 \end{array}$$

Add "0"s as placeholders.

So, 40 – 9.731 = **30.269** .

Placeholders are especially important in subtraction. Without them, you may find it difficult to find the answers.

Application

Last week, Mr. Koch earned \$493.08 and spent \$309.40, and Mrs. Koch earned \$643.83 and spent \$136.77. They both put the remaining money in their savings account. How much did they save last week?

Solution:

$$\text{Total savings: } \underbrace{(493.08 - 309.40)}_{\text{Mr. Koch's savings}} + \underbrace{(643.83 - 136.77)}_{\text{Mrs. Koch's savings}}$$

$$= 183.68 + 507.06$$

$$= 690.74$$

They saved \$690.74 last week.

5.2 Multiplying Decimals

In this unit, you will learn to multiply decimals. You will also learn to apply the distributive property of multiplication when calculating with decimals.

Steps to Multiplying Decimals

- **1st** Multiply the numbers as if there were no decimal points.
- **2nd** Find the total number of decimal places in the decimals being multiplied.
- **3rd** The sum is the number of decimal places the product has.

e.g. 14.23 x 56 = ?

```
    1 4.2 3  ← 2 decimal places
x       5 6  ← 0 decimal places
    8 5 3 8
  7 1 1 5 0
  7 9 6.8 8. ← 2 decimal places
        2 1
```

So, 14.23 x 56 = **796.88** .

e.g. 14.23 x 5.6 = ?

```
    1 4.2 3  ← 2 decimal places
x       5.6  ← 1 decimal place
    8 5 3 8
  7 1 1 5 0
  7 9.6 8 8. ← 3 decimal places
      3 2 1
```

So, 14.23 x 5.6 = **79.688** .

As you can see in the examples, the number of decimal places in each product is the sum of the decimal places in the multipliers.

You may also use the distributive property of multiplication to find answers. This property states that one of the numbers can be broken down into two numbers, which are then multiplied separately and added.

e.g. 7.5 x 0.4

= 7 x 0.4 + 0.5 x 0.4 ← Break 7.5 into 7 and 0.5.

= 2.8 + 0.2

= 3

Using this property to do multiplication can sometimes make calculations easier, especially when it is done mentally.

Application

I earn $18.75 an hour for the first 40 hours per week and 1.5 times the hourly rate for each hour I work after that.

How much did Ava earn if she worked 52 hours last week?

Solution:

Overtime hourly rate: 18.75 x 1.5 = 28.125

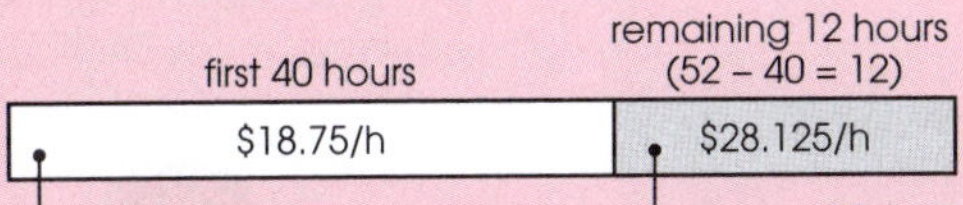

earnings: 18.75 × 40 = 750 earnings: 28.125 × 12 = 337.5

Total earnings: 750 + 337.5 = 1087.5

Ava earned $1087.50 last week.

5.3 Dividing Decimals

In this unit, you will learn to divide decimals. You will also apply the distributive property in certain division questions for efficiency.

Steps to Dividing Decimals

1st If the divisor is a whole number, go to **2nd**; otherwise, make sure the divisor is a whole number by moving the decimal point to the right. Then move the decimal point in the dividend the same number of places.

2nd Do the division as if there were no decimal points.

3rd Align the decimal points in the answer.

A common mistake is forgetting to move the decimal point in the dividend after moving the decimal in the divisor. Remember to avoid this mistake as it will yield an incorrect answer.

e.g. $4.45 \div 5 = ?$

```
    0.89
 5 ) 4.45
     4 0
     ----
       45
       45
     ----
```

So, $4.45 \div 5 =$ **0.89**.

e.g. $4.45 \div 0.5 = ?$

Think Change the divisor, 0.5, to a whole number.

$0.5 \rightarrow 5$

$4.45 \rightarrow 44.5$

```
     8.9
 5 ) 44.5
     40
     ----
      4 5
      4 5
     ----
```

So, $4.45 \div 0.5 =$ **8.9**.

For some division questions, it is more efficient to solve them using the distributive property. Use the following example to learn when it is beneficial to apply this property.

e.g. $4.45 \div 0.5 = ?$

Think $4.45 \div 0.5 = 44.5 \div 5$

40 is divisible by 5, and 4.5 is divisible by 5. So, break 44.5 into 40 and 4.5.

$4.45 \div 0.5$
$= 44.5 \div 5$
$= 40 \div 5 + 4.5 \div 5$
$= 8 + 0.9$
$= 8.9$

Application

Kate and her three cousins went to a concert together by taxi. The ride cost \$12.45 for the first 2 km and \$0.75 per 0.5 km for the rest of the trip. They travelled 8.5 km. How much did each person pay if the cost was split evenly?

Solution:

first 2 km	remaining 6.5 km (8.5 – 2 = 6.5)
\$12.45	\$0.75 per 0.5 km

cost: 12.45

cost: 0.75 x (6.5 ÷ 0.5)
= 0.75 x 13
= 9.75

Total cost: 12.45 + 9.75 = 22.2

Cost per person: 22.2 ÷ 4 = 5.55

Each person paid \$5.55.

5.4 Relating Decimals, Fractions, and Percents

In this unit, you will learn how fractions, decimals, and percents are related. You will then learn to convert among the three forms.

Fraction ⟷ Decimal

Divide the numerator by the denominator of the fractional part.

e.g. Write $1\frac{2}{5}$ as a decimal.

$2 \div 5 = 0.4$

$1\frac{2}{5} = \underline{\mathbf{1.4}}$

Write the decimal with a denominator of 1. Multiply the numerator and the denominator by powers of 10 (i.e. 10, 100, 1000, etc.) so that the numerator is a whole number.

e.g. Write 1.4 as a fraction.

$\frac{1.4}{1} \overset{\times 10}{=} \frac{14}{10} = \frac{7}{5} = 1\frac{2}{5}$

$1.4 = \underline{\mathbf{1\frac{2}{5}}}$

Percent ⟷ Fraction

Write the percent as a fraction with a denominator of 100. Then simplify.

e.g. Write 140% as a fraction.

$140\% = \frac{140}{100} = 1\frac{2}{5}$

$140\% = \underline{\mathbf{1\frac{2}{5}}}$

Find the equivalent fraction of the fractional part with 100 as its denominator. Then write it as a percent.

e.g. Write $1\frac{2}{5}$ as a percent.

$1\frac{2}{5} = 1\frac{40}{100} = 140\%$

$1\frac{2}{5} = \underline{\mathbf{140\%}}$

Percent ⟷ Decimal

Drop the "%". Then move the decimal point 2 places to the left.

e.g. Write 140% as a decimal.

$140.\cancel{\%} = 1.4$

$140\% = \underline{\mathbf{1.4}}$

Move the decimal point 2 places to the right. Then add the "%".

e.g. Write 1.4 as a percent.

$1.4\_\_ = 140\%$ (1 2)

$1.4 = \underline{\mathbf{140\%}}$

Application

A car has just arrived at my auto shop for an emergency repair. I want the mechanic who is closest to finishing his current task to deal with the emergency.

Leo says, "I've done $\frac{1}{5}$ of the job."

Joe says, "I still have $\frac{3}{4}$ of the job left."

Ken says, "There's still a half way to go."

Use a fraction, a decimal, and a percent to show how much of each mechanic's task is done. Who should be assigned the new task?

Solution:

Find how much of each mechanic's task is done.

Leo: $\frac{1}{5}$	Joe: $1-\frac{3}{4}=\frac{1}{4}$	Ken: $1-\frac{1}{2}=\frac{1}{2}$
0.2	0.25	0.5
20%	25%	50%

Ken should be assigned the new task because he is the closest to finishing his current task.

Chapter 6

Proportional Relationships

6.1 Ratios

This unit introduces the concept of ratios. You will learn to write ratios in proper format and find equivalent ratios.

Writing Ratios

A ratio is a comparison between two or more quantities of similar units.

e.g. Zoe has 3 blue marbles and 2 green marbles. Find the ratios.

- blue marbles to green marbles = 3:2
- green marbles to all marbles = 2:5

Remember, the order of the quantities in a ratio matters.

Finding Equivalent Ratios

To find an equivalent ratio, multiply or divide both sides of the ratio by the same number.

e.g. Find two equivalent ratios of 2:6.

$2 : 6 = 4 : 12$ (× 2 on both sides)

2:6 = **4:12**

$2 : 6 = 1 : 3$ (÷ 2 on both sides)

2:6 = **1:3**

Application

Mrs. Cory's class had 48 fiction books and 30 non-fiction books. She then received 1 fiction and 5 non-fiction books from the library. Mrs. Eston had 40 fiction books and 30 non-fiction books. She then gave a total of 10 books to the library. If the ratio of fiction to non-fiction books is the same for both classes, how many of each type of book did Mrs. Eston give to the library?

Solution:

Books in Mrs. Cory's class

Number of fiction books: 48 + 1 = 49
Number of non-fiction books: 30 + 5 = 35

The ratio of fiction to non-fiction books: 49:35 = 7:5

Books in Mrs. Eston's class

Number of books: 40 + 30 − 10 = 60
(40: fiction; 30: non-fiction; 10: given away)

Both classes have the same ratio of fiction to non-fiction books, which is 7:5.

Find an equivalent ratio of 7:5 with its two numbers having a sum of 60.

7:5 = 35:25 ← 35 + 25 = 60 (× 5, × 5)

Number of fiction books Mrs. Eston gave away: 40 − 35 = 5
Number of non-fiction books she gave away: 30 − 25 = 5

So, Mrs. Eston gave 5 fiction books and 5 non-fiction books to the library.

6.2 Rates

In this unit, you will be introduced to two common applications of rates. You will also learn to do conversions when comparing rates with different units.

Finding Speed

Speed is a rate that describes how fast someone or something moves by comparing distance to time.

Speed = Distance ÷ Time

e.g. Joanne drives 102 km in 1.5 h. What is her speed?

102 km ÷ 1.5 h = 68 km/h

So, her speed is **68 km/h**.

e.g. Jake drives at 1.5 km/min. Who drives faster, Jake or Joanne?

To compare the speeds, they must have the same unit.

Think Convert Jake's speed from km/min into km/h.

1.5 km/min
= 90 km/h (x 60)

So, **Jake** drives faster.

Finding Unit Price

Unit price is a rate that describes the price of one unit of an item.

Unit Price = Cost of Item ÷ Number of Units

e.g. Mr. Ali sells 2.5 L of detergent for $12. What is the unit price in L?

$12 ÷ 2.5 L = $4.8/L

So, the unit price is **$4.8/L**.

e.g. Mrs. Louis sells 1500 mL of the same detergent for $9. Who offers a better deal?

Think Compare the prices using the same unit. Convert 1500 mL into 1.5 L.

$9 ÷ 1500 mL
= $9 ÷ 1.5 L
= $6/L

So, **Mr. Ali** offers a better deal.

Application

On day 1, it took Sarah 80 min to run 10 km. On day 10, it took her 3 h 12 min to run 20 km. On day 20, it took her 5 h to run 30 km. Find her speeds per hour. How likely is it that Sarah can complete the marathon in 6 hours?

Solution:

Day 1

80 min = $1\frac{1}{3}$ h

Speed: $10 \div 1\frac{1}{3} = 7\frac{1}{2}$ (km/h)

Day 10

3 h 12 min = $3\frac{1}{5}$ h

Speed: $20 \div 3\frac{1}{5} = 6\frac{1}{4}$ (km/h)

Day 20

Speed: $30 \div 5 = 6$ (km/h)

Find the speed needed for running 40 km in 6 h.

Speed: $40 \div 6 = 6\frac{2}{3}$ (km/h)

Sarah's overall running speed decreases as the distance run increases. So, it is unlikely that she can complete the marathon in 6 hours.

Chapter 7

Measurement

7.1 Area

This unit reviews finding the areas of triangles and parallelograms. You will apply your understanding of parallelograms to derive the formula for finding the areas of trapezoids.

To find the area of a parallelogram or a triangle, identify its base and height, which always make a right angle.

Area of a Parallelogram

Area of a Parallelogram = **Base** x **Height**

e.g. Find the area.

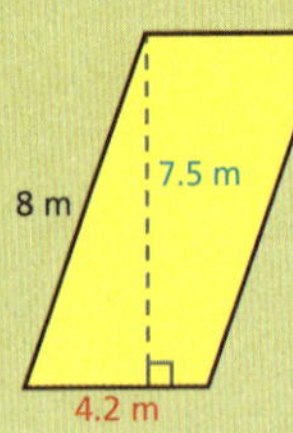

Area: **4.2** x **7.5**
= 31.5 (m^2)

The area is **31.5 m²** .

Area of a Triangle

Area of a Triangle = **Base** x **Height** ÷ 2

e.g. Find the area.

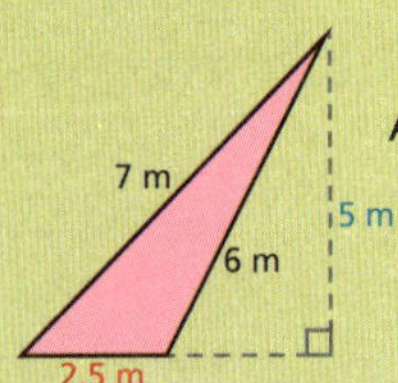

Area: **2.5** x **5** ÷ 2
= 6.25 (m^2)

The area is **6.25 m²** .

Area of a Trapezoid

To understand how to find the area of a trapezoid, you must know how to find the area of a parallelogram.

Consider this parallelogram and how it is split into two equal trapezoids.

e.g.

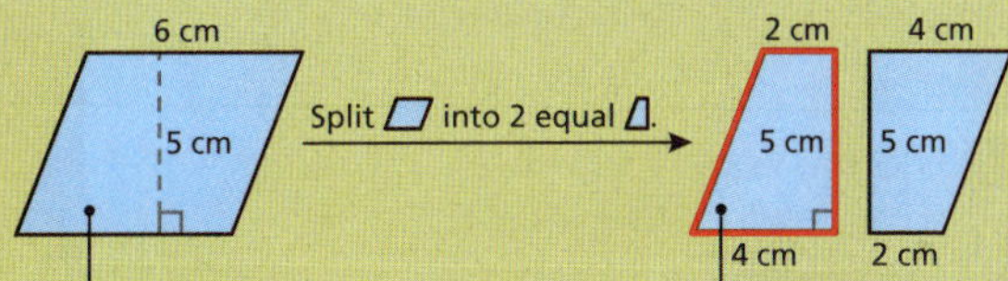

Area: 6×5
$= 30\ (cm^2)$

Area: area of ▱ $\div 2$
$= 30 \div 2$
$= 15\ (cm^2)$

The area of a trapezoid is found by multiplying the sum of its two bases by its height and then dividing the product by 2.

Area of a Trapezoid = $(a + b) \times h \div 2$

Consider the reasoning below.

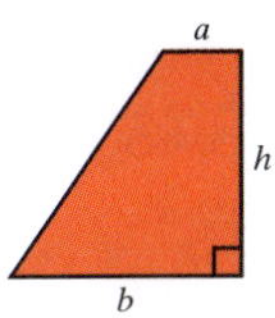

Area of a trapezoid = area of a parallelogram $\div 2$
= base x height $\div 2$
= sum of bases of ⏢ x height $\div 2$
$= (a + b) \times h \div 2$

e.g. Find the area.

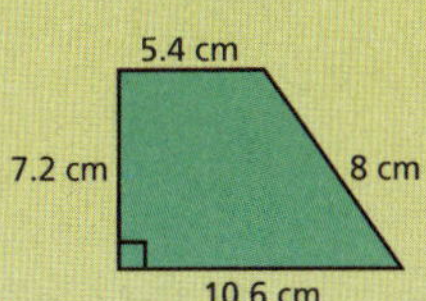

Area: $(5.4 + 10.6) \times 7.2 \div 2$
$= 16 \times 7.2 \div 2$
$= 57.6\ (cm^2)$

The area is **57.6 cm²**.

Application

If Olivia wants to add trimming around the scarf, how many metres of trimming does she need?

Solution:

Let a represent the measurement of the missing length. There are two ways to find a.

Way 1 Use the guess-and-check method to find the missing length.

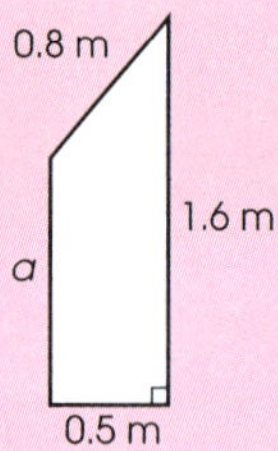

$(a + 1.6) \times 0.5 \div 2 = 0.7$

Guess a	Check
1	$(1 + 1.6) \times 0.5 \div 2 = 0.65$
1.5	$(1.5 + 1.6) \times 0.5 \div 2 = 0.775$
1.4	$(1.4 + 1.6) \times 0.5 \div 2 = 0.75$
1.2	$(1.2 + 1.6) \times 0.5 \div 2 = 0.7$ ✔

So, the missing length is 1.2 m.

Way 2 Relate the trapezoid to the parallelogram to find the missing length.

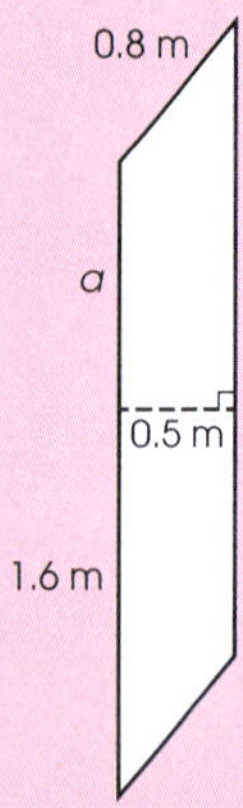

Visualize putting two trapezoids together to make a parallelogram. Then use the area of the parallelogram to find the length of its base.

Let b represent the length of the base of the parallelogram.

Area of parallelogram: $0.7 \times 2 = 1.4$

$b \times 0.5 = 1.4$

$b = 2.8$

The length of the base of the parallelogram is the sum of the two bases of the trapezoid.

$a + 1.6 = 2.8$

$a = 1.2$

Total trimming needed: $1.2 + 0.8 + 1.6 + 0.5 = 4.1$

Olivia needs 4.1 m of trimming for her scarf.

7.2 Volume

In this unit, you will learn to find the volumes of prisms by relating the areas of their bases to their heights, and to calculate the volumes of prisms with simple polygonal bases.

In general, for a prism that has a simple polygonal base (e.g. a parallelogram or a trapezoid), its volume is the product of the area of its base and height (or thickness).

Volume of a Prism = Area of Base x Height

e.g.

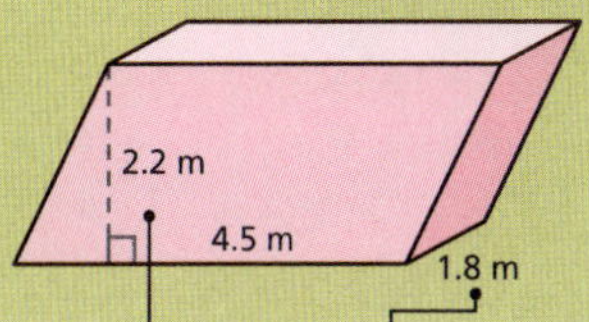

V = [area of base] 4.5 x 2.2 x [height] 1.8
= 9.9 x 1.8
= 17.82 (m³)

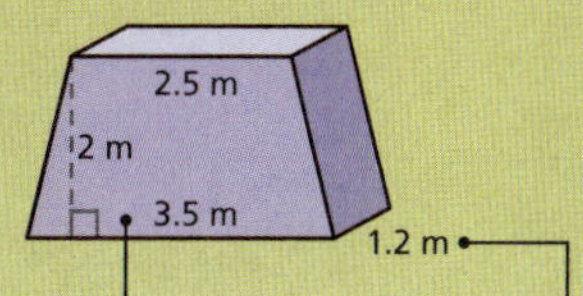

V = [area of base] (2.5 + 3.5) x 2 ÷ 2 x [height] 1.2
= 6 x 1.2
= 7.2 (m³)

For prisms that do not have simple polygonal bases, decompose them into prisms with simple polygonal bases.

There can be more than one way to decompose a prism.

e.g. Find the volume.

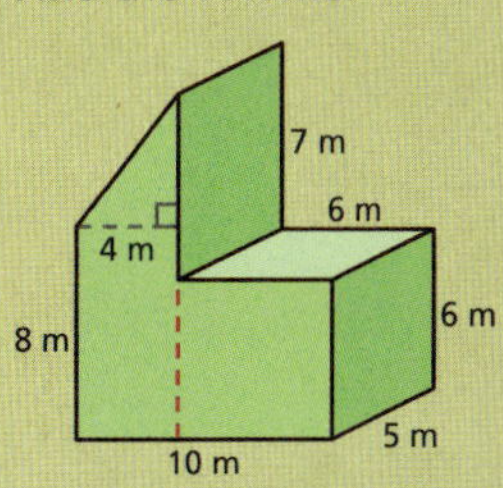

Think Decompose the prism (as shown by the red line).

Volume of ▯: (8 + 7 + 6) x 4 ÷ 2 x 5 = 210 (m³)
Volume of ▢: 6 x 6 x 5 = 180 (m³)
Total volume: 210 + 180 = 390 (m³)

The volume is **390 m³**.

Application

A princess is sleeping on a stack of mattresses. Each mattress has a base of 1.5 m by 2 m. If each mattress is 20 cm thick and the total volume of the mattresses is 5.4 m³, how many mattresses is the princess sleeping on?

Solution:

20 cm = 0.2 m

Volume of each mattress: $1.5 \times 2 \times 0.2 = 0.6$

Number of mattresses: $5.4 \div 0.6 = 9$

The princess is sleeping on 9 mattresses.

7.3 Surface Area

In this unit, you will find the surface areas of prisms with bases of different shapes and investigate the relationship between surface area and volume.

Finding Surface Area

Surface area is the total area of all the faces of a solid. You should be familiar with finding the surface areas of rectangular prisms. At this level, you will learn to find the surface areas of prisms with bases of different shapes.

It usually helps to draw out the faces of a prism and find their areas before adding them up to find the surface area.

e.g. Find the surface area.

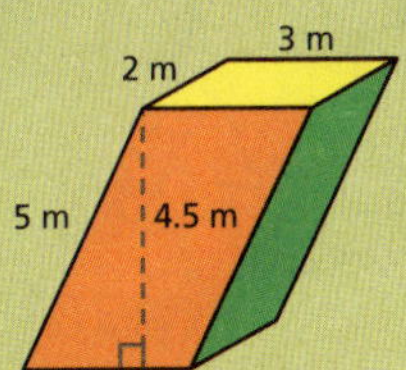

Areas of faces:

2 ▱ : 3 x 4.5 x 2 = 27 (m^2)

2 ▯ : 5 x 2 x 2 = 20 (m^2)

2 ▭ : 3 x 2 x 2 = 12 (m^2)

Surface area: 27 + 20 + 12 = 59 (m^2)

The surface area is **59 m^2**.

Relating Surface Area and Volume

Once you are able to find surface areas, investigate some relationships between surface area and volume. Consider the solids on the right and ask these questions:

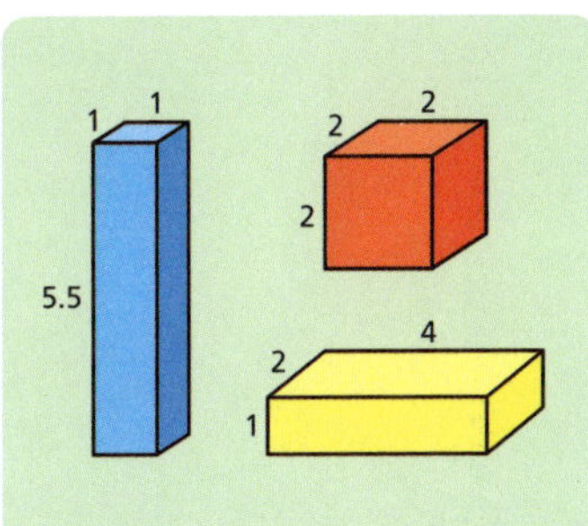

- Do solids with the same volume imply that they have the same surface area as well? No.
- Do solids with the same surface area imply that they have the same volume as well? No.

Application

Dorothy built a staircase out of Styrofoam cubes, each with a side length of 10 cm. How many cubes did she use? What is the total area to be painted if all sides will be painted except the bottom?

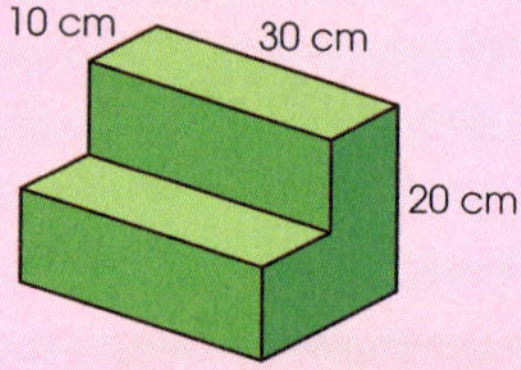

Solution:

"Cut" the solid into 10-cm blocks to find the number of cubes used.

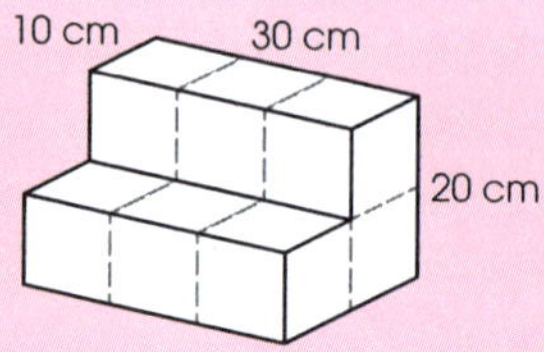

9 cubes were used.

Area of 1 face of each small cube: $10 \times 10 = 100$

There are 24 faces in total (except the bottom).

Surface area (except the bottom): $100 \times 24 = 2400$

The total area to be painted is 2400 cm^2.

Chapter 8

2-D and 3-D Geometry

8.1 Properties of Quadrilaterals

In this unit, you will learn to identify and use the markings and symbols that represent the various properties of quadrilaterals.

Below are some markings that are used to show some properties of shapes such as right angles, equal angles, equal sides, and parallel sides.

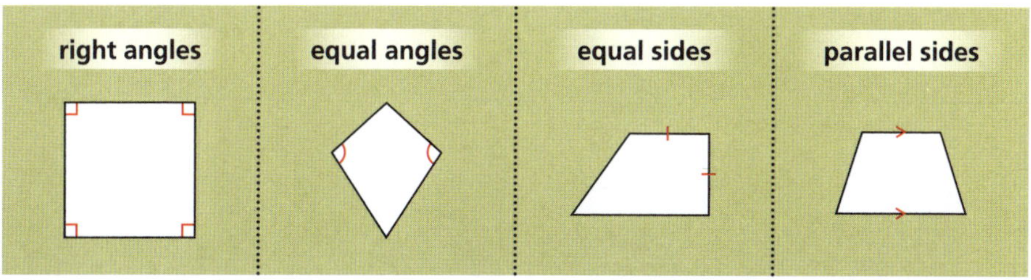

Identify the properties of these shapes according to their markings.

To indicate "another pair", double the markings. For example, > indicates the first pair, whereas >> indicates the second pair.

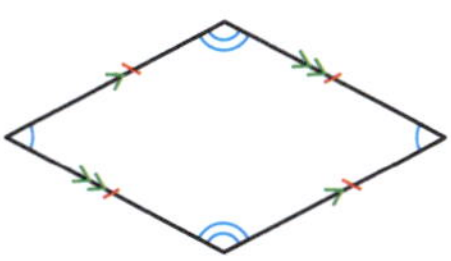

- 2 sets of **equal angles**
- 4 **equal sides**
- 2 pairs of **parallel sides**

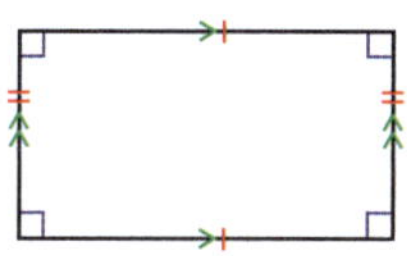

- 4 **right angles**
- 2 pairs of **equal sides**
- 2 pairs of **parallel sides**

Application

Is what the girl says true? If so, draw the quadrilateral and label the sizes of the angles.

Solution:

Yes, what the girl says is true. It is possible to draw a quadrilateral with three 45° angles.

A quadrilateral must have 4 angles that have a sum of 360°. If three angles are 45°, the last angle must be:

$360^\circ - 45^\circ \times 3 = 225^\circ$

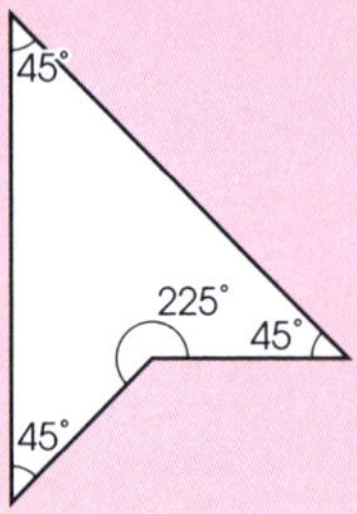

8.2 Properties of Triangles

In this unit, you will learn to categorize triangles according to their side lengths and angles. You will also investigate what information is needed in order to describe a unique triangle.

Classifying Triangles

A triangle can be named in two ways: by its angles and by its sides.

By Angle

Acute Triangle
- all acute angles

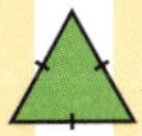

Right Triangle
- has a right angle

Obtuse Triangle
- has an obtuse angle

By Side

Equilateral Triangle
- all sides equal

Isosceles Triangle
- two equal sides

Scalene Triangle
- no equal sides

e.g. Name the triangle in two ways.

- Obtuse triangle
  (It has an obtuse angle.)
- Isosceles triangle
  (It has two equal sides.)

Describing Unique Triangles

You need to be able to identify the minimum side and angle information to describe a unique triangle. Consider the questions below. The answers are either "one" or "many". Through this activity, you will learn that the minimum information needed to describe a unique triangle is: the lengths of 3 sides (side-side-side), the lengths of 2 sides and 1 angle (side-angle-side), or the length of 1 side and 2 angles (angle-side-angle).

How many triangles can you make if you know...

Set A
- the length of one side? Many.
- the lengths of two sides? Many.
- the lengths of all sides? One.

Set B
- the length of one side? Many.
- the length of one side and the size of one of its angles? Many.
- the length of one side and the sizes of its angles on both ends? One.

Set C
- the size of one angle? Many.
- the size of one angle and the length of one of its arms? Many.
- the size of one angle and the lengths of both of its arms? One.

Application

Read how the children describe the triangles that they saw. Are they describing the same triangle?

Solution:

Draw a triangle for each description.

A 90° angle with 2-cm and 3.5-cm sides:

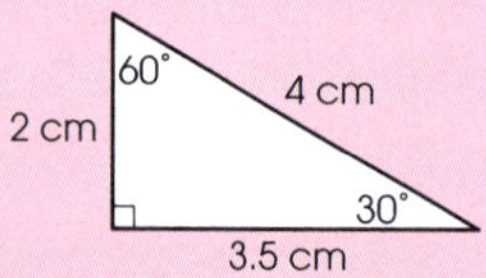

A 4-cm side with angles of 30° and 60°:

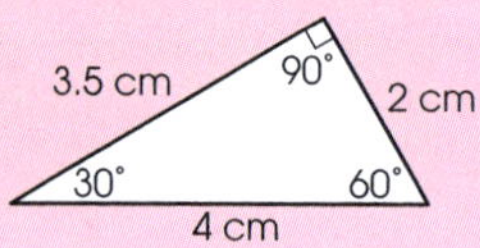

The side lengths and angle sizes are the same for both triangles. So, they are describing the same triangle.

8.3 Congruent and Similar Shapes

In this unit, you will learn to identify and differentiate between congruent and similar shapes.

Identifying Congruent and Similar Shapes

Congruent Shapes

- figures that are identical in shape and size

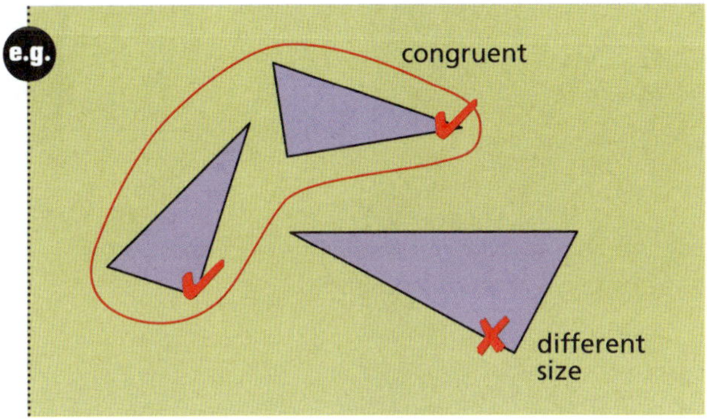

Similar Shapes

- figures that are the same shape but are different in size

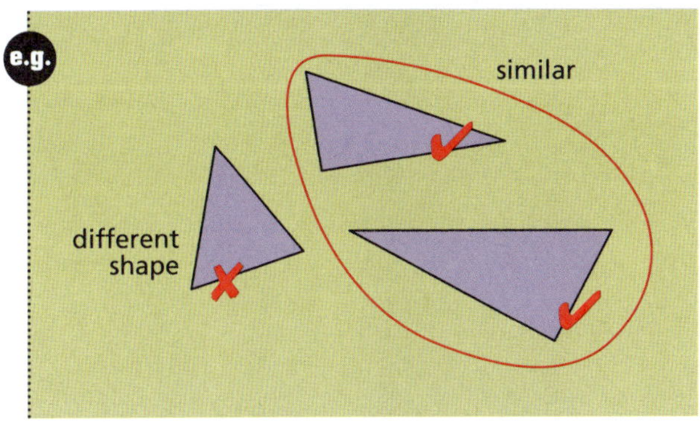

Application

My desk is made up of two congruent trapezoids.

Can the area of the desk be found with the given measurements? If so, what is the area?

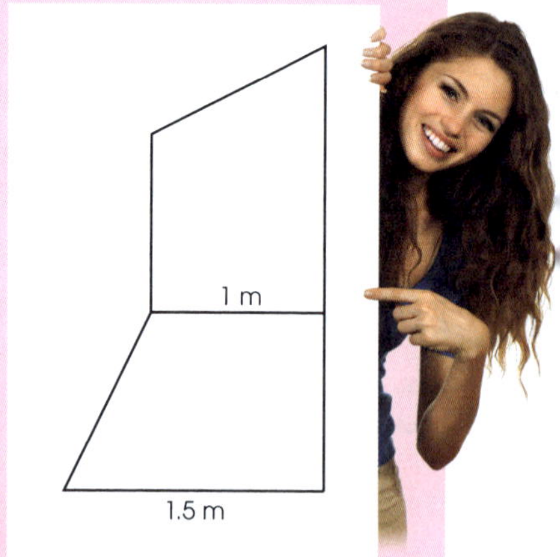

Solution:

The area of the desk can be found.

Since the two trapezoids are congruent, their corresponding sides are equal.

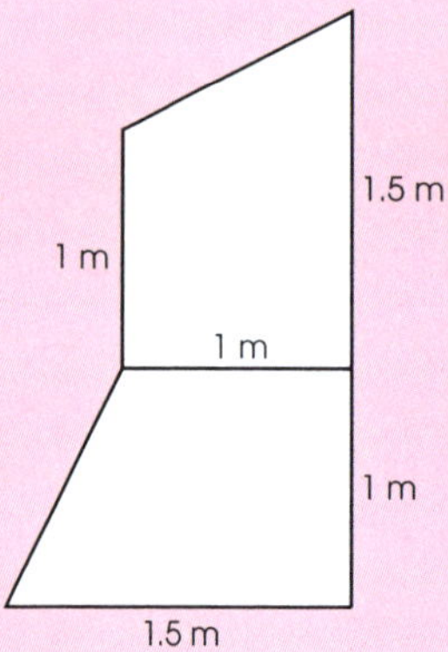

Area of 1 trapezoid:

$(1 + 1.5) \times 1 \div 2$

$= 1.25$

Since the two trapezoids are congruent, their areas are also the same.

Area of the desk:

1.25×2

$= 2.5$

The area is 2.5 m^2.

8.4 Constructing Angles and Bisectors

In this unit, you will learn how to draw angles using a protractor and how to use a compass to draw perpendicular bisectors and angle bisectors.

Constructing an Angle

Follow the steps below to draw angles with a protractor.

Steps to Drawing an Angle

1st Draw an arm.

2nd Place the centre of the protractor on one end of the arm and mark the angle.

3rd Draw another arm to join the mark to that end.

The following tips will help you draw precise angles.

Tip 1 Always use a sharp pencil to draw angles for precision.

Tip 2 To prevent using the wrong scale on the protractor (which is a common mistake), determine whether the angle is acute or obtuse before marking the angle.

Tip 3 Once drawn, measure the angle again to ensure accuracy.

Drawing a Perpendicular Bisector

Perpendicular lines: lines that intersect at a 90° angle

Bisector: a line that divides something into two equal parts

Perpendicular bisector: a line that divides a line into two halves at 90°

Which red line is a perpendicular bisector?

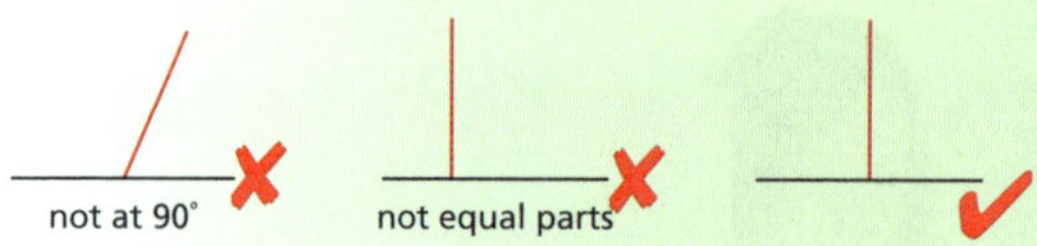

Steps to Drawing a Perpendicular Bisector

1st Centre the compass on one end of the line and draw an arc. Repeat for the other end of the line.

2nd Draw a line to connect the two points where the arcs intersect. This line is the perpendicular bisector.

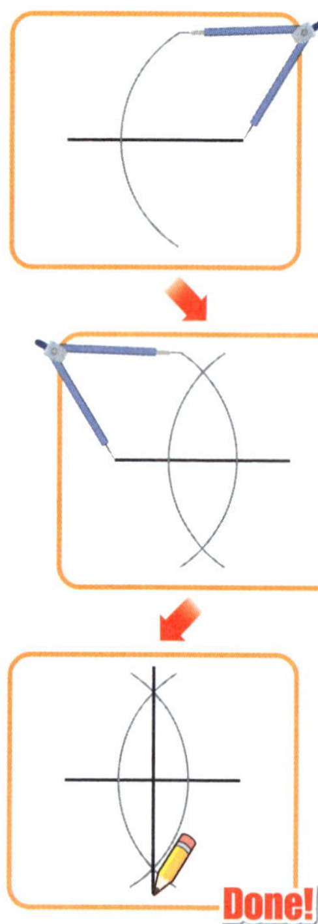

As you can see in the example, the bisector cuts the line in half at a 90° angle.

Drawing an Angle Bisector

Angle bisector: a line that cuts an angle into two halves

Steps to Drawing an Angle Bisector

1st Centre the compass on the angle's vertex and draw an arc that intersects the angle's arms.

2nd Centre the compass at the two intersections and draw two arcs.

3rd Draw a line to join the intersection of the arcs and the angle's vertex. This line is the angle bisector.

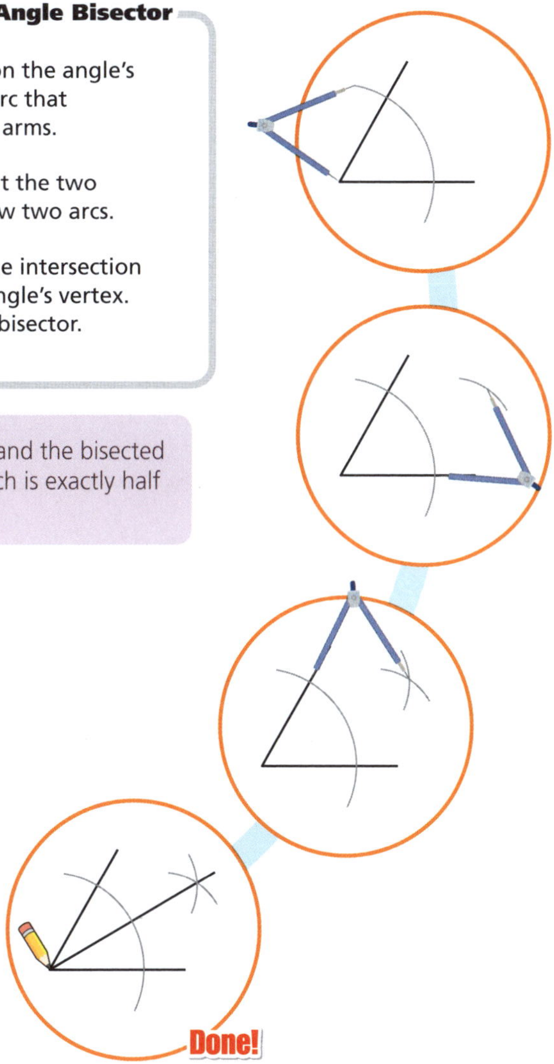

The original angle is 60° and the bisected angles are 30° each, which is exactly half of the original.

Application

Is what Kenneth says true? If so, draw an isosceles triangle using a compass and a ruler.

Solution:

What Kenneth says is true. An isosceles triangle can be drawn using a compass and a ruler.

1st Draw a line (Line AB) with a ruler.

2nd Draw a perpendicular bisector with a compass.

3rd Pick any point (Point P) along the perpendicular bisector and draw to connect the point (Point P) to the two ends (Points A and B) of the line.

Measure the lengths of PA and PB. They should be the same.

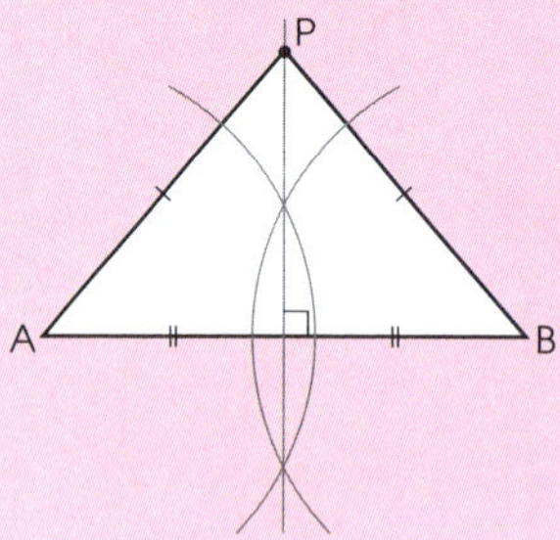

This is an isosceles triangle because two of its sides are equal.

Chapter 9

Locations and Movements

9.1 Transformations

This unit introduces two new transformations: enlargement and reduction.

Enlargement and Reduction

In addition to translation, reflection, and rotation, you will learn to identify, perform, and describe enlargement and reduction.

Enlargement: increasing the size of a shape to form a similar shape
Reduction: decreasing the size of a shape to form a similar shape

Investigate the properties of enlargement and reduction that are common to and different from other transformations.

- How are enlargement and reduction different from other transformations (i.e. position, orientation, etc.)?
- Are translated, reflected, or rotated images congruent to their original shapes? How about enlarged or reduced images?

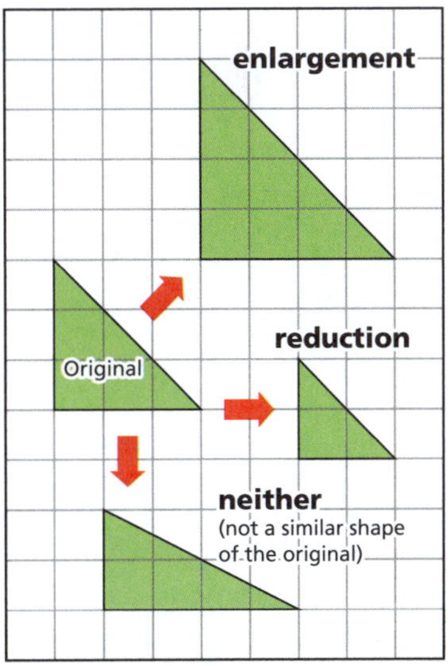

9.2 Cartesian Coordinate Plane

This unit introduces the four quadrants of Cartesian coordinate planes. You will investigate how coordinates differ from quadrant to quadrant and graph points on the quadrants.

A Cartesian coordinate plane is divided into four quadrants. You should have already learned how to plot and write coordinates for points in the first quadrant (or quadrant I). Observe how the four quadrants are numbered and how the signs (positive and negative) for the coordinates differ from one quadrant to another.

The Four Quadrants

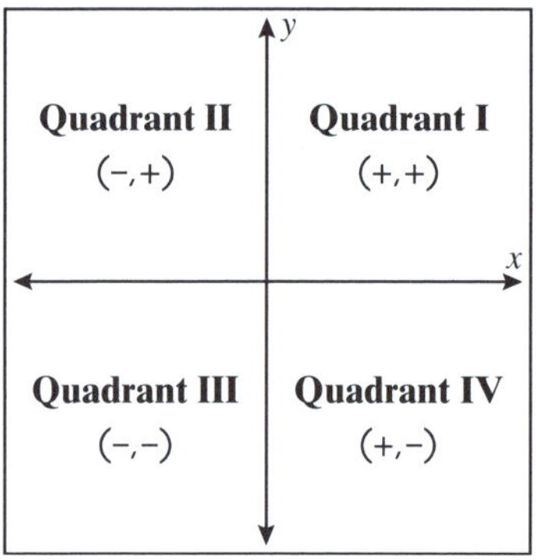

Remember, a Cartesian coordinate plane has a horizontal x-axis and a vertical y-axis. Any point on the plane is represented by its coordinates in the form of (x,y).

(x, y)

↑ no. of units across the x-axis ↑ no. of units along the y-axis

e.g. Plot the points.

A (4,3) B (-4,1)

C (-5,-3) D (2,-4)

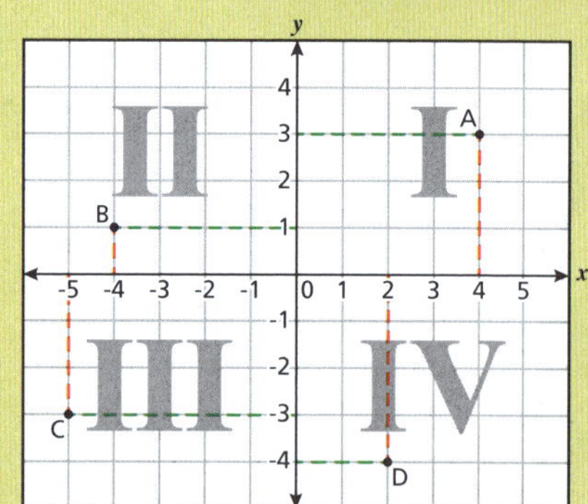

A common mistake you might make is switching the x and y axes in an ordered pair. Remember to be extra cautious to avoid this mistake.

Application

A right triangle has an area of 6 square units. Two of its vertices are (-2,-5) and (2,-5). What are the possible coordinates of its third vertex?

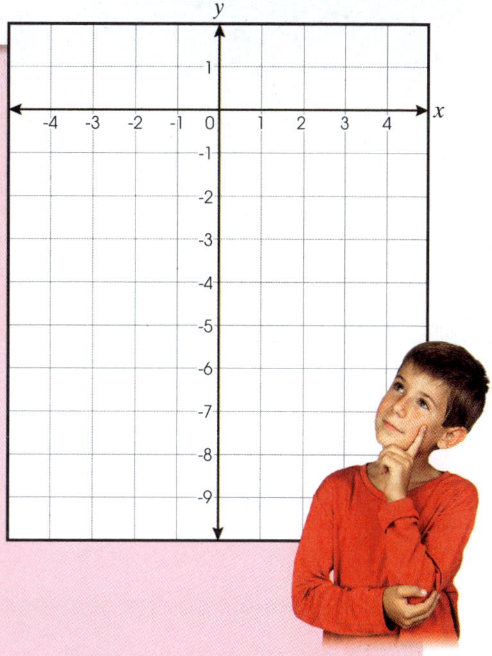

Solution:

1st Plot the known vertices of the triangle.

The base is 4 units.

2nd Find the height of the triangle.

$$4 \times h \div 2 = 6$$
$$h = 3$$

The height is 3 units.

3rd Plot the points that would make right triangles with a height of 3 units.

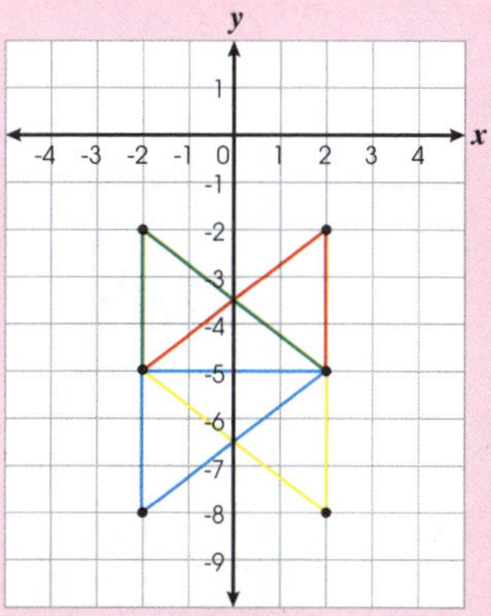

The possible coordinates of its third vertex are (-2,-2), (2,-2), (-2,-8), or (2,-8).

Chapter 10

Patterning

10.1 Number Patterns

At this level, you will describe patterns in two ways. You will also determine a term with a given term number, and vice versa.

A number pattern can be described in two ways:

Way 1 adding, subtracting, multiplying, and/or dividing a constant to get the next terms

Way 2 describing all terms by referring to their term numbers

e.g. Describe the pattern in two ways.

2 5 8 11 14

Way 1 Start at 2. Add 3 each time.

Way 2 Multiply the term number by 3 and subtract 1.

e.g. Use the expression to find the 50th term.

$$50\text{th term} = 50 \times 3 - 1$$
$$= 149$$

So, the 50th term is <u>149</u>.

As you can see, finding a term using **Way 2** is a lot more efficient than using **Way 1**.

Application

Jenny and Lewis are weight training. In Week 1, Jenny lifts 2 lb and Lewis lifts 3 lb. Jenny and Lewis increase their weights by 2 lb and 1 lb each week respectively. Write two expressions to describe the weights they lift in relation to the week number. Who will lift 18 lb first and in which week?

Solution:

Make a table to represent the first few weeks and the weights.

Week	Jenny	Lewis
1	2	3
2	4	4
3	6	5

Let w represent the week number.

Jenny's expression: $2w$
Lewis's expression: $w + 2$

Find out who will lift 18 lb first and in which week using the guess-and-check method.

Jenny

Guess w	Check
7	$2 \times 7 = 14$
8	$2 \times 8 = 16$
9	$2 \times 9 = 18$ ✔

Lewis

Guess w	Check
14	$14 + 2 = 16$
15	$15 + 2 = 17$
16	$16 + 2 = 18$ ✔

Jenny will lift 18 lb in week 9 and Lewis will lift 18 lb in week 16. So, Jenny will lift 18 lb first.

10.2 Patterns in Graphs

In this unit, you will learn to describe patterns in a graph algebraically. You will also learn to derive algebraic equations from pattern rules and relationships of x and y values in ordered pairs observed from a graph.

To describe a pattern in a graph algebraically, you must first be able to identify the pattern and describe it in words.

e.g.

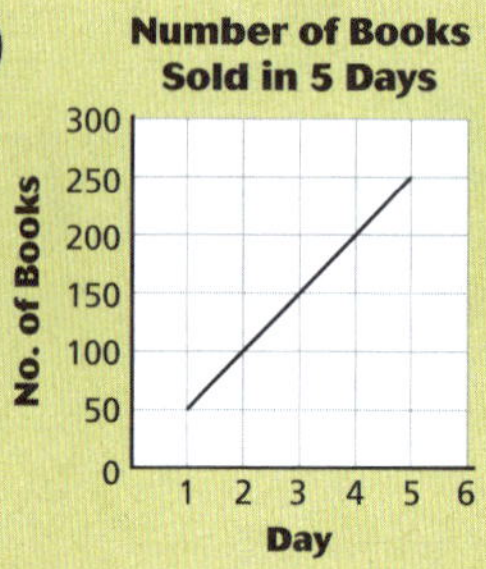

Write a pattern rule and an equation to describe the pattern shown in the graph.

Pattern Rule

Start at 50. Increase the number of books sold by 50 for each day.

Equation

$b = 50d$

(b = no. of books; d = no. of days)

You also need to learn how to identify the relationship of the x-coordinate and y-coordinate in an ordered pair on a Cartesian coordinate plane.

e.g.

The best way to identify the relationship between x and y is to make a table.

(x,y)	x	y
(1,1)	1	1
(2,3)	2	3
(3,5)	3	5
(4,7)	4	7
(5,9)	5	9

x- and y-coordinates of the ordered pairs

Pattern Rule

Multiply x by 2 and subtract 1 to get y.

Equation

$y = 2x - 1$

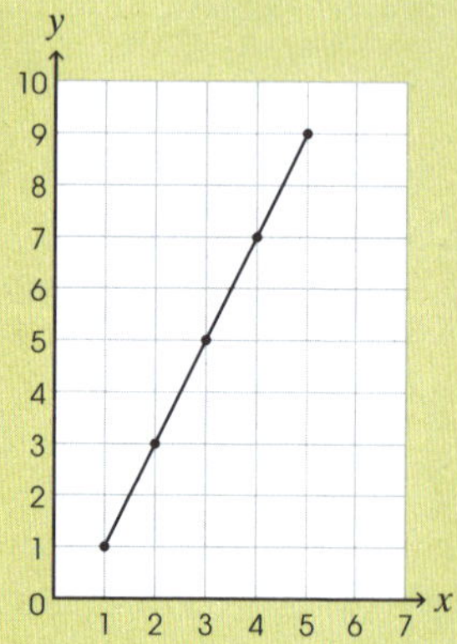

Chapter 11

Algebra

11.1 Algebraic Expressions

In this unit, you will learn to formulate algebraic expressions and evaluate algebraic expressions by substituting variables with different values.

Formulating an Algebraic Expression

An algebraic expression is a number sentence that consists of variables, numbers, and operations, where variables represent unknowns.

Steps

1st Identify the unknown and assign a letter to it.

2nd Find out how the other quantities relate to the unknown.

3rd Write a number sentence to represent the relationships.

e.g. Write "2 times a number and add 3" as an algebraic expression.

2 times | a number | and add 3

$2 \times n + 3$

2 times | the sum of a number and 3

$2 \times (n + 3)$

Be careful with the order of operations. Add brackets when necessary.

It is common practice to omit the multiplication sign in multiplication problems that involve variables.

e.g.
$2 \times n + 3 \rightarrow 2n + 3$
$2 \times (n + 3) \rightarrow 2(n + 3)$

Evaluating an Algebraic Expression

To evaluate an algebraic expression, substitute the variable with its value into the expression. Then do the calculations.

e.g. Evaluate $2n + 3$ when $n = 1$.

$2n + 3$
$= 2 \times 1 + 3$ ← Substitute 1 for n.
$= 5$

Evaluate $2n + 3$ when $n = 3$.

$2n + 3$
$= 2 \times 3 + 3$
$= 9$

A variable can take on different values. Therefore, the value of an expression can differ depending on the value that the variable represents.

As you can see in the examples, the value of an expression depends on the value that the variable represents. Evaluate the expression with different values of n.

Application

The regular price of snorkelling gear rentals will increase by $\$d$. Eva plans to go snorkelling 10 times. She is debating whether she should buy the 10-day pass or a set of snorkelling gear that costs $196. What increase in rental price will make buying a set of snorkelling gear worthwhile?

Solution:

Cost of a new 10-day pass: $(22.5 + d) \times 10 \times (1 - 20\%)$

$= (22.5 + d) \times 10 \times 0.8$

$= (22.5 + d) \times 8$

Use the guess-and-check method to find out what increase in price would result in a rental cost of $196.

Guess d	Check
1	$(22.5 + 1) \times 8 = 188$
2	$(22.5 + 2) \times 8 = 196$ ✔

It will be worthwhile for Eva to buy a set of snorkelling gear if the increase in price is $2 or more.

11.2 Algebraic Equations

In this unit, you will build upon your knowledge of the previous unit and apply it to model real-life scenarios as algebraic equations. You will also solve for unknown variables using different strategies.

Formulating an Algebraic Equation

Formulating an algebraic equation is similar to formulating an algebraic expression. Therefore, make sure that you are familiar with the previous unit before starting this unit.

e.g. Write an equation that represents the scenario.

> Kelly made 12 Popsicles. She made 4 more than half of the number I made. How many Popsicles did I make?

Let p be the number of Popsicles Janice made.

$$p \div 2 + 4 = 12$$

($p \div 2 + 4$: 4 more than half of p; 12: no. of Popsicles Kelly made)

Solving an Algebraic Equation

Way 1 Using the Guess-and-check Method

e.g. $a + 8 = 12$

Guess		Check
$a = 2$	$2 + 8 = 10$	✗
$a = 3$	$3 + 8 = 11$	✗
$a = 4$	$4 + 8 = 12$	✓

Way 2 Using an Algorithm

To solve for a variable, isolate it by performing the opposite operation on both sides of an equation.

e.g.

$$a + 8 = 12$$
$$a + 8 - 8 = 12 - 8 \quad \leftarrow \text{Isolate } a \text{ by subtracting 8 from both sides.}$$
$$a = 4$$

e.g.

$$7k = 14$$
$$7k \div 7 = 14 \div 7 \quad \leftarrow \text{Isolate } k \text{ by dividing both sides by 7.}$$
$$k = 2$$

Application

How many kilometres did she jog in June?

I jogged a total of 21 km in June and July. I jogged 3 km more in July than in June.

Solution:

Let j represent the distance she jogged in June.

$j + 3$ would be the distance she jogged in July.

June: j; July: $j + 3$

$$j + j + 3 = 21$$

Guess j	Check
7	$7 + 7 + 3 = 17$
8	$8 + 8 + 3 = 19$
9	$9 + 9 + 3 = 21$ ✔

She jogged 9 km in June.

Chapter 12

Data Management

12.1 Interpreting Graphs

In this unit, you will learn to classify data according to its source. Additionally, you will review measures of central tendency and learn to describe trends observed in graphs. You will also learn to recognize biases in presentations of data.

You need to be able to identify two types of data sources.

Identifying Sources of Data

Primary Data	or	Secondary Data
a set of data that is collected by conducting a survey or an experiment		a set of data from other sources such as books and websites

Census	or	Sample
a set of data from an entire population		a set of data from a representative group of a population that reflects the entire population

Finding Central Tendency and Trend

The measures of central tendency, namely mean, median, and mode, are important in summarizing a set of data.

- mean: the sum of a set of data values divided by the number of data values
- median: the middle value in a set of data that is ordered from least to greatest
- mode: the value(s) in a set of data that occur(s) most often

At this level, you should be familiar with finding mean, median, and mode.

Trends are usually present in line graphs. Words that are commonly used to describe trends are: increase, decrease, steady, stable, sharp, and significant.

Supply and Demand of Pearls over the Past 10 Years

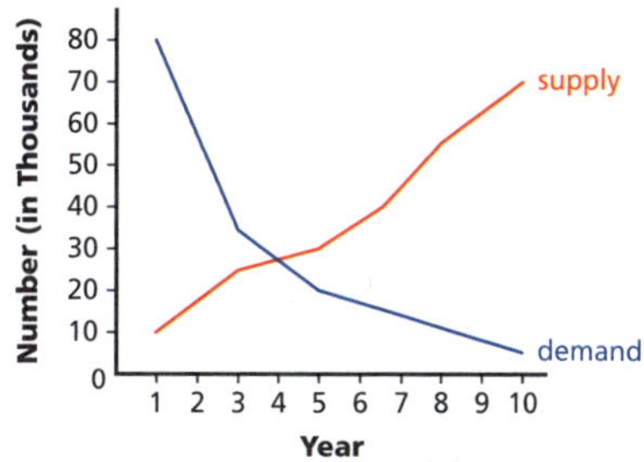

e.g. The supply of pearls has **increased steadily** over the past 10 years.

The demand of pearls **decreased sharply** in the first three years and continued to decrease at a steady rate.

The type of graph used affects the way we interpret the graph. If it is a line graph, look for a trend; if it is a circle graph, compare the sizes of the different sections.

Identifying Biases in Graphs

Some graphs are intentionally displayed in a way that favours a specific viewpoint or persuades others to interpret the data in a certain way. In the example below, both graphs show exactly the same data. However, the scales on the y-axes are different.

Number of People Affected by Smoking (2000 to 2015)

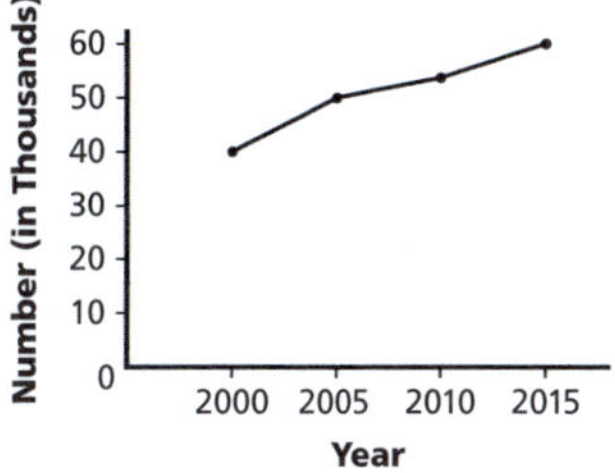

Graph A

Number of People Affected by Smoking (2000 to 2015)

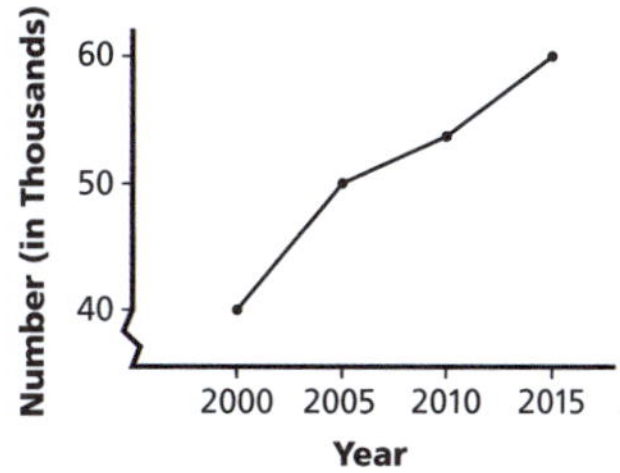

Graph B

A group that is against the use of cigarettes would use Graph B to show that the number of people affected had increased significantly over the years, whereas a company that sells cigarettes would use Graph A to show that the impact was present but not significant.

12.2 Making Graphs

In this unit, you will learn the different characteristics that distinguish bar graphs, line graphs, and circle graphs. You will also learn to recognize when it is suitable to use a certain type of graph.

Knowing the Characteristics of Different Graphs

Before making a graph, you must choose the most appropriate type of graph for a given set of data. Below are the three most commonly used graphs. Each one has characteristics that make it a better choice over the others in different situations.

Bar Graph

- can be vertical or horizontal
- is suitable for comparing values, including those that involve time
- Double bar graphs allow direct comparisons, for example, between the number of boys and the number of girls in Grade 7 classes.

Line Graph

- is commonly used to show data that involves time
- effectively reveals trends and relationships in data
- Double line graphs allow for direct comparisons of data of the same type over a period of time.

A bar graph is effective if there are just a few items that need to be shown. For more than 8 items, it is usually a better idea to use a line graph.

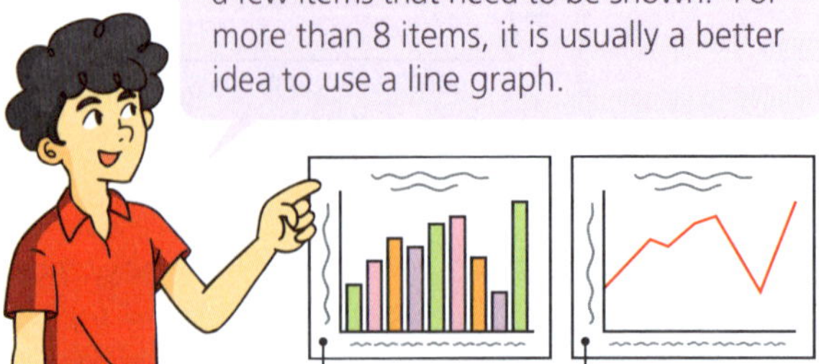

bars too tightly packed

a better representation of the data

Circle Graph

- provides a visual concept of a whole
- uses percents to compare information
- is suitable for components that have significant differences in their values

Steps to drawing a circle graph:

1st Find the relative frequency of each component by dividing its value by the whole.

2nd Multiply the relative frequency by 360°.

3rd Draw the component with the size of the angle.

Chapter 13

Probability

13.1 Finding Probability

In this unit, you will learn to differentiate between experimental probability and theoretical probability. You will also use a tree diagram to find possible outcomes to determine theoretical probabilities.

Experimental probability and theoretical probability are closely related, but are determined differently.

- **experimental probability:**
  the probability of an event occurring that is determined from actual experiments

$$\text{Probability of an Event} = \frac{\text{No. of Times the Event Occurred}}{\text{Total No. of Trials}}$$

- **theoretical probability:**
  the probability of an event that will occur in theory

$$\text{Probability of an Event} = \frac{\text{No. of Favourable Outcomes}}{\text{Total No. of Possible Outcomes}}$$

In most cases, experimental probability and theoretical probability are not equal, but as more trials are conducted, they should become relatively close.

e.g. If a coin is tossed 3 times, what is the probability of getting at least 2 heads?

Determine the total number of possible outcomes using a tree diagram.

Probability $= \frac{4}{8} = 50\%$

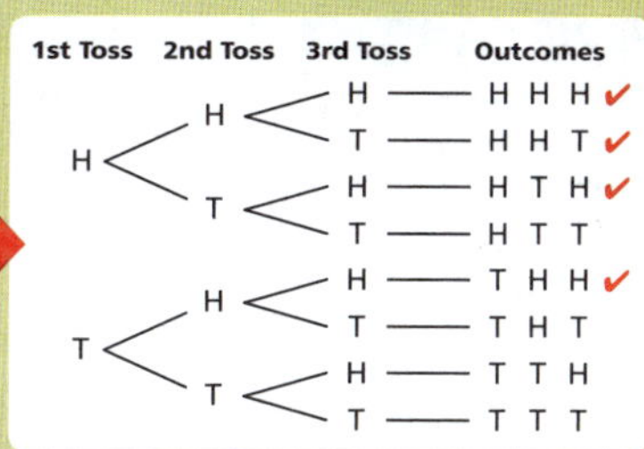

So, the probability of getting at least 2 heads is 50%.

13.2 Predicting Outcomes

In this unit, you will learn to predict the number of times an event will occur using probability.

In order to predict the number of times an event will occur, find its probability of occurring first. Then multiply the number of trials by the probability.

e.g.

Predict how many times the dice will land on 2 if I roll it 30 times.

Probability of landing on 2 $= \frac{1}{6}$ ← no. of times it will land on 2 (numerator); ← total no. of outcomes (denominator)

Prediction $= 30 \times \frac{1}{6} = 5$

So, it is predicted that the dice will land on 2 **5 times**.

e.g.

Predict how many times the spinner will land on red if I spin it 60 times.

Measure the angle of the red section with a protractor to find the probability of landing on red.

Probability of landing on red $= \frac{30^\circ}{360^\circ} = \frac{1}{12}$ (30° ← red; 360° ← a whole)

Prediction $= 60 \times \frac{1}{12} = 5$

So, it is predicted that the spinner will land on red **5 times**.

Grade 8

Chapter 1

Numbers

1.1 Exponential Notation

Exponential notation is a simplified way of expressing repeated multiplication. It is particularly useful when writing large numbers. In this unit, you will learn to write numbers in exponential notation and solve problems involving exponents.

For 2^3, we say "2 to the power of 3" or "2 to the third power".

exponent

$2^3 = 2 \times 2 \times 2$

base

2 multiplies itself 3 times.

y^n

exponent/power the number of times the base multiplies itself

base the number being multiplied

Any number raised to the power of zero equals one.

e.g. $5^0 = \underline{1}$; $21^0 = \underline{1}$

Writing numbers to the power of 10 is a very useful way of expressing large numbers such as 1 million and 10 billion.

e.g. $10^5 = 10 \times 10 \times 10 \times 10 \times 10$

$= 100\ 000$ ← 5 zeros

powers of 10 = the number of zeros in a number

e.g. $10^5 = 100\ 000$ (5 zeros)

Application

What are the missing exponents? What is the relationship between the number of zeros in multiples of 10 and the exponents?

1	= 10^0
10	= 10^1
100	= 10^2
1000	= 10^3
10 000	= $10^{\square}$
100 000	= $10^{\square}$
1 000 000	= $10^{\square}$
10 000 000	= $10^{\square}$

Solution:

1 = 10^0

10 = 10^1
1 zero

100 = 10^2
2 zeros

1000 = 10^3
3 zeros

10 000 = 10^4
4 zeros

100 000 = 10^5
5 zeros

1 000 000 = 10^6
6 zeros

10 000 000 = 10^7
7 zeros

The missing exponents are 4, 5, 6, and 7. The number of zeros in each multiple of 10 is equal to the exponent.

1.2 Whole Numbers

You have learned to write whole numbers in standard form, expanded form, and words. In this unit, you will learn to express whole numbers in expanded form as powers of ten. Practise using a place value chart to record numbers. This can help you visualize the value of each digit and read numbers in groups of three.

Numbers in Expanded Form

A place value chart can help you locate the value of each digit in a number.

e.g. 15 236 407

Place Value Chart

Millions			Thousands					
Hundred	Ten	One	Hundred	Ten	One	Hundreds	Tens	Ones
100 000 000	10 000 000	1 000 000	100 000	10 000	1000	100	10	1
10^8	10^7	10^6	10^5	10^4	10^3	10^2	10^1	10^0
	1	**5**	**2**	**3**	**6**	**4**	**0**	**7**

powers of 10

- in **Expanded Form:**

  10 000 000 + 5 000 000 + 200 000 + 30 000 + 6000 + 400 + 7

- in **Expanded Form Using Powers of 10:**

  $1 \times 10^7 + 5 \times 10^6 + 2 \times 10^5 + 3 \times 10^4 + 6 \times 10^3 + 4 \times 10^2 + 7 \times 10^0$

The powers of 10 represent the number of zeros.

e.g. $1\underbrace{000\ 000}_{6\text{ zeros}} = 10^6$

$5\ 000\ 000 = 5 \times 1\ 000\ 000$
$= 5 \times 10^6$

Application

The price of a house is $\$(1 \times 10^6 + 2 \times 10^5 + 8 \times 10^4 + 3 \times 10^2)$ in 2018. The price of the house will be 10 times its current price every 5 years. What will the prices of the house be in 2023 and 2028?

Solution:

Price in 2018 = $\$(1 \times 10^6 + 2 \times 10^5 + 8 \times 10^4 + 3 \times 10^2)$

In 2023, 5 years will have passed and the price of the house will be 10 times the price in 2018. This means that each exponent will go up by 1.

Price in 2023 = $\$(1 \times 10^7 + 2 \times 10^6 + 8 \times 10^5 + 3 \times 10^3)$ = $12 803 000

In 2028, another 5 years will have passed and the price of the house will be 10 times the price in 2023. So, each exponent will go up by 1 again.

Price in 2028 = $\$(1 \times 10^8 + 2 \times 10^7 + 8 \times 10^6 + 3 \times 10^4)$ = $128 030 000

The prices of the house in 2023 and 2028 will be $12 803 000 and $128 030 000 respectively.

1.3 Integers

Integers include zero and all positive and negative whole numbers, such as -3 and +4. In this unit, you will learn to add and subtract integers, and then multiply and divide them. Use a number line to learn about addition and subtraction of integers. For multiplication and division, memorize the rules outlined below.

+ or - Integers

Use the first number in an expression as the starting point. Then move the correct number of units to the left or right to find the answer.

Adding a Positive Integer

- Move the units to the right.

e.g. +2 + (+3)
= **+5**

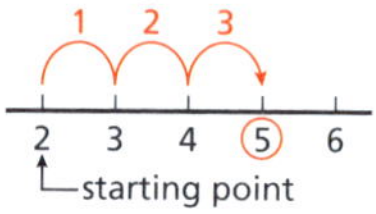

Adding a Negative Integer

- Move the units to the left.

e.g. -3 + (-4)
= **-7**

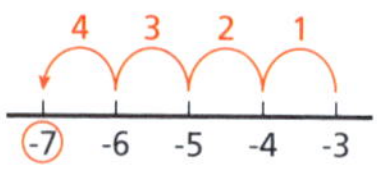

Subtracting a Positive Integer

- Move the units to the left.

e.g. +2 – (+3)
= **-1**

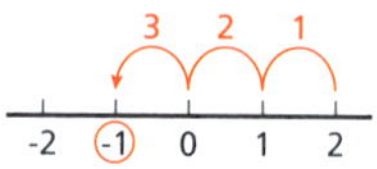

Subtracting a Negative Integer

- Move the units to the right.

e.g. -1 – (-4)
= **+3**

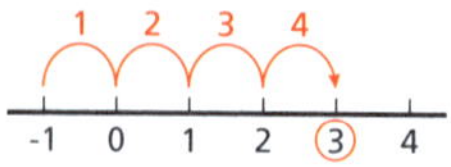

x or ÷ Integers

Rules to Remember

(+) x (+) = +	(+) ÷ (+) = +
(+) x (–) = –	(+) ÷ (–) = –
(–) x (+) = –	(–) ÷ (+) = –
(–) x (–) = +	(–) ÷ (–) = +

If the signs of the integers being multiplied or divided are the same, the answer is positive. If the signs are different, the answer is negative.

e.g. (+2) x (-5)
= **-10** ← **1st** 2 x 5 = 10
2nd (+) x (–) = –

(-20) ÷ (-4)
= **+5** ← **1st** 20 ÷ 4 = 5
2nd (–) ÷ (–) = +

Application

In the past 2 weeks, there were 4 days at 3°C, 7 days at -8°C, and 3 days at -18°C. What was the daily average temperature over the past 2 weeks?

Solution:

"In the past 2 weeks" = 14 days

Daily average temperature: $\frac{4 \times 3 + 7 \times (-8) + 3 \times (-18)}{14}$

$= \frac{12 + (-56) + (-54)}{14}$

$= \frac{(-98)}{14}$

$= -7$

The daily average temperature over the past 2 weeks was -7°C.

1.4 Order of Operations

In Grade 7, you learned to evaluate expressions involving whole numbers, decimals, brackets, and exponents using the order of operations. In this unit, you will evaluate expressions that also contain integers. You can review the order of operations to make sure you are able to apply it when evaluating complicated expressions.

Follow the order of operations to evaluate the expressions.

Order of Operations

B E D M A S

B – Brackets
E – Exponents
D – Division
M – Multiplication
A – Addition
S – Subtraction

e.g. $9^2 \div (1 + 2) \times 2 - 15$

$= 9^2 \div \mathbf{3} \times 2 - 15$ ← Do the **brackets** first.

$= \mathbf{81} \div 3 \times 2 - 15$ ← Evaluate the **exponent**.

$= \mathbf{27} \times 2 - 15$ ← Do ÷/x from left to right, so do ÷ first.

$= \mathbf{54} - 15$ ← **Multiply**.

$= \underline{\mathbf{39}}$ ← **Subtract**.

Watch the signs closely when evaluating expressions. Try to evaluate the following expressions and see whether or not you can get the correct answers.

Try These!

- $3 \times (8^2 - 6^2) \div (-4) + 10 = \underline{-11}$
- $3 \times 8^2 - 6^2 \div (-4 + 10) = \underline{186}$
- $3 \times 8^2 - (6^2 \div (-4) + 10) = \underline{191}$
- $(3 \times 8^2 - 6^2) \div (-4) + 10 = \underline{-29}$

Some calculators do not consider the order of operations, so do not rely on a calculator to find answers.

Application

One day in December, the mean temperature of these four western Canadian cities was -17.25°C. What was the temperature in Regina?

City	Temperature (°C)
Calgary	-13
Edmonton	-16
Regina	
Saskatoon	-19

Solution:

The mean temperature of -17.25°C is the average temperature of the 4 cities.

Sum of the temperatures of the 4 cities: $(-17.25) \times 4 = -69$

The temperature in Regina: $(-69) - (-13) - (-16) - (-19) = -21$

The temperature in Regina was -21°C.

1.5 Common Factors and Common Multiples

In Grade 6, you learned how to write composite numbers as products of prime factors using factor trees. In this unit, you will learn to find the greatest common factor (GCF) and the least common multiple (LCM) of two numbers using prime factors. These important concepts will help you do operations with fractions.

Composite Number

a number that has factors in addition to 1 and itself

e.g. Factors of 9: **1, 3, 9**

9 is a composite number.

A Factor Tree

e.g.

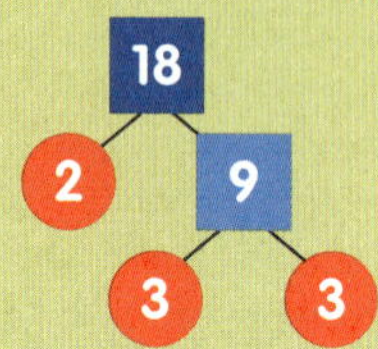

18 = **2 x 3 x 3**

↑ a product of prime factors

Finding the GCF Using Prime Factorization

Steps:

1st Write each number as a product of prime factors.

2nd Circle the common prime factors.

3rd Multiply them to find the GCF.

e.g. Find the GCF of 12 and 30.

1st

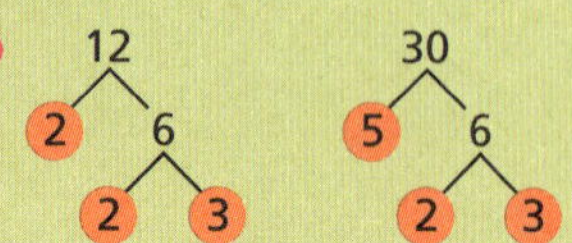

2nd 12 = 2 x 2 x 3

30 = 2 x 3 x 5

common prime factors: 2 and 3

3rd GCF = 2 x 3

= **6**

The GCF of 12 and 30 is **6**.

Finding the LCM Using Prime Factorization

Steps:

1st Write each number as a product of prime factors.

2nd Multiply the common factors to find the GCF.

3rd Multiply the GCF by the remaining factors to find the LCM.

e.g. Find the LCM of 12 and 30.

1st

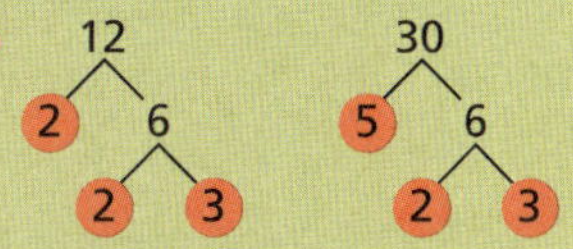

2nd (common prime factors)

$12 = 2 \times 2 \times 3$

$30 = 2 \times 3 \times 5$

3rd $\text{LCM} = 2 \times 3 \times 2 \times 5$

$= \underline{60}$

So, the LCM of 12 and 30 is $\underline{60}$.

Try This!

It is even easier to find the GCF and the LCM when the factors are written in a neat and orderly way.

e.g.

$12 = 2 \times 2 \times 3$ ← Each factor has its own column.

$30 = 2 \times \quad 3 \times 5$

Write down the common factors.

$\text{GCF} = 2 \times 3 = \underline{6}$

$\text{LCM} = 2 \times 2 \times 3 \times 5 = \underline{60}$

Write down each remaining factor.

Application

The GCF of a pair of numbers is 12 and the LCM is 84. What are the two numbers?

Solution:

GCF = 12 = 2 × 2 × 3
LCM = 84 = 2 × 2 × 3 × □

So, 84 = 12 × □
□ = 7

We know that the common prime factors 2 × 2 × 3 are in both numbers because they form the GCF, 12. For the LCM, 7 is the only non-common prime factor, and must belong to one of the two numbers. So,

first number = 2 × 2 × 3 × 7 = 84
second number = 2 × 2 × 3 = 12

The two numbers are 12 and 84.

1.6 Squares and Square Roots

You should already be familiar with perfect squares and square roots (e.g. 25 is a perfect square and the square root of 25 is 5; $\sqrt{25} = 5$). In this unit, you will learn to estimate and find the square roots of whole numbers with and without a calculator.

Square of a Number

e.g. Square of 10 $= 10^2$

$= \underline{\textbf{100}}$

Square Root of a Number

e.g. Square root of 10 $= \sqrt{10}$

$\approx \underline{\textbf{3.16}}$

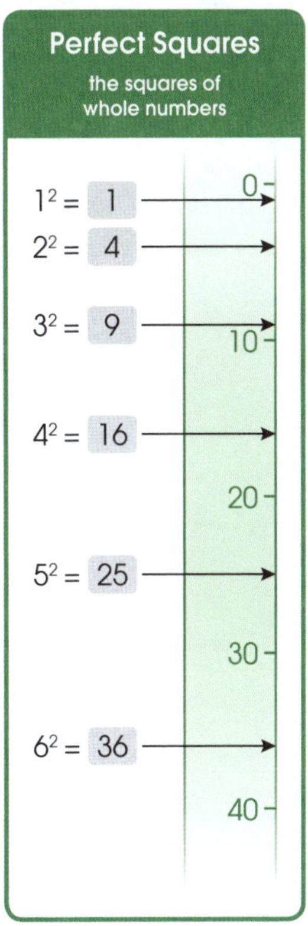

You may find it difficult to find the square root of a number without using a calculator. See how to use a number line to find the answer.

e.g. Evaluate $\sqrt{30}$.

1st 30 is between the two perfect squares, 25 and 36.

2nd $\sqrt{30}$ must be between 5 and 6.

3rd Guess and check the answer.

Guess	Check
5.6	$5.6^2 = 31.36 > 30$
5.5	$5.5^2 = 30.25 > 30$
5.4	$5.4^2 = 29.16 < 30$

So, $\sqrt{30}$ is about $\underline{\textbf{5.5}}$.

Application

Josie has two squares. She cuts the yellow one along the dotted lines. Then she combines the pieces with the pink square to form one big square. What is the side length of the big square?

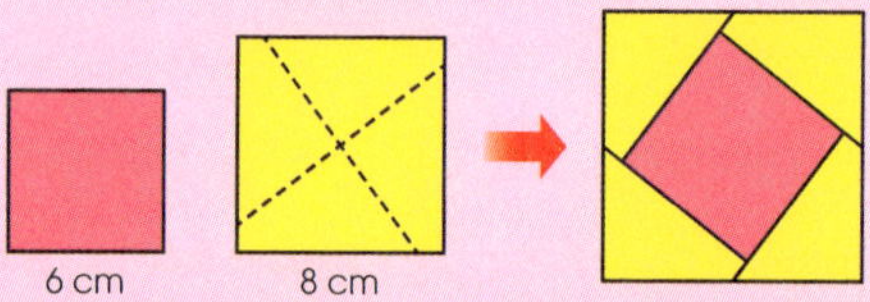

Solution:

The area of the new square is the sum of the areas of the two smaller squares.

$6^2 + 8^2$
$= 36 + 64$
$= 100$

Side length of the big square: $\sqrt{100} = 10$

The side length of the big square is 10 cm.

1.7 Rational Numbers

In this unit, you will learn about rational numbers and distinguish them from other types of numbers. You will also learn to represent, compare, and order rational numbers. Knowing the definition of rational numbers can help you understand how mathematicians sort numbers into categories and prepare you for solving algebraic problems in high school.

Rational Numbers

numbers that can be written as fractions with integers where the denominator is not zero

A rational number = $\frac{a}{b}$,

where a and b are integers and $b \neq 0$.

Integers – zero and all positive and negative whole numbers

e.g. ... -3, -2, -1, 0, 1, 2, 3, ...

Examples of Rational Numbers

- **Integers and Fractions**

e.g. 5 ← can be written as the fraction $\frac{5}{1}$ (5 and 1 are integers.)

-3 ← can be written as the fraction $\frac{-3}{1}$ (-3 and 1 are integers.)

$\frac{2}{5}$ ← in the form of a fraction already

So, 5, -3, and $\frac{2}{5}$ are rational numbers.

- **Terminating Decimals** – a decimal that ends

e.g. 0.4 ← can be converted into a fraction

$= \frac{4}{10}$ ← 4 and 10 are integers.

So, 0.4 is a rational number.

- **Repeating Decimals** – a decimal that does not end, but instead repeats digits

e.g. 0.33333... ← This can be written as the fraction $\frac{1}{3}$. We can also write it as $0.\overline{3}$.

$= \frac{1}{3}$ ← 1 and 3 are integers.

So, 0.33333... is a rational number.

Numbers that are not rational are called irrational numbers.

Examples of irrational numbers:

$\sqrt{2}$, $\sqrt{6}$, 3.1415...

Application

Tammy received a note from her classmate asking her to make a monster green solution with household items for their science project. Tammy read the note and said that it was impossible to make the solution with one of the amounts listed. Explain why.

Monster Green Solution

2^{10} mL **red cabbage juice**

$\frac{45}{\sqrt{324}}$ mL **vinegar**

$\sqrt{400}$ **cotton balls**

$\sqrt{60}$ **grapes**

$\frac{\sqrt{1089}}{4}$ g **baking soda**

Solution:

Red cabbage juice: $2^{10} = 1024$ (mL)

Vinegar: $\frac{45}{\sqrt{324}} = \frac{45}{18} = 2.5$ (mL)

Cotton balls: $\sqrt{400} = 20$

Grapes: $\sqrt{60} = 7.74596...$ ← irrational number

Baking soda: $\frac{\sqrt{1089}}{4} = \frac{33}{4} = 8.25$ (g)

It is impossible to get $\sqrt{60}$ grapes because $\sqrt{60}$ is an irrational number that is equivalent to 7.74596...

Chapter 2

Fractions, Decimals, and Percents

2.1 Addition and Subtraction of Fractions

By Grade 8, you should have a clear understanding of adding and subtracting fractions with like and unlike denominators. In this unit, you will apply the concept of the least common multiple (LCM) to find equivalent fractions for addition and subtraction and the concept of the greatest common factor (GCF) to write fractions in simplest form.

Adding / Subtracting Fractions with Unlike Denominators

Rewrite mixed numbers as improper fractions if needed.

- **1st** Find the LCM of the denominators.
- **2nd** Rewrite the fractions as equivalent fractions with the LCM as the denominators.
- **3rd** Add / subtract the fractions.
- **4th** Simplify the answer by dividing the numerator and denominator by their GCF.

e.g.

$1\frac{7}{15} - \frac{11}{12}$ ← They are unlike denominators, so find the LCM of 15 and 12, which is 60.

$= 1\frac{28}{60} - \frac{55}{60}$ ← $\frac{7 \times 4}{15 \times 4} = \mathbf{\frac{28}{60}}$; $\frac{11 \times 5}{12 \times 5} = \mathbf{\frac{55}{60}}$

$= \frac{88}{60} - \frac{55}{60}$ ← Rewrite $1\frac{28}{60}$ as $\frac{88}{60}$ and subtract.

$= \frac{33}{60}$ ← Divide 33 and 60 by their GCF, 3.

$= \mathbf{\frac{11}{20}}$ ← Show the answer in simplest form.

Application

Kristen's phone has 16 gigabytes of memory for photos. $7\frac{5}{6}$ gigabytes had already been used before Kristen took some more photos, which used another $4\frac{7}{10}$ gigabytes. After deleting some photos, there are $8\frac{2}{3}$ gigabytes of unused memory. How many gigabytes of photos did she delete?

Solution:

First look at how much memory was unused before photos were deleted.

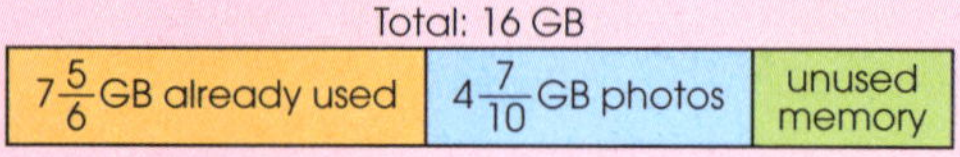

Unused memory: $16 - 7\frac{5}{6} - 4\frac{7}{10}$

$= 16 - 7\frac{25}{30} - 4\frac{21}{30}$

$= 3\frac{14}{30}$

$= 3\frac{7}{15}$

The deleted memory is equal to the difference between the amount of unused memory before and after deleting.

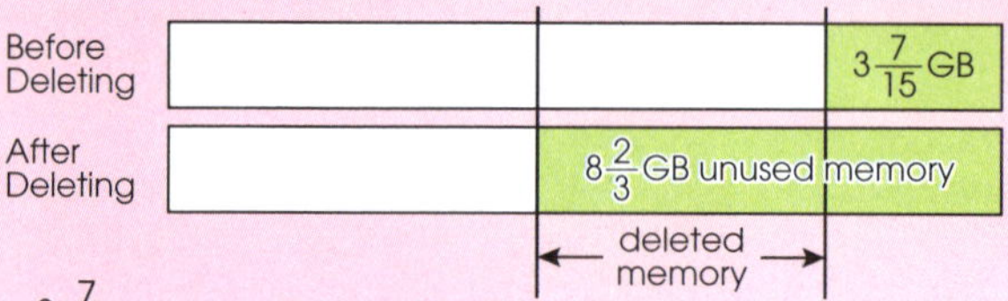

$8\frac{2}{3} - 3\frac{7}{15}$

$= 8\frac{10}{15} - 3\frac{7}{15}$

$= 5\frac{3}{15}$

$= 5\frac{1}{5}$

So, Kristen deleted $5\frac{1}{5}$ gigabytes of photos.

2.2 Multiplication of Fractions

In this unit, you will multiply fractions. The rules below show the correct steps for multiplying fractions. Once you grasp the basic idea, you can find the answers more effectively using the trick as shown.

Rules for Multiplying Fractions

1st Change all mixed numbers or whole numbers (if any) into improper fractions.

2nd Multiply the numerators.

3rd Multiply the denominators.

4th Reduce the answer to its simplest form.

e.g.

$2\frac{1}{7} \times \frac{3}{5}$ ← Change $2\frac{1}{7}$ to an improper fraction.

$= \frac{15}{7} \times \frac{3}{5}$ ← Multiply the numerators (15 x 3) and the denominators (7 x 5).

$= \frac{\cancel{45}^{\,9}}{\cancel{35}_{\,7}}$ ← Reduce 45 and 35 by their GCF, 5.

$= \frac{9}{7}$ ← Rewrite it as a mixed number.

$= \mathbf{1\frac{2}{7}}$

e.g.

$2\frac{1}{7} \times \frac{3}{5}$

$= \frac{\cancel{15}^{\,3}}{7} \times \frac{3}{\cancel{5}_{\,1}}$

A Trick! Reduce between any numerators and any denominators if possible. In this question, divide 15 and 5 by their GCF, 5.

$= \frac{9}{7}$ ← numerator: 3 x 3; denominator: 7 x 1

$= \mathbf{1\frac{2}{7}}$

Here is a trick to help you find the answer faster.

Application

Carmen wants to use $\frac{7}{8}$ of her savings to buy a gift. She thinks that if the gift is sold at half price, she will have \$20 left. Is her thinking correct?

Solution:

Cost of gift:

$$30\frac{2}{5} \times \frac{7}{8}$$
$$= \frac{\overset{19}{\cancel{152}}}{5} \times \frac{7}{\cancel{8}_1}$$
$$= \frac{133}{5}$$
$$= 26\frac{3}{5}$$

Discounted price of gift:

$$26\frac{3}{5} \times \frac{1}{2}$$
$$= \frac{133}{5} \times \frac{1}{2}$$
$$= \frac{133}{10}$$
$$= 13\frac{3}{10}$$

Money left after purchase:

$$30\frac{2}{5} - 13\frac{3}{10}$$
$$= 30\frac{4}{10} - 13\frac{3}{10}$$
$$= 17\frac{1}{10}$$

Carmen will have $\$17\frac{1}{10}$ left, so her thinking is incorrect.

2.3 Division of Fractions

In this unit, you will learn to divide fractions. The three simple steps below help you grasp the concept of dividing a number by a fraction.

Reciprocal of a Fraction

To find the reciprocal of a fraction, just swap the numerator and the denominator.

Before doing the division, I need to know how to find the reciprocal of a fraction.

e.g.

Fraction	Reciprocal
$\frac{3}{8}$	$\frac{8}{3}$
$\frac{2}{1}$	$\frac{1}{2}$

Dividing by a Fraction

1st Change all the mixed numbers or whole numbers (if any) into improper fractions.

2nd Change ÷ to x and the divisor to its reciprocal.

3rd Multiply and simplify the fraction.

e.g.

$2\frac{2}{5} \div \frac{8}{15}$ ← Rewrite $2\frac{2}{5}$ as $\frac{12}{5}$.

$= \frac{\cancel{12}^{3}}{\cancel{5}_{1}} \times \frac{\cancel{15}^{3}}{\cancel{8}_{2}}$ ← Change ÷ to x and $\frac{8}{15}$ to $\frac{15}{8}$.

Simplify the numerators and the denominators.

Divide 15 and 5 by their GCF, 5.

Divide 12 and 8 by their GCF, 4.

$= \frac{9}{2}$ ← 3×3 ; ← 1×2

$= \underline{\mathbf{4\frac{1}{2}}}$

Application

Jack the farmer has a rectangular field with an area of $16\frac{4}{5}$ km^2. If he divides his field into 3 equal sections, what will be the dimensions of each section?

Solution:

Length of the field: $16\frac{4}{5} \div 3\frac{1}{2}$

$= \frac{84}{5} \div \frac{7}{2}$

$= \frac{\cancel{84}^{12}}{5} \times \frac{2}{\cancel{7}_1}$

$= \frac{24}{5}$

$= 4\frac{4}{5}$

Width of each section: $4\frac{4}{5} \div 3$

$= \frac{\cancel{24}^{8}}{5} \times \frac{1}{\cancel{3}_1}$

$= 1\frac{3}{5}$

So, the dimensions of each section will be $3\frac{1}{2}$ km by $1\frac{3}{5}$ km.

2.4 Multiplication and Division of Decimals

At this level, you should be familiar with multiplying and dividing decimals. In this unit, you will learn to multiply and divide decimals to various powers of ten. You will also apply this to conversions among various metric units.

Multiplying or Dividing by a Power of 10

a decimal x **a power of 10**

Move the . to the **right** as many places as the number of **0**'s there are in the power. Add 0's as placeholders if needed.

e.g. 0.53×10^5 ← Move the . 5 places to the right.

= **53 000**

0.5 3 0 0 0.
Add 3 zeros.

a decimal ÷ **a power of 10**

Move the . to the **left** as many places as the number of **0**'s there are in the power. Add 0's as placeholders if needed.

e.g. $5300 \div 10^6$ ← Move the . 6 places to the left.

= **0.0053**

.0 0 5 3 0 0.
Add 2 zeros.

Metric Conversions

Length

1 km = 1000 m = 10^3 m
= 100 000 cm = 10^5 cm
= 1 000 000 mm = 10^6 mm

Area

1 m^2 = 100 cm x 100 cm
= 10 000 cm^2
= 10^4 cm^2

To convert a big unit into a small unit, we use multiplication. To convert a small unit into a big unit, we use division.

e.g. Convert 0.25 m^2 into cm^2.

$0.25\ m^2 = 0.25 \times 10^4\ cm^2$ ← $1\ m^2 = 10^4\ cm^2$

= **2500 cm^2**

0.2 5 0 0.
Move . 4 places to the right.

Application

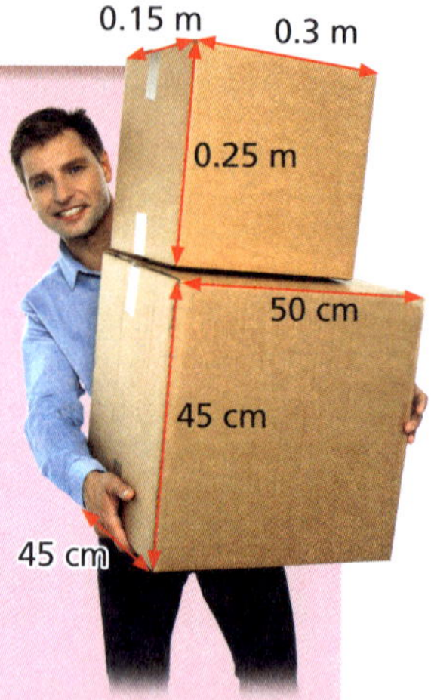

Uncle Sam has 100 small boxes and 10 big boxes. Do the 100 small boxes or the 10 big boxes take up more space?

Solution:

Volume of a small box:

$0.15\text{ m} \times 0.3\text{ m} \times 0.25\text{ m}$
$= 0.01125\text{ m}^3$

Volume of 100 small boxes:

$0.01125\text{ m}^3 \times 100$
$= 1.125\text{ m}^3$

Volume of a big box:

$45\text{ cm} \times 50\text{ cm} \times 45\text{ cm}$
$= 101\ 250\text{ cm}^3$
$= 0.10125\text{ m}^3$ ← $101\ 250 \div 10^6$
Convert into the same unit as the small box for comparison.

Volume of 10 big boxes:

$0.10125\text{ m}^3 \times 10$
$= 1.0125\text{ m}^3$

100 small boxes have a volume of 1.125 m^3 and 10 big boxes have a volume of 1.0125 m^3.

$1.125 > 1.0125$

So, 100 small boxes take up more space.

2.5 Percents

In previous grades, you learned to solve simple percent problems, such as finding a part of a whole (e.g. Find 15% of 80; 80 x 15% = 12). In Grade 8, you will learn to solve percent problems in a variety of real-life contexts, such as percent increase / decrease, discounts, and taxation on purchases.

Finding Percent Increase / Decrease

Percent Increase =

$$\frac{\text{amount increased}}{\text{original amount}} \times 100\%$$

Percent Decrease =

$$\frac{\text{amount decreased}}{\text{original amount}} \times 100\%$$

e.g. What is the percent increase for the number of tablets?

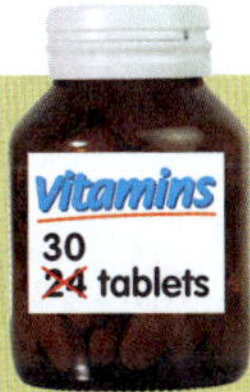

Increase: 30 – 24 = 6

Percent increase $= \frac{6}{24} \times 100\%$

$= \underline{\textbf{25\%}}$

Finding Discount and Sale Price

Discount =

Original Price x Discount in Percent

Sale Price =

Original Price – Discount

Finding Tax and Total

Tax = Price x Tax Rate

Total = Price + Tax

A shortcut for finding the sale price:

Sale Price = Original Price x (1 – Discount in Percent)

A shortcut for finding the total:

Total = Price x (1 + Tax Rate)

e.g.

$16.50

Sales Tax 13%

30% off

Discount = $16.50 x 30%
= $4.95

Sale Price = $16.50 – $4.95
= $11.55

Tax = $11.55 x 13%
= $1.50

Total = $11.55 + $1.50
= **$13.05**

Application

The cost of a pair of headphones on promotion is \$203.40 after a 13% tax. The regular price after tax would have been 25% more than the total. What is the regular price of the headphones? What is the percent discount?

Solution:

Regular price after tax: $\$203.40 \times (1 + 25\%)$
$= \$254.25$

Regular price before tax: $\$254.25 \div (1 + 13\%)$
$= \$225$

Promotion price before tax: $\$203.40 \div (1 + 13\%)$
$= \$180$

Discount amount: $\$225 - \$180$
$= \$45$

Discount in percent : $\frac{\$45}{\$225} \times 100\%$
$= 20\%$

The regular price of the headphones is \$225 and the discount is 20% off.

2.6 Equivalent Forms of Fractions, Decimals, and Percents

Fractions, decimals, and percents are different representations of the same value. In this unit, you will convert among fractions, decimals, and percents using 100-square grids, strip diagrams, multiplication, and division.

e.g.

0.35

$= \frac{0.35}{1}$

$= \frac{0.35 \times 100}{1 \times 100}$

$= \frac{35}{100}$

$= \frac{7}{20}$

- Write the decimal over 1.
- Multiply the numerator and the denominator by 10, 100, or 1000 to make the numerator a whole number.
- Simplify the fraction.

You may have difficulty deciding on the correct operation to convert among fractions, decimals, and percents. You can grasp the concept using this diagram.

Decimals

Divide the numerator by the denominator.

e.g. $\frac{2}{5} = 0.4$ $\quad 5\overline{)2\,0}$ → 0.4; 2 0

Fractions

Multiply the decimal by 100%.

e.g. $0.35 = 0.35 \times 100\%$

$= 35\%$

Remove the % sign. Put the number over 100. Simplify the fraction.

e.g. $28\% = \frac{28}{100}$

$= \frac{7}{25}$

Percents

Divide the numerator by the denominator. Then multiply the answer by 100%.

e.g. $\frac{3}{8} = 3 \div 8$

$= 0.375$

$= 0.375 \times 100\%$

$= 37.5\%$

Divide the percent by 100. Then remove the % sign.

e.g. 78%

$= 0.78$

$78 \div 100$

$= 0.78.$

Application

Sue conducted a music survey among her clients. She found that 0.42 prefer pop music, and more than 30% prefer rock music. What fraction of the clients prefer country music? Suggest one possible fraction.

Solution:

Pop music: 0.42 = 42%

Since the total percent must equal 100%,

Pop + Rock + Country = 100%

42% + Rock + Country = 100%

Rock + Country = 58%

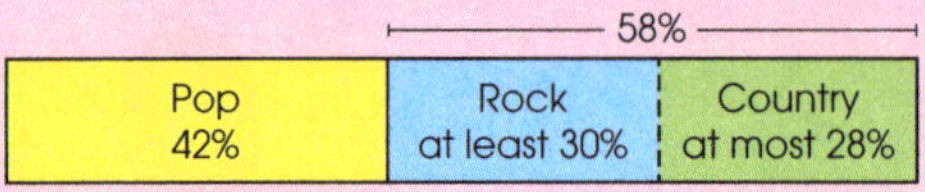

At most 28% of clients would have preferred country music.

(Suggested answer)
A possible percent would be 25%.

$25\% = \frac{25}{100} = \frac{1}{4}$

So, $\frac{1}{4}$ of the clients prefer country music.

Chapter 3

Proportions and Rates

3.1 Proportions

A proportion is a mathematical comparison between two quantities. In a direct proportion, as one quantity increases, the other increases at the same rate, and vice versa. In this unit, you will relate proportions to real-life contexts.

We can make 3 cakes with 2 bananas. This is an example of a direct proportion. The number of bananas is always related to the number of cakes at a rate of 1.5.

No. of Bananas		No. of Cakes
2	x 1.5 →	3
4	x 1.5 →	6
6	x 1.5 →	9
8	x 1.5 →	12

e.g. How many bananas are needed to make 24 cakes?

$\frac{2}{3} = \frac{x}{24}$ (bananas / cakes) ← Set up a proportion in fraction form.

$\frac{2}{3} = \frac{x}{24}$ (x 8 on top and bottom) ← Find the equivalent fraction.

$x = \underline{16}$

So, **16 bananas** are needed to make 24 cakes.

Cross Multiplication

$\frac{2}{3} = \frac{x}{24}$ ← Multiply the numbers as shown by the arrows.

$3x = 48$ ← Isolate x by dividing both sides by 3.

$x = 48 \div 3$

$x = 16$

Here is an example that does not represent a directly proportional relationship.

Sue is 12 years old and her father is 38.

Sue's age	12	13	14
	x 3.17	x 3	x 2.86
Her father's age	38	39	40

Their ages are not related by multiplication because the rates are different.

Application

Mrs. Martin's car covers 52 km with 4.8 litres of gas. How much gas does each car need to cover a distance of 100 km? Whose car is more fuel-efficient?

Solution:

Mrs. Martin's car:

km / litres: $\frac{52}{4.8} = \frac{100}{x}$

$52x = 4.8 \times 100$

$x = \frac{4.8 \times 100}{52}$

$x = 9.23$

Mrs. Martin's car needs 9.23 L of gas to cover 100 km.

Mr. Martin's car:

km / litres: $\frac{112}{8} = \frac{100}{y}$

$112y = 8 \times 100$

$y = \frac{8 \times 100}{112}$

$y = 7.14$

Mr. Martin's car needs 7.14 L of gas to cover 100 km.

Mr. Martin's car needs less gas to cover the same distance than Mrs. Martin's car. So, Mr. Martin's car is more fuel-efficient.

3.2 Rates

A rate is a ratio that compares two quantities of different units. For example, Tim runs 6 laps in 2 minutes, so he runs 6 laps/2 min. When rates are expressed as a quantity of 1, such as 3 laps in 1 minute and $25 per ticket, they are called unit rates. Problems involving rates can be solved using proportions.

Rates are used in many situations, such as finding speed with a given distance and time, and comparing unit prices when grocery shopping.

e.g. Abby cycles 34 km in 2 h. At this speed, how far can she cycle in 5 h?

$\frac{\text{distance}}{\text{time}}$ $\frac{34}{2} = \frac{y}{5}$ ← Set up a proportion.

$\frac{34}{2} = \frac{y}{5}$ ← Cross-multiply.

$2y = 170$ ← Divide both sides by 2.

$y = 85$

So, Abby can cycle **85 km** in 5 h.

Steps to Solving Rate Problems

1st Set up a proportion.

2nd Solve it using cross-multiplication.

We use rates in everyday life.

You can see how rates are applied with the examples below. Then consider how rate problems can be solved mentally.

e.g. Which is a better deal?

- grapefruit at 3 for $1.99 or 5 for $2.49

Which is a better deal?

- $84 for 7 h or $77 for 5.5 h

Application

Wendy and Marvin are comparing their heights. Marvin has grown 2.5 cm over the last 2 months while Wendy has grown 0.12 m over the past year. If their growth rates remain constant, how many months will it take for them to be the same height?

Solution:

Find the growth rates of both kids in the same unit.

Marvin: $2.5 \div 2 = 1.25$ (cm/month) ← growing faster

Wendy: $12 \div 12 = 1$ (cm/month)

Marvin grows faster than Wendy by 0.25 cm per month.

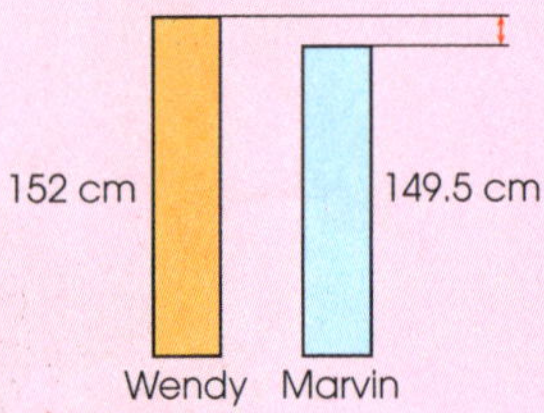

difference:
$152 - 149.5 = 2.5$ (cm)

Number of months needed to catch up: $2.5 \div 0.25 = 10$

So, it will take 10 months for them to be the same height.

Chapter 4

Circles and Cylinders

4.1 Constructing Circles

This is the first unit that introduces circles and attributes of circles. You will learn the terminology used to describe the attributes of a circle, and use a compass to construct circles and create simple circle designs.

Circle

centre –
the middle of a circle

diameter –
a line that joins two points on a circle and passes through the centre

radius –
the distance from the centre to a point on a circle

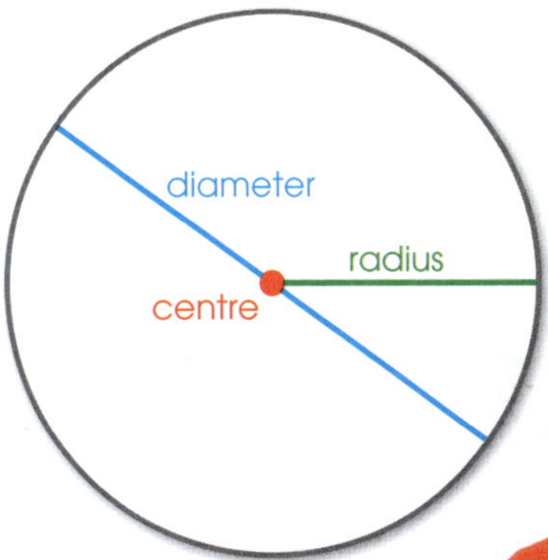

A circle is a 2-dimensional shape where all points along the circle are the same distance from its centre.

* Note that the diameter is twice as long as the radius.

$d = 2 \times r$

Constructing Circles with a Compass

e.g. Draw a circle with a radius of 4 cm using a compass.

Steps:

1st

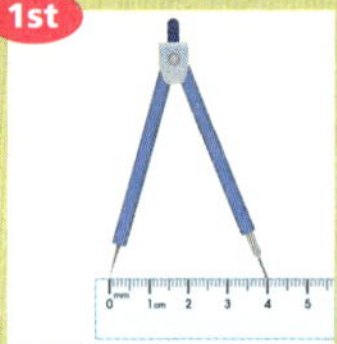

Open the arms of the compass 4 cm wide.

2nd

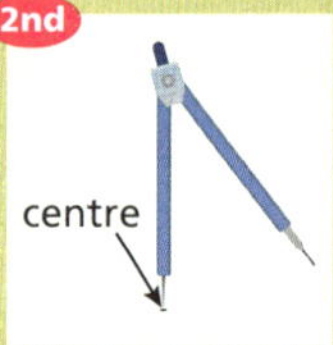

Press down the compass's needle on a piece of paper (this will be the centre of the circle).

3rd

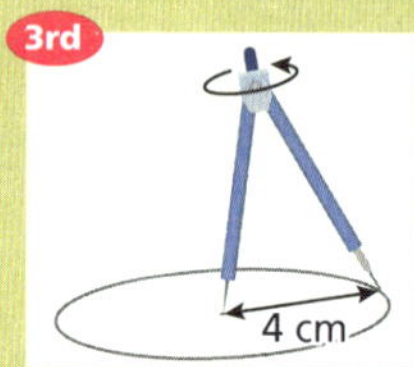

Draw the circle by turning the knob at the top of the compass 360°.

Circle Designs

We can use circles to create many beautiful designs. You can practise using a compass to draw the circles on a piece of paper.

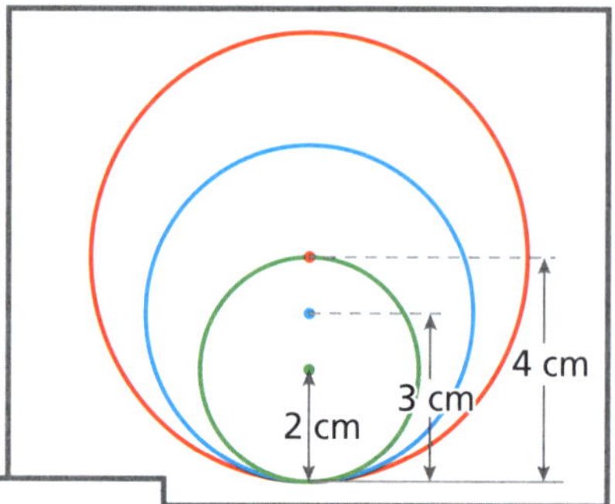

green – 2-cm radius
blue – 3-cm radius
red – 4-cm radius

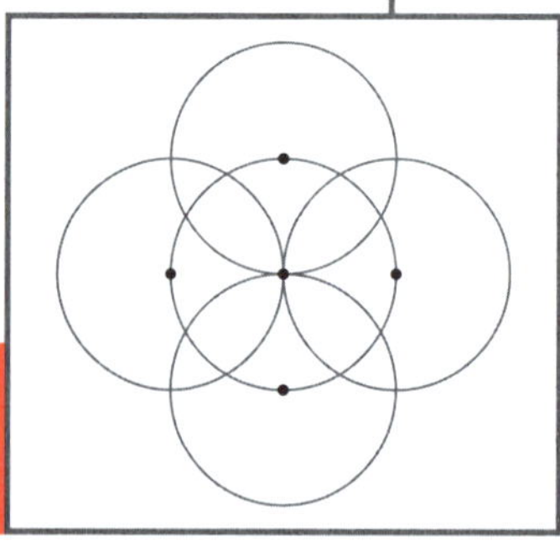

5 identical circles; each with a 4-cm radius

Application

Describe how to draw this circle design.

Solution:

There are 5 circles in the design: 1 big circle, and 4 small circles that each have a radius of half of that of the big circle.

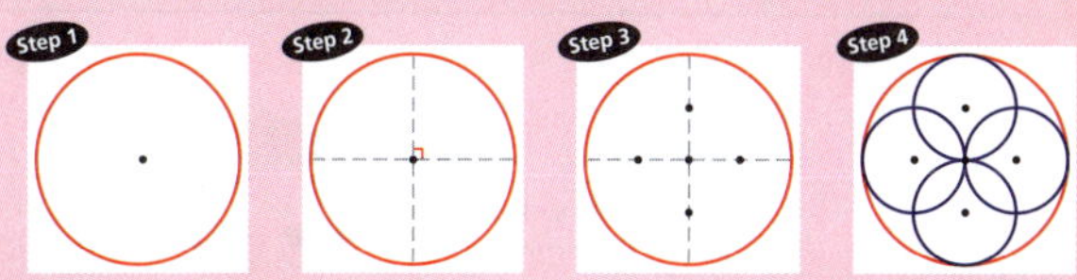

Step 1 Draw a centre and a big circle.

Step 2 Draw 2 diameters that intersect at a 90° angle.

Step 3 Draw 4 points on the diameters that are halfway from the centre.

Step 4 Use the new points as centres to draw 4 small circles.

4.2 Circumference of Circles

The circumference of a circle is the distance around its edge. It can also be considered as the perimeter of a circle. In this unit, you will learn the formula for finding the circumference of a circle and apply the formula to solve a variety of circle-related problems.

The ratio of circumference to diameter is the same for all circles.

$$\frac{\text{circumference}}{\text{diameter}} = \pi\ (3.14159...)$$

So, circumference = π x diameter.

Circumference of a Circle

$C = \pi d$ or $C = 2\pi r$ ($d = 2r$)

π (pronounced "pi") is an irrational number with infinite decimal places. At this level, you can consider π to be 3.14.

e.g.

How many times must the wheel turn to cover a distance of 1000 cm?

the distance covered by turning once = the circumference of the wheel

$= \pi \times 75$

$= 235.5$ (cm)

number of turns $= \frac{1000}{235.5}$

$= 4.25$

The wheel must turn 4.25 times.

Application

The London Eye is a Ferris wheel with a diameter of 120 m. The wheel rotates at a speed of 26 cm per second. How many minutes does it take to complete 1 revolution?

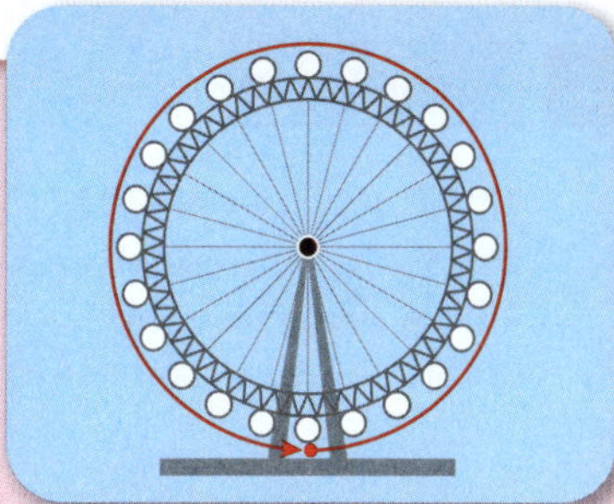

Solution:

The distance travelled in 1 revolution is equal to the circumference of the wheel.

Circumference: 120 m × 3.14 = 376.8 m = 37 680 cm

Time it takes for 1 revolution:

Time: 37 680 cm ÷ 26 cm/s = 1449 s = 24.15 min

It takes 24.15 min to complete 1 revolution.

4.3 Area of Circles

In this unit, you will learn to apply the formula $A = \pi r^2$ to find the area of a circle, and will solve problems involving the area of a circle given its radius, diameter, or circumference. When finding the radius of a circle using its area, remember to find the square root of a number first.

Area of a Circle

$A = \pi r^2$

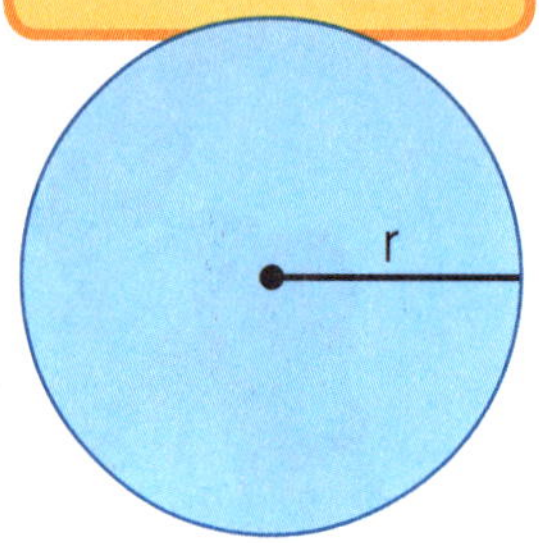

$A = \pi \times 5^2$

$= 3.14 \times 25$

$= \underline{78.5 \text{ (cm}^2\text{)}}$

Below is an example of a complex problem to show you how multiple steps are involved in solving the problem.

e.g. The circumference of a circle is 62.5 cm. What is its area?

Think

- To find the area of the circle ($A = \pi r^2$), we need to know its radius, which is not given.
- We know the circumference ($C = 2\pi r$) instead, so find the radius using the circumference first.

$C = 2\pi r$

$62.5 = 2 \times 3.14 \times r$

$r = 9.95$

$A = \pi r^2$

$A = 3.14 \times 9.95^2$

$= 310.87$

So, the area of the circle is 310.87 cm^2.

Application

Enzo wants to paint a target to practise archery. He paints a yellow circle with an area of 78.5 cm² in the middle of a 35 cm by 50 cm board. Each subsequent circle of the target is 4 cm longer in radius. How many circles can Enzo fit on the board? What is the area of the completed target?

Solution:

1st Find the radius of the yellow circle.

$78.5 = 3.14 \times r^2$

$r = 5$

2nd Find the dimensions of the subsequent circles.

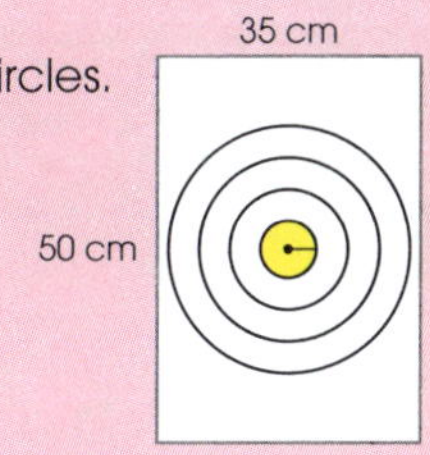

Circle	Radius (cm)	Diameter (cm)
1	5	10
2	9 (+4)	18
3	13 (+4)	26
4	17 (+4)	34
5	21 (+4)	42 > 35

← A circle with a diameter of 42 cm will not fit on a board of 35 cm by 50 cm.

The board can fit 4 circles.

Area of the target: $3.14 \times 17^2 = 907.46$

Enzo can fit 4 circles on the board and the area of the target is 907.46 cm².

4.4 Volume of Cylinders

A cylinder is a 3-D figure with a circular base. In previous grades, you learned to find the volume of a prism using the formula: V = area of base x height. In this unit, you will learn to apply this concept to find the volume of a cylinder using the same formula.

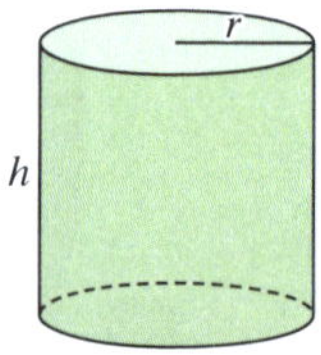

Volume of a Cylinder

V = area of base x height

$V = \pi r^2 \times h$

r = radius h = height

Both ends of a cylinder are congruent circles.

e.g. What is the volume of the container?

$V = \pi r^2 \times h$

$= 3.14 \times 7^2 \times 10$

$= 1538.6\ (cm^3)$

Remember to illustrate word problems whenever possible. This will help you better understand the problem.

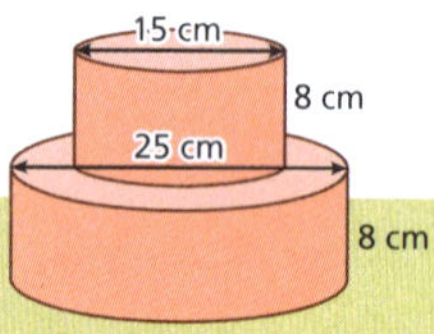

e.g. A cake has two tiers. The top tier has a diameter of 15 cm and the bottom tier is 10 cm longer. Each tier has a height of 8 cm. What is the volume of the cake?

Steps

1st Illustrate and label the dimensions of the cake.

2nd Apply the formula twice to find the volume.

V (top) $= \pi r^2 \times h$

$= 3.14 \times 7.5^2 \times 8$

$= 1413$

V (bottom) $= 3.14 \times 12.5^2 \times 8$

$= 3925$

Total Volume $= 1413 + 3925$

$= 5338$

The volume of the cake is 5338 cm^3.

Application

Agatha's bakery has boxes with dimensions of 25 cm x 25 cm x 12 cm for cakes. Each cake has to be at least 3 cm away from each side of the box. What is the largest volume a cylindrical cake can be to fit into the box?

Solution:

In order to fit into the box, the cake must leave space all around the sides and from the top.

The largest possible diameter: $25 - 3 - 3 = 19$

The largest possible height: $12 - 3 = 9$

Volume of cake: $3.14 \times 9.5^2 \times 9 = 2550.47$

Top View of Box

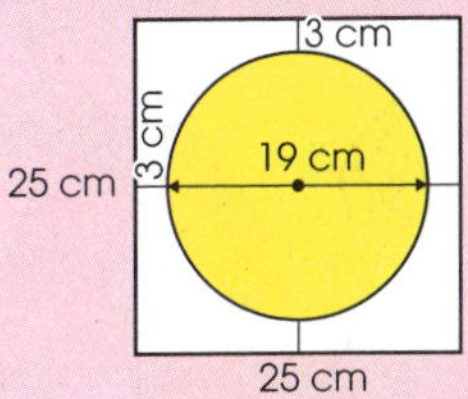

Side View of Box

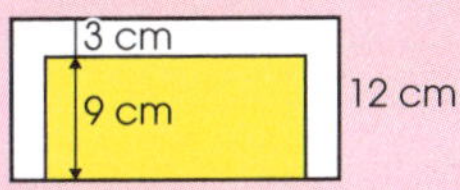

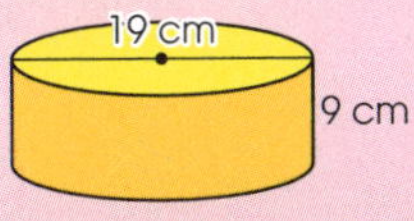

The largest volume a cake can be to fit into the box is 2550.47 cm³.

4.5 Surface Area of Cylinders

In this unit, you will learn to find the surface area of a cylinder. You should develop a better understanding of how the circumference of a circle is equal to the length of the rectangle.

Surface Area of a Cylinder

S.A. = sum of the areas of all the faces

= area of the 2 circles + area of the rectangle

= $\mathbf{2\pi r^2 + 2\pi rh}$

Sometimes, working backward is a good strategy to help us solve problems.

e.g. Tina has used 591.89 cm² of wrapping paper to wrap a cylindrical can with a radius of 6.5 cm. How tall is the can?

$$\text{S.A.} = 2\pi r^2 + 2\pi rh$$

$591.89 = 2 \times 3.14 \times (6.5)^2 + 2 \times 3.14 \times (6.5)h$ ← Substitute S.A. = 591.89 and $r = 6.5$.

$591.89 = 265.33 + 40.82h$ ← Multiply.

$40.82h = 326.56$ ← Isolate h.

$h = 8$ ← Divide to find h.

The can is 8 cm tall.

Application

Eric has a can of tennis balls. Each tennis ball has a radius of 3.4 cm. What is the total surface area of the can?

Solution:

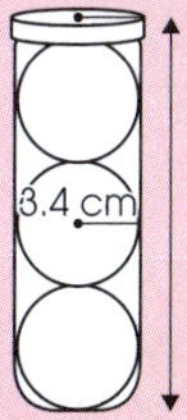

3.4 cm (The radius of the can is equal to the radius of 1 tennis ball.)

20.4 cm (The height of the can is equal to 6 times the radius of a tennis ball: $3.4 \times 6 = 20.4$.)

The dimensions of the can is 3.4 cm in radius and 20.4 cm in height.

Surface Area: $2\pi r^2 + 2\pi rh$

$$= 2 \times 3.14 \times 3.4^2 + 2 \times 3.14 \times 3.4 \times 20.4$$
$$= 72.6 + 435.58$$
$$= 508.18$$

The total surface area of the can is 508.18 cm^2.

4.6 Volume and Surface Area of Cylinders

This unit provides an overall review on finding the volumes and surface areas of cylinders. You should understand how the formulas for the volume and surface area of a cylinder are derived and apply the right formulas when solving problems. Additionally, you should be able to solve problems that require unit conversions of volume and capacity.

Volume is measured in cm^3 and m^3, whereas capacity is measured in mL and L. It is important to be able to convert among the units.

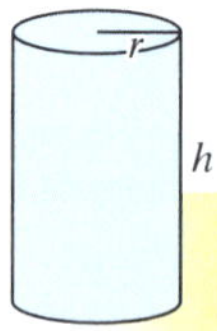

Volume $= \pi r^2 h$

Surface Area $= 2\pi r^2 + 2\pi rh$

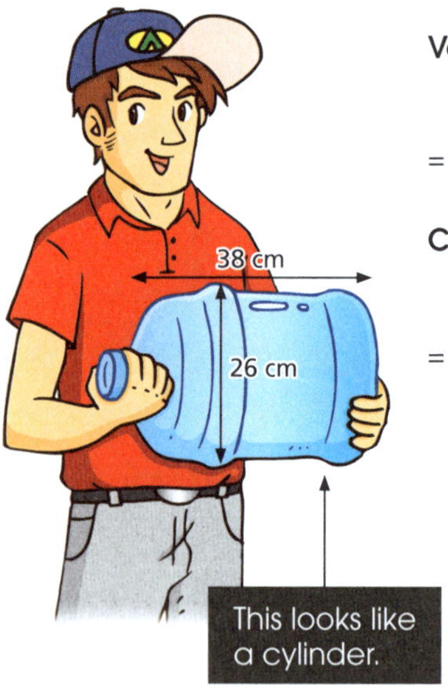

Volume of the water jug:

$3.14 \times 13^2 \times 38$

$= 20\ 165.08\ (cm^3)$

Capacity of the water jug:

20 165.08 mL

= **20.17 L**

Unit Conversions

$1\ cm^3 = 1\ mL$

$1000\ cm^3 = 1000\ mL = 1\ L$

$1\ m^3 = 1\ 000\ 000\ cm^3 = 1000\ L$

Application

Lenora is decorating the side of her cake with 2-mm thick roll-up candy. How many rolls does she need to completely cover the surface of the side of the cake?

Solution:

1st Find the volume of each roll-up candy.
Volume: $3.14 \times 2^2 \times 2 = 25.12$

2nd Find the length of the roll-up candy (in cm). When the roll-up candy is unrolled, it becomes a prism. Its volume equals the product of its length, height, and thickness.
Volume: $l \times 2 \times 0.2 = 25.12$
$l = 62.8$

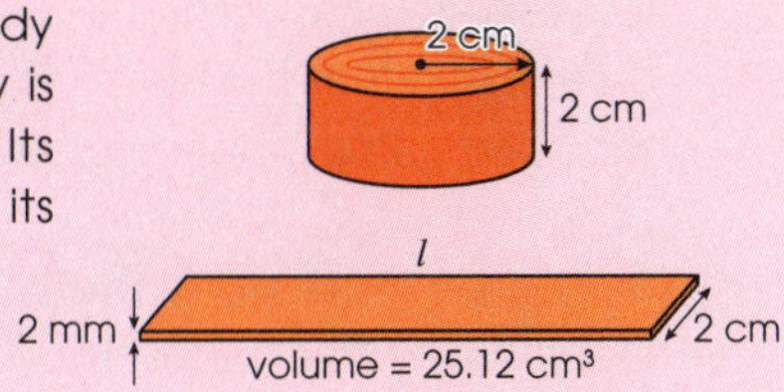

3rd Find the area covered by 1 roll of roll-up candy.
Area: $62.8 \times 2 = 125.6$

4th Find the surface area of the side of the cake.
Area: $2 \times 3.14 \times 10 \times 12 = 753.6$

5th Find how many rolls are needed to cover the surface of the side of the cake.
$753.6 \div 125.6 = 6$

Lenora needs 6 rolls of roll-up candy to completely cover the surface of the side of the cake.

Chapter 5

2-D and 3-D Geometry

5.1 Sorting and Classifying Quadrilaterals

In Grade 6, you learned to identify, compare, and sort different types of quadrilaterals. Therefore, you should be able to classify quadrilaterals by their geometric properties, such as equal sides, parallel sides, and number of right angles. At this level, you will learn to sort quadrilaterals by their diagonals. You will learn to draw the diagonals of a quadrilateral and identify whether or not the diagonals bisect each other.

There are six types of quadrilaterals.

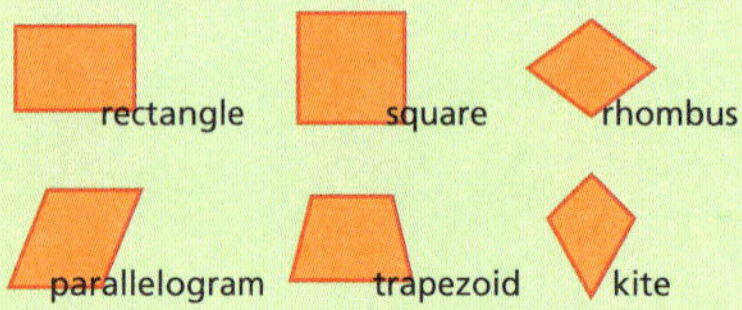

Quadrilateral

– a polygon with four sides

A Diagonal of a Quadrilateral

– a line drawn from one vertex to the opposite vertex

e.g. Draw the diagonals of the kite.

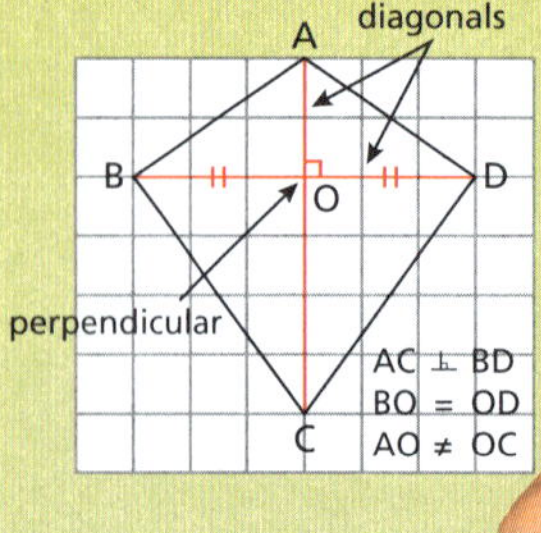

e.g. A rectangle is a quadrilateral.

AC and BD are the diagonals.

The diagonals of a kite are perpendicular to each other, but only one diagonal is bisected.

Application

Malcolm is designing a shield using two 1-m bars. He measures 30 cm from the end of each bar and ties them together at a 90° angle to make an "X". The bars are the diagonals of the shield's shape. What is the shape of the shield? Write about its geometric properties.

Solution:

The shape of the shield is an isosceles trapezoid.

Geometric properties of the shield:

- 1 pair of parallel sides 
- 1 pair of equal sides 
- diagonals of equal length 
- perpendicular diagonals 
- 1 line of symmetry 

5.2 Properties of Similar Figures

In this unit, you will learn to identify similar figures. You will apply the properties of similar figures to find unknown measurements and solve problems involving construction of similar figures. To begin, you should understand the characteristics of similar figures.

When two figures are similar,

- their corresponding angles are equal.
- the ratios of the corresponding sides are equal.

These two squares are similar.

$\frac{A}{B} = \frac{5}{10} = \frac{1}{2}$

The ratio of square A to B is 1:2.

e.g.

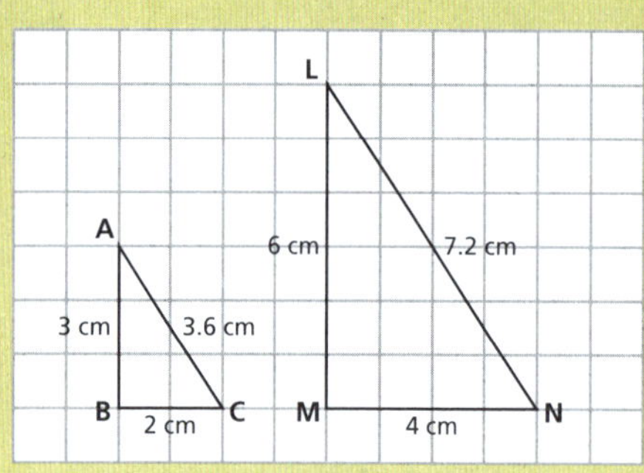

Are the triangles similar?

By Checking the **Angles**

$\angle A = 34^\circ \qquad \angle L = 34^\circ$

$\angle B = 90^\circ \qquad \angle M = 90^\circ$

$\angle C = 56^\circ \qquad \angle N = 56^\circ$

$\angle A = \angle L$; $\angle B = \angle M$; $\angle C = \angle N$

The corresponding angles are equal.

So, ΔABC and ΔLMN are similar.

By Checking the **Side Lengths**

$\frac{AB}{LM} = \frac{3}{6} = \frac{1}{2}$

$\frac{BC}{MN} = \frac{2}{4} = \frac{1}{2}$

$\frac{AC}{LN} = \frac{3.6}{7.2} = \frac{1}{2}$

ratio: $\frac{1}{2}$

The ratios of the corresponding sides are equal.

So, ΔABC and ΔLMN are similar.

You can practise finding unknown measurements using the properties of similar figures.

e.g. The triangles below are similar. Find the lengths of AC and NO.

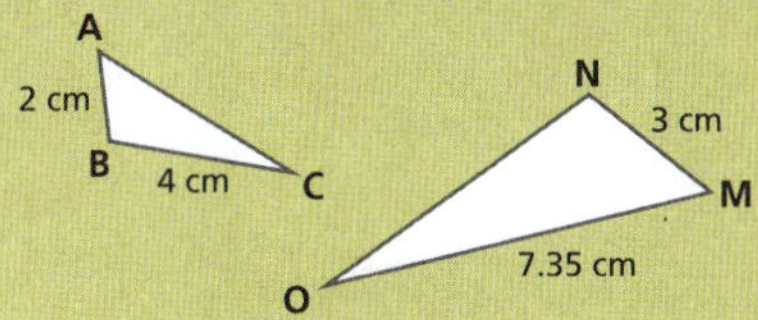

Corresponding sides:

$$\frac{AB}{MN} = \frac{BC}{NO} = \frac{AC}{MO} = \text{ratio}$$

Finding AC

$$\frac{AB}{MN} = \frac{AC}{MO}$$

$$\frac{2}{3} = \frac{AC}{7.35}$$

AC = 4.9 (cm)

Finding NO

$$\frac{AB}{MN} = \frac{BC}{NO}$$

$$\frac{2}{3} = \frac{4}{NO}$$

NO = 6 (cm)

When the figures are not in the same orientation, you can sketch the figures on a piece of paper in the same orientation to identify their corresponding angles and sides.

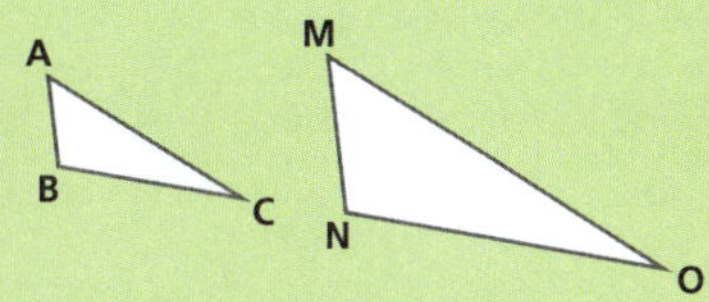

We can also use the properties of similar figures to determine perimeters and areas.

Similar Figures

Their perimeters are proportional to the ratio of their sides.

Their areas are proportional to the ratio of their sides squared.

e.g.

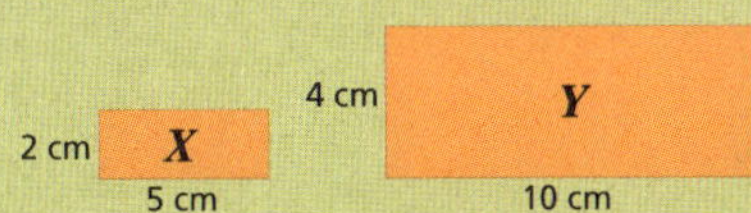

ratio $\frac{2}{4} = \frac{1}{2}$

The ratio of these two rectangles is 1:2.

$$^{*}\frac{P_x}{P_y} = \frac{14}{28} = \frac{1}{2}$$

P_y is 2 times P_x.

$$^{**}\frac{A_x}{A_y} = \frac{10}{40} = \frac{1}{4} = \left(\frac{1}{2}\right)^2$$

A_y is 4 times A_x.

*P_x : perimeter of rectangle x

**A_x : area of rectangle x

Application

Jenny uses her flashlight to project an image onto a wall. What is the ratio of the height of the projected image and the height of the design on the flashlight? What is the area of the projected image?

Solution:

The projected image and the design on the flashlight are similar figures.

Ratio of the heights: $\frac{150\text{ cm}}{3\text{ cm}} = \frac{50}{1}$

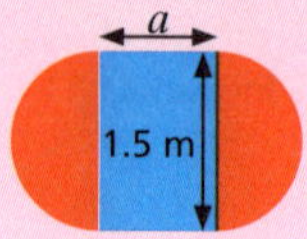

Length of a: $\frac{a}{2} = \frac{50}{1}$

$a = 100$ (cm)

Area of the projected image: $150 \times 100 + 3.14 \times 75^2$ ← radius of circle in cm

$= 32\ 662.5$

The ratio of the heights of the projected image and the design on the flashlight is 50:1. The area of the projected image is 32 662.5 cm².

5.3 Properties of 3-D Figures

In previous grades, you learned to identify the faces, vertices, and edges of all 3-D figures. In this unit, you will learn about the relationships among the faces, vertices, and edges of polyhedrons and develop a formula to model their relationships.

You can build the following 3-D figures with modelling clay and sticks. You can organize the information as shown in the table below. Then develop a general formula to model the relationships among the faces, vertices, and edges.

Polyhedron

a 3-D figure that has polygons as faces

e.g.

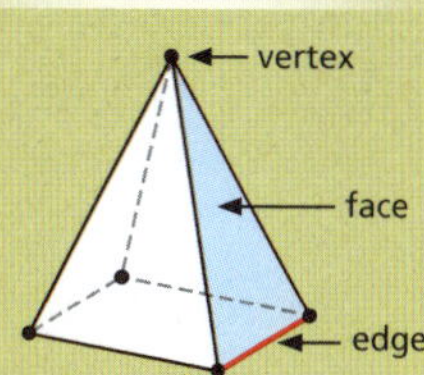

rectangular pyramid

Prism	Number of faces	vertices	edges
triangular prism	5	6	9
rectangular prism	6	8	12
pentagonal prism	7	10	15
hexagonal prism	8	12	18
heptagonal prism	9	14	21
octagonal prism	10	16	24

Pyramid	Number of faces	vertices	edges
triangular pyramid	4	4	6
rectangular pyramid	5	5	8
pentagonal pyramid	6	6	10
hexagonal pyramid	7	7	12
heptagonal pyramid	8	8	14
octagonal pyramid	9	9	16

*Compare the number of edges with the total number of faces and vertices to see what you can find.

For any polyhedron:

faces + vertices = edges + 2

Application

There are special types of polyhedrons called Platonic Solids, on which all the faces are of the same regular polygon. A dodecahedron, which has 12 faces, and an icosahedron, which has 20 faces, are examples of Platonic Solids. Both of these have 30 edges. How many vertices does each have? Give another example of a Platonic Solid and state the number of faces, vertices, and edges it has.

Solution:

Dodecahedron:

faces + vertices = edges + 2
12 + vertices = 30 + 2
vertices = 20

Icosahedron:

20 + vertices = 30 + 2
vertices = 12

A dodecahedron has 20 vertices and an icosahedron has 12 vertices.

The remaining Platonic Solids:

Name	Shape	Faces	Vertices	Edges
Tetrahedron (or triangular pyramid)	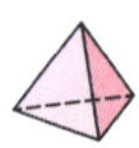	4	4	6
Hexahedron (or cube)	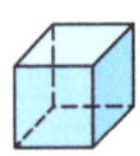	6	8	12
Octahedron		8	6	12

Chapter 6

Properties of Triangles

6.1 Related Angles

In this unit, you will learn about angle relationships among intersecting lines, parallel lines, and transversals. There are six major types of angle pairs that you need to know. You can draw intersecting lines, parallel lines, and transversals and measure the angles formed. Then identify the angle pairs and their relationships. Additionally, you will learn that the sum of all angles in a triangle is always 180°. You will then apply this concept to solve problems related to the angles of a triangle.

6 Major Types of Angle Pairs

Angle Relationships for Intersecting Lines

1. **Opposite Angles**

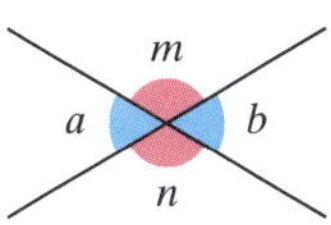

$\angle a = \angle b$

$\angle m = \angle n$

opposite angles:

$\angle a$ and $\angle b$

$\angle m$ and $\angle n$

2. **Complementary Angles**

- 2 angles that add up to 90°

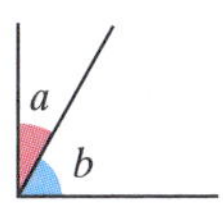

$\angle a + \angle b = 90°$

complementary angles:

$\angle a$ and $\angle b$

3. **Supplementary Angles**

- 2 angles that add up to 180°

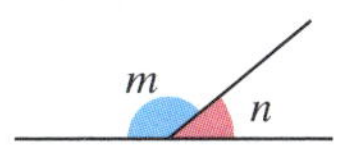

$\angle m + \angle n = 180°$

supplementary angles:

$\angle m$ and $\angle n$

Angle Relationships for Parallel Lines and Transversals

Parallel Lines and Transversals

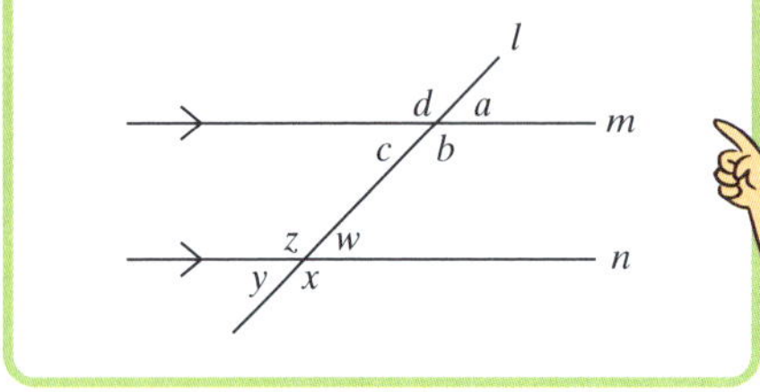

Lines m and n are parallel. Line l is a transversal.

4. **Corresponding Angles** 
("F" angles)

Corresponding angles are congruent and have the same position along the parallel lines and the transversal.

e.g. $\angle a = \angle w$
$\angle b = \angle x$
$\angle c = \angle y$
$\angle d = \angle z$

5. **Alternate Angles** 
("Z" angles)

Alternate angles are congruent and are on opposite sides of the transversal.

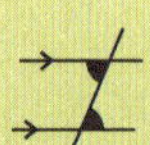 interior alternate angles

e.g. $\angle c = \angle w$
$\angle b = \angle z$

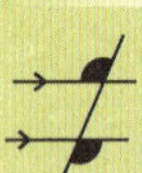 exterior alternate angles

e.g. $\angle d = \angle x$
$\angle a = \angle y$

6. **Consecutive Interior Angles** 
("C" angles)

Consecutive interior angles are on the same side of the transversal and are supplementary.

e.g. $\angle b$ and $\angle w$
$\angle b + \angle w = 180°$

$\angle c$ and $\angle z$
$\angle c + \angle z = 180°$

The sum of the angles in a triangle is 180°.

A + B + C = 180°

e.g.

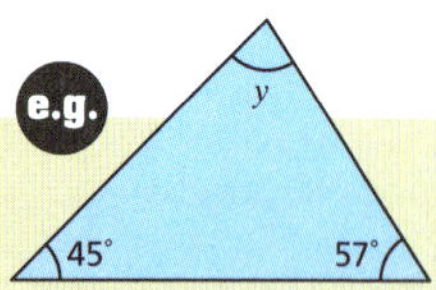

$y + 45° + 57° = 180°$
$y = 78°$

6.2 Pythagorean Relationship

The Pythagorean relationship is an important mathematical concept that relates the lengths of the three sides of a right triangle. In this unit, you will learn to apply this relationship to solve problems involving right triangles and other geometric problems.

Before introducing the Pythagorean relationship, make sure you are able to identify the hypotenuse of a right triangle.

e.g.

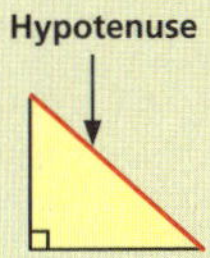

Hypotenuse

- the longest side of a right triangle
- the side opposite to the right angle

The Pythagorean Relationship

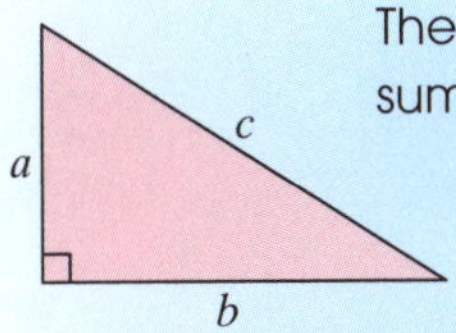

The square of the hypotenuse is equal to the sum of the squares of the other two sides.

$$a^2 + b^2 = c^2$$

Remember that the Pythagorean relationship can be applied to right triangles only!

e.g. Find the perimeter of the triangle.

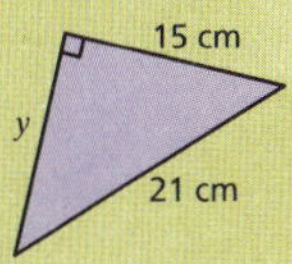

Think: 1st Find the missing side. "21 cm" is the hypotenuse.
2nd Add the three sides to find the perimeter.

1st
$$y^2 + 15^2 = 21^2$$
$$y^2 + 225 = 441$$
$$y^2 = 216$$
$$y = 14.7$$

2nd
$$P = 14.7 + 15 + 21$$
$$= 50.7$$

The perimeter is __50.7__ cm.

Application

What is the length of Diagonal AB?

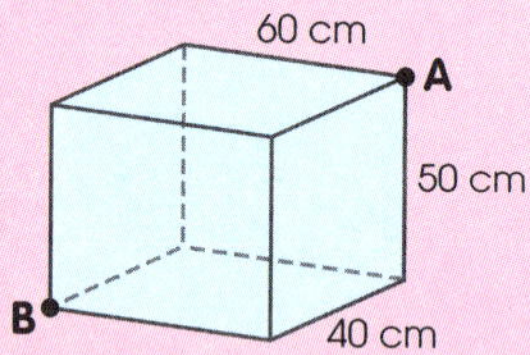

Solution:

Label Vertices C and D to help visualize the diagonals and the right triangles they form.

We need to use the Pythagorean relationship twice.

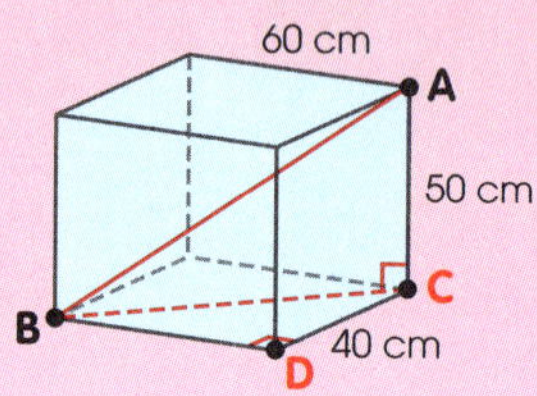

1st Find the diagonal of the base BC.

2nd Find Diagonal AB.

1st Diagonal BC

$BC^2 = 60^2 + 40^2$

$BC^2 = 5200$

$BC = 72.11$

2nd Diagonal AB

$AB^2 = (72.11)^2 + 50^2$

$AB^2 = 7700$

$AB = 87.75$

The length of Diagonal AB is 87.75 cm.

Chapter 7

Locations and Movements

7.1 Graphing on Cartesian Coordinate Planes

In Grade 7, you learned to plot points on the four quadrants of a Cartesian coordinate plane. This unit reviews how to plot points and find the coordinates of points on a Cartesian coordinate plane. You will learn to find the distance between two points using the Pythagorean relationship.

The Cartesian Coordinate Plane

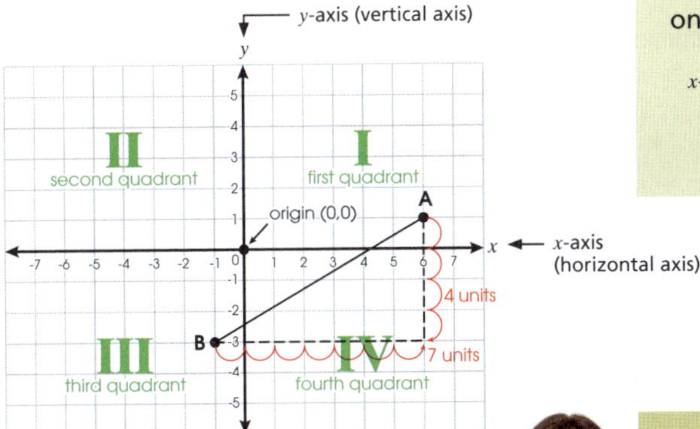

The coordinates of Point A on the coordinate plane:

x-coordinate → A (6,1) ← *y*-coordinate

Find the distance between Points A and B.

$AB^2 = 7^2 + 4^2$

$AB = 8.06$

The distance between Points A and B is 8.06 units.

Finding the distance between two points:

1st Draw a right triangle with 2 points forming the hypotenuse.

2nd Use the Pythagorean relationship to find the hypotenuse.

7.2 Transformations

In this unit, you will learn to graph a shape formed by a set of points after applying a transformation to the original shape. There are three types of transformations involved.

Types of Transformations:

1. 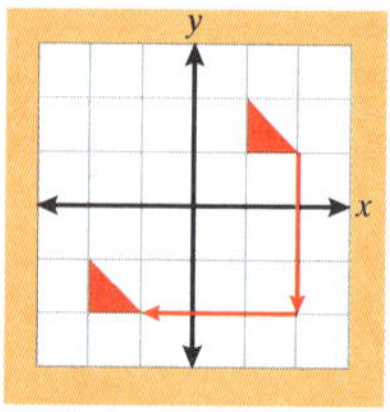

Translation

Move up or down, and/or left or right.

2. 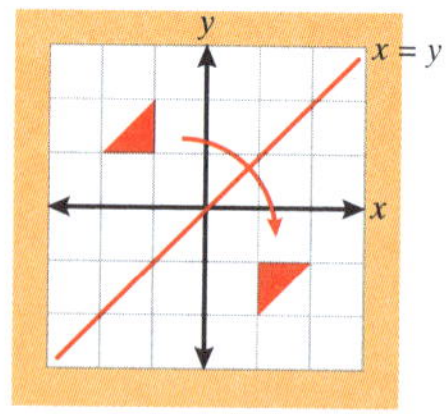

Reflection

Reflect in the x-axis, the y-axis, or the line $x = y$.

3. 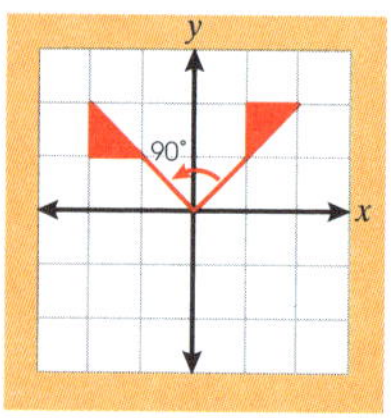

Rotation

Rotate 90°, 180°, or 270° about the origin.

Review the following examples and remember the rules for determining the coordinates of points for different transformations.

You can also trace a congruent figure on a piece of paper and perform the transformation to visualize the result.

Translation

e.g. Translate: 4 units to the left (x-coordinate decreases by 4) and 1 unit up (y-coordinate increases by 1)

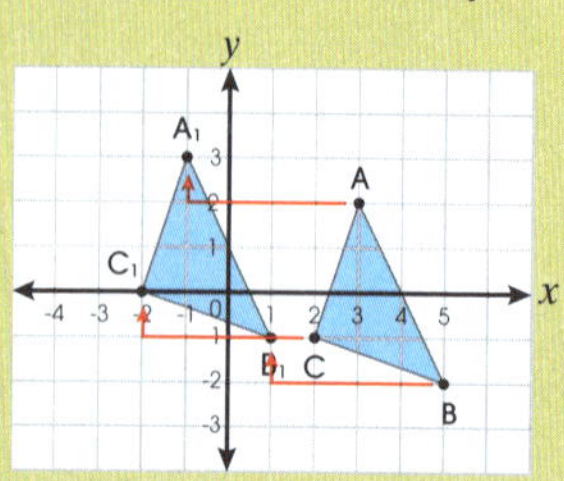

A (3,2) → A_1 (-1,3)

B (5,-2) → B_1 (1,-1)

C (2,-1) → C_1 (-2,0)

Reflection

The original point and its corresponding point are the same distance from the line of reflection.

e.g.

in the x-axis

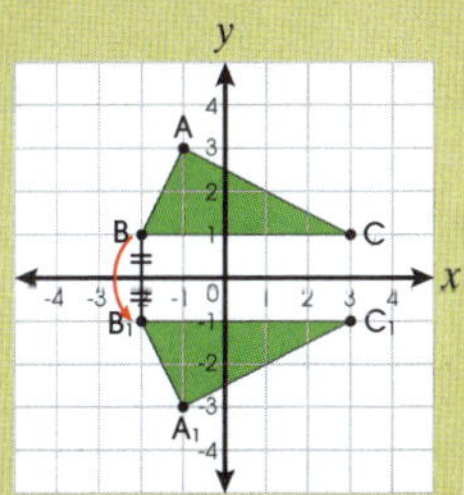

The x-coordinates stay the same but the y-coordinates are the opposite of the originals.

A (-1,3) → A_1 (-1,-3)

B (-2,1) → B_1 (-2,-1)

C (3,1) → C_1 (3,-1)

in the y-axis

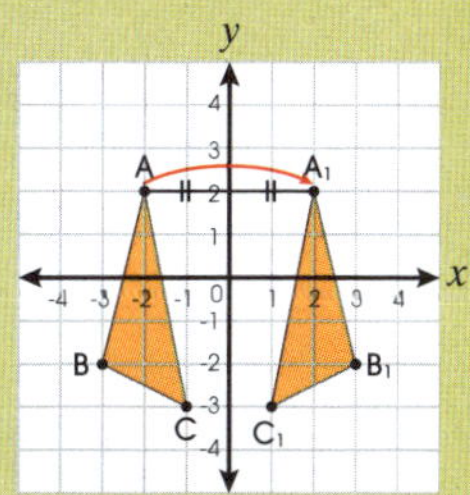

The y-coordinates stay the same but the x-coordinates are the opposite of the originals.

A (-2,2) → A_1 (2,2)

B (-3,-2) → B_1 (3,-2)

C (-1,-3) → C_1 (1,-3)

in the line $x = y$

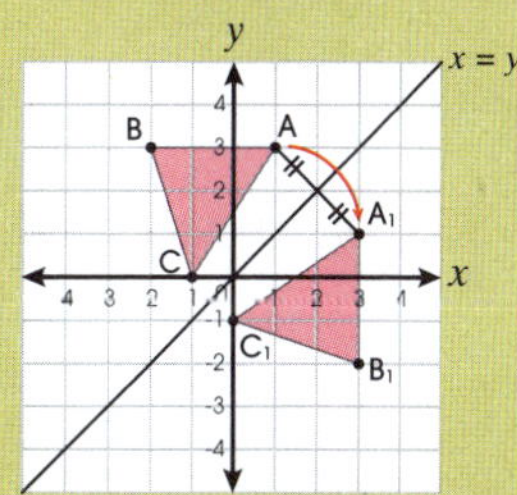

Swap the x-coordinates and the y-coordinates.

A (1,3) → A_1 (3,1)

B (-2,3) → B_1 (3,-2)

C (-1,0) → C_1 (0,-1)

Rotation

e.g. 270° clockwise rotation about (0,0)

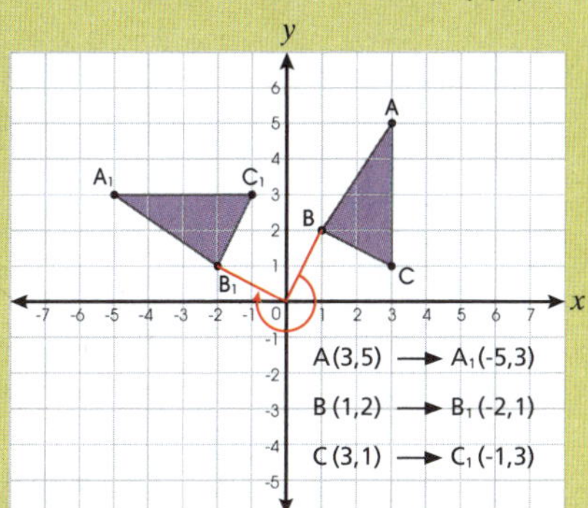

90° clockwise rotation

(a,b) → (b,-a)

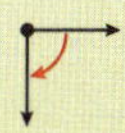

180° rotation

(a,b) → (-a,-b)

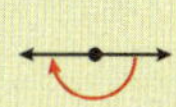

270° clockwise rotation

(a,b) → (-b,a)

Chapter 8

Patterning

8.1 Representing Linear Patterns

A linear pattern is a pattern that increases or decreases at a constant rate. In this unit, you will learn to write algebraic expressions to describe linear patterns and use them to find terms and term numbers.

e.g. Describe the relationship between the frame number and the number of squares with an algebraic expression.

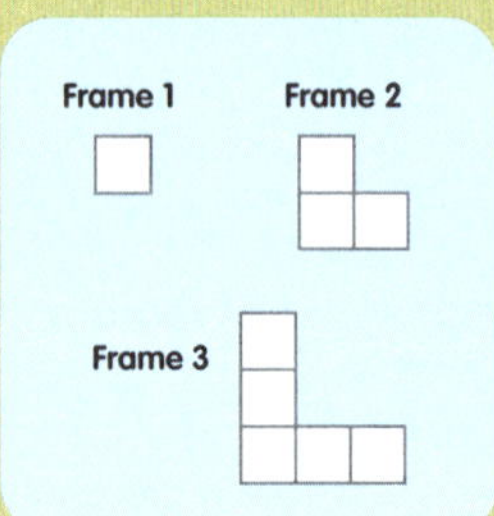

Make a table to see how the frame number and the number of squares relate.

Frame Number	Number of Squares
1	1
2	3
3	5

Think

1 x 2 – 1 → 1

2 x 2 – 1 → 3

3 x 2 – 1 → 5

So, the number of squares is twice the frame number minus 1.

If n is the frame number, then the number of squares in Frame n is $2n - 1$.

Once the algebraic expression is determined, you can use it to find the number of squares with the given frame number and vice versa.

e.g. How many squares are in Frame 30?

$2n - 1$

$= 2 \times 30 - 1$ ← Substitute 30 into n.

$= 59$

So, there are **59 squares** in Frame 30.

8.2 Graphing Linear Patterns

Graphing is a useful method to visualize linear patterns and extract information from them. Every term number and its term can be plotted on a Cartesian coordinate plane as a pair of coordinates. For linear patterns, all points lie on a straight line. This line can then be used to find terms and term numbers.

Steps to Graphing Linear Patterns

1st Consider each term number as the x-coordinate and its term as the y-coordinate.

2nd Plot each point on a Cartesian coordinate plane. Then draw a line to connect the points.

e.g. Graph the pattern below.

Term Number	Term
1	2
2	4
3	6
4	8

1st →

Coordinates
(1,2)
(2,4)
(3,6)
(4,8)

2nd →

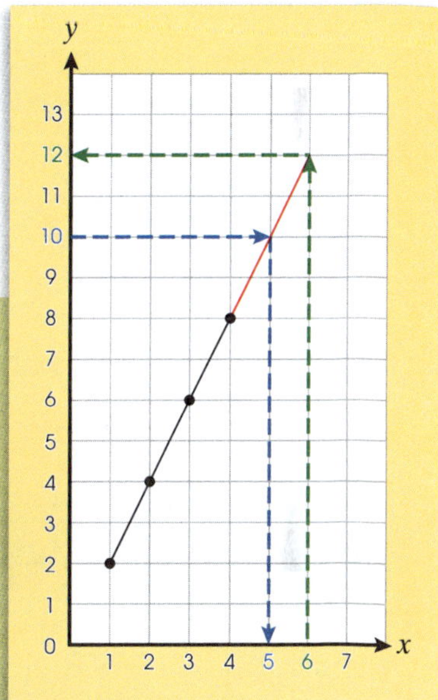

What is the 6th term? What is the term number of 10? Use the graph to find the answers.

To answer the questions, extend the line as shown with the red line and use it to find the term and the term number.

As you can see from the graph, the **6th** term is <u>12</u> and the term number of **10** is <u>5</u> .

Chapter 9

Expressions and Equations

9.1 Evaluating Algebraic Expressions

In Grade 7, you learned to evaluate an algebraic expression by substituting an integer for a variable. At this level, you will substitute fractions and decimals into multiple variables.

To evaluate an algebraic expression, substitute the variables with their values into the expression. Make sure you follow the order of operations in the calculations.

Brackets
Exponents
Division
Multiplication
Addition
Subtraction

e.g. Evaluate $2x - y^2 + (z - 1)$ with the given values.

$x = 2.5 \qquad y = -3 \qquad z = \frac{5}{4}$

$2x - y^2 + (z - 1)$

$= 2(2.5) - (-3)^2 + (\frac{5}{4} - 1)$ ← Substitute the variables.

$= 5 - (+9) + (\frac{1}{4})$

$= 5 - 9 + \frac{1}{4}$

$= -3\frac{3}{4}$

$2x - y^2 + (z - 1)$

$= 2(-3) - 2.5^2 + (\frac{5}{4} - 1)$

$= -6 - 6.25 + (\frac{1}{4})$

$= -6 - 6.25 + \frac{1}{4}$

$= -12$ ✗ The values of x and y were swapped.

Remember that it is important to substitute the given values into the correct variables. As shown in this example, not doing so will yield an incorrect answer.

9.2 Solving Equations

In previous grades, you learned to solve equations by inspection, using the guess-and-check method, and using a "balance" model. At this level, you will solve equations that involve multiple operations using a "balance" model.

All equations have two sides: left-hand side (LHS) and right-hand side (RHS). The LHS and RHS must always be equal. So, when solving an equation, make sure that what is done to one side is also done to the other side to maintain equality.

Solving Equations Involving 1 Operation

In Grade 7, you learned to solve for a variable by performing the opposite operation on both sides of the equation to isolate the variable. The opposite operations are addition and subtraction, and multiplication and division.

e.g.

$$y + 4 = 20$$

$$y + 4 - 4 = 20 - 4$$ ← "− 4" cancels out "+ 4" so that y is isolated.

$$y = 16$$

e.g.

$$x \div 4 = 5$$

$$x \div 4 \times 4 = 5 \times 4$$ ← "x 4" cancels out "÷ 4".

$$x = 20$$

To check whether or not an answer is correct, substitute the variable with the answer and evaluate. If the LHS and RHS are equal, the answer is correct. For example, check whether or not $x = 20$ is correct for $x \div 4 = 5$.

LHS	RHS
$20 \div 4$ $= 5$	5 ✔

LHS = RHS
So, $x = 20$ is correct.

Solving Equations Involving More Than 1 Operation

It is important to isolate a variable in a particular order when solving equations with more than 1 operation. To maintain the "balance", perform the operation in reverse BEDMAS order.

e.g.

$5x + 2 = 12$ ← Isolating x involves subtraction and division.

$5x + 2 - 2 = 12 - 2$ ← Perform subtraction first.

$5x = 10$

$5x \div 5 = 10 \div 5$ ← Perform division.

$x = 2$

Reverse BEDMAS Order

Subtraction
Addition
Multiplication
Division
Exponents
Brackets

Some equations have more than 1 of the same variable. These variables are called like terms. Like terms can be added or subtracted to make one term.

e.g.

$\mathbf{2x + x} - 6 = 9$ ← $2x$ and x are like terms.

$\mathbf{3x} - 6 = 9$ ← $2x + x = 3x$

$3x - 6 + 6 = 9 + 6$

$3x = 15$

$3x \div 3 = 15 \div 3$

$x = 5$

Like terms must have the same exponents.

e.g. $x, 3x$ ← like terms

x, x^3 ← unlike terms

It does not matter which side of the equation the isolated variable ends up on, though it is more common to have it on the LHS.

Chapter 10

Data Management

10.1 Analyzing Graphs

Once data is represented in a graph, information can be interpreted and inferred from it. In this unit, you will learn to determine whether or not a measure of central tendency is a good representation of a set of data. You will also identify trends in graphs, including scatter plots.

Choosing Representative Measures of Central Tendency

As you should know, there are three measures of central tendency.

- **Mean**: the sum of a set of data values divided by the number of data values
- **Median**: the middle value in a set of data that is ordered from least to greatest
- **Mode**: the value(s) in a set of data that occur(s) most often

Depending on the data being analyzed, there might only be one measure of central tendency that is a good representation of a set of data.

e.g. Is the mean a good representation of the score?

Game	1	2	3	4	5	6	7	8	9	10
Score	2	5	21	68	68	78	86	86	86	86

Mean: 58.6 Median: 73 Mode: 86

The mean score is 58.6. However, the mean might not be a good representation because most scores are in the 68 to 86 range.

Describing Trends

You should be familiar with describing trends presented in bar graphs and line graphs. At this level, you will identify trends in scatter plots.

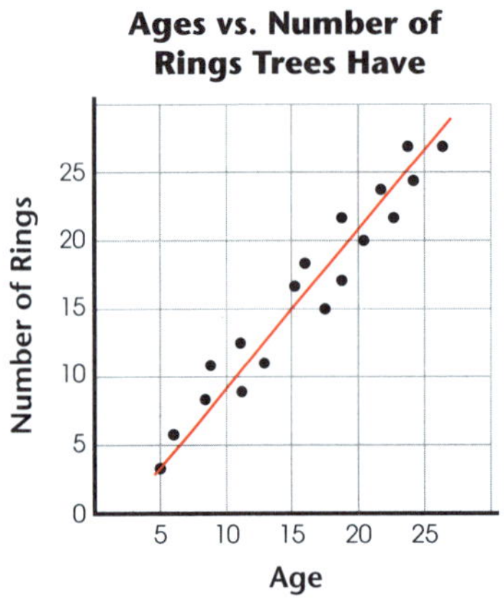

The points on a scatter plot show the relationship between two sets of data. The example on the left shows the relationship between the ages of trees and the number of rings they have. You should see that as the ages of trees increase, the number of rings they have also increases.

A line of best fit is a straight line that best represents the data on a scatter plot. The red line in the example is the line of best fit. According to this line, a tree that is 15 years old has 15 rings.

Here are the three types of trends in a scatter plot.

Increasing Trend

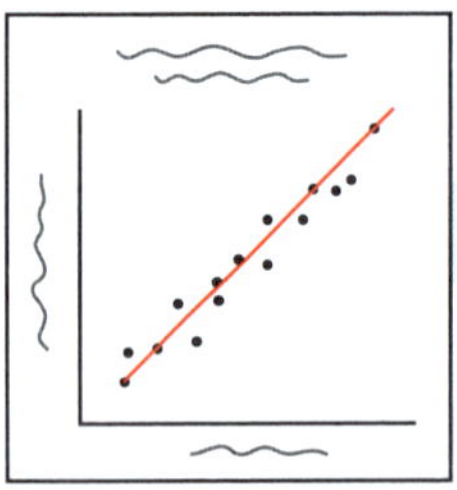

As one set of data increases, the other set increases as well.

Decreasing Trend

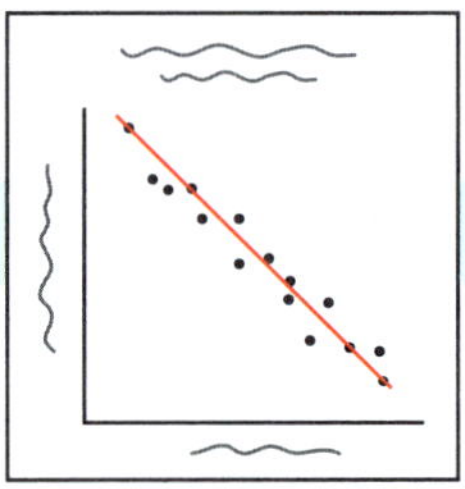

As one set of data increases, the other set decreases.

No Trend

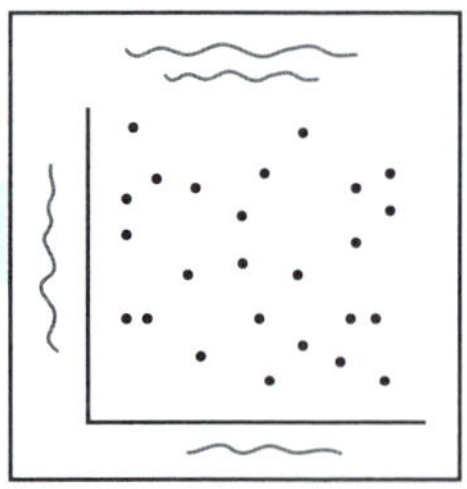

There is no correlation between the two sets of data.

10.2 Representing Data in Graphs

In this unit, you will identify the source and the type of a set of data. You will learn to organize a set of data before representing it in graphs, including histograms and scatter plots.

Identifying the Sources and Types of Data

Being able to identify the source and type of data will help you choose the most appropriate method to organize and graph a set of data.

Primary Data	Secondary Data
a set of data that is collected by conducting a survey or an experiment	a set of data from other sources such as books and websites

Sample	Census
a set of data from a representative group that represents the entire population	an entire population that is examined

Discrete Data	Continuous Data
data that includes only whole numbers	data that includes any numerical values including fractions and decimals

e.g. Identify the source and types of the set of data.

Joshua found some data on a website (secondary data). It is from an experiment for a study on growth rates of a virus at room temperature.

Temperature	20°C	21°C	22°C	23°C	24°C
Growth Rate	12.5%	10.8%	10.2%	9.5%	8.9%

continuous data

Since it is impossible to conduct the experiment on all viruses, this set of data must be from a **sample**.

Organizing a Set of Data into Intervals

After data is gathered, the next step is to organize it so that information can be derived and represented meaningfully in a graph. You have already learned to organize data in a stem-and-leaf plot. At this level, you will learn to organize data into intervals.

Steps

1st Find the range of the values.

2nd Determine the appropriate number of intervals to have.

3rd Create a table and organize the data into correct intervals.

Remember these rules when determining the number of intervals.

- The range of each interval must be the same.
- Each data value must only be present in one interval.
- No data value can fall on the boundary of any two intervals.

e.g. Organize this set of data.

12.5	20.1	17.3	8.4
25.1	21.3	16.2	18.5
2.1	22.4	4.2	15.2

Think Range: 25.1 – 2.1 = 23

It is appropriate to have 4 intervals each with a range of 6.

Intervals	Frequency
2 – 7.9	2
8 – 13.9	2
14 – 19.9	4
20 – 25.9	4

Representing Data in Histograms and Scatter Plots

You should be able to determine the most appropriate graph for a set of data. At this level, you will be introduced to two types of graphs: histograms and scatter plots.

Histogram

- similar to bar graphs except for having no space between the bars
- suitable for data that is continuous

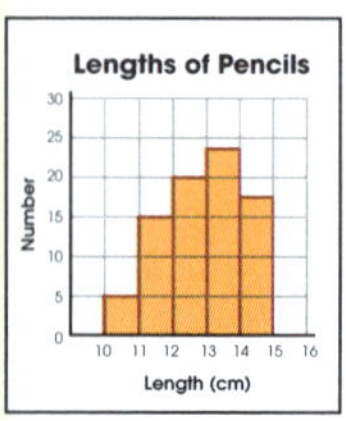

Scatter Plot

- similar to line graphs except the points are not connected
- suitable for comparing two sets of data

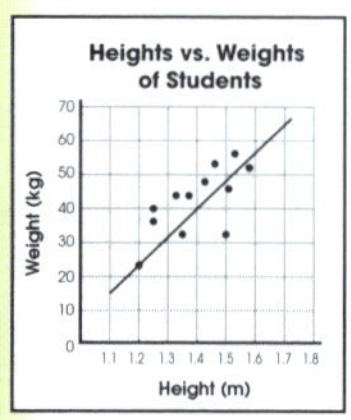

Chapter 11

Probability

11.1 Finding Probability

Previously, you learned to find the probabilities of events. In this unit, you will learn to identify complementary events and find their probabilities.

Identifying Complementary Events

Complementary events are two or more outcomes that make up all possible outcomes. The sum of the probabilities of these events must be 1.

For example, flipping a head or a tail is the only possible outcome. Therefore, the two complementary events are flipping a head and flipping a tail. The sum of the probabilities of these two complementary events is 1.

There can be more than one set of complementary events.

e.g. Spin the wheel once.

Complementary events

Set 1 spinning red, not spinning red ($\frac{1}{3} + \frac{2}{3} = 1$)

Set 2 spinning yellow, not spinning yellow ($\frac{1}{3} + \frac{2}{3} = 1$)

Set 3 spinning a primary colour, not spinning a primary colour ($\frac{2}{3} + \frac{1}{3} = 1$)

As you can see in the example, there can be multiple sets of complementary events.

11.2 Theoretical Probability and Experimental Probability

When performing a probability experiment, the outcome may differ from what is expected. This is due to differences between the theoretical probability and the experimental probability. In this unit, you will learn about these two types of probabilities and how they are related in terms of the number of trials.

Theoretical Probability

- the chances that an event will occur in theory

Probability =

$$\frac{\text{No. of favourable outcomes}}{\text{Total no. of possible outcomes}}$$

e.g. Find the probability of getting a red ball from the box below in one draw.

Probability of getting a red ball:

$$\frac{2}{8} = \frac{1}{4}$$

Experimental Probability

- the chances that an event will occur based on experimental results

Probability =

$$\frac{\text{No. of times an outcome occurs}}{\text{Total no. of trials}}$$

e.g. Use the results of eight draws below to find the probability of getting a red ball.

Draw	1	2	3	4	5	6	7	8
Colour	R	B	R	Y	B	B	R	R

Probability of getting a red ball:

$$\frac{4}{8} = \frac{1}{2}$$

As shown in the example, the probabilities of the same event may differ. However, as the number of trials increases, the effects of random events decrease and the experimental probability and theoretical probability tend to be closer to each other.

acute angle – an angle between 0° and 90°

acute triangle – a triangle that contains only acute angles

addition – a mathematical operation that represents combining two or more numbers; the opposite of subtraction

alternate angles – a pair of angles on opposite sides of a transversal in a "Z" shape; if the transverse lines are parallel, then the angles are equal

angle bisector – a line that cuts an angle into equal halves

area – the size of space contained by a shape

associative property – a property of addition and multiplication that allows numbers to be regrouped without changing the answer

axis – a line in a graph that denotes the quantities depicted; plural form: axes

bar graph – a type of graph in which the length of a bar represents the quantity in a category

base – (geometry) the side of a polygon or the face of a 3-D figure considered the "bottom" and is perpendicular to the height; (exponent) the number which is multiplied by itself

BEDMAS – a mnemonic device to help remember the order of operations; it stands for Brackets, Exponents, Division, Multiplication, Addition, and Subtraction

bias – a representation or interpretation of data that leads to misleading conclusions

bisector – a line that cuts something into two equal halves

capacity – a measure of how much liquid a container can hold; measured in litres and its related units

cardinal directions – the four main points of a compass: north, east, south, and west

Cartesian coordinate plane – a system to determine the location through a horizontal x-axis and a vertical y-axis

census – a collection of data from an entire population

centre – the point that is the same distance from every point on a circle

circle graph – a type of graph in which the size of a slice represents the quantity in a category

circumference – the perimeter of a circle

clockwise – the direction of rotation that follows the hands of a clock

coefficient – a numeric factor of a variable

commutative property – a property of addition and multiplication that allows numbers to be reordered without changing the answer

complementary angles – two angles that have a sum of 90°

complementary events – two events that have no outcome(s) in common and together account for all possible outcomes

composite number – a number that has more than two factors; it has factors other than 1 and itself

congruent shapes – two or more shapes that are identical; they are the same size and shape but can be of differing orientation

consecutive interior angles – a pair of angles on the same side of a transversal in a "C" shape; if the transverse lines are parallel, then the angles are supplementary

continuous data – a type of data that can include any numerical values, including decimals and fractions

coordinates – an ordered pair that describes a location on a grid or plane

correlation – a statistical relationship

corresponding angles – a pair of angles on the same side of a transversal in an "F" shape; if the transverse lines are parallel, then the angles are equal

corresponding sides – the related sides between congruent or similar shapes

counterclockwise – the direction of rotation that is opposite of clockwise

data – a set of information

data management – a strand of mathematics that analyzes data

data value – a numeric quantity of a single data point

decimal number – a number that contains parts of a whole in base-ten

decimal point – a point in a decimal number that separates the ones digit and the tenths digit

denominator – the number at the bottom of a fraction; the number of equal parts in a whole

dependent variable – a variable that changes based on the independent variable

diagonal – a line segment joining two vertices in a polygon that are not next to each other

diameter – a line segment that joins two points on a circle and crosses the centre; it is twice the radius

digit – a position of place value within a number

discrete data – a type of data that can only include certain values, like whole numbers

distributive property – a property of multiplication that allows a number to be decomposed into two or more numbers

division – a mathematical operation that represents separation into equal parts; the opposite of multiplication

double bar graph – a type of bar graph in which two sets of data are compared using bars

edge – a line where two faces meet in a three-dimensional figure

equally likely – a probability of two or more outcomes having the same chance of occurring

equation – a mathematical sentence in which the values on both sides of an equal sign are equal

equilateral triangle – a triangle that has three equal sides and angles

expanded form – a way of writing numbers that shows the value of each digit

experimental probability – a probability derived from the results of an experiment

exponent – the number of times a number multiplies itself

exponential notation – a way of writing the product of a number multiplied by itself

expression – a representation of a quantity that may include numbers, variables, and operations

face – a flat surface of a three-dimensional figure

factor – a whole number that divides exactly into another whole number

factor tree – a diagram that shows the factors of a number

fraction – a way of representing part of a whole; contains a numerator and a denominator

frequency – the number of times an event or outcome occurs

geometric pattern – a sequence of pictures that follow a pattern rule

geometry – a strand of mathematics that involves shapes, sizes, and positions

greatest common factor – the largest factor that two or more numbers have in common

grid – a diagram of equal squares used to show location

height – the distance from the base of a polygon or a 3-D figure to its farthest point; is perpendicular to the base

histogram – a type of bar graph in which each bar represents a continuous interval; has no spaces between bars

hundreds chart – a diagram that shows the numbers from 1 to 100; organized into rows and columns of 10

hypotenuse – the longest side of a right triangle opposite its right angle

improper fraction – a fraction in which the numerator is greater than or equal to the denominator

independent variable – a variable that does not change due to other variables

integer – any positive or negative whole number, including zero

interval – the set of numbers between two given end points

irrational number – a number that cannot be represented as a fraction using integers

isosceles triangle – a triangle that has two sides of equal length

least common multiple – the smallest number that two or more numbers can be divided into evenly

length – a measure of how long something is; measured in centimetres and its related units; in a rectangle, it is typically longer than the width

line graph – a type of graph in which a line segment joins points representing data; the line can be continuous or broken

line of symmetry – a line that divides a shape into two congruent parts

line segment – a straight line that connects two points

linear equation – an algebraic equation that represents a relationship with one or more first-degree variables

mass – the amount of matter in an object; measured in grams and its related units

mean – the average of a set of numbers; a measure of central tendency

measure of central tendency – a value that summarizes a set of data; an approximation of the central value of a set of data

median – the middle value in a set of data when arranged in order; a measure of central tendency

mixed number – a number that consists of a whole number and a fraction

mode – the value that occurs most frequently in a set of data; a measure of central tendency

multiple – a product of a whole number by another whole number

multiplication – a mathematical operation that represents repeated addition; the opposite of division

negative integer – an integer that is less than zero; denoted by a negative sign "-" before the number

net – a diagram that can be folded to create a three-dimensional figure

number pattern – a pattern that consists of a sequence of numbers

numerator – the number at the top of a fraction

obtuse angle – an angle between 90° and 180°

obtuse triangle – a triangle that contains an obtuse angle

opposite angles – a pair of angles formed when two lines intersect; they lie opposite each other and are equal

order of operation – the rules for performing more than one operation

ordinal number – a number that shows a relative position or place

outlier – a data point that is separate from the rest of a set

parallel sides – the sides in a shape that do not intersect when extended

pattern – a sequence of pictures or numbers that follows a rule

pattern rule – a set of number operations that dictates how a pattern changes

percent – a numerical value expressed out of 100 using the symbol "%"

perfect square – a number that is the product of two identical numbers

perimeter – the length of the boundary of a shape

perpendicular bisector – a line that cuts another line into two equal parts and forms a 90° angle with it

perpendicular lines – two lines that form a 90° angle

pictograph – a type of graph in which a symbol represents a certain quantity

place value – the value of a digit in a number based on its position

place value chart – a diagram that displays a number's place values

polygon – a closed shape formed by three or more line segments

polyhedron – a three-dimensional figure with polygons as faces

population – the total number of individuals or objects in a set

positive integer – an integer that is more than zero; can be denoted by a "+" before the number

power – a number written in exponential form; consists of a base and an exponent

primary data – information that is collected directly or first-hand

prime factorization – an expression showing a number as the product of prime numbers

prime number – a whole number greater than 1 that has only two factors, 1 and itself

prism – a three-dimensional figure with two parallel and congruent faces

probability – a description or a value from 0 to 1 that shows the likelihood that an event will occur

proper fraction – a fraction in which the numerator is less than the denominator

proportion – an equation showing equivalent ratios in fraction form

pyramid – a polyhedron whose base is a polygon with all other faces as triangles that meet at a common vertex

Pythagorean relationship – the relationship of the sides of a right triangle in which the sum of the squares of two sides is equal to the square of the hypotenuse

quadrant – one quarter of the Cartesian coordinate plane bounded by the axes

quadrilateral – a polygon with four sides

radius – a line segment that joins the centre and a point on a circle; also half the diameter

range – the difference between the highest and lowest numbers in a set of numbers

rate – a comparison of two measurements in different units

ratio – a comparison of quantities in the same unit

rational number – a number that can be written as a fraction using integers

reciprocal – a fraction in which the numerator and the denominator are swapped

reflection – a type of transformation that flips a shape over a line to create a congruent image

related fact – an equation that expresses the same relationship between numbers

remainder – the number left over from a division

right angle – an angle of 90°

right triangle – a triangle with a right angle

rotation – a transformation that turns a shape about a fixed point

rotational symmetry – a geometric property such that when a shape is rotated, it returns to its original position

sample – a representative group chosen from a population

scale factor – a number multiplier that represents the size of the image from an enlargement or a reduction

scalene triangle – a triangle with three different side lengths

scatter plot – a type of graph in which each point represents a data value

scientific notation – a way of writing very large or very small numbers

secondary data – information that is not collected first-hand

shape – a two-dimensional picture

similar shapes – two or more shapes that share the same form but are of different sizes

simplest form – a way for writing a number such that it cannot be reduced or simplified any further

square root – a factor that, when multiplied by itself, equals the number

standard form – a way of writing a number in which each digit has a place value according to its position

statistics – a strand of mathematics that involves the collection and analysis of data

stem-and-leaf plot – an organization of data into categories based on place values

straight angle – an angle that is 180°

substitution – a method of problem solving that involves replacing an expression with another that has the same value

subtraction – a mathematical operation that represents reducing one number from another; the opposite of addition

supplementary angles – two angles with a sum of 180°

surface area – the total combined area of the faces of a three-dimensional figure

tally chart – a chart that uses tally marks to record the quantities of data

theoretical probability – the likelihood of an outcome based on calculations

three-dimensional figure – an object that spans in three dimensions; typically consists of geometric shapes

tiling pattern – a series of pictures that fills a space without gaps or overlaps

transformation – a change in a shape that results in a different position, orientation, or size

translation – a transformation that moves every point on a shape the same distance

transversal – a straight line that crosses two lines

tree diagram – a branching diagram that shows all possible outcomes

trend – a relationship within a set of data; can be increasing, decreasing, or without correlation

unit price – the cost of a single item

unit rate – a special rate with one as the unit in the denominator

variable – a letter or symbol used to represent an unknown quantity

Venn diagram – a diagram consisting of overlapping circles that shows elements that are in common and not in common between sets of data

vertex – a point in a three-dimensional figure; plural form: vertices

volume – a measure of space taken up by an object; measured in cubic centimetres and its related units

whole number – a positive number without decimals

Photo Credits

All the photos below are from 123RF.

front cover/boy/Vitaly Valua; **4**/boy/Vitaly Valua; **24**/woman/Ivan Mikhaylov; **25**/man/auremar; **25**/girl/Dmitriy Shironosov; **27**/boys/Jose Manuel Gelpi Diaz; **27**/mother and three children/vitalinka; **30**/boy/windu; **32**/students/Jacek Chabraszewski; **35**/boy/Valeriy Lebedev; **38**/kid/Oksana Kuzmina; **38**/girl/auremar; **41**/teddy bear/Serhii Odarchenko; **42**/woman/Andres Rodriguez; **43**/girl/Xavier Gallego Morell; **44**/girl/jirkaejc; **45**/girl/Paul Michael Hughes; **45**/girl/darko64; **48**/boy/Suzanne Tucker; **51**/boy/annunna1; **54**/little cook/Sergiy Bykhunenko; **56**/girl/Noam Armonn; **59**/young man/George Muresan; **61**/kid/davepot; **63**/garden scissors/Elnur Amikishiyev; **65**/pattern/pacpumi; **65**/photo frame/Mr.Smith Chetanachan; **65**/family/epicstockmedia; **65**/tile/PaylessImages; **65**/paper/Patrick M. Pelz; **66**/girl/Denys Prokofyev; **68**/student/ximagination; **72**/girl/andersonrise; **74**/girl/Nicolaas Traut; **77**/girl/Wavebreak Media Ltd; **80**/boy/Sergiy Bykhunenko; **84**/girl/Jose Manuel Gelpi Diaz; **87**/girl/Lyubov Kobyakova; **94**/woman/szefei; **96**/boy/pat138241; **98**/girl with child/Evgeniya Tiplyashina; **102**/girl/Jacek Chabraszewski; **103**/girl/Roman Gorielov; **107**/boy/Tetiana Vitsenko; **109**/boy/Veronica Louro; **111**/girl/Vera Kuttelvaserova Stuchelova; **116**/girl/Thomas Perkins; **118**/girl/Dmitry Naumov; **121**/cook/Sergiy Bykhunenko; **122**/child pointing/windu; **123**/child pointing/Waraporn Sang-Arwut; **125**/girl/auremar; **127**/man/My Make OU; **128**/boy with watermelon/Elena Blokhina; **130**/grandmother with grandchildren/Tetiana Kolinko; **132**/girl with cubes/Nikolay Turkin; **134**/man/Alexander Raths; **135**/girl/Gino Santa Maria; **136**/girl/Anurak Ponapatimet; **138**/schoolboy/Jasmin Merdan; **140**/woman/Jatuporn Amorntangsati; **142**/boy/Vitaly Valua; **144**/farmer/Ljupco Smokovski; **146**/man/Vadim Guzhva; **148**/teenager/darkbird; **150**/boy pointing/pahham; **153**/girl/랑 최; **156**/girl/Borges Samuel; **158**/woman pointing/maridav; **159**/girl cook/Goce Risteski; **161**/boy pointing/sergein; **162**/boy/Paul Michael Hughes; **164**/businesswoman/Liubov Vadimovna (Luba) Nel; **168**/boy/xalanx; **169**/woman/Erik Reis; **170**/girl/Sergiy Bykhunenko; **172**/girl holding blocks/Olena Afanasova; **173**/teenager/Dndavis; **173**/girl/slplondon; **174**/boy thinking/Mohamed Osama; **176**/woman pointing/nobilior; **177**/woman/paffy; **178**/woman/auremar; **180**/woman pointing/mathom; **181**/girl/phartisan; **182**/woman pointing/Edyta Pawlowska; **182**/woman/Waroot Tangtumsatid; **183**/boy/HONGQI ZHANG; **183**/girl/pat138241; **184**/girls thinking/Jose Manuel Gelpi Diaz; **184**/girl/Jose Manuel Gelpi Diaz; **185**/woman/Gino Santa Maria; **186**/delivery man/Vadim Guzhva; **187**/woman pointing/maridav; **188**/boy/get4net; **189**/boy thinking/Teeravut Atthasak; **191**/woman/fuzzbones; **192**/couple enjoying pizza/stockyimages; **193**/woman/Erik Reis; **193**/businesswoman/Dean Drobot; **194**/teenager thinking/Deborah Kolb; **197**/woman with shopping cart/Ivonne Wierink; **198**/baseball cap/Anton Starikov; **198**/shoes/Ruslan Kudrin; **199**/laptop/Maxim Basinski; **199**/woman/blueskyimage; **200**/girl/Ljupco Smokovski; **201**/woman/123RF Limited; **202**/woman/auremar; **204**/woman/stokkete; **205**/woman/vgstudio; **206**/woman/Boris Ryaposov; **207**/woman/Sergejs Rahunoks; **208**/farmer/Jeanne McRight; **209**/woman/Diana Eller; **210**/girl/Tomasz Trojanowski; **211**/man/Fiona Lynch; **212**/girl/Serhiy Kobyakov; **213**/woman/vgstudio; **214**/woman holding box/Vadim Guzhva; **216**/woman/Piotr Marcinski; **217**/delivery man/rido; **219**/girl/bloomua; **220**/child pointing/Jose Manuel Gelpi Diaz; **222**/girl/phartisan; **223**/teacher/Veronica Louro; **224**/girl/simsonne100; **225**/girl/gekaskr; **226**/woman/Marcel Braendli; **227**/woman/paffy; **228**/woman/vgstudio; **228**/girl/Blaj Gabriel; **230**/girl pointing/Jacek Chabraszewski; **231**/woman/Leung Cho Pan; **232**/boy/Olga Sapegina; **233**/woman/vgstudio; **233**/boy/Edyta Pawlowska; **234**/woman/HONGQI ZHANG; **235**/girl/HONGQI ZHANG; **237**/boy playing/auremar; **238**/man/pablocalvog; **239**/worker/Lisa Young; **240**/woman/Freddy Cahyono; **241**/girl/Dmitry Iatsenko; **242**/woman/Andres Rodriguez; **243**/schoolboy/xalanx; **245**/woman/zhudifeng; **247**/teenage girl/Edyta Pawlowska; **249**/couple/HONGQI ZHANG; **250**/boy/Borges Samuel; **253**/child/Jose Manuel Gelpi Diaz; **254**/girl pointing/Edyta Pawlowska; **255**/woman/Piotr Marcinski; **256**/child/Jose Manuel Gelpi Diaz; **257**/man reading/Piotr Marcinski; **258**/girl/Borges Samuel; **259**/woman/Edyta Pawlowska; **260**/woman/Leung Cho Pan; **260**/man/Edyta Pawlowska; **261**/woman/kurhan; **262**/woman/Leung Cho Pan; **263**/girl/Edyta Pawlowska; **265**/boy playing/Jose Manuel Gelpi Diaz; **266**/woman/phartisan; **268**/girl/Piotr Marcinski; **269**/message in a bottle/philipus; **269**/girl/Glenda Powers; **270**/student/Edyta Pawlowska; **271**/students/kurhan; **273**/woman/Edyta Pawlowska; **273**/student/Edyta Pawlowska;

Photo Credits

274/man/auremar; **275**/girl/Elena Elisseeva; **276**/boy/Maksym Topchii; **277**/schoolgirl/agencyby; **278**/girl/Luis Louro; **279**/woman/ariwasabi; **280**/girl/Piotr Marcinski; **281**/children/Vitaly Valua; **283**/mother and daughter/get4net; **284**/man/Hyunsu Kim; **286**/woman/lithian; **287**/girl/Jacek Chabraszewski; **289**/girl pointing/Edyta Pawlowska; **290**/man/Leung Cho Pan; **291**/man/Edyta Pawlowska; **294**/girl/HONGQI ZHANG; **295**/man pointing/Edyta Pawlowska; **297**/girl/Kirill Ryzhov; **298**/boy/Vitaly Valua; **299**/girl/szefei; **300**/woman/kurhan; **301**/girl/Cathy Yeulet; **302**/schoolgirl/agencyby; **304**/girl/Luis Louro; **306**/girl pointing/Edyta Pawlowska; **309**/woman/Leung Cho Pan; **310**/woman/Wavebreak Media Ltd; **311**/man/Edyta Pawlowska; **312**/child/Jose Manuel Gelpi Diaz; **314**/woman/HONGQI ZHANG; **315**/boy/get4net; **317**/girl/Piotr Marcinski; **318**/girl/HONGQI ZHANG; **318**/woman/HONGQI ZHANG; **319**/brothers/tobkatrina; **320**/girl/Lana Langlois; **321**/girl with books/Sergey Novikov; **322**/woman/kurhan; **323**/woman/Serhiy Kobyakov; **324**/woman/Freddy Cahyono; **325**/child/Jose Manuel Gelpi Diaz; **326**/woman tossing coin/citalliance; **327**/woman/Diana Eller; **328**/woman/Ferli Achirulli; **330**/woman/bruno135; **331**/man/Maris Kiselov; **332**/girl/Andres Rodriguez; **333**/woman/imagesbavaria; **334**/girl/Nicoleta Ifrim-Ionescu; **336**/woman/Piotr Marcinski; **338**/gardener/Andriy Popov; **340**/boy/James Flint; **341**/boy/Joerg Hackemann; **344**/girl/Alexander Raths; **345**/man/Vitaly Valua; **346**/friends/Oleksandra Borsuk; **347**/man/Edyta Pawlowska; **348**/woman/Ferli Achirulli; **349**/woman/Edyta Pawlowska; **350**/woman/Sergejs Rahunoks; **351**/man/Edyta Pawlowska; **352**/girl/My Make OU; **353**/girl/Edyta Pawlowska; **354**/boy/Tetiana Vitsenko; **355**/woman/Edyta Pawlowska; **356**/man/Edyta Pawlowska; **357**/car/Alex Varlakov; **359**/couple/goodluz; **361**/woman/stylephotographs; **362**/woman/Anton Todorov; **363**/friends/Manav Lohia; **365**/mechanic/kurhan; **366**/woman/Acha Yhamruksa; **367**/librarian/Daniel Kaesler; **368**/boy/pat138241; **369**/trainer/Anton Gvozdikov; **370**/woman/Edyta Pawlowska; **371**/girl/Borges Samuel; **372**/female/Vitaly Valua; **373**/boy/HONGQI ZHANG; **374**/girl/IrinaSolo; **375**/woman/ariwasabi; **376**/woman/Irina Chirkova; **378**/woman/Edyta Pawlowska; **379**/boy/Martin Allinger; **380**/girl and boy/sergein; **382**/woman/gmast3r; **383**/woman/Daniel Kaesler; **384**/woman/Antonio Guillem; **384**/woman pointing/Antonio Guillem; **385**/woman/Andres Rodriguez; **386**/boy/sergein; **387**/woman/Andres Rodriguez; **388**/woman/Jason Stitt; **389**/boy/Jose Manuel Gelpi Diaz; **391**/children/Jose Manuel Gelpi Diaz; **392**/girl/Konstantin Chagin; **393**/girl/Ashwin Kharidehal Abhirama; **394**/girl/Edyta Pawlowska; **395**/girl/Gennadiy Poznyakov; **396**/girl/Sergiy Bykhunenko; **397**/female/Ljupco Smokovski; **398**/woman/stokkete; **399**/man/Viorel Sima; **401**/man/George Muresan; **402**/man/Elena Elisseeva; **402**/woman/Theepatheep Kawinpathawee; **404**/girl/Edyta Pawlowska; **405**/woman/Edyta Pawlowska; **407**/man/Edhar Yuralaits; **408**/woman/Serhiy Kobyakov; **409**/woman/neonshot; **410**/woman/SORAPONG CHAIPANYA; **411**/woman/Olena Yakobchuk; **412**/female student/Edyta Pawlowska; **413**/woman/Ferli Achirulli; **414**/student/arekmalang; **415**/woman/Acha Yhamruksa; **416**/girl/Serhiy Kobyakov; **417**/woman/SORAPONG CHAIPANYA; **418**/girl/Jose Manuel Gelpi Diaz; **419**/man/Edyta Pawlowska; **420**/teenagers/My Make OU; **421**/woman/Piotr Marcinski; **422**/girl/goodluz; **423**/schoolgirl/agencyby; **424**/farmer/Ljupco Smokovski; **425**/construction worker/Vitaly Valua; **426**/man/stockyimages; **427**/bottle/Jeeragone Inrut; **427**/teddy bear/Brian Weed; **427**/woman/Antonio Guillem; **428**/woman/Borges Samuel; **429**/businesswoman/miszaqq; **430**/girl/Balazs Biro; **431**/woman/Luis Molinero Martínez; **432**/male/antikainen; **433**/woman/Luis Molinero Martínez; **434**/children/xalanx; **435**/female student/Edyta Pawlowska; **438**/young woman/stockyimages; **438**/bicycle/Ljupco Smokovski; **439**/man/Ferli Achirulli; **441**/man/Edyta Pawlowska; **442**/woman/imagesbavaria; **443**/chef/stockyimages; **444**/man/Wavebreak Media Ltd; **445**/man/agencyby; **446**/little girl/jirkaejc; **447**/cake/Ivan Kmit; **447**/chef/kurhan; **448**/schoolgirl/Viktor Pravdica; **449**/man/Dean Drobot; **450**/businesswoman/Marcel Braendli; **451**/woman/Piotr Marcinski; **452**/model/bruno135; **453**/businesswoman/citalliance; **454**/woman/Piotr Marcinski; **454**/solids/timurd; **456**/businesswoman/tomwang; **458**/woman/123RF Limited; **459**/woman/Serhiy Kobyakov; **460**/student/warrengoldswain; **461**/woman/Freddy Cahyono; **462**/young man/Edyta Pawlowska; **463**/thinking girl/Anastasia Vish; **464**/woman/Lammeyer; **465**/girl/Maksym Topchii; **465**/woman/Edyta Pawlowska; **466**/student/Edyta Pawlowska; **467**/teen girl/HONGQI ZHANG; **468**/woman/Leung Cho Pan; **469**/girl/Edyta Pawlowska; **470**/teen girl/Piotr Marcinski; **471**/woman/Serhiy Kobyakov; **472**/man/Leung Cho Pan